Myths of the North-East Frontier of India

Myths of the North-East Frontier of India

Verrier Elwin

GYAN

ISBN : 978-81-212-9028-9 (HB)

First Published, 1958

Indian Reprint in 2017

Published by

Gyan Publishing House
5, Ansari Road
Daryaganj, New Delhi-110002
Phone: 9811692060
E-mail: books@gyanbooks.com

Printed at: G. Print Process, Delhi.

TO

THE MEMBERS

OF THE

INDIAN FRONTIER ADMINISTRATIVE SERVICE

If I have harboured love within my breast,
'Twas for my comrades of the dusty day,
Who with me watched the loitering stars at play,
Who bore the burden of the same unrest.

CONTENTS

PREFACE

THIS is the first of what I hope will be two or more volumes dealing with mythology and folklore of the North-East Frontier Agency of India (NEFA). The Philological Section of the NEFA Research Department will produce other volumes containing the original versions of these and similar stories. Dr B. S. Guha, formerly Director of the Department of Anthropology, is engaged in recording and translating the great Adi (Abor) myths, the *abhangs*, especially those known in the Pasighat area, and these will form the subject of yet another volume. I have, therefore, not attempted to reproduce any of the *abhangs* as such here, though I have included certain episodes from those chanted in the northern Siang villages, and I have left the task of printing the originals of the stories to our philologists, who are far more qualified to do so than myself.

This book, therefore, has the modest and restricted purpose of making available English versions of nearly 400 tales, many of which are of exceptional and some of unique interest, and all of which throw a great deal of light on the thought and poetic imagination of tribes about whom little has hitherto been written.

In all tribal areas, there is a great divergence of ideas, especially in the realm of folklore, mythology and religion: stories and the names of gods and heroes vary from place to place; the same informant may even pronounce a word, or use a name differently on two successive days. This is inevitable in a region where there is no fixed deposit of doctrine, no sacred books to carry traditions from one generation to another, and where the repositories of knowledge are human beings exposed to the inspirations of their dreams and fancies.

In northern Subansiri, for example, I found the name of a great tribal ancestor pronounced in several different ways. The Tagins said something between Abo-Tani and Abo-Teni; the Miris said Abo-Teni or Ab-Teni; and the Apa-Tanis and Gallongs said Abo-Tani. It was equally difficult to decide the proper transliteration of the Wancho name of the Supreme Being; informants would say Rang, Jang and Zang almost in the same breath.

In translating I have followed the principle described in my *Tribal Myths of Orissa*. 'My custom was to translate the stories on the spot, as they were narrated or interpreted to me. I have translated them literally, as if I was translating poetry: that is to say, I have inserted no new symbol or image, and I have tried to avoid words which, though neutral in themselves, carry associations alien to the tribal consciousness. I have never, of course, tried to make the stories intelligible or attractive to my readers.'

In making a collection of this kind a scholar is bound to incur many debts of gratitude. My chief debt is to the tribal interpreters who travelled with me and went to enormous pains not only to make the meaning of the stories clear but to persuade informants to tell stories at all. For, although the Sherdukpens and some of the Adis were forthcoming and even eager to explain their traditions, others, especially in Tirap and Tuensang, were reluctant to do so. NEFA is not an easy place for research; it does not give up its secrets readily. A common attitude was summed up by one of my assistants: 'he doesn't know and if he did know, he wouldn't tell'. In the Khamlang Valley only the priests can tell stories, and for nearly the whole of my visit there, no priest was to be found—until, at the very end, one was proudly produced, and he proved deaf and dumb!

In an area where a fantastic variety of dialects is spoken it was inevitable that I should have had to depend on interpreters, except in a few cases where informants told stories directly in Hindi. But I was fortunate in obtaining the services of exceptionally good official interpreters, among whom I must make special mention of Shri Wangdun of Tirap, Shri Tapang Taki of Siang, Shri Ita Pulu of Lohit and Shri Bini Jaipur of Subansiri. To them, and many others, I tender my grateful thanks.

The stories were collected mainly on long tours in the frontier mountains during the four years 1954 to 1957. Others were recorded for me by my indefatigable assistant,

Shri Sundarlal Narmada, who has now worked with me for nearly a quarter of a century. He is responsible for collecting the Singpho, Bugun, Hrusso and Dhammai myths (most of which I personally verified later) and he went with me on most of my tours. A few other stories were collected by the Assistant Research Officers of the NEFA Administration and in particular by Shri T. K. Barua, who has spent a number of years among the Mishmis, and who accompanied me on arduous tours along the Patkoi Range and in the Khamlang Valley, and by Shri B. K. Shukla who has been working for the past year in Subansiri. I must also express my appreciation of the loyal and tireless work of my stenographer, Shri S. Lahiri, and typists, Shri P. Banerji and Shri Higher Land Syiem, in the preparation of the manuscript.

I am grateful to the Asiatic Society for permission to reproduce a number of stories from G. D. S. Dunbar's 'Abors and Galongs', which appeared in the *Memoirs of the Asiatic Society of Bengal,* Vol. V (1913-17).

In the second volume I hope to give much more introductory material, and in particular a full account of the various tribes. But in view of the keen interest that the tribal people are themselves taking in the preservation of their own oral literature, it seemed desirable to produce this preliminary collection as soon as possible, and I hope that its publication will encourage others also to record the NEFA mythology before its clear and original outlines become dimmed by the external influences which inevitably accompany the march of material progress and development. A Motif-Index to cover both books will be included in Volume Two.

VERRIER ELWIN

SHILLONG
29TH DECEMBER 1957

INTRODUCTION

THE North-East Frontier Agency is a wild and mountainous tract in the Assam Himalayas which covers some 27,000 square miles bounded by Bhutan to the west, Tibet to the north and Burma to the south-east, and into which the Valley of the Brahmaputra projects like a great spur. It is now divided into five Frontier Divisions, Kameng, Subansiri, Siang, Lohit and Tirap and accommodates about four hundred thousand people. Some parts, such as central Siang, are heavily populated; others, like northern Subansiri and Lohit, are sparsely inhabited in isolated villages along the river valleys. The rainfall is heavy, as much as 200 inches in Subansiri. The countryside offers almost every possible type of mountain scenery. On the 14,000-foot Se-La Pass on way to Tawang, with its masses of rhododendrons and other multi-coloured flowers, the traveller is reminded of Kashmir; in the lovely valleys of Siang with their background of snow-capped mountains, you are at one moment in Austria, at another in Wordsworth's Lakes. Nor are the formidable slopes of the Patkoi, the wide and open glories of Tirap, the dark jungles of Lohit, easily forgotten. An early traveller described this country as 'back-breaking': I would rather call it 'heart-warming', for though the marches are long and difficult, the people's welcome and hospitality quickly wipes away the memory of fatigue.

This area, which was almost completely isolated until very recently, is populated by a large number of tribes speaking different languages and dialects of the Tibeto-Burman family and exhibiting a great diversity of culture, dress and custom. It may be divided into three main cultural areas. The first is largely inspired by Buddhist ideas and includes the people of Western Kameng, small tribal groups living all along the northern frontier through Subansiri, Siang and Lohit, and the Buddhist Khamptis and Singphos in the foot-hills near Tezu and Margherita. The second cultural province consists of the great central block of territory—

eastern Kameng, Ṣubansiri, Siang and Lohit and the third to the south-east, is a small but important area, now consisting only of part of the Tirap Frontier Division which is populated by the Wanchos and Noctes. Although each of these provinces has much in common with the others, there are a number of definite cultural traits which distinguish them.

The Buddhist or near-Buddhist tribes have a developed civilization which has been considerably influenced by Tibet and Burma. In western Kameng live the Monpas and Sherdukpens, gentle, courteous people who cultivate on terraces, maintain large numbers of cattle, sheep and horses and are to a great extent under the influence of the lamasery of Tawang. Both tribes combine in their religion and mythology traditional tribal ideas with the Buddhist theology. In fairly close geographical proximity live the Buguns (Khowas), Hrussos (Akas) and Dhammais (Mijis) who, although not Buddhists, share some aspects of their neighbours' culture. The Membas and other tribes living along the northern frontier may be conveniently grouped with them and so may be the Buddhist Khamptis and Singphos who migrated in historical times from the Irrawady Valley and have lived for some generations in close proximity to the Assam plains.

The great central area is populated by a large number of tribal groups who have been divided from one another by the difficulty of communications and by the state of war in which they lived for centuries before they were brought under regular administration. In the east of the Kameng Division is a fairly large population of Daflas, who are here known as Bangnis; the same tribe extends into the west of the Subansiri Frontier Division. The wild and desolate hills of Subansiri are also inhabited by the Tagins and Gallongs in the north, by a tribe which for want of a better name is usually called the Hill Miri and by the Apa Tanis whose system of cultivation would be remarkable even in a fully settled area. The life of the people in the northern and western mountains, where puny man fights an arduous battle against the giant forces of nature, is in striking contrast to that of the Apa Tanis on their beautiful plateau where nature has been largely dominated and controlled by tribal genius.

Siang, the happiest of the NEFA Divisions, is the home of bright colours, lovely weaving, dancing, singing and an enchanting people formerly known collectively by the Assamese word 'Abor', which means 'independent', but who now call themselves Adi or hillmen. Here too are striking contrasts. On one side is Pasighat, now a prosperous little township, with a High School, a fine Hospital and various training establishments. On the other, are the remote valleys to the north inhabited by Ashings, Pailibos, Ramos, Bokars, Boris and other tribes of whom we still know comparatively little.

Also included in the central area are the Mishmis of Lohit who are divided into three main groups—the Idus (Chulikattas), the Taraons (Digarus) and the Kamans (Mijus). The Taraons and Kamans differ only in dialect and are not easily distinguished. The 'crop-haired' Idus, however, who represent an earlier wave of migration from Burma, differ in many ways and resemble in appearance (though not in culture) the Padams who are their neighbours. All Mishmis, however, live in very small villages, some of which consist of a single great house in which as many as forty to sixty persons may be accommodated. They have few social virtues and are the most individualistic of the NEFA tribes. On the other hand, their weaving is probably the finest in the whole area and the Taraon and Kaman women are distinguished by their attractive hand-woven cloth and the coiffure and silver ornaments which give them an unusual and striking appearance.

In Tirap are the virile and picturesque Wanchos, who are organized under influential and wealthy Chiefs; the Noctes, who have adopted a very elementary form of Vaishnavism and have been more in contact with the outside world than any others, with a resultant loss of much of their traditional culture; the many small groups collectively known as Tangsa, a charming friendly people who have migrated from Burma, and still have many links across the border; and small populations of Singphos and Khamptis.

Throughout NEFA the unit of social organization is the patrilineal family; polygamy is fairly common, a fact which is often emphasized in the tales, and there are traces of polyandry among the Gallongs. Each tribe is divided into a number of exogamous clans and, as a general rule, the tribes do not intermarry, although there are many examples of this rule being ignored. The people all live in villages, but the Mishmis and Daflas tend to make the house rather the village the centre of their social interests. Village government varies from the autocracy of the great Wancho and Nocte Chiefs to the highly democratic system of the Adi tribes, which are governed by a Kebang or Council of the leading members of the village clans. The people are generally well organized, at least within the clan or village, a state of affairs which is encouraged by the existence of communal dormitories among the Wancho, Nocte and Adi groups.

All the tribes live by what is known in Assam as *jhuming*, or shifting cultivation, the harvests of which they supplement by a wide variety of forest produce. Many of them are also skilled hunters and fishermen. Few of them drink distilled spirit, but everywhere they make a light and nourishing rice-beer which is used on all ceremonial and social occasions. Many of them grow their own tobacco and some grow opium for their own consumption and for trade. Although formerly suspicious and hostile to strangers, they have, under the present policy of the Government of India, become friendly and co-operative. They are in the main hospitable and well-disciplined, hard-working, truthful and honest. Former customs of inter-village wars, head-hunting, kidnapping and slavery have largely disappeared and in the new era of peace there is an increased inter-mingling of the tribes, a fact which will undoubtedly have its influence on their mythology and folktales in time to come.

Until Independence such contacts as the people of NEFA had were with soldiers, the merchants to whom they sold their goods, a few explorers and members of the

Topographical Survey and, in the later years of the British period, with a few Political Officers who visited their villages and settled some of their disputes.

There is no space here to recall the long and distressing story of tribal raids on the inoffensive plains or of the punitive expeditions that went into the hills to rescue captives or avenge the dead. In the thirties of the last century, for example, Tagi Raja, the Chief of the Kapaschor Akas or Hrussos, led his followers to murder and pillage and in 1835 wiped out a British outpost at Balipara. The Adis made frequent attacks on the plains villages throughout the century, and their hostility culminated in the murder of Williamson and Gregorson with forty-two of their followers in 1911. The first official record of the Mishmis, in 1825, declares that they were 'very averse to receive strangers' and in 1854 the intrepid Father Krick with a fellow-priest who had successfully crossed the pass at the head of the Zayul Valley was murdered on their way home. Forays by the Daflas and Apa Tanis were less serious, but the Khamptis and Singphos proved worthy antagonists of British arms in their early raids on Sadiya, though they later settled down to the pacific life to which their Buddhist faith naturally inclined them. The tribes of the Tirap hills have always had more friendly relations with the plains people, and except for an occasional kidnapping of individuals for slavery or sacrifice, the only outstanding tragedy was the massacre of Holcombe's Survey party by the Wanchos in 1875. The people of Tuensang further south lived in almost complete isolation; they were visited by Dr J. H. Hutton in 1922, and in 1936 Mr J. P. Mills led an expedition to punish a village called Pangsha, which had taken 400 heads in a few months.

The policy of Government in the pre-Independence period was to attempt no more than a skeleton administration in the foothills; to send out punitive expeditions in reaction to the more serious raids; to impose blockades and establish fortified posts at strategic points; and in certain cases to pay what is called *posa* to the Chiefs on condition that they kept their people under control.

Another form of external contact was through the explorers who from the earliest times pressed into the interior.

In 1826, for example, Wilcox reached the Upper Irrawady from Assam and the following year went into the Kaman Mishmi country as far as the point where the Brahmaputra, 'after flowing nearly south from Tibet suddenly changes its course and flows in a westerly direction'. Ten years later the botanist Griffith succeeded in travelling as far as the village of Ghalum on the Lohit, but was unable to enter the Kaman hills. In 1845, Rowlatt went up the Du river as far as Tuppang where he met a number of Tibetans. E. T. Dalton, later to become famous as the author of one of the classics of Indian anthropology, the *Descriptive Ethnology of Bengal,* made a trip up the Subansiri River in 1845 and visited the Adi country, though not very far in, ten years later. Perhaps the most remarkable of these early travellers was T. T. Cooper, a British businessman who, in 1868, was invited by the Shanghai Chamber of Commerce to attempt to reach India from China through Tibet. In this he failed and the following year attempted the journey in reverse, starting out from Sadiya. He came to within twenty miles of Rima, but was then compelled to return.

The first person to visit the Apa Tanis was an adventurous Tea Planter, H. M. Crowe, who went into their hills in 1889 and got on very well with them, an experience which was not shared by the German explorer von Ehlers who followed him a few years later but was robbed and driven out of the country. Another Tea Planter, who made extensive explorations with the idea of extending the trade of Assam beyond the frontier, was J. Errol Gray who left Saikwa at the end of 1892 in an attempt to cross into western China. He travelled unarmed with a comparatively small party and succeeded in crossing the Nam-Kiu and entering the valley of the Tisang, an important affluent of the Irrawady.

When the Topographical Survey of India directed its attention to this area a number of survey parties went far into the interior and the leaders of some of them such as R. G. Woodthorpe, H. J. Harman, and C. R. Macgregor established friendly relations with the tribes.

Another way in which the hill people came in touch with the outside world was through trade. The Mishmis have always been keen traders and they brought down musk, *Mishmi teeta* which was at one time widely used as a febrifuge, ivory and skins. At one time, the Apa Tanis brought large quantities of rubber for sale. The Adis bartered skins, cane and wool for salt. The Mishmis and some of the tribesmen in Tirap also used to smuggle opium into the plains areas. The Hrussos and Sherdukpens have had trade-contacts with Assam for generations.

From the middle of the last century annual fairs were held at Udalgiri, Doimera, Sadiya and elsewhere, and were visited by large numbers of hillmen.

Finally, there was the impact on the people of Government officials. It was not until 1894 that a Political Officer, J. F Needham, was appointed to study the languages and politics of the tribal people and try to win their goodwill by sympathy and contact. He made many promenades (as they were then called) to within a few miles of Rima, to the Hukong Valley, to Burma across the Patkoi Range, and accompanied two disastrous military expeditions, one in the Abor Hills and another in the last year of the century to the Idu Mishmi country. There is no doubt that he, as well as his successor Williamson, made many friends on the frontier and contributed to the more hospitable reception which visitors received in later years. During the present century the number of visitors as well as the gradual expansion of some sort of administration naturally increased and we may mention the work of the Miri Mission in northern Subansiri in 1911 and the still more adventurous expedition of Dr C. von Furer-Haimendorf in 1944 to the Upper Kamla Valley and beyond.

These varied contacts had remarkably little effect on the life and culture of the people. They were probably too transient and occasional to have a deep effect, but they did succeed in slowly bringing the inhabitants to realize that the greater world outside their hills was not hostile to them but only wished them well. At least the isolation of NEFA was not complete.

This may account for the fact that, although many of the NEFA stories are original and most of the common motifs of Indian folklore are absent, there are some traces of external influence. A very few myths show traces of missionary teaching, heard on visits to the plains; there is an occasional echo of the Ramayana; one Singpho myth is based on a Jataka tale; a fable from a school primer finds its way, greatly altered, into the body of the mythology.

Among the motifs common in other parts of tribal India which will be found in NEFA are those of an original primaeval ocean out of which the world was formed, of earthquake as caused by the great animal on whose back the world rests, of lightning as the pursuit of a girl by an unwanted lover, traditions of a Land of Women, of opium as the reincarnation of a girl whom nobody loved in her lifetime, the taboo on opening something during a journey, the Fox Woman, the Trickster cycle and the widespread idea that monkeys were originally human beings who lost their status through idleness or breach of a taboo.

But on the whole the tales are remarkably original and seem to be genuine products of tribal creativity and imagination. There are no moral tales, though a few suggest the possibility of divine punishment for sin. There are very few formulistic or cumulative tales; there is little stress on sacred numbers; not a hint of astrology; and only one reference to the 'soul index' motif so popular in Indian folklore.

The myths are told on a variety of occasions: some are chanted during the dance, as for example the Adi *abhangs*, and the Sherdukpen tales; some are repeated at ceremonies, at a funeral or harvest thanksgiving or to save the life of a child; others are told round the fire in the Naga *morung* or Adi *moshup;* yet others are perhaps not told publicly at all, but are passed down from shaman to shaman as a kind of traditional wisdom or history.

Long ago Tylor suggested that myth was primitive

history and ethnology expressed in poetic form. The poet contemplates the same natural world as the man of science, but he expresses his discovery in a different way. And the primitive poet who puts his inspiration in the form of myth shapes it out of 'those endless analogies between man and nature which are the soul of all poetry.' The truth of a myth is thus in a way irrelevant. 'Myth is the history of its authors, not of its subjects; it records the lives, not of superhuman heroes, but of poetic nations.'

Many tribal people have a deep vein of poetic imagination, and only the difficulty of interpretation prevents us from enjoying it as we should. Many of the NEFA myths are rich in 'poetic' ideas, an expression which can hardly be defined, but which most readers will appreciate.

The NEFA stories of the origin or creation of the world, the sky, and the heavenly bodies have an almost Miltonic grandeur of conception. Earth and Sky are lovers and when the Sky makes love to the Earth every kind of tree and grass and all living creatures come into being. But the lovers must be separated, for so long as they cling together there is nowhere for their children to live. In a Minyong tradition, after their separation, the Earth always longed to return to her husband to be one with him again. But as she was raising herself to the Sky, the Sun and Moon appeared, and she was ashamed and could go no further. That part of her which was reaching towards her lord became fixed for ever, as the great mountains. In a Singpho story the rainbow is a ladder by which a god climbs from earth to meet his wife in the land of the Moon, high in the sky, and in Tagin stories the rainbow is a bridge by which a bride goes to her husband's house.

There is poetic inspiration in the Sherdukpen story about rainbows which tells how there are four water-spirits, white, black, yellow and red, who live in springs among the hills and from time to time wander across the heavens for ever seeking wives as lovely as themselves. The rainbow is the path of blended colours that they make across the sky.

The people of NEFA have a strong sense of beauty and love bright colours and flowers. There is a Nocte tale of two brothers, one of whom lives on earth and the other, the younger, in the sky. 'From time to time the younger brother dances and throws showers of rain-drops down to earth. Then he asks the lovely fair-coloured girls of earth whether they have such beads on their necks. Sometimes too he throws the lightning down and asks the earth-people if they have such wondrous magic as this. Sometimes he beats his drum and when it thunders across the sky, he asks the earth-people if they have any music to match it.' Lightning always delights the tribal poets and myth-makers; it is, say the Minyongs, the flashing of a divine mother's eyelids; to the Mishmis it is the beauty of a star-girl running across the sky; to the Buguns, it is the long hair-pin with which a girl threatens an undesired lover.

The tribesmen are realists and there are plenty of ugly people in their stories, women with, for example, only one eye, one ear, one breast and one leg, but there are also many lovely creatures whose memory has come down from generation to generation. The Singphos, for example, speak of Raja Sitte-Charka whose queen shone like the light. 'When he went anywhere at night he used to take her with him so that her beauty could lighten the path by which he had to go. Not only light but a delicate scent came from her body.' Even after her death her body lay for months with its scented beauty unimpaired.

Such ideas, and others similar to them which will be found in this book, are the material of true poetry. It is consoling to reflect that Imagination, which is the light of the finest and most cultured minds, illuminates also the hard lives of the people of the hills.

PART ONE: HEAVEN AND EARTH

CHAPTER ONE

THE CREATION OF THE WORLD

NEFA traditions about the Creation of the World are of five main types, all of which can be paralleled in both the classical and the tribal literature of India.

Very common is the idea that the world arose from a primaeval ocean or was formed upon its surface. Also common is the notion of the world as a macrocosm, transformed from some great personage or even a tree. A few stories speak of a direct creation by heavenly beings; there are Hill Miri, Hrusso and Khampti tales of a cosmic egg; and there are traditions of earth and sky being 'born' of a universal Mother.

It is remarkable that people who have never seen the sea nor even, so far as we can tell, large sheets of water of any kind, should have devised the idea of a primaeval ocean from which all things have emerged. This tradition, of course, is as old as the Upanishads, several of which declare that the original material of the world was water. The Ramayana maintains the tradition, saying that all was water at first and that the earth was formed beneath it. Then Brahma arose and, becoming a boar, raised up the earth.

Throughout central India, Orissa and Bihar, tribal creation myths echo this belief. In some of these the world develops from the primal sea directly; in others there is an original world which is destroyed by flood or fire and is then created afresh. The NEFA stories are usually of the first pattern, although one Kaman Mishmi tale describes a great flood succeeded by fire which destroys the original world as a punishment for sin, and a Singpho tale tells how the Supreme Being rebukes man's iniquities by fire and flood. Bori, Gallong, Hill Miri, Nocte, Sherdukpen, Minyong and Taraon Mishmi stories describe how at first everything was water. The Gallongs attribute the emergence of the earth to the prawn and the crab: the prawn collected a great pile of rubbish on the surface, the crab dug a pit below to drain off the water. The Hill Miris say that an enormous tree grew out of the sea and worms ate the wood until, by the constant falling of the dust into the water, the world was formed. In Minyong tradition, a great mithun dug a pit into which the waters poured and allowed the dry earth to appear. In two Nocte stories, the water subsided of its own accord, allowing the earth to rise above it. Among the Sherdukpens, it is believed that two heavenly brothers threw a lotus down onto the surface of the ocean, whereupon it was covered with flowers, over which the four winds blew clouds of dust until the earth was formed. A Taraon Mishmi tale describes how there was a lot of mud below the waters and a god erected in it a pillar, up which a swarm of white ants climbed with their mouths filled with earth. This idea of animals bringing earth from the bottom of the primal ocean to make the world is common in central India.

A more remarkable idea found in some of the NEFA stories is that of creation by sacrifice or the transformation of some great personage into the world, an idea which echoes the famous Purusha-Sukta in the Rigveda. 'Far, far back out of the recesses of the Vedic cultus the figure of Maha-Purusha emerges as the symbol of creation by sacrifice. A vast cosmic Man, human in person but divine in nature, submits to be offered up by the gods. . . The Purusha has a thousand heads, a thousand eyes, a thousand feet, expressive of omniscience and omnipresence. He envelops the earth and transcends it; he is identical with the whole universe; he is the sum of all existence: he includes all that is and all that shall be. From this exalted Person spring all the objects and beings of the world.'[1]

This was the beginning, and the macrocosmic idea of the world as a vast personage transformed is frequently repeated. The Atharva-Veda (10.7.32-34) describes the earth as the base of the highest Brahma, the air is his belly, the sky his head, the Sun and Moon his eyes, fire his mouth, the wind his breathing. In the Brihad-Aranyaka Upanishad

[1] J. E. Carpenter, *Theism in Mediaeval India* (London, 1921), p. 43.

(1.2) the demiurge Death dismembers himself. 'The eastern direction is his head. Yonder one and yonder one are the fore-quarters. Likewise the western direction is his tail. Yonder one and yonder one are the hind-quarters. South and north are the flanks. The sky is the back. The atmosphere is the belly. This earth is the chest. He stands firm in the waters.' The magnificent and mysterious opening of the Aitareya Upanishad (1.1) describes how fire comes from the mouth of the world person, 'from his nostrils the wind, from his eyes the sun, from his heart the moon, from his navel death, from his male generative organ water.' A later Upanishad—the Mundaka—describes 'the issue of all kinds of beings from the Imperishable, like sparks from a fire. From him, as he became personalized in creation, were born breath, and all organs of sense, ether, air, light, water, earth. Fire is his head; the Sun and Moon his eyes; the wind his breath; his heart the universe. From him come the devas, men, cattle, birds, the up and down breathings.'

In central India the Bhuiyas, Juangs, Gonds, as well as the Madigas of southern India, repeat this tradition, but more commonly with the motif that the world is made from a human sacrifice rather than from a divine transformation. In NEFA, however, the stress is rather on the sacrifice of some great creature for the sake of the world or on the formation of the world out of some person or animal who has died. Thus the Apa Tanis tell how the original human beings lived on the surface of the belly of the giantess Kujum-Chantu (a primitive version of Mother Earth) until one day she realized that if she got up and walked about, they would fall off and be killed, and so she died of her own accord. Every part of her body became part of the world and her eyes turned into the Sun and Moon. In a Bori story the only creatures in the early world were two spirits, one of whom had the form of a mithun and the other the form of an elephant. They fought and killed each other and from their flesh and bones the world was formed. In the Hill Miri story of the tree, to which I have already referred, the tree itself finally falls to the ground and its bark becomes the skin of the world, the trunk turns into rocks and the branches into hills. In another Apa Tani story there is a great Wiyu in the form of an earthen ball. When she dies, her thighs turn into the earth and her eyes into the Sun and Moon.

Other stories attribute the origin of the world to some kind of direct creation. The Buguns describe how the two sons of the Supreme Zongma made the earth and sky. The Sherdukpens similarly describe how two brothers, neither of whom is the Supreme Being, created the world by throwing a lotus onto the primal ocean. The Kaman Mishmis tell of two powerful spirits who do not actually create the world, but come down from the sky and make the hills and mountains. The Taraon Mishmis have a similar tradition and, in their case, the god Techimdun, who lived at first below the great waters, plays an important part in creation by setting up the pillars which support the earth laid by white ants on the surface.

In many cases the tribal story-tellers are concerned to explain how it is that part of the world is flat and part mountainous, and in general, whatever may have been the origin of the world itself, the piling up of part of it in the form of mountains and hills is attributed to certain gods or spirits.

It is interesting to note that the creation of the world is not usually attributed to a Supreme Being, but to lesser gods who often act in pairs.

Two Hill Miri stories speak of a cosmic egg—in one the earth and the mountains come from it, in the other the first rivers flow when it is broken. Hrusso tradition tells of two great eggs, forever revolving in space. They collide and break open: from one comes the Earth, from the other the Sky, her husband. This idea is echoed in a Khampti myth. Here we have an interesting parallel with the Gond tradition that the first human beings were born from the eggs of great birds who lived on the face of the ocean, an idea which appears again in Santal and Saora mythology.[3]

[3] See my *Myths of Middle India*, pp. 16 ff.

Finally, there is a tradition that earth and sky have descended from a sort of universal Mother. For example, in an interesting Singpho story, a woman in the form of a cloud is born out of the primaeval fog and mist. She has a son and a daughter, who are like snow, and from them the earth and sky are born. At first the earth is only mud and the sky lies upon it as a thick cloud, but when the wind is born, it dries the mud, thus making the earth solid and drives the sky far away. Similarly, in a Dhammai story, earth and sky are born of parents whose nature is not revealed. A worm swallows them, but is caught by the father and split open. The children are still in the worm's belly, the upper part of which becomes the sky and the lower the earth. Earth and sky then come together and produce the mountains; from their next encounter are born frogs, and from the frogs are born beings who, though human, are entirely covered with hair.

Stories about the beginning of the world are rarely consistent. In a Bugun story, we find an elderly man living with a young wife who deserts him for an attractive water-god. The husband then goes to Lhasa and on the way meets the hideous Nikauma-Madongma. From their union the first rock is born and from it flow the first rivers. Then she bears a son who goes into the sky and makes the thunder and lightning and another who goes below the earth to cause the earthquake. A fourth son is a rain-maker, the fifth originates the four winds and the sixth causes the rainbow. Other children are snakes, poisonous insects and demons of disease. Last born is the pathetic child of death who unknowingly kills his own parents and then, in searching for them, kills everyone he meets.

Some of these Creation stories have an almost Biblical dignity and are inspired by the very spirit of poetry.

1

APA TANI

Reru, Subansiri F.D.

At first Kujum-Chantu, the earth, was like a human being ; she had a head, and arms and legs, and an enormous fat belly. The original human beings lived on the surface of her belly.

One day it occurred to Kujum-Chantu that if she ever got up and walked about, everyone would fall off and be killed, so she herself died of her own accord. Her head became the snow-covered mountains ; the bones of her back turned into smaller hills. Her chest was the valley where the Apa-Tanis live. From her neck came the north country of the Tagins. Her buttocks turned into the Assam plain. For just as the buttocks are full of fat, Assam has fat rich soil. Kujum-Chantu's eyes became the Sun and Moon. From her mouth was born Kujum-Popi, who sent the Sun and Moon to shine in the sky.

2

BORI

Gasheng, Siang F.D.

At first there was nothing but water. There were two brothers, Poling the elder and Tering the younger. They lived separately in the water and neither of them knew that the other existed. Tering had the form of a mithun and Poling had the form of an elephant. Each thought that he was the only creature living in the world.

But after many years had passed, as they moved about the lonely ancient waters, they met each other, and Poling said, 'Who are you and where do you come from?' Tering asked, 'Who are *you* and where do *you* come from?' Though there were only these two in all the world, they did not make friends ; each accused the other of invading his territory, they quarrelled and in the fight that followed they killed each other.

From the flesh of Tering, the earth was formed, from his bones came the trees and from his hair the grass. From Poling's bones came the rocks and from his flesh the mountains.

After the world had been formed in this manner, Sedi-Melo was born, and he set himself to put it in order. In one place he made it flat, in another he piled up hills. He made the rivers flow between them. When he had finished, he came to Assam and while he was resting there he caused the English to be created.

3

BUGUN (KHOWA)

Senchong, Kameng F.D.

Long ago, before the earth or the sky was made, Zongma, who is the greatest of all, had two sons, Nipu and Nili.

Nipu and Nili were without form ; they were not human beings, they were not animals, nor were they like the rocks. Many ages passed and then Nili made the earth and Nipu made the sky. When it was ready the earth was very big and Nipu put the sky like a lid above it. But the lid was too small and Nipu said, 'Brother, make the earth smaller so that the sky will fit it.' So Nili pushed and pulled the soil together until the sky and earth were the same size, and as a result parts of the world stood up as mountains.

4

BUGUN (KHOWA)

Senchong, Kameng F.D.

There was a man called Apuphulwa whose wife's name was Muinini. Apuphulwa was rather elderly, but Muinini was still young and she was not happy with him. Every day when she went to the stream to fetch water she would put her bamboo-tubes down on the bank and sit there singing and weeping. In her song she sang—

My husband is old and I am young,
When he dies, what shall I do ?

Now in the water of the stream beside which Muinini used to sit and weep there lived a god who heard all that she said and he thought, 'Muinini's husband is old but I myself am young. If I can marry her, she will live very happily with me.'

One day when Muinini went for water to the stream, she took off her clothes and put them on the bank and went into the water to bathe. The water-god seized her and took her to his house and married her.

When Muinini did not return from the stream Apuphulwa grew impatient and went down to search for her. There on the bank he saw her clothes and the bamboo water-tubes. He called loudly for her, thinking that she might have gone somewhere to catch fish, but when he got no reply he began to look for her desperately.

His search was long and arduous and took him all the way to Lhasa. One day as he was returning he met a very ugly girl, whose name was Nikauma-Madongma. She had only one ear and one eye, no nose and no chin and only one arm and one leg. But when Apuphulwa saw her he thought, 'I am an old man now and there is little chance of my getting a pretty wife. I may as well keep this girl, for she will probably stay with me, as she's hardly likely to get a handsome husband.' So he took her as his wife.

After some time Nikauma-Madongma conceived and in due course gave birth to a son. But the child was a rock and though the parents tried to talk to him, naturally he could not reply.

When the child absolutely refused to speak, his parents were exasperated and decided to punish him. First they piled five loads of wood upon him. Then when this had no effect, they put five loads of bamboo-tubes full of water. When this had no effect, they added five loads of cane. When this had no effect, they put five loads of bamboo. And when this too had no effect, they piled up five loads of grass.

But when nothing they could do made the child speak, Apuphulwa threw him away into the jungle. And then at last the child spoke. 'My parents,' he said, 'you have done well in throwing me into the forest. Now from me rivers will flow and on my body trees and grass will grow. Where I am a rock, your other children will make their houses beneath my shelter. Where I am a river many fish will live in me and, when your children go fishing, I will help them.' This is why, when people go to catch fish, they are able to put up a wall of stones as a dam to hold the water.

Some time afterwards Nikauma-Madongma gave birth to another son, whom they called Takiong. They could not tell what sort of creature he was, for he was always running about and wherever he went he made a noise *dudung-dhadang,* and when they lit a fire to cook their food he used to blow the flames in all directions. This was a great bother to his parents and one day Apuphulwa kicked the boy and told him to get out. Takiong took one of his father's daos and a burning log from the fire and went into the sky. As he went he said, 'Now I am going. In the sky there is a great snake who prevents the rain from falling. I will fight with this snake and your children will get plenty of rain.'

This is why when Takiong fights with the snake we hear the thunder and when he threatens the snake with his burning brand we see the lightning.

Some time afterwards Nikauma-Madongma gave birth to a third son, whose name was Kallao. When he was born he went round and round in a circle, making a noise *gurur-ghara.* When he went round, his father and mother had to go round with him. Unfortunately, this meant that they could not do any work and had no chance to eat. At last in despair Apuphulwa kicked Kallao and told him to get out and the boy went down below the earth.

As he went down he said, 'I am not an easy one to be offended and you have kicked me. As you are angry, so I also will be angry. I will make the earth as if it were not and will destroy your children.' So now, when Kallao goes round like a grindstone, there is an earthquake.

Some time afterwards Nikauma-Madongma gave birth to a fourth son called Chakmao. When he was born everything became dark, so dark that Apuphulwa and Nikauma-Madongma could not see each other. This time they both kicked the child and he, taking a bamboo full of water, went up into the sky. As he went he said, 'My elder brother Takiong and I will send rain upon the earth, and we will help whatever children you may have.'

After some time Nikauma-Madongma gave birth to a fifth child called Hassam. He, like the first boy, did not speak but he kept very close to his mother . nd wherever he was, a strong whirlwind made it impossible for anyone to talk or do any work. The wind blew so strongly that all Apuphulwa's things were blown about in every direction. They tried to catch hold of him and put him in some place where he would not do any damage, but they could not get their hands on him. So they said to him, 'Since you will not stay in one place, go to the four corners of the world. But at all events go away from here.' As he went Hassam said, 'I am going, but I will give you every kind of help. Wherever there is dirt I will blow it away. When the leaves dry on the trees, I will blow them away so that new leaves can come. I will bring the cold, I will bring the heat and I will bring the rain.'

After some time Nikauma-Madongma gave birth to a snake and when they saw it his parents were afraid and were about to run away. But the snake said, 'Don't be afraid. I will be the king of the water and will live in streams and rivers. When the water runs low, I will call for more.' So saying, he left his parents and went down into the water. This is why when there is scarcity of water the snake goes up into the sky as the rainbow to call for rain.

After some time Nikauma-Madongma gave birth to a poisonous snake. The mother, thinking that this would be a good child, put him to her breast but he bit her and she fell unconscious to the ground. Apuphulwa gave her some medicine and she recovered, but now wherever she went the snake followed her, trying to return into her body by the way he had come out. At last Nikauma-Madongma wearied of this and threw the snake into the forest, telling him to live in a hole in the ground. So the snake went to live in a hole beneath the rock that was the eldest brother.

After this Nikauma-Madongma gave birth to thorny trees and bushes and threw them away into the forest. Some time afterwards she gave birth to every kind of poisonous insect and threw them too into the forest.

After this Nikauma-Madongma gave birth to disease-children of every kind, and Apuphulwa and Nikauma-Madongma fell ill. But the hornet[3] came and cured them. When they were quite well again,

[3] There are a number of helpful hornets in the NEFA stories. Here a hornet cures the first people to fall sick ; in a Hrusso tale (p. 263) a hornet warns men, by stinging them on the back of the neck, that the demons of disease are approaching ; the Boris describe how a hornet helps Awing-Kare to recover his lost pig (p. 283) ; a Hill Miri hornet, after a drink of rice-beer, gives Abo-Teni some of the earth from his children's grave, thus unwittingly bringing the boon of death to mankind (p. 288) ; and in a Taraon story, a hornet assists an elder against a younger brother who is stealing his honey. In world-folklore, there are, of course, plenty of helpful ants and bees, and even helpful fleas, locusts and dung-beetles, but the hornet does not often appear in this amiable role.

they said to the disease-children, 'Don't stay here, but go away. You will never find a place where you can all live together.' So the children have ever since wandered through the world making people ill, and have found no place to rest.

Then after a time Nikauma-Madongma gave birth to the child of death, and when he was born both his parents died. The child went weeping to find them, but wherever he went people died when he spoke to them.

The children of Nikauma-Madongma were sometimes good and sometimes bad, because she herself was good on one side of her body and bad on the other.[4]

5

DHAMMAI (MIJI)

Nakhu, Kameng F.D.

At first there was neither earth nor sky. Shuzanghu and his wife Zumiang-Nui lived above. One day Shuzanghu said to his wife, 'How long must we live without a place to rest our feet?' Zumiang-Nui said, 'What can I say to you? You always live apart from me and don't love me. But if you truly love me and will stay with me, I will tell you what to do.' So Shuzanghu went to his wife and she conceived.

In due time Zumiang-Nui gave birth to a baby-girl, Subbu-Khai-Thung, who is the Earth and to a baby-boy, Jongsuli-Young-Jongbu, who is the Sky. But there was no place for them. So they fell down, down to where Phangnalomang the Worm and his wife were living, and the Worm swallowed them both.

Zumiang-Nui tried to find her children and asked her husband, 'What has happened to them? Where have they gone?' But he could not tell her. Then she said, 'Next time I have a child, make a clear flat place where I can keep him safely and set traps all round it.' Shuzanghu made such a place and when his wife was delivered of her next child, there was somewhere for him to stay. And now when Phangnalomang came to devour the child he was

[4] Another, shorter and rather different, version of this story will be found in Chapter VII.

caught in one of the traps. Shuzanghu found him there and split his body open. The two children were still in his belly and the lower part of his body became the Earth and the upper the Sky.

Now Earth and Sky lived together. The Sky went to his wife, the Earth, and she gave birth to a son, Subjang-Gnoi-Rise and a daughter, Jubbu-Jang-Sangne. These were gods but they had the shape of mountains. After they were born Earth and Sky separated and as they were parting Earth gave birth to two other children, a boy, Lujjuphu, and a girl named Jassuju, who had the form of frogs. They mated and from them a boy and a girl in human form, Abugupham-Bumo and Anoi-Diggan-Juje, were born. They were human but were covered with hair. They married each other and in time had three sons, Lubukhanlung, Sangso-Dungso and Kimbu-Sangtung.

6

GALLONG

Don, Subansiri F.D.

In the sky were the old man Puk and his woman Yuk. At that time the earth was covered with water. The prawn and the crab tried to dry it up. The prawn used his antennae to collect the rubbish, leaves, grass and bits of wood that were floating on the surface and the crab dug a deep pit down below. The water poured into the pit and the earth appeared. The prawn's pile of rubbish turned into mountains.

But the earth was very soft at first. Then the Sun and the Moon came up and hardened it by their heat. Puk and Yuk looked down from the sky and saw the earth bare and dry: there were no trees, no grass. Puk said to his wife, 'There is nothing green there: water the earth that grass and trees may grow.' Yuk objected. 'How can I water the earth?' she said. In a temper she pulled up her cane-girdle and exposed herself. Now her parts were bright as the Sun and they flashed across the sky as lightning. Puk too was angry, and he beat his pipe on his water-tube and made the sound of thunder. Then the rain fell and the earth was green.

7

HILL MIRI

Chemir, Subansiri F.D.

Long ago, before the world was made, the Wiyu Chungum-Irum was living with his wife Chingum-Erum. One day when this woman was lying asleep, a little water fell and flowed into her. She woke up and felt bitterly cold inside. She looked everywhere to see what had made her so cold, but there was nothing. She told her husband about it, how she was shivering with the cold thing that had entered her body, but he too could not make out what it was.

Twenty days later, Chingum-Erum laid an egg. Husband and wife looked at it in wonder and put it carefully aside. After six months it broke open of its own accord, and out of it came Sichi the earth, Togle the great mountains and Togji the little hills.

8

HILL MIRI

Lomdak, Subansiri F.D.

Everything was water, water as far as the eye could see. But above the water rose the tree Teri-Ramula. As time passed a worm was born in the tree and it began to eat the wood. The dust fell into the water, year after year, until slowly the world was formed.

And then at last the tree fell to the ground. The bark on the lower side of the trunk became the skin of the world: the bark of the upper side became the skin of the sky. The trunk itself turned into rock. The branches became the hills.[5]

9

HRUSSO (AKA)

Buragaon, Kameng F.D.

At first there was no earth and sky ; there were only two great eggs. But they were not ordinary eggs, for they were soft and

[5] In a Godak variant (Sarak Miri), it was the overflowing of the waters of the Subansiri River that flooded the world. The only dry land left was in Tibet.

shone like gold. They did not stay in one place, but went round and round. At last, as they went round, they collided and both the eggs broke open. From one came the Earth, from the other the Sky, her husband.

Now the Earth was too big for the Sky to hold in his arms and he said, 'Though you are my wife, you are greater than I and I cannot take you. Make yourself smaller.'[6]

The Earth accordingly made herself pliable and the mountains and valleys were formed, and she became small and the Sky was able to go to her in love.

When the Sky made love to the Earth, every kind of tree and grass and all living creatures came into being.

10

KAMAN MISHMI

Lohit Valley, Lohit F.D.

Long long ago there were two powerful spirits named Draku and Supaidang. They were strong and powerful but rather lazy and spent their days in a free and happy way.

One day Draku met Supaidang on the bank of a river and said, 'Look brother, let us do some real work which will remain on earth in token of our strength and power.' Supaidang agreed and after some discussion they decided to level down the hills and make the surface of the earth equal. They each went to opposite corners of the earth and crushed the hills and mountains to sand and dust.

But there was a bird called Cherrai who with his wife had built a nest on the branch of a lofty tree. When he saw the spirits levelling the hills and mountains and making the whole earth one great plain he was frightened, for he thought that if they went on like this there would be no hills on earth, and if the hills were destroyed

[6] There is a similar Angami tradition that the Sky is really smaller than the Earth. 'In the beginning the Sky said to the Earth, "You are so big, I cannot cover you, wrinkle up your feet." So the Earth wrinkled to let the Sky cover it, and that is why there are hills and valleys in the earth while the sky is smooth.'—J. H. Hutton, *The Angami Nagas* (London, 1922), p. 260. Compare also the Bugun story at page 9.

there would be no trees, and if there were no trees the birds would have no shelter. So he went to the spirits and said, 'Look, you are no doubt doing a wonderful job of work breaking down mountains and turning everything into dust, but you forget what you are missing at home. Don't you know that while you are doing all this your wives have fallen sick and your parents have died?'

When Draku and Supaidang heard this, they sat down silent in grief and did not move or speak for a long time. Then Supaidang said to his brother, 'Look, brother, by doing a little work you can get anything in the world, but it is very difficult to get a wife. Even if one's parents live to a great age they become a burden to the son, but a man can enjoy his wife's company till his death, for a woman is a very precious thing.'

Draku agreed and the two brothers gave up the idea of levelling the hills and mountains and went back home. Because they abandoned their task before it was complete, the surface of the earth remained uneven, with plains in one part and with mountains in another.[7]

11

KHAMPTI

(From C. R. Macgregor, *Military Report on the Khampti-Singpho Countries*, 1887, p. 69)

In the beginning all was water. Phra (God) placed some earth on a fish's back, and ordered a female to give birth to an egg. God cut the egg in two equal portions, placing one portion on the earth. He, by means of a hill which he constructed, ascended and fixed the other half of the egg above, and this upper part formed the sky.

In the beginning there was a tree. From the berry of this tree grew a flower, and out of this flower came a pair of human beings, a male and a female.

The Rajas are said to have had their origin in the egg which Phra ordered to be produced, and which was the origin of the world.

[7] Recorded by T. K. Barua.

12

MINYONG

Riga, Siang F.D.

At first there was nothing, nothing at all, but rocks and water. The first living beings were the rocks, but they were not as rocks are now: they were soft and they could move about. From the rocks, a female rock Eling-Litung-Tune was born and from her another female rock Peddong-Nane was born. When Peddong-Nane grew up she was ashamed, for she was naked. She married another rock, Eling-Limuk-Muktum, and her first child was the fish ; it went to live in a mountain stream. Then she gave birth to the big frog, and then to Etut-Tigling, the little frog, and then to the land-frog. After that she gave birth to the insect Kungung-Pangam, which lives in water, and then to another fish.

But now Peddong-Nane left her husband and went to the sky-village Engo-Takar among the stars, where she married Karba-Bojong. By him she had many children—Ninur-Botte, Lomang-Botte, Doini-Nibu and Darro-Rabbo—and when she had borne them all she died. Doini-Nibu and Darro-Rabbo prepared rice-beer for her funeral. When the millet was ready and they poured water over it, a great cloud arose, and from the cloud was born Polung-Sabbo, the mithun.

They held a Kebang to discuss how to make an earth. 'There is nothing but water. Who will dry it up and let the earth appear?' 'I can do it,' said Polung-Sabbo and forthwith he dug a great pit with his horns, and when the water had poured into the pit, the dry land appeared. After this the rocks became hard as they are today.

13

NOCTE

Laju, Tirap F.D.

In the beginning, the earth was covered with water. Deep down in the water there lived a snake called Pu. As the years passed, slowly slowly the water sank down and the earth appeared. At first, everything was mud and when the snake moved over it, there was a long winding track which became a valley through which the rivers could flow. When the mud dried up, part of the earth became flat and part turned into hills.

In those days, there was only Joban, who is the greatest of all, in the sky. There were no men on earth but only spirits. In the sky was another god, Yang. He had a very pretty daughter who was married by one of the spirits on earth. In time, she bore chidren and these were the first men.

The first men were called Nocte and their descendants were the Ahoms. Joban gave them life and food and death.

Down in the plains there was a sort of monkey with a very long tail. One of the Noctes married her and their children are the English.

These first men lived in caves and made fire by rubbing bamboos together.

14

SHERDUKPEN

Shergaon, Kameng F.D.

Before the earth was made everything was water. There were two brothers who were supreme in the sky. The elder was Lopong-Rimbuche and the younger was Chom-Dande. One day they said to each other, 'When men are created, how will they live if there is nothing but water in the world?' There was a lotus flower growing in the sky. The brothers threw this down and immediately the water was covered with flowers. Then they called the winds from the four quarters. The east wind brought white dust and scattered it on the flowers. The west wind blew yellow dust, the south wind red dust and the north wind black dust. The wind blew the dust round and round and mixed it up together until the earth was formed. This is why the earth is of different colours.

The wind scattered the dust unevenly and the two brothers levelled it with their hands, piling it up here and making a hole there, with the result that there are today hills and valleys on the face of the earth.

15

SINGPHO

(From J. B. Neufville, *On the Geography and Population of Assam*, 1828, p. 15)

The race of men having fallen into every kind of iniquity, the Supreme Being, called by us Soari Mittia, but worshipped by all nations under different names, determined on destroying it, and creating it anew. With this in view, he gave warning in a vision to four holy Goheins, directing them to take shelter in the heaven. Meru (called by the Khamtis Noi Sao Pha) then caused seven suns to appear, which burnt up the whole earth, and destroyed everything on it. After this there came violent rains which washed away all the cinders and ashes, and refreshed and re-fertilized the earth.

The four Goheins then descended, and re-peopled it with a new race.

16

SINGPHO

(From C. R. Macgregor, *Military Report on the Khampti-Singpho Countries*, 1887, p. 70)

In the beginning there was a great flood, and all the wicked people who dwelt in the plains were drowned. This flood lasted for the eight ages of a man's life. In the ninth age Chirun and Woisin, two Nats, dried up the flood with their hair which was very thick and long. Modoi, the eldest son of Mutum, kept one family of seven people on top of a high hill, and they were not drowned.

17

SINGPHO

Imbu, Tirap F.D.

At first there was no earth nor sky, but only cloud and mist. From it a woman called Khupning-Knam was born, and since she came from the mist she was a sort of cloud. In time she gave birth to a girl called Ningon-Chinun and a boy called Tung-Kam-Waisun. They had the appearance of snow. When they grew up they married each other and from them were born a girl called Inga (Earth) and a son called Mu (Sky). Inga was mud and Mu, a cloud. These two also married and had a boy called Imbung, the Wind. When he was born, he blew so strongly that he raised the cloud, his father, into the sky and dried up his mother, the mud. In this way heaven and earth were made.

18

TARAON (DIGARU) MISHMI

Machima, Lohit F.D.

At first there was nothing but water in the world. Below the water there lived the god Techimdum. He came up to the surface and saw nothing but water.

Now below the water there was a lot of mud and in this Techimdum erected a great pillar. White ants swarmed round and crawled up to the top with their mouths full of earth, which they spread over it. When it was dry, the wind blew the earth all over the surface of the water.

Techimdum said to the ants, 'I will put up four more pillars and you must help to bring the earth up from the bottom of the ocean.' He put one pillar in each corner of the world and the ants became very busy carrying earth up above the surface of the water. Along with the earth they brought the seeds of flowers and trees. In some places they put too much earth and there were hills and mountains.

When the whole face of the water was covered with earth, two gods Drakob and Daiyunga came and levelled it in some places and piled it up high in others. In one place they made a high mountain called Ring-Lembum (Land of the Sun). The Lohit River flowed from this mountain, but after going a little way it was stopped by a range of hills. The crab cut a channel through the hills and the river flowed on again until it was stopped once more and became a great lake.

Then a wood-louse came to drink the water. It flew up into the air like a bird and let the water fall like rain back into the lake. Then came a wild cat hungry and thirsty searching for food. Wherever the cat went, the water followed. But again it had to return and now the lake overflowed all but the tops of the highest mountains, destroying villages and fields and drowning many people.

A man and his sister collected some seed and escaped to the top of the highest hill crying, 'All are dead but ourselves and our seed, and we too will soon die.' The god Drakob came to them and said, 'Why don't you light a fire and dry up the water?' 'But we don't know how to make fire,' they said. So Drakob made it for them by rubbing bits of wood together and set fire to the forest. It was so hot that the waters were dried up, and this frightened the brother and sister. They said to each other, 'At first everybody died of water, but now we will die of fire.' They made a fence of plantain leaves round their house and the fire could not pass it and they were saved.

There was no one else in the world. So brother and sister came together and they went along the valley of the Lohit, Drakob making a path for them.

Since all the trees were burnt they had no wood to make a house in which they and their children could shelter. So the wife went to Ring-Lengum and brought every kind of tree-seed and the forests grew again. So they were able to make a house.

When they had done this they planted flowers and fruit-trees and in time the wind blew the seed all over the world.

CHAPTER TWO

THE FIRMAMENT

'IT is a common belief of primitive people that sky and earth were originally joined together, the sky either lying flat on the earth or being raised so little above it that there was no room between them for people to walk upright. Where such beliefs prevail, the present elevation of the sky above the earth is often ascribed to the might of some god or hero, who gave the firmament such a shove that it shot up and has remained up above ever since. In some parts of Polynesia this exploit is attributed to the famous hero Maui; in Micronesia it is said to have been the work of various deities.'[1] In India this idea goes back to the Vedic mythology; the Aitareya Brahmana, for example, speaks of the two worlds of heaven and earth as once joined together. 'Subsequently they separated. After their separation there fell neither rain, nor was there sunshine. The five classes of beings then did not keep peace with one another. Thereupon the gods brought about a reconciliation of both these worlds. Both contracted with each other a marriage according to the rites observed by the gods.'[2]

Throughout tribal India there are stories describing the union and separation of heaven and earth, and their subsequent re-union in marriage.[3] This tradition may also be found in NEFA. To the Boris earth and sky are wife and husband: the Minyongs describe how at first Sedi, the earth, and Melo, the sky, lay close together in the marriage-bond: to the Dhammais, earth and sky are brother and sister, but live as man and wife and have children before they separate. The mountains are children of the sky, and from

[1] J. G. Frazer, *The Worship of Nature* (London, 1926), p. 26, where full references are given. Frazer also quotes, at pp. 96 and 109, similar legends from Africa.

[2] *Aitareya Brahmana*, iv. 27, quoted and translated by J. Muir, *Original Sanskrit Texts* (London, 1858-72), v. 23.

[3] A detailed account will be found in my *Myths of Middle India*, pp. 78ff.

the earth all mankind is descended. The Hrussos regard earth and sky as husband and wife: when they first loved each other, every kind of tree and grass and living creature came into being.

But so close was the union that there was no room for mankind to live, and so—according to the Boris—the sky rose up that the children of earth could move about; according to the Hill Miris, the first Wiyu to be born from the womb of the earth emerged waving his arms above his head and pushed the sky away; according to the Minyongs, the first mithun tossed the sky up with his horns.

An interesting variant, which I do not remember having seen elsewhere, occurs in the Minyong tradition. After the separation of the sky from his wife Sedi, she desired to return to him, to be one with him again. But as she was raising herself towards him, the Sun and Moon appeared, and she was ashamed and could go no farther. That part of her which was reaching towards her lord became fixed for ever, as the great mountains.

Another variant will be found in a Hrusso story. The sky quarrels with his wife, the earth, and men and animals are put to great trouble as a result. It is only when the wind is born and blows the sky far up into the heavens that the earth is left in peace. Similarly, in a Bori story at page 151 there is a reference to a mysterious being called Higgu-Doggu who carries the sky on his head. It is said that if he drops it, everyone on earth will be killed.

The same idea occurs in a Tagin story, which also represents earth and sky as enemies rather than as lovers. The sky comes down and hangs threateningly above the earth's surface, and men and animals are afraid that they will be crushed to death. After a meeting of the World Council it is decided that the opponents should each sacrifice a mithun and there is a great feast. Earth and Sky are each laid under a ten day's taboo. The Earth broke the taboo and as a result her body became deformed with hills and rocks. But the Sky kept the rules and so he is still as beautiful as ever.

1

HILL MIRI

Muri, Subansiri F.D.

At first Sichi, the Earth, and Nido, the Sky, lay close together. But when Dige-Wiyu was born from the womb of the Earth, he came out waving his arms above his head, and pushed the Sky away so that it went far off as it is now.

2

HRUSSO (AKA)

Buragaon, Kameng F.D.

Long long ago the Sky quarrelled with his wife, the Earth, and men and animals could not get any food or water, for the Sky troubled his wife in every way he could.

At this time a boy called Nejlieu was born: he was like an interpreter who puts things right. When he saw what was happening he came strongly as the wind and blew the Sky far away from the Earth. This is why the Sky is now so far away from the Earth and why men and animals today can get sufficient food and water.

Even today Nejlieu, the wind, acts as an interpreter. When it is cold he brings the heat, when it is hot he comes as a cool refreshing breeze.

3

MINYONG

Riga, Siang F.D.

Formerly Sedi, the Earth, and Melo, the Sky, lay close together, for they were wife and husband. But when Polung-Sabbo, the mithun, was born and wandered over the hills, his horns hit the clouds and in his anger he tossed them away, far above the Earth.

But afterwards, when the dry land appeared, Sedi desired to return to Melo, to be one with him again. As she was raising her body towards him, Doini, the Sun, and Pollo, the Moon, came out and there was light. Sedi was ashamed and could go no farther. That part of her which was reaching towards her lord, the Sky, became fixed for ever, as the great mountains.

4

SINGPHO

Imbu, Tirap F.D.

There are three kinds of heaven. The happiest is Likpan in the sky. Here go the great followers of Dharma who never return again to earth. They have no bodies to trouble them and live in peace and without care. The Lord of Likpan is Phan-Ningsang. The second heaven is called Mungsang. It lies on earth to the north and here go those who are not sinners and who follow Dharma, but not greatly. They have bodies, and the cares that bodies bring, and after a time return in another birth to earth. The Lord of Mungsang is Chaukhun-Phi-Phara. The third heaven is Mungphi, and this too is on earth. Here go the people who give meagre charity and who follow Dharma without zeal and they are sent back in another birth very quickly.

But sinners go to a hell which is called Gorai Indi and is in a place called Pitapum.

5

TAGIN

Bagbi, Subansiri F.D.

Nido lived in the sky and Sichi lived on earth. One day they quarrelled and Nido tried to frighten Sichi by showing her his army of the Sun, Moon and Stars. On her side Sichi displayed her army of all the animals living on earth and in the water and the snakes.

When Nido saw Sichi's mighty army he exclaimed in anger, 'You have won and I am defeated. But I will not allow you to exist any longer, even though it may be that I will be killed when I kill you.'

As he said this he came down towards the earth but checked himself a little above the surface, threatening to squash every living creature to death. But the animals of the earth and water begged him to spare them. Nido refused to listen and cried, 'I am coming. I am coming.' And for several days he hung threateningly above the earth. Animals of earth and water and the snakes gathered in Kebang (council) to decide what to do.

Presently a little bird called Chichin Jarin came to the animals and asked if they had finished their Kebang and, if so, what they had decided. One of the big animals said, 'All of us here have been considering the matter and what business has a little creature like you to say anything?' Chichin Jarin flew away but, since the animals in the Kebang would not listen to one another and could not come to any decision, they resolved to call him back for his opinion. When the bird returned, they said, 'Tell us now what you have to say.' The bird replied, 'We all should try to live. Why must you determine to get yourselves killed?'

They then decided that Nido should sacrifice his mithun called Dumir Sobo, and Sichi should sacrifice her mithun Chimir Sobo, and they should all feast together. After the feast both Sichi and Nido should remain inside their houses for ten days. If they came out of their houses before the end of that time their bodies would be deformed and they would lose their beauty. Nido and Sichi then sacrificed their mithuns and they all feasted together. Nido and Sichi returned to their houses, but after three days Sichi came out of her house and as a result her body was deformed and hills and mountains appeared all over it. Even today rocks fall and her body quakes from time to time. But Nido, the Sky, remained in his house for the full ten days, and so he is still as beautiful as ever.[4]

6

WANCHO

Khassa, Tirap F.D.

It is better to live in heaven than on earth. Once there were two brothers in the sky. One day the elder asked the younger to go

[4] Recorded by B. K. Shukla.

down to earth and see what it was like. The younger brother came down and after staying for a few days went back and said it was much better than the sky. So the elder brother made a ladder of rope and climbed down to earth. Directly he stepped from the ladder onto the ground, the younger brother pulled up the rope and the elder had to remain on earth.

From time to time the brothers compete with each other. To show that the sky is the better place, the younger brother blows his trumpet and it sounds on earth like thunder. Then the elder brother beats a great drum to show that the earth is better.

CHAPTER THREE

THE SUN AND MOON

IN his Gifford Lectures, *The Worship of Nature,* Frazer gives a convenient summary of ideas about the Sun and Moon held by the tribal people of Assam, though at that date he did not, of course, have the evidence from NEFA before him. Had he known of the assiduous interest of the Abors, Mishmis, Daflas and other tribes in the heavenly bodies, he would have modified the opening statement in the following passage.

Among the Mongoloid hill-tribes of Assam, he says,[1] 'the worship of the heavenly bodies, including the Sun and Moon, appears to be either absent or very little developed. Thus of the Lushais we are told that they do not worship the Sun or Moon or any of the forces of nature, though when wishing to emphasize a statement they frequently say, 'If what I say is not true, may the Sun and Moon desert me."[2] Similarly of the Sema Nagas we read that "the forces and phenomena of nature, though not definitely deified by the Semas, are often regarded as the manifestations or abodes of spirits. In the case of the Sun and Moon they are not worshipped or deified, and no clear conception at all is entertained of their nature. They are regarded as phenomena, and their existence is taken as a matter of course, but they are called upon to witness oaths and asseverations, and cannot be falsely invoked with impunity."[3] In all oaths it is deemed essential by the Semas that the swearing should take place between sunrise and sunset, "that the Sun may see the oath."[4] The implication seems to be that the Sun is a conscious and powerful being who can punish perjury. A being so conceived is on the highroad to divinity. The Angami Nagas so far personify the Sun that they regard him

[1] J. G. Frazer, *The Worship of Nature* (London, 1926), where all references will be found.
[2] J. Shakespear, *The Lushei Kuki Clans* (London, 1912), p. 65.
[3] J. H. Hutton, *The Sema Nagas* (London, 1921), pp. 249 ff.
[4] ibid., p. 166.

as female, the wife of the Moon, whom they look on as a male. Being a woman, she is afraid to go about in the dark and only shows herself by day; whereas her husband the Moon, being a man, moves fearlessly about in the gloom of night.[5] The Lhota Nagas think that the Sun is a flaming plate of hard metal, as big as a piece of ground on which one basket of a seed-rice is sown; by day it travels along its path in the sky, and at night it returns back under the earth and lights up the Land of the Dead; and the Moon is just such another plate of flaming metal.[6] Conceived in this materialistic way, the luminaries are far indeed from being deified. The Mikirs regard the Sun and Moon as divine, but do not specially propitiate them.[7] However, among the hill-tribes of Assam the one which seems to have approached most nearly to a worship of the Sun is the Ao. Of this tribe we are told that "among the Aos, although there is no distinctive nature worship, there is something which closely approaches it. In a way there is a Sun worship, but it would be more accurate to say that they worshipped the deity who controls it and its beneficent rays. When the weather is inclement for several days, the priests collect a number of eggs, and, going to a particular spot, break them and eat them raw, hanging up the shells for the deity. Then they implore the Sun deity to grant favourable weather; otherwise the villagers must suffer from lack of food. This is followed by a rest day, when the priests go from house to house, drinking rice-beer and singing praises to the Sun. At times they sacrifice cows and pigs to the ruling spirits of the Sun and Moon. According to the Aos this has been a customary practice from the beginning of time, and should it not be kept up, the pigs and cattle would die and the crops fail. At some of the other festivals they appeal to the deities of heaven and earth, of the Sun and of the Moon, to be favourable unto them."[8]

When we turn to NEFA, however, although we find

[5] Hutton, *The Angami Nagas*, pp. 410 ff.
[6] J. P. Mills, *The Lhota Nagas* (London, 1922), p. 172.
[7] E. Stack, *The Mikirs* (London, 1908), pp. i, 33.
[8] W. C. Smith, *The Ao Naga Tribe of Assam* (London, 1925), pp. 87. ff.

comparatively little attention paid to the Sun and Moon as deities in the Naga or Buddhist areas, there is a strong cult of the great luminaries right through the central mountains, in the Lohit, Siang and Subansiri Divisions, and in eastern Kameng.

The Adis of the Siang Valley, for example, visualize their life on earth as surrounded by a great company of good and evil spirits, above whom rises the majestic figure of the Sun-Moon, Doini-Pollo. Doini-Pollo is not indeed the Creator or the Prime Mover of creation. That dignity belongs to the enigmatic Kayum, the Great Mother, whose character and activity is shrouded in the mists of antiquity, who is not worshipped, who does not intervene in human life and who is but rarely remembered except in the great geneological songs of the Miris. From Kayum descended a line of mysterious beings down to Peddong-Nane, the living rock from whom Wiyus, men and animals were born. Doini-Pollo emerged rather late in the scheme of things, and his origin was not altogether dignified: there were at first two Suns, of an unbearable brightness, but the Frog shot at one of them with his arrow and reduced its radiance to the cool and gentle light of the Moon. The Sun-Moon was created after the Wiyus and, according to some traditions, later even than mankind.

But today, Doini-Pollo is the nearest approximation to a Supreme Deity known to the northern Adis. He reigns unchallenged in the heavens; he is the 'eye of the world'; he is as important to man as the eye is to the body. He watches everything; he is the witness; he shows men the way to go; he protects them; he shows them mercy. Above all, he is the lord of truth, and an oath taken on his name is the most binding of all. Though he is not offered special sacrifices, for he does not need them, his name is invoked on every ritual occasion. He is the unifying force behind all Adi theology.

The religion of the so-called Hill Miri groups of Subansiri is of the same general type as the Adi. At the head of a large and varied pantheon of spirits (Wiyus or Uis) will again be found the august figure of the Sun-god, or rather Sun-goddess, for in this area the Sun is a woman, who in some villages appears to stand by herself without the support of the Moon. With her is often bracketed Si, the Earth-god. 'Duinye the Sun lives in the sky and sees all things. Si lives in the earth. Together they protect man and care for him.' Duinye is the wife of Si, but they live so far apart that they can never come together.

Tagin religion is also, in its general pattern, of the Adi type. There is a pantheon of gods headed by Daini-Pol, the Sun-Moon, who has below him a great number of Wiyus. The Tagin idea of the Supreme Being may be gathered from the terms of an invocation which I noted down at Serra village during a test when someone had accused a neighbour of stealing his knife. The shaman killed a chicken and addressed the Sun:

> You are the greatest of all; you are above all; you see all. You see the lost things, the stolen things. By day you watch the world of the living, at night you watch the world of the dead. From the world below, having feasted well, you come in your finest clothes, with splendid ornaments, a coloured hat on your head, a shining dao in your hand. You look on every side; you know everything. If a man's mithun has strayed, if anyone is ill, then from this fowl speak the truth. So say now whether so-and-so stole my goods or not. If he stole them, let the marks of feathers be on the liver of this fowl. If he is innocent, let the liver be clean.

The shaman then removed the liver of the fowl, spat on it and examined it. In this case it was found unmarked, and the accused was declared innocent.

In the Mishmi pantheon, the Sun-god is called Ringya and some idea of how he is regarded will be gathered from an invocation used by the Taraon Mishmis at the time of a funeral: 'You made all; you see all; you are greatest of all; care for us all, both animals and men; protect the crops and make them grow.'

The myths recorded in this book interest themselves especially in certain problems:

(1) How did the Sun acquire its present temperature?
(2) Why is the Moon so pale and cool?
(3) What are the marks on the Moon?
(4) What is the relationship between the Sun and Moon?
(5) What causes an eclipse?

There is a very common belief, which is shared by many tribes in other parts of India, that originally the Sun was too hot. It is sometimes supposed that at first there were two or more Suns which shone together at the same time, thus creating excessive heat, or in turn so that there was no night. The Moklums, for example, say that the Sun and Moon used to shine both day and night. The Taraons say that two Suns were always in the sky and never gave any hope of darkness. The Wanchos have a tradition that the Moon also was very hot until someone threw mud at it and cooled it.

There are many ways by which this destructive heat of the Sun and even of the Moon was lessened. There is an Apo Tani tale that one of the original Suns was killed by an angry father, whose child had been withered by the heat. The Daflas say that someone shot out one of the Sun's eyes and thus halved his power. The Singphos say that at first there were Suns who caused great distress to the world. The great god Mathum-Matta destroyed all but two who hid behind the Himalaya Mountains. Here the Sun made a golden and the Moon a silver boat and now come alternately to light the world. The Moklums say that god arranged the duties of the Sun and Moon, allocating one to the day and the other to the night. The Taraons suppose that somebody caught and killed one of the two Suns who were making life intolerable for mankind. The Kamans say there were at first four Suns and eight brave men went to destroy three of them.

According to some traditions, the Moon was at first a Sun. In a Minyong story, one of the original two Suns was hit by a poisoned arrow and became the pale Moon. The Padams say that in the days when the Moon was very hot, his father hit him and tore out one of his eyes, a tradition which is known also to the Gallongs. The Taraons say that a great tree stands between the earth and the Moon and quenches his rays. The Wanchos say that someone threw mud at the Moon and cooled it. In a Singpho story, the Moon became pale and saintly as a Lama, when his sister the Sun, hot with passion, tried to force him into an incestuous marriage with her.

The marks on the Moon are attributed by many tribes to something which has been thrown at it. Sometimes it is dung, sometimes ashes or even a hare. According to the Daflas, the marks were caused by a beating given him by his wife, the Sun. There is a Miri tradition that the marks were caused by human dung thrown at the Moon by another deity in the course of a public quarrel at a festival. In a Mishmi story the Sun threw the Moon into a pond and the mud still clings to his face, because he was angry at his persistent request for a share of his heat.

Ideas about the relations between the Sun and Moon vary greatly from tribe to tribe. In the first place, there is much confusion about their sex. In Assam generally the Sun is often recorded as feminine and the Moon masculine, a view which is held by the Angami and Sema Nagas and the Khasis. Hutton notes that outside Assam the idea of the Moon as male and the Sun female is widespread. It appears to have been held by some of the early Scandinavians; the Moon is masculine and the Sun feminine in Western Germany; the Moon is masculine in all Semitic languages; the Uraons make the Moon masculine; so do the Fijians, and the Guarayo Indians. The Nagas of the Patkoi state that the Sun and Moon were originally sister and brother. They quarrelled, and the Moon in a fit of temper burnt up everything on earth. A tree fell on him and he died, after which the Sun died of grief for her brother, and eventually they were reborn with their sexes reversed. Here we have the idea of the interchange of functions between the two orbs, as also in the case of the Eskimo, who make the sun smear with soot the face of her incestuously-minded brother the Moon.[9]

[9] From a note by J. H. Hutton, where the authorities are given, in J. P. Mills, *The Ao Nagas*, p. 301.

In the stories recorded here, the Boris make the Sun feminine and the Moon masculine; so do the Singphos. The Padams say that Sun and Moon are brother and sister; some Minyongs declare them to be two brothers, others to be two sisters. The Dhammais regard them as two sisters. The Buguns say that the Sun is the Rani of the day and the Moon the Raja of the night. The Tator-Tanis regard the Sun as their mother. In an Idu Mishmi story the Moon is the younger brother of his sister, the Sun. In Nocte and Taraon Mishmi tales, Sun and Moon change their sex from time to time. In a Singpho story, Sun and Moon are twins; the Sun is the girl. A Hrusso story about the origin of death, recorded in Chapter XV, assumes more complicated relationships. There are two Suns—a male Sun and his wife, and two Moons—a male Moon and his wife. The Sun's wife and the Moon's husband fall in love, but have to come to earth to meet one another.

Ideas about the eclipse have a remarkable similarity throughout the whole of India.[10] The traditional Puranic account is, of course, that Rahu, the Asura, takes vengeance on the Sun and Moon by swallowing them from time to time, and many of the central and southern Indian tribes hold this tradition in one form or another. The Todas, for example, say that a snake devours the hare that lives on the surface of the Moon. The Muthuvans say that a solar eclipse is caused when a serpent coils round the Sun. There are frequent references to the great snake or frog which devours the Sun and then has to let it go.

A completely different tradition, however, holds that an eclipse is due to the fact that the Sun and Moon are either in debt themselves or have stood surety for a debt from a money-lender who duns them and thus causes darkness by shutting them up. This may be found all over India and in Assam is represented by the Angami belief that an eclipse is caused by the Sun and Moon having to repay a loan of borrowed light.[11] In the present collection there is an interesting variant of this in the Bori story which attributes

[10] There is a detailed account in my *Myths of Middle India*, pp. 68 ff.
[11] J. H. Hutton, *The Angami Nagas*, p. 411.

an eclipse to an attempt on the part of men, animals and Wiyus to liberate the Sun and Moon who are working as slaves in the house of a great black Wiyu like a bear. The Wiyu demands a heavy price for his slaves and, though most of it is paid, the whole amount has never yet been found. From time to time, therefore, the Wiyu comes to claim his debt and this causes the eclipse.

Generally, however, the 'Devouring' motif is the most popular. In the Tagin and Gallong stories a demon called Tame eats the Sun, who ultimately escapes through his vent. In Moklum, Nocte and Wancho stories it is a great Frog who attacks the heavenly bodies.

A Minyong tradition, however, is quite different. A Wiyu finds the Sun too hot and throws his shade on it. He abuses the Moon and she veils part of her face. Whenever this occurs there is an eclipse. On the other hand, in a Kaman Mishmi story, the Sun (after losing his three comrades in the sky) has gone too pale and a dog has to bite him from time to time to remind him to do his work properly.[12]

[12] I have remarked on the absence of Sun-myths in the Naga groups, but the following passage by C. R. Stonor on certain festivals observed by the Northern Sangtams suggests I may be wrong.

'A remarkable feature of the ritual is the very strong element of Sun worship: (1) the night dance is accompanied by flaring torches lit at the new fire, (2) a sacred fire is lit at the place of sacrifice, (3) it is lit precisely at sunrise, (4) the mithun heads must be so oriented as to catch the first rays of the risen Sun, (5) a little meat is put aside specifically for the Sun and the Moon, (6) beer is heated symbolically over the sacred fire, (7) I was told that the invocations before dancing and before feasting are addressed to the Sun and the Moon, and in the latter case the two celebrants had every appearance of addressing the Sun, (8) among the ornaments of the Sangtam women (and neighbouring tribes) are large, saucer-like discs of white shell, worn as necklaces. There seems a definite connection between these discs and the Sun. When I asked the meaning of the sacred fire at the place of sacrifice I was informed: "if there was no fire lit at the festival, the women would not be able to wear the shell discs." I was also told in another village that there is a connection between these discs and the torches used at the night dance.'—C. R. Stonor, 'The Feasts of Merit among the Northern Sangtam Tribe', *Anthropos*, Vol. XLV (1950), p. 11.

1

APA TANI

Reru, Subansiri F.D.

First of all there was Kenku, but no one can say what it was or what it was like. From Kenku was born a female Wiyu in the form of an earthen ball. She said to Kenku, 'I am Chantu.' Kenku said, 'You have been born from me. Who will be born from you?' 'I will give birth to Abo Tani,' said Chantu. Then Abo Tani was born. Chantu said to him, 'I am going to die. You must give birth to mankind.' 'If you die', said Abo Tani, 'where will all men live? Everything will be dark and where will we get our food and water?' Chantu said, 'My thighs will become the earth on which you can move about and cultivate your fields. My eyes will become the Sun and Moon and my blood will become water.'[13]

2

APA TANI

Reru, Subansiri F.D.

In the days of Abo Tani there lived the Wiyus—Doini, Polo and Si. Of these Si was the stronger and very wicked and he had many quarrels with Doini and Polo. One day he asked Tamu[14] to go to Doini and Polo and devour them. Tamu took the form of a frog and when Doini and Polo saw him approaching them they cried, 'We will give you fowls, dogs and cats. We will give you *tai* and *kra* leaves so long as you do not eat us.' But Tamu took no notice of them.

Then a priest of the Wiyus called Karcha went to Tamu and said, 'Don't devour Doini and Polo. If they do not give you the things they have promised, I will give them to you instead.' 'Very well,' said Tamu. 'If you will give me these things I will leave Doini and Polo alone.' In this way Karcha made peace between

[13] Recorded by B. K. Shukla.

[14] Tamu is described by the Apa Tanis as the body-guard of Si. He is like 'an Assam Rifles jawan who looks after and protects his officer'.

them and Abo Teni made offerings to Tamu and Karcha as well as to Doini and Polo.[15]

But Tamu is a very wicked creature and still from time to time tries to devour Doini and Polo and sometimes succeeds.[16]

3

APA TANI

Reru, Subansiri F.D.

One day while the Sun was playing with her brother the Moon, they found the carcass of a mithun lying beneath some bushes. They were delighted and at once set to discussing how to divide the flesh. They agreed to share it exactly. When they had cut it up and divided it, the Moon said to the Sun, 'You take your share and go ahead, and I'll follow with mine.' So the Sun went home first and shared the meat with her father. But the Moon, lagging behind, ate up every morsel of his share. When he reached home empty-handed, his father, who had heard all about it from the Sun, asked him where his meat was. The Moon said that he had eaten it all. His father lost his temper and beat him. His stick caught one of the Moon's eyes and tore it out. This is why the light of the Moon is less than the Sun's light, for he has only one eye.

4

APA TANI

Reru, Subansiri F.D.

Before our Sun was made, there was another, earlier, Sun.

Dacha-Untre had a son named Ari-Untre. Father and son never got on very well together, and one day they had a violent quarrel.

[15] At the time of an eclipse the Apa Tanis behave very much like people all over India, except that there is no taboo on pregnant women watching it as there is elsewhere. Everybody goes out of doors and make as much noise as possible. The Apa Tanis shoot arrows into the air to frighten Tamu away ; women poke the pigs with their sticks to make them scream and they pull feathers out of the fowls so that they too may make a noise and divert Tamu's attention. Nobody goes indoors until the eclipse is over. Then they extinguish all the fires in the houses for fear that Tamu will set their houses on fire, and the priests sacrifice fowls.

[16] Recorded by B. K. Shukla.

Dacha-Untre was so angry that he shot his son with an arrow and killed him. As the blood flowed from the boy's body it turned into fire. His bones turned into iron.

The arrow with which Dacha-Untre shot his son went into one of his eyes ; that is how it killed him. But there was one eye left, and it was bright and shining as the Sun. Presently it went into the heavens and wandered about as our Sun does today. But it was so hot that the trees and grasses were withered and men died of the heat.

Wiyu Middo-Kojim had three pretty sisters, Dule-Yasu, Dule-Yaba, and Dule-Yape. One day some strangers met them as they were gathering wood in the forest and raped them. Not only that: they took them away and forced them into marriage. These girls had many cows and goats and used to eat *pan, supari* and *chuna.* This is why the Assamese today have many cows and goats, but no mithuns, and why they eat *pan.*

Middo-Kojim also had a son, Kojim-Ludi, and a daughter, Kojim-Taker. One day the two children were playing together, when the Sun came up into the sky. They had no time to take shelter, and its heat burnt their heads to ashes and they died.

Middo-Kojim was very angry at this and he said to the Sun, 'How great you are, but how proud you are! Are you willing to fight me? Otherwise I am going to kill you.' Before the other could answer he raised his gun and shot him dead. Then all the world became dark until the new gentler Sun came to shine in the sky.

5

BORI

Gatte, Siang F.D.

There is a great black Wiyu like a bear and when the Sun and Moon go out on their course he catches them and keeps them as slaves. When this happens the world becomes dark. When this happened first, men, animals and Wiyus held a Kebang and decided to go in search of the missing deities. They came to the house of the great Wiyu and found that the Sun and Moon were working as slaves in his fields. Men and animals and Wiyus said,

'If you keep these as slaves, how will we be able to live on the earth?' The Wiyu said, 'I paid the parents of my two slaves a great price for them, beads and mithuns and coats and dishes. If you pay back to me what I paid to them then I will let them go.' Men and animals and Wiyus paid most of the things that the Wiyu demanded, but they have never been able to pay the whole debt. And so from time to time even now the Wiyu comes to demand his debt and this causes the eclipse.[17]

6

BORI

Gasheng, Siang F.D.

Sitking-Kedding (the earth) and her husband Peddo-Dodum (the sky) used formerly to live together. Their first daughter was Doini, and after her a son, Pollo, was born. As the children grew taller, Peddo-Dodum rose slightly above the earth so that they could move about.

Presently Doini got hungry and begged her mother to give her something to eat. At that time Tani was in the womb of Sitking-Kedding and she was afraid that when Tani was born Doini would eat him. So she said to her husband, 'Take these two children up into the sky with you.' But he said, 'How can I leave you and go away?' Sitking-Kedding was angry and kicked her husband up into the sky. As he went he took Doini and Pollo with him.

When Tani was born, Peddo-Dodum hid Doini and the whole world became dark and the child could not see his way about. Then another son was born called Taro. Sitking-Kedding was very worried because her two sons had to live in the dark and she went to her husband and begged him not to hide Doini any longer Peddo-Dodum said, 'I will let Doini and Pollo out of hiding on condition that Tani will belong to Doini and Taro will belong to Pollo.' He said, 'Doini will eat nothing. She will only drink blood and Pollo will also drink blood.' But when he heard that, Pollo

[17] The institution of slavery has existed from times immemorial among the Boris and other tribes of northern Siang. Slaves, however, can be redeemed. sometimes by their own efforts, sometimes by members of their clan who repay the initial expenditure of the owner. Many slaves have been freed by officers of the NEFA Administration in the past few years.

came out and declared that he would only drink blood for one day in a month. Sitking-Kedding agreed to these conditions.

Peddo-Dodum brought Doini out of her hiding-place and the whole world became full of light. All mankind is descended from Tani and since he belongs to Doini she cares for men. The Wiyus are descended from Taro and since Taro belongs to Pollo, it is Pollo who looks after the Wiyus.

In one day Doini drinks blood many times and that is why she is so strong and hot, and on her account many human beings die. But Pollo only drinks blood once a month, on the day when he rises red into the sky, and for this reason the Wiyus only die once in a month.

7

BUGUN (KHOWA)

Senchong, Kameng F.D.

The Sun is the Rani of the day and the Moon is the Raja of the night. But the great serpent, Ettong, is jealous of them and wishes to kill them and become Lord of the Sky in their place. From time to time he goes into the sky and seizes the Sun or Moon, thus causing an eclipse.

But whenever he does this all the people on earth shout, 'Let go, let go,' and he is frightened and lets them alone.[18]

8

DAFLA

(From G. D. S. Dunbar, *Abors and Galongs*, p. 65)

Now in those early days the Sun was much bigger and far hotter than he is now. So hot was he that he burnt up everything,

[18] The Buguns, like people all over India, shout, beat gongs and light fires at the time of an eclipse of the Moon or a partial eclipse of the Sun. But for a total eclipse of the Sun, they go outside their houses and throw off all their ornaments and clothes, hide themselves and their children under bamboo baskets and do not allow any animal to come near them. For they think that at the moment of darkness their clothes, ornaments, daos or domestic animals will turn into demons and destroy them. After the eclipse they bathe and only then resume their clothes.

trees and harvest alike, and the people in their distress cried out for someone to lessen the fiery heat. So a god Tamo ate up a portion of the Sun, and Debo-Kombu took his bow and shot an arrow into the eye of the Sun and put it out. And the Sun became very angry and went and hid himself under the earth.

9

DHAMMAI (MIJI)

Sachung, Kameng F.D.

At the very begining of the world a woman lived alone. Her name was Sujang-Nui and she gave birth to a girl-child whom she called Biuri-Riang. This child was like a white stone and from her were born two sisters who were the Sun and Moon.

In time the Sun gave birth to a girl whom she called Laolang and the Moon gave birth to a daughter whom she called Jong-Dang. These two children were human beings.

The daughter of the Sun, being the greatest, was regarded as a Rani and she had the finest clothes and ornaments and was given the best food. But the daughter of the Moon lived like a peasant-girl and worked as her servant. The daughter of the Sun was so beautiful in her bright clothes and ornaments that her mother was afraid somebody would kidnap her. So she always kept her shut up in a silver box. Jong-Dang was just as beautiful, but in her poor clothes and cheap ornaments she did not look so attractive, and she had to work hard, cooking, washing clothes and making rice-beer for her mistress.

After a time Biuri-Riang had another child, this time a son called Abbu-Bullu and he in turn had two sons Dung-Riang and Jibru. When Dung-Riang grew up he wanted a wife, but there were no people then in the world. Dung-Riang had a servant called Jowang and one day he sent him to fish in a stream among the hills. On that very day Laolang sent Jong-Dang to the same stream to get her some fish for supper, the girl fishing up-stream and Jowang was fishing down-stream. Jong-Dang made the water muddy and it flowed down to where Jowang was fishing. When he saw the muddy water he wondered what could have caused it. Presently Jong-Dang spat on the water and the spittle flowed down and when Jowang saw it he said to himself that there must be some human being there and went up-stream until he saw the girl. Both of them were young and in search of love. Jowang asked the girl if she was married and she replied, 'I am the daughter of the Moon and I am not yet married.' Then he asked if her elder sister was married and she replied that she was not.

The servant said, 'My master's name is Dung-Riang. He too is unmarried.' After some more talk they went to their different homes and then day after day they used to meet and gradually came to love each other. One day Jowang followed Jong-Dang home but could not see Laolang anywhere in the house. Jong-Dang said to him, 'Don't come here. Run for your life. If my mother sees you, she will burn you to ashes.' 'But I want to see Laolang,' he said. 'Nobody can do that,' she replied, 'for she is hidden in that silver box.' When he heard that, Jowang went home quickly and told everything to his master who got very excited and said, 'Take my younger brother Jibru and a lot of rice-beer and give it to the Sun and Moon. When they have drunk enough, they will probably let you see Laolang.'

So the next day they took a lot of rice-beer to the house of the Sun and gave it to the Sun and Moon to drink. But before she accepted it, the Sun asked, 'Why have you come here and why are you giving us all this beer?' The visitors said, 'We have heard of your beautiful daughter and we want her in marriage for Dung-Riang.' The Sun was very angry when she heard this and was about to burn them to ashes but the Moon said, 'What is the use of destroying these people. We have only one girl here in the house. Let them look at her and if they like her, they can have her.' She called her own daughter Jong-Dang and said, 'This is Laolang.' But Jowang, of course, knew Jong-Dang well and was not deceived. He tried again to persuade the Sun to show her own daughter but she refused.

At last they went home unsuccessful, but they went on trying and used to go often with gifts of beer, but they were never able to see the hidden girl. Then one day Jibru played a trick. When they came to the house he said to Jowang, 'Go and fetch some wood and I will wait for you here.' When Jowang was on the way back and quite near the house, Jibru fell down and pretended to be dead. Jowang threw his wood away and wept crying, 'We came for your daughter and now my master's son is dead.' He spread a cloth over Jibru's body and sat by him weeping.

When Laolang heard the sound of weeping, she came out of the silver box and cautiously went to look at what she thought was the corpse. But when she lifted up the cloth, Jibru jumped up and seized her. Jowang caught hold of Jong-Dang and they carried off the two girls to Dung-Riang's house. There Dung-Riang married Laolang and Jowang married Jong-Dang. This is why among the Dhammais there is the custom that only rich men's sons can marry rich men's daughters and the sons of servants must marry the daughters of other servants.

In time Laolang had many children and these were the first human beings.

10

GALLONG

Don, Subansiri F.D.

Hindu-Doini and Hingar-Pol were born of Hindu and Hingar. Doini the Sun was born first. Mochu-Pada the Wiyu had two sons. One day they went out to see the Sun, but he killed them with his heat. Mochu-Pada Wiyu was angry and went to shoot him with his bow and arrow. But by the time he reached the path, Doini the Sun had already passed and Pol the Moon came instead. In those days the Moon was hot as the Sun and Mochu-Pada mistook her for him and shot out one of her eyes. Since then her light has been pale and cool.

Hingar-Pol was very angry and said, 'What have I done to you that you should shoot me?' The Wiyu was sorry and said, 'When you grow old, you will grow young again.' This is why the Moon is now young, now old.

Mochu-Pada called Tame to catch the Sun and bring him to him. Tame caught him, but the Sun escaped through his vent. And so it goes on, Tame catches the Sun, but he always escapes in the end. This is an eclipse.

11

IDU MISHMI

Dibang Valley, Lohit F.D.

There was no Moon at the beginning but there were two Suns who gave light and heat to the world. Epanja was the father of the Suns and their mother was Lanbbai.

Now the younger of the two Suns was bad and one day he said to his elder brother, 'Why should we not burn the earth with our great heat?' The elder brother replied that it would be wrong to do this and that in any case his brother's body was too small for it. But the younger Sun took no notice and left his home and went to the middle of the sky and there began to pour his heat upon the earth.

As a result, grasses and trees dried up and the farmers in the fields died of sunstroke. Even the houses could not give shelter to the wives and children. The animals wandered about searching for shade and water, but it was no use and the streams and rivers soon dried up.

When Anya[19] saw the suffering of the earth and of the living creatures on it, he called the gods of the sky for a meeting and they decided to send someone to talk to the elder Sun about what was going on. But none of them knew how to find the way to his home. Anya then said, 'I have little knowledge of the path but I will tell you what I know. First go in an eastern direction until you reach a place where two rivers meet. From here a track goes to Laliya where the god Nyu Anjoro lives. Thence you must go through many villages until you reach the gate of the Sun's house.' Anya advised the messenger to take some presents to offer to the elder Sun. One of the gods suggested that some rice-beer would be a suitable gift, but Anya thought that would not be proper. He told them to give the bamboo in which they had put the rice-beer to the Mishmis, and this is how the Mishmis learnt to drink beer. Instead of this Anya suggested that they should take pigs and fowls and birds as presents. This is why the Mishmis worship the Sun with pigs, fowls and birds whenever it is necessary.

[19] Anya is one of the greatest Idu gods, second only to the supreme Inni Taya.

Anya's messenger reached the elder Sun and offered his presents. The elder Sun received him hospitably but when he heard the story of misery caused to the people of the earth by his brother he was filled with anger and he seized the younger Sun and threw him into a pool of mud. Ever since then the younger Sun has never dared to go into the sky so long as his elder brother was present. He only comes when the elder, greater, Sun goes to take his rest. As a result of being thrown into the pool of mud the younger Sun grew pale and the marks of the mud may still be seen on his face.

The elder Sun gave the messenger a silk-worm so that men could weave their garments from it and a white jewel for their necklaces. He said to the Mishmis, 'I will always be in the stones as Madu-Lalaya and will give you fire.'[20]

12

KAMAN MISHMI

Lohit Valley, Lohit F.D.

Long long ago there were four Suns in the sky and these used to give so much heat that no crops could grow and everything was dried up. So one day the people held a meeting and resolved to destroy three of the four Suns, for the heat and light of one would be quite enough. They chose eight brave men and sent them with two dogs to destroy the Suns up in the sky.

The party set out on their long journey to the sky and when they reached there, they fought with the three Suns after defeating them, threw their bodies into a river.

But this took a long time and the climate of the sky did not suit them. So they left one of the dogs whose name was Tafyeo in the sky to guard the Sun and went back home. On this terrible journey seven of them died and only one man and one dog returned to earth to tell the people what had happened to the three Suns. When the people heard the news there was great rejoicing on earth, for they had suffered greatly from the heat of the Suns.

The fourth Sun who remained in the sky was very sad at the death of his comrades and wept day and night for them. This made

[20] Recorded by T. K. Barua

him pale and thin and he did not give enough heat and light to the world. When the dog Tafyeo saw this he jumped up at him and tore off a bit of his flesh. Even since then Tafyeo bites the Sun once a year to remind him to perform his duties. This is what causes the eclipse.[21]

13

MINYONG

Ratung, Siang F.D.

(From G. D. S. Dunbar, *Abors and Galongs*, p. 65)

Once upon a time there were two Suns, brothers, each taking it in turn to shine for twelve hours. So it was day all the time. But a frog shot one of the Suns with an arrow and killed the fire that was in it, so now it has no warmth, but as the Moon it shines at night. And the splinters made by the arrow became stars. And now in revenge the two Suns shoot their arrows down upon the earth and bring death to the children of men. But the frog, to escape from the wrath of the Sun, hides in the water.

14

MINYONG

Komsing, Siang F.D.

When Kayum-Sedi-Sedi-Irkong-Komi-Manne died, though his body perished, his eyes remained alive and fierce. The Wiyus thought that a clever craftsman might perhaps make something beautiful out of them. They sent for Sedi-Digir-Irkong-Komong-Yongmo and he removed the eyes from the corpse and told them to go into the sky. They flew up above the clouds and became the two Suns. Thereafter there was no night and the heat was so great that the harvests failed and great rivers dried up.

The frightened Wiyus assembled in their Kebang. 'If this goes on,' they said, 'we will all die, for there is no night when we can get our food. Let us beat one of the Suns and frighten him away.'

[21] Recorded by T. K. Barua.

They built a platform and Silling-Pai, the maker of rainbows, climbed upon it and shot with his bow at one of the Suns. The arrow was poisoned and the Sun grew weak and pale. The Wiyus said to him, 'Go after the other Sun. Follow it round. You will be the Moon.' Slowly and wearily Pollo, the Moon, rose from the earth and followed the Sun across the sky.

But Silling-Pai was frightened at what he had done and jumped into the Siang River, bow in hand. He still lives there as a frog crying *'Kik-kik-kik-kik'*. Ladang Laiyu, the water-spirit, took the bow from him and gave it to Go-Eng, a Wiyu in the form of an insect which says *'Go-eng-gorio'*. Go-Eng took the bow and arrows to a clearing in the forest and hung them on the stump of a tree. When men came to work Go-Eng killed them. Ever since, at the beginning of the season, when people first go to work in the fields, they fall ill. It is all Go-Eng's doing.

15

MINYONG

Riu, Siang F.D.

The Wiyu Tameng-Tamak gets angry with the Sun for being too hot and casts his shadow on it. He abuses the Moon for shining so brightly and she veils part of her face.

16

MINYONG

Komkar, Siang F.D.

Sedi is the Earth: Melo is the Sky. The Earth is a woman. the Sky is a man. These two married, and when they came together, Wiyus, men and animals held a Kebang to consider how they could save themselves from being crushed between them. Sedi-Diyor, one of the greatest of the Wiyus, caught hold of the Sky and beat him so that he fled far up into the heavens leaving the Earth behind. As he went away, the Earth gave birth to two daughters. But she was so sad at losing her husband that she could not bear to look at them. Sedi-Diyor, therefore, found a woman to nurse them.

When the little girls were old enough to walk, light began to shine from them, and day by day the light grew brighter. After a while the nurse died and Sedi-Diyor buried her in the ground. The children wept for her as for their mother: they wept so much that they died, and the light they gave died with them.

Now it was dark again, and Wiyus, men and animals were afraid. The Wiyus thought that the nurse must have stolen something from the children and that it was this that had made them weep so much. So they dug up her body to see what it was. They found that it had rotted away, all except the eyes. They saw the eyes great and shining in the darkness, and their own reflection was mirrored in them. They thought that they saw the dead children in the eyes. They took them to a stream and washed them in the water for five days and five nights, and made them shine more brightly. But they could not remove the images looking back at them from the eyes.

The Wiyus sent for a carpenter and he cut the eyes open with great care and removed the reflections, which turned into living children. They called one girl Sedi-Irkong-Bomong and the other Sedi-Irkong-Bong. They did not let them go out of their house.

But one day, when they were grown up, the elder girl, Bomong, dressed herself in gaily-coloured clothes and many ornaments, and went out in her beauty to wander through the world. As she came out of the house, there was light all round her, and it was day. She went across the hills and did not return.

After a long time, her sister Bong went to look for her, tracing the path by her footsteps. But when she came out, there was so much light that she caused the rocks to break, the trees to wither and men to faint in the heat.

Wiyus, men and animals held yet another Kebang and decided that the only thing to do was to kill one of the sisters. They were afraid to do it and argued for a long time, but at last the frog went to sit by the path and waited bow in hand for the girl to come. When Bong came shining and lovely he shot her with an arrow in each side and she died. Then it was not so hot, the light was not so dazzling. The trees revived and men went again about their work.

But the girl's body lay where it had fallen. Then there came along Kirte, a Wiyu in the form of a rat: he dragged the corpse to Bomong on his back. As he went along, he fell over and ever since the rat's legs have been crooked. But he got up and took the body to a river where Bomong was due to pass. He showed her sister's body and she wept for sorrow and fear that she herself would be killed. She took a path that no one knew and sat down, placing a big stone on her head. With the shadow of the stone, the world became dark.

At this, Wiyus, men and animals were afraid and they went to search for light. For a long time they found nothing. Then Nginu-Botte caught a rat, a wild bird and a cock and sent them to find Bomong. The cock went first, but its parts were so heavy that it could not walk. It met Banjibanman and told him its trouble, and he cut off its organ and threw it away. Its testes went into its body. This is why the cock has no parts outside its body.

The cock's organ turned into the earthworm.

The cock went on and at last found Bomong and begged her to come back. 'No', she said, 'they killed my sister and they'll kill me. Tell them that I willl only come if they make my sister alive.' The cock returned and told Nginu-Botte what the girl had said. He found a carpenter who fashioned Bong's body, making it small and putting life into it. When Bomong heard that her sister was alive again, she threw the stone down from her head and stood up. The day returned and as the light blazed out, the cock cried *'Kokoko-kokoko'* ; the wild bird sang *'Pengo-pengo'* : the rat squeaked *'Taktak-taktak'*. For they were glad at the light and heat.

17

MOKLUM

Khimiyang, Tirap F.D.

The cock at first lived in the sky. He was the chief minister of Rang. Now Rang had two children. They were twins, a boy and a girl. The cock said to them, 'If you keep apart, you will never have children, so why not live together even though you are brother and sister.' So they came together and in due time the girl gave birth to a lump of flesh like the fleshy part of a man's leg. The girl did not know what to do with it, for it was neither dead nor living. So she put it by the fire and it gradually dried up. At last it burst and the bits flew in all directions. From these came all mankind scattered about the world.

The name of Rang's son was Rangsa and his daughter's name was Yappi. They used to walk night and day across the sky and so there was never any night. When Rang saw that this caused mankind a great deal of trouble, he appointed separate times when the boy and the girl should walk in the sky and when they should stay at home. Since then they have not come out together in the sky.

18

MOKLUM

Longke, Tirap F.D.

A great frog called Luk lives in Rang's village in the sky. He has an enormous mouth and can never get enough to eat. So from time to time he tries to eat the Sun and the Moon, taking them between his jaws.

Directly the Sun or the Moon become hidden in the great creature's mouth, people on earth fire guns and beat drums and beg him not to eat them. After a time the frog gets frightened and lets the Sun or the Moon go.

19

NOCTE

Tut, Tirap F.D.

At first the earth was very small and completely surrounded by water. A woman fell from the sky. At that time there was no man living. Gradually the water went down and more and more earth appeared. Then a man came down from the sky. The man and the woman came together and they had many children. Rango-Kotakrang, who is greatest of all, put the Sun and the Moon in the sky as without them the first man and woman could not have lived.

Formerly the Sun was a man and the Moon was a woman and they were living together as husband and wife. The Moon had many children but the Sun killed them by his heat. The Moon used to cultivate her crops in her forest-clearing but the Sun's heat destroyed them. One day in a temper, the Moon threw mithun-dung at the Sun. Then the Sun said, 'Henceforth we will change our sex for a few days every month. I will be a woman and you will be a man ; then we will change and I will be a man and you will be a woman.' This is why the Moon sometimes is smaller and sometimes larger. Husband and wife had another quarrel later on and this time it was the Sun who threw the mithun-dung at the Moon and the marks of this can still be seen.

20

NOCTE

Tut, Tirap F.D.

One day men and animals gathered together to make a Chief. Everyone put forward his claim in turn and then the cock said, 'The Sun and Moon come into the sky at my command, so I should be the Chief.' They agreed and made the cock their Chief.

Early in the morning the cock used to cry, *'Boo-boo'* and in the evening, *'Nok-nok'*. But as years went by the tigers began to kill other animals and even human beings at night and men began to kill each other in the day-time. When the cock heard this he was very angry. He put on his red hat and fixed daos to his feet and cried, *'Boo-boo nok-nok'*. When they heard this the Sun and Moon were confused and rose into the sky together. The day became dark and everyone was afraid. So now whenever the cock is angry, he cries, *'Boo-boo nok-nok'* and there is an eclipse.

21

PANGGI

Geku, Siang F.D.

In the time of Doini and Dopo, Pollo and Poyo it was always day: there was no night then. They had no eyes, no hands, for it was always day. Then they got eyes and limbs, but they had no food. 'How can we get food', asked the Wiyus, 'so long as there is no night?' So the Frog killed Doini the Sun and it was dark.

The Wiyus did not like this. They held a Kebang and declared that Doini must be made alive again. They told men and animals to make him alive. But Doini said, 'You killed me for no reason. I won't become alive. Why did you kill me?' They replied, 'At least become alive: you may eat what you will, you may go where you will.'

At that Doini rose up and the day returned. But now death came to the world. If someone dies in the daytime, we say he has been devoured by the Sun, if the night, that he has been devoured by the Moon.

22

PASI

Siang Frontier Division

(From G. D. S. Dunbar, ***Abors and Galongs***, p. 66)

There were two Suns, and a god, to lessen the scorching heat, took his bow and shot an arrow at one of them, and killed it. And so its blazing light turned into the pale fire of the Moon.

When the Sun went and hid under the earth the land was plunged into darkness and a great fear fell upon all and men went to ask the Sun to appear again. But the Sun was angry and hid below the earth. Now there was a bird with a long tail perching on the sun as he lay sulking just below the horizon, and the bird talked to the men. When the Sun heard the talking he called out, 'Who do I hear talking?' and, out of curiosity, rose to look. And he saw the men who had come to petition him sitting on the ground, and they implored him to return and shed his light over the world. After a little while the Sun spoke and said, 'If you will give me a daughter of the gods to eat, then I will return and lighten the earth.' The men agreed and went back to their homes, but the bat followed them and said, 'It is a daughter of men that the Sun wants, not a daughter of the gods.' So the men took one of their daughters and brought her to the Sun as a sacrifice ; and he devoured her and arose in his strength to give light and warmth to the world. But from that day death has come into world to destroy the children of men ; for before that they, like the gods, were immortal.

23

SINGPHO

Wakitna, Tirap F.D.

When the earth and sky were first made they were close together. Ningun-Chinun and her mate Tungkam-Waisun appeared on earth and loved each other. Soon Ningun-Chinun gave birth to twins, a boy called Sita the Moon and a girl called Chan the Sun. The mother cut the cord and threw it to the ground and from it came every kind of grass and tree. Tungkam-Waisun made a ladder for the children to play with, and the Sun and Moon climbed on it into the sky.

Then Ningun-Chinun gave birth to a human child called Machang, a being like a gourd called Wakum, and Lung-Nin-Chang who was a rock.

The three children used to play together. One day, as they were playing, Lung-Nin-Chang broke open his gourd-brother Wakum and many little people came out of him. When the Sun and Moon climbed into the sky, the little people were happy and content, but when the Sun and Moon came down again, they suffered in the great darkness. So next time that the Sun and Moon went into the sky, Tungkam-Waisun broke the ladder and they could not go back to earth.

When the Sun grew up she wanted a husband and tried to marry her brother, the Moon. But he said, 'We are brother and sister and I can't possibly marry you.' The Sun tried to take him by force and he ran away ashamed, and became a Lama, pale and saint-like. But the Sun is a woman, always hot with desire and shines brightly.

24

SINGPHO

Imbu, Tirap F.D.

Formerly there were nine Suns. Naturally they made everything very hot and men, trees and animals became variously coloured. When Mathum-Matta saw that men and animals were suffering terribly from the heat, he killed seven of the Suns. He tried also to kill the Sun and Moon, but they hid behind the Himalaya Mountains in the place called Majoi-Singrabhum. Here the Sun made a golden boat and the Moon made a silver boat. The Sun sits in his boat and goes round and round the Himalayas. When he comes to this side of the mountains, it is day and when he goes to the far side, it is night. It is his golden boat which makes the world so full of light.

The Moon sits in his silver boat and goes round and round the mountains. But sometimes he is tired and sleeps, sometimes he stands up and sometimes he sits down. This is why at one time we see more of the Moon and at other times less.

25

TAGIN

Dasi, Subansiri F.D.

The mighty Wiyu Tamu has four legs, a tail and an enormous head, but he is not like any animal on earth. He had two sons, Muiyu and Murro. One day, while they were still small, they went out along the path of the Sun and sat there waiting for him to pass.

The Sun finished his feast and dressed in all his finery. Then with his flaming hat and dao in hand,[22] he came down the path, but his heat was too great and killed the two children.

When Tamu heard of it, he was furious and decided to devour the Sun in revenge for what he had done. One morning he went

[22] In this story, the Sun is regarded as male.

and sat with open jaws in the path of the Sun. When the Sun came, he came so swiftly that he did not see who was sitting there and went directly into his mouth. As he went in, darkness came to the world.

But the Sun was able, by his magic, to prevent Tamu from devouring him. He turned himself into a green leaf and escaped through Tamu's nose. Tamu saw the leaf and wondered what it was, but thought little of it. The Sun, still in the form of the green leaf, crept slowly home. There he hid in a corner of his house and did not go out.

There was darkness all over the world. Then Wiyus, men and animals gathered in council and said, 'Unless the Sun comes out of his house, we shall all die.' So they went to find the Sun.

But when they found him, the Sun turned his head aside and would not look at them. Men said to him, 'You are the greatest of all. You know all things. If you are angry, we will die. Come out and don't be angry any more.' The Sun replied, 'I will come out on one condition. Abo-Teni has a son called Niddin. Bring this child to me so that I can eat him and then I will come out.' The men returned and told the council what the Sun had said. They said to Abo-Teni, 'Give us your son.' But he refused.

So the men caught a wild beast and dressed it up like Abo-Teni's son, Niddin. They took it to the Sun and said, 'Here is Niddin.' The Sun was about to eat it, when Tapeng the bat came and said, 'Look they are deceiving you. This is only some wild beast of the forest.'

The Sun was angry and said, 'If you deceivers will not give the boy, I will never come out.' The men returned and told the council. They tried again to persuade Abo-Teni to give his son, but he still refused. Then they took another boy and dressed him to look like Niddin, but when they offered him to the Sun, the bat again betrayed them.

Finally, the council of Wiyus, men and animals said to Abo-Teni, 'It is by the Sun that we live. If one boy dies so that all may live, there is no loss to you, for you and he will die in any case without the Sun. But if Niddin dies, through him all will be born and live. Give us your son and in his place we will give you mithuns, pigs and fowls.' At this Abo-Teni relented and gave them his son.

The men took Niddin to the Sun. Tapeng the bat flew with them and the Sun asked him, 'Is this the boy?' When the bat said it was, the Sun devoured him. Then he took his own form and put on his best clothes, his ornaments, his flaming hat and with his dao in his hand went out to give light to the world.

Before the Sun devoured Abo-Teni's son, men lived for ever. But since then they have died. And now, every morning before he rises, the Sun devours a man and then takes his path across the sky. That is why, somewhere in the world, a man dies every day.

But Tamu is still angry with the Sun, and when the memory of his son returns to him, he goes to the path and waits there with open mouth. The Sun enters Tamu's mouth, but by his magic he escapes through his vent.

When this happens, the Tagins shout, 'Tamu, let him go.' The Gallongs to the south shoot arrows into the sky to frighten Tamu.

26

TARAON (DIGARU) MISHMI

Tetuliang, Lohit F.D.

Every day the Sun goes for a walk. There are two paths across the sky and in the morning he takes the upper path and in the evening the lower. Sometimes the Sun is a man and sometimes he is a woman. When the Sun is a woman, the day is long and when he is a man, he goes away quickly to rest at home.

Once there were two Suns. One used to come up first and then as he went down, another Sun came up in his place. The result was that there was never any night, but it was always hot and shining and for this reason many men and animals died, and men everywhere longed for darkness. In the end, a man caught one of the Suns and killed him. So now there is only one Sun and half of every day is dark.

The Moon shows one half to earth and the other half to the Land of the Dead. There is a great tree which stands before her and this makes her light cool.

27

WANCHO

Ninu, Tirap F.D.

At first the Moon was very hot and shone all through the night so that, what with the Sun by day and the Moon by night, many people died of heat and the trees and grasses dried up. One day human beings and animals held a meeting and told Jang-Tai how much they were suffering. He threw some mud at the Moon and this partly covered his face and made it weak and cool. Even today you can see the dirt on it.

To celebrate this the people killed a pig and divided the meat, some to one, some to another, and they gave a portion also to the Moon. The Moon did not eat all his share but took some to his parents whom he loved greatly. When they got the meat they loved him in return and blessed him saying, 'Although Jang-Tai threw dirt at you, you will be seen for ever by the people on earth and all men will love you. Every month for one day they will see your face entire and those born on that day will be lucky. But those who are born when your face is not visible will die young, and will be short and mean in appearance.'

28

WANCHO

Ninu, Tirap F.D.

Luk is the great enemy of the Sun and Moon and once a year he devours them. He has a long face and a thin belly and when he swallows the Sun it quickly passes through his body and comes out through the vent. This is one cause of an eclipse, but some people say that the Sun is devoured by a great Frog and the Serpent comes to save him. Others again say that just as men keep count of time so does Rang-Bau, but he sometimes forgets to do this or he counts wrongly and then the Sun and Moon do not appear in their proper shape.

CHAPTER FOUR

THUNDER AND LIGHTNING

STORIES about thunder and lightning in NEFA, though they differ in detail, belong to the same family of ideas as those recorded in other parts of India. Thunder is associated with anything that makes a loud noise—someone shouts in fear, an angry husband beats his arm-shield, an old woman weeps for a dead son, a god chops at a tree, pigs grunt as they fight—and lightning is associated with anything that makes a flash —a girl beats her brother with a hair-pin, a great spirit in the sky blinks her eyes, chips of wood fly through the air, a god waves his shining dao.

In just the same way popular Hinduism declares that lightining is one of the weapons of the Maruts or the breath of the King of the Snakes. In Western India, according to Enthoven, thunder is now Indra's angry voice, now his loud laughter. It is the noise he makes when playing tip-cat with the clouds. He is getting married, at war, shooting his arrow to bring rain, beating the clouds with his whip.

Other tribal traditions are of the same pattern. The Muthuvans say that thunder is caused by Devas rolling a stone across the sky; the Kannikars attribute it to a demon who strikes a stone against a tree. The Dhurwas of Bastar have a curious legend that it is caused by the childless dead who drag a chariot of iron oddments across the heavens. The Binjhwars say it is the noise of the hoofs of Raja Indra's horse as he dances with delight in the sky. The Jhorias of Orissa associate it with the sound of supernatural drums, the Konds with the blows of an angry god beating his wanton wife.

Similarly lightning to the Cheros is the flash of the sword of Indra, to the Khasis it is the stolen silver sword of U Kui the lynx which U Pyrthat the thunder-giant brandishes in the sky, to the Dhurwas it is play of sky-fish among the clouds.

But the most common myth is that of the escape of a

girl from her lover. Sometimes this is associated with incest, as in the Bugun and Kachari tales, where a sister flees from her brother; in central India it is often Lakshman who desires to marry a girl who escapes from him into the sky: her beauty flashes like lightning and the noise of his pursuit is the thunder. The Juangs say that Raja Indra married a daughter of the Sun, but he is so ugly that she laughs at him and her teeth flash like lightning. He beats her and the sound of his blows is the thunder.[1]

It is only in NEFA, however, that these examples of domestic infelicity are connected with the woman's exposure of herself. For a woman to do this is regarded as the greatest of insults, yet the typical tribal attitude to sex as a natural and beautiful thing transforms it and the exposure shines in the loveliness of lightning across the sky.

1

BORI

Gatte, Siang F.D.

Earth and Sky are husband and wife. Between them lives the Wiyu Neli-Bo who is very black and fat with great ears and big eyes. When the sky wants to approach his wife the Wiyu knows it is going to happen and is so afraid that he will be squashed to death in the mighty encounter that he shouts for fear and men hear the sound as thunder.

2

BUGUN (KHOWA)

Senchong, Kameng F.D.

In the sky lived the girl Halia and the boy Haklum. Though they were brother and sister, they lived far away from one another,

[1] For references, see my *Myths of Middle India*, pp. 88 ff, and *Tribal Myths of Orissa*, pp. 67 ff.

for both were virgin. But although Halia did not like boys, her brother was very fond of girls. The trouble was that, apart from his sister, there was no other girl in all the earth or sky.

So Haklum tried and still tries to make love to his sister. For fear of him she usually hides among the white clouds. But sometimes she comes out to wash her hair and it covers the sky and makes it dark. When Haklum sees this he knows that his sister is coming out and he tries to catch her. She is very angry at this and pulls the long pin from her hair and beats him with it. He runs away roaring like the thunder. Men on earth see the pin flashing as lightning across the sky. Sometimes Halia drops the pin and when this happens the lightning falls to earth and destroys a house or a tree.[2]

3

DHAMMAI (MIJI)

Sachung, Kameng F.D.

Above the sky there is the tree called Chingnui which bears a great quantity of fruit. When the fruit is ripe and ready for eating, the god Subbo-Grang chops at the tree with his dao so that he can get at the fruit more easily, but it is so broad that he cannot cut it through. The chips of wood fly into the air as the lightning ; the sound of his blow is the thunder. Although he cannot bring the tree down, he shakes it and the fruits fall as the hail.

4

HILL MIRI

Lomdak, Subansiri F.D.

Dugum and his wife Dorak are in the sky. They have a great tank there and this is usually full of water. But sometimes there

[2] The Kacharis also associate thunder and lightning with a brother who wishes to marry his sister. Raona is in love with Raoni and when she hears of it, she flies into the sky and he shouts to her to return. 'It is these loud shouts and threats of Raona that men call thunder ; and when Raoni occasionally look back to see if her pursuer is gaining upon her, she in so doing reveals for an instant the brightness and beauty of her face, glowing like fire ; and it is this bright, dazzling beauty that men call lightning.' —S. Endle, *The Kacharis* (London, 1911), p. 70.

is very little water, though sometimes there is so much that it overflows. When it overflows, the water falls to the earth as rain. When there is too little water, Dugum and his wife quarrel. Dugum says, 'You have wasted so much water that there's none left.' 'That's not my fault,' says Dorak. 'I have to use up the water to make the beer that you're always drinking.'

At that Dorak lifts her cane-belt and her body shines out dazzlingly. This always makes Dugum furious and he puts on his armour and with spear in hand does a war-dance before his wife, threatening to kill her. She flies for her life and her body's beauty flashes across the sky. Dugum beats his arm-shield and the *ting-tang* noise he makes is the thunder.

There is a river that flows across the earth, then curves up into the sky and fills Dugum's tank with water.

5

HILL MIRI

Bini, Subansiri F.D.

Chungum-Irum and Chingum-Erum his wife, who laid the egg from which the world was born, live in the sky. They do not get on very well nowadays and there are constant rows between them. When they quarrel, Chingum-Erum expresses her opinion of her husband by lifting her cane-belt and exposing herself, and she shines in beauty as the lightning. Wiyu Dungum-Irum, who lives with them, does not like this at all, and abuses her for a dirty wanton. He spits at her in disgust and his spittle falls to earth as hail.

6

HRUSSO (AKA)

Buragaon, Kameng F.D.

Chou-Siphu and Khrao-Lijji were born of the great creature Phum-Badra who lives under the earth. After they were born they came from below to the surface. They killed the Sun and Moon who were doing evil on the earth and the arrows they fired still fall to the ground as thunderbolts.

7

IDU MISHMI

Taraon, Lohit F.D.

In the land of the sky, which is called Etombro, there is a great gate. Storms live behind it and from time to time the wind blows it open and the lightning flashes out across the world. At the same time the god Eto-Anjaya comes out as thunder to take the life of a man.

8

KAMAN MISHMI

Lohit Valley, Lohit F.D.

There was a man by the name of Awawa who had a lovely daughter called Omflan. Near Awawa's home there was a hill where the spirit called Singfung lived. This spirit desired to devour Awawa's daughter but Awawa, who was strong and resourceful, guarded her very carefully.

But one day when Awawa had gone somewhere, the girl went out to pick the ripe fruit of the *aman* tree. She climbed up and had just began to eat the fruit, when she saw Singfung coming towards her. She hurriedly climbed down and ran towards her house, but Singfung followed her. Just as he was catching her up, she went for refuge into the hollow of a tree. Singfung stood outside and called to her to come out. But she remained inside weeping. When night fell and the stars appeared in the sky the girl called to them to help her. One of the stars took pity on her and took her up to the sky.

When Singfung saw this he tried to follow her. He went into the hollow tree and prayed the star to take him to the sky. When she heard this the girl was frightened and asked the star to save her from her enemy and the star asked Tama-ok to kill him. Tama-ok hurled a thunderbolt which struck the tree and burnt it and the spirit to ashes. He then took the girl from the star and made her his bride.

Since then Awawa's daughter lives in the sky above the clouds with her husband. Since she came from earth she sometimes goes with her husband to see what is happening there. But when she rushes across the sky, her thighs and feet are seen by men and the Kaman Mishmis say, 'Awawa's daughter is lifting her skirt.'[3]

9

MINYONG

Komsing, Siang F.D.

There was a mighty Wiyu who was born from his mother Sedi-Nane. He was chief of the Wiyus: he ruled them as a king. But the other Wiyus grew jealous and said, 'Why is he great? Why should we obey him? Let us kill him.' But they had no sword or daos.

There was a craftsman who knew how to make daos and arrowheads. He prepared a poisoned arrow and gave it to Doing-Idu-Dudeng, who killed the great Wiyu with it.

When his mother, Sedi-Nane, heard of her son's death, she wept loudly as she remembered him. *Heen-heen-heen*, she wept. The sound of her weeping is the thunder. She blinks through her tears and the movement of her flashing eyelids is the lightning.

10

MOKLUM

Longke, Tirap F.D.

Rang had a daughter who was so lovely that a man climbed all the way to the sky to win her. He brought her down to earth and married her there. Rang sent his sons for the bride-price. But the man was a tricky fellow and when Rang's sons came, he received them with friendliness and hospitality and promised to pay everything they demanded. While they were sitting and drinking, however, he secretly collected a pile of wood and dry leaves and set fire to them. This frightened the sons of Rang and they flew back to the sky. When they told their father how they had been cheated he threw a thunderbolt down to the earth in his rage. From time to time when he remembers this he still throws a thunderbolt, for his anger has never ceased.

[3] Recorded by T. K. Barua.

11

NOCTE

Tut, Tirap F.D.

One brother lives on earth and the younger brother lives in the sky. From time to time the younger brother dances and throws showers of rain-drops down on to the earth. Then he asks the lovely fair-coloured girls of earth whether they have such beads on their necks. Sometimes too he throws the lightning down and asks whether the earth-people possess such marvellous magic. Sometimes he beats his drum and when it thunders across the sky he asks whether the earth-people have any music to match it.

12

TARAON (DIGARU) MISHMI

Machima, Lohit F.D.

The clouds are the pigs of the sky. There is a road of chains across the sky and the cloud-pigs wander about on it. When two pigs meet, they fight each other and when the bristles scrape against each other, lightning flashes across the sky. The pigs grunt loudly as they fight and this is the thunder.

13

WANCHO

Watnu, Tirap F.D.

The lightning is the dao of Rang. He waves it about while he is dancing and it flashes across the sky.

Men got their guns from Rang, who at first had all of them in the sky. Men learnt to shoot by seeing how the lightning hits a tree. In just the same way a bullet from a gun hits the mark.

CHAPTER FIVE

WATER

WATER is under the control of the spirits; some dwell in streams and rivers; others are in the sky, making the world hot or cold, sending or restraining rain, snow and hail; they can all be influenced by the shamans. Chief among the Adi water-spirits are the Nippongs, who live in marshy places and among wild plantains and may terminate a mother's pregnancy, cause excessive menstruation in young girls and give every kind of disorder to a woman's body. They have the habit of keeping their fingers clenched close together. When a Nippong attacks a woman, she raises both her hands to her hair and clutches it. You cannot drive the Nippong away with a dao or stick; the only thing to do is to put fire on the woman's head.

Ladang Laiyo is the Wiyu of streams and rivers and often appears in the mythology. Both he and Silising, whose home is in the great rivers, cause men to drown and fall to their death from bridges.

Adi control of rain, storm and hail is effected in ways that may be paralleled in other parts of the world. In time of drought, the people combine to buy a mithun for sacrifice. They take it to the nearest stream, tether it there, and then pour water over its head until it collapses and dies. As they do so, they shout, '*Peddonge-hoe-he*! O water come!' They feast on the flesh and perform the dance called Peddong-Miri.

On the other hand, if the rain is too heavy, a special Doini-Miri leads a dance for two successive nights in the dormitory. He ties a leaf over the door in the hope that, as it dries, the weather too will become dry.

To stop hail at harvest-time, boys gather before the dormitory and shoot arrows into the air at Doitang Wiyu, the spirit of hail. They tie gourds to a forked branch and set it up in front of the building.

In Miri tradition rain is due to the overflowing of the great sky-tank of Dugum and Dorak. But sometimes the tank goes dry and there is a drought. When this happens, the people of a number of neighbouring villages gather together and go down to the nearest large stream. There they throw poisonous bark into the water and many fish are killed. This angers Nitpor Wiyu who is lord of the fish and he tells Tetik the frog to weep for his dead brothers. But Tetik is the son of water, which gets angry when it hears Tetik crying and rushes into the sky, filling the great tank and overflowing it so that it falls to the earth as rain.

Another method of getting rain is to sacrifice to Niddo-Pumpo Wiyu.

If on the other hand, the rains are too heavy, the Nibo sacrifices to the Sun. The people build a very high altar, 'high enough to reach to the sky' and decorate it with bamboo 'stars' and a bamboo hat for the Sun. The Nibo offers a white goat or a fowl—white is everywhere regarded as the proper colour for offerings to the Sun-God. Men and women bring eggs and rice-beer and greet the Sun 'as if they were giving salami to an officer' and say, 'Save us. We cannot get dry wood, we cannot light our fires, we cannot go from place to place.'

For the Sherdukpens, Gyapu Medeng is a water-spirit, who is worshipped at the great festivals. When dysentery or any other water-borne disease attacks a village, the Lama or Jiji-priest ties a string of flags across a stream in his honour. At the confluence of two streams there lives a spirit called Du, the black god, who is found where the water is muddy and dark through the conflict of contending currents.

Nanwang (Numwang) is the water-god of the Wanchos. 'He lives in the deep pools of streams and looks after the fish. Sometimes he attacks men. If someone drinks the water of his pool, he may slip into the belly and make it swell.' Lamlongkan is god of the rainbow. He comes down into small streams to eat frogs. He may also devour the child in the womb and cause miscarriage. Pregnant women, therefore, never look at a rainbow, and when one appears in the sky, they run for shelter and cover themselves with palm-leaves.

NEFA is a country of a thousand rivers, and the life of the people is in many ways dominated by them, for they are the natural boundaries between cultivation and hunting areas; they seriously interrupt communications; and the fish in their waters is an important source of food. A number of stories, therefore, describe how rivers first began to flow and how they made their way through the obstacles that faced them. In a Bori tale a Wiyu falls into a deep pond in Tibet and breaks its banks, allowing the water to flow out as the Siyom River. A curious Hill Miri tale traces rivers to the eggs laid by a Wiyu living on the snow-clad mountains of the north. The origin of the Tirap and Dihing Rivers was in a great mass of water surrounded by hills, through which the Cock and the Snake dug a channel. The Hrussos say that all the water in the world was at the beginning confined within the coils of a great snake who lived in the country of the sunrise. Men and animals, driven to despair by thirst, send a bird to bring them water. The bird pecks out the snake's eyes and in its agony it uncoils and lets the water flow out as a great river for the benefit of mankind. In a Mishmi tradition, the Brahmaputra (who is described as a sister of the Sun) also escaped from its mountain prison, but this time with the help of the Cat who made the channel and showed it the way to go.

There is a pretty Sherdukpen tale about rainbows, but most of the stories about them are of the conventional type. The rainbow, in a Taraon story, grows out of the head of a great water-snake. According to the Wanchos, Rang, the sky-god, is fond of fishing and travels by the rainbow down to earth to fish in its rivers. One Singpho tale declares the rainbow to be a ladder whereby those who have suffered a tragic death mount to the sky: another says it is a ladder used by a god to meet his wife.

1

BORI

Gameng, Siang F.D.

The Wiyu Sitking-Kinnier-Nirpo-Padang lives on earth and his wife, the Wiyu Peddo-Dudu-Duming, lives in the sky. Whenever he goes to his wife in the sky, rain falls on earth.

Daini-Igum-Guming-Gumdeng is the Wiyu who gives heat and Dimmu-Tayang is the Wiyu who makes things cold and sends snow. These two Wiyus cultivate their fields and whenever they get a good harvest, there is a lot of snow and it is very cold.

One day Dimmu-Tayang planted a *tirgum* tree which sometimes bears a lot of fruit and sometimes has none. When a shaman dies he goes to Dimmu-Tayang's village, and when he sees the fruit he beats the trunk of the tree to shake it down. The fruit falls to the earth as hail.

2

BORI

Gatte, Siang F.D.

At the beginning there was no water. But one day the Wiyu Babing-Sunne fell sick and vomited, and from his vomit a small pond of water was formed. It was at a place called Tunker-Siddo in Mimet (Tibet). The pond was very deep and none of the water flowed out.

But after some years, another Wiyu, Sedi-Botte, accidentally fell into the pond there was such a splash that the bank broke and the water flooded out and ran down between the hills as a river which to-day is called the Siyom.

3

DAFLA

Solo (Palin Valley), Subansiri F.D.

Tarngum Sung-Sung was the ancestor of all the priests in the world, priests of men, priests of earth, priests of tigers and all animals. Originally he lived with the Sun and rose and set as the Sun does, but once it rained so heavily that he fell down from the sky and since then he has lived in the earth and waters. His house has doors and windows and, after he has eaten, he often blows wind from his mouth out of the doors and windows. In the winter he does not blow so much but in the summer when the people are growing their crops he blows a great deal, for he wants to eat the rice. This is why during the summer there are great winds and sometimes storms.[1]

4

DHAMMAI (MIJI)

Nakhu, Kameng F.D.

Long ago there were two sisters, Nulo and Anoi-Midge-Juje. Nulo was married to a man called Sichung but the younger girl was virgin.

One day when the god Abbu-Bullu-Nuchu was out hunting, he shot his arrow at a deer but missed, and the arrow fell between the two sisters where they were sitting at their looms in the bright sun. They jumped up wondering where the arrow had come from and presently Abbu-Bullu-Nuchu came and sang to them:

'Give me the beer your father drinks,
Give me the roots your father eats,
Give me the bed on which he sleeps.'

When they heard this, the sisters wondered what to do and sang in reply:

'We have no beer such as our father drinks,
We have no roots such as our father eats,
We have no bed where our father sleeps,
How then can we feed you and give you a place to sleep?'

Abbu-Bullu-Muchu said, 'But I am very thirsty. At least give me some water to drink.' Nulo said to Anoi-Midge-Juje, 'Get a hollow bamboo and bring some water and give him to drink.' The girl went down to a stream but found that she could not fill the bamboo, and presently the god grew impatient and said, 'Why is

[1] Recorded by B. K. Shukla.

your sister taking so long to bring a little water? I am dying of thirst ; I'd better go myself to the stream.'

He went down to the stream and found Anoi-Midge-Juje trying to fill the bamboo. He took it from her and broke it to pieces and threw them into the water, where they turned into various kinds of fish. He caught the girl by the hand, but she was frightened and bit him to make him let her go. The blood was scattered in the water and on the stones and trees of the forest, where it turned into leeches.

But the god would not let the girl go and took her away. Nulo waited a long time for them to return and then went down to the stream to find them. But all she saw were the fish in the water and wondered how they had come there. In her astonishment she forgot all about her sister.

In the meantime, Abbu-Bullu-Nuchu and Anoi-Midge-Juje had gone a long way and Nulo thought she would never catch them up. But she ran along, following their foot-prints, crying and shouting to them to return.

On the way she met a very old god with white hair, a big belly, but no feet. He had a fire burning in front of him and a pot on it. He asked Nulo why she was crying and she replied, 'Some god has carried off my sister. Have you seen them?' 'Yes', he said, 'a little while ago, but he has cut her up and eaten her flesh and only her bones are left.'

Now it was true that Abbu-Bullu-Nuchu had got tired to dragging Anoi-Midge-Juje along and, as he was hungry and thirsty, he killed her and ate the flesh and drank the blood. He did not really like doing this, for he wanted to marry her, but he was so hungry that he had no choice.

When the old god told Nulo what had happened she cried loudly and asked him if he could make her sister alive. He sent her to collect the bones and said, 'I will make her alive, but you must not look at me or watch what I am doing. Sit quite still with your back towards me,'

Then the old god put the bones in his pot and boiled them to a fine liquid. He went on with his boiling till the liquid thickened and then made it into an image of the dead girl. But before he was able to complete the head, Nulo said to herself, 'He is taking a very long time,' and turned round for a quick look. Directly she did so, the image turned to water and the old god was annoyed and said, 'Now I'll never be able to make your sister alive.' Nulo protested saying, 'But I didn't look properly, I only peeped. If you really try you'll be able to make her.'

So the old god made another image and put nails into the joints of its bones and then made it alive. He said, 'Now have a look and tell me whether this is your sister or not.' Nulo at once clasped Anoi-Midge-Juje in her arms and the god said, 'You may go home now, but if your sister asks you to do her hair or take lice from it, don't do anything until you get home. If you do anything on the way you will lose your sister and I won't be able to help you.'

The two sisters set out on their long journey and as they went along they got very hot and tired and sweat poured down their faces. After a time they sat down to rest and Anoi-Midge-Juje said, 'My head is itching. Do look and see what's the matter; there may be nits.' Nulo forgot what the old god had told her and began to search in her sister's hair for nits. Presently she found a nail sticking into the head and pulled it out. Directly she did this and Anoi-Midge-Juje turned into a river and flowed down to the plains.

This is the Suturulu (Brahmaputra).

5

DHAMMAI (MIJI)

Nakhu, Kameng F.D.

In the Phong-Langra Mountains[1] there were living long ago in a place called Jangdaphang-Nadmu two brothers, Tamajang-Debiang and Pama-ji-Dinyang. Tamajang-Debiang's wife was Lale-Jumo and Pamaji-Dinyang's wife was Silye-Bingbo. The two families had many children, but no food. So one day the two brothers with their wives and children climbed high in the Phong-Langra Mountains, but there too they found no food. In despair they left their children and went away. The children lifted their faces to the sky and cried for hunger.

High in the sky the gods Lujuphu and Jasuju gathered a great quantity of cooked rice, and when they heard the children's cries they threw it down for them and it fell to the earth as snow.

[1] Himalayas.

6

DOBANG (GALLONG)

Siang Frontier Division

(From G. D. S. Dunbar, *Abors and Galongs*, p. 65)

Now whilst gods and men were living together on the earth, there was much distress because there was no water, and gods and men alike were lean and thin. But it was noticed with a good deal of wonder that the rat was always fat and sleek. So one day a man followed the rat and tracked it to a big stone in which it found water to drink. Then the man came back and told what he had seen. But when the men came to break the stone and get the water out for themselves they found that the stone was very hard, so hard that it broke the tools they brought with them. So the god Debo-Kombu took his bow and shot at the stone with an arrow and a trickle of water—the stream of the arrow—came welling out of the rock. And so Debo-Kombu is worshipped with his bow and his arrow to this day. But only a tiny flow of water ran out of the stone. Then the god Nurupur took an axe, and broke the stone and the water gushed out freely over the thirsty earth. And he too is worshipped for ever in the water he gave to gods and men.

7

HILL MIRI

Bini, Subansiri F.D.

The elder brother of Sichi, the earth, is the great snow-covered mountain Chabobi. On Chabobi lived two Wiyus, Hak-Tajum and his wife Sip-Gilli. They came together and Sip-Gilli conceived. In due time she laid an egg. But they were living on such a steep and slippery slope that the egg rolled down, down to the valley below. There it broke and from it flowed a river. Presently Sip-Gilli laid another egg and another, and another, and from each flowed water until the land was full of rivers.

8

HRUSSO (AKA)

Buragaon, Kameng F.D.

At the beginning, when the earth and the sky were first made, there was no water and men and animals suffered greatly.

Men and animals, therefore, assembled to see what could be done. They said, 'Who is the wisest among us who will be able to find water?' They all replied, 'We are ignorant people and do not know where water can be had. So how can we go and fetch it?'

But there was a bird called Horsi-Basam who said, 'I know where there is water.' Men and animals asked, 'Tell us where.' The bird replied, 'It is to be found in the place where the Sun rises, for there is a great snake there who is holding a great lake in his coils. If you wish I will go and fetch water from it.' Men and animals were pleased and begged the bird to go.

The bird set out on its journey, but when it reached the place and saw the great snake it was frightened and decided to wait until dark and then steal some of the water.

Accordingly in the evening, when the snake fell asleep, the bird pecked out both its eyes and in its pain the snake uncoiled itself and let the water escape and it poured down as a great river.

Ever since the bird Horsi-Basam has lived on the banks of rivers.

9

IDU MISHMI

Harangam, Lohit F.D.

Tallao (which is what we called the Brahmaputra River) is the sister of Ringya, the Sun. The Sun is fortunate because he travels in the sky where there are no obstacles to make his path difficult and he can go about as he feels inclined. But at the beginning Tallao found it very difficult to move about on earth. At that time she lived in Nimtubram, which is at the very end and limit of the world. Here there was a great lake. But in other parts of the world, there was no water and men and animals fainted for lack of it.

A worm called Taiyu was thirsty and came to drink. It dug a little channel and a trickle of water flowed down from it. A wild cat saw it and tried to drink the water, but there was too little and it was too muddy. So the cat went to the Nimtubram Lake and made a big channel and after drinking as much as he could, went away. Tallao followed him, wandering about the country as a cat wanders.

But when Drakub saw what was happening, he came hastily to stop them. He brought a basket full of earth and built a wall across the path. Chainye heard about this and was angry that men should be deprived of the water they needed so badly. He went to Drakub and said, 'Brother, you are a wonderful worker. You made the world and now you want to stop Tallao from wandering about. All your work is good but I have bad news for you. In your own home your wife has died. Go back and see to it.'

Drakub said, 'What does it matter? If one wife dies, I can get a thousand more.' Chainye who had hoped to break down the dam when Drakub was away, had to go home disappointed.

But he tried again and this time he said, 'I have more bad news for you. Your son is dead.' Drakub replied, 'What does it matter? If one son dies, I can get a thousand more.' Chainye again went away disappointed.

But he was so worried about men (for, as he said, 'How can they live without water?') that he tried yet again and this time he said, 'Your wife is dead and I agree that it does not matter. Your son is dead, and that doesn't matter either. But today your mother has died.' Drakub said to himself, 'It is true that I can get plenty of other wives, and sons too, but I can never get another mother. I must go and see her.' So he stopped his work and went away.

At once Chainye broke down the dam and Tallao continued on her way wandering through the mountains, until she came down into the plains of Assam. Wherever she brought her waters, men and animals revived.

10

KAMAN MISHMI

Lohit Valley, Lohit F.D.

Khrane created the birds and when they were ready he called a man called Brassa from the earth and said to him, 'Look, the birds that I have created will go to the earth to warn you that the rain is coming. So when you see these birds in your fields, get ready to cultivate immediately, for showers of rain will follow.'

When Brassa returned to earth the neighbours gathered round and asked him what Khrane had told him. But he, being a man anxious for his own profit, kept the matter secret and said that Khrane had merely asked how they all did.

After a time the birds created by Khrane came flying round the village and Brassa went immediately to clear the jungle for cultivation. A few days later a shower of rain fell for the first time on the earth and made it soft. When the other people saw the rain falling, it seemed to them a wonderful thing and with great joy they collected the water and drank it.

Now when Brassa left his house to cultivate his fields, his wife was expecting a child and he said to her, 'Before long, water will fall from the sky. If the child has been born before then, wash his body with the heavenly water.' Actually on the very day the rain first fell the woman gave birth to a male child, and after he was born the mother took him out of the house to wash him, but as the people had drunk all the water she could not get so much as a single drop for him and in a little while he died.

When Brassa returned home and heard of the death of his child, he was full of grief and said to himself, 'I'll make these fools drink as much water as they want.' He went to Khrane and begged him to send more rain and Khrane, not understanding what Brassa had in mind, poured rain incessantly on the earth for several days, and there were great floods.

Now everyone held Brassa responsible for the heavy rain and reproached him. Some of them came to his house and beat him till he was half dead. Then they flayed him alive and threw his flesh in different parts of the country. The Kaman Mishmis believe that the earth got its fertility from Brassa's flesh.[1]

[1] Recorded by T. K. Barua.

11

MINYONG

Parong, Siang F.D.

Nomkir and Nomnang were the sons of Peddo-Donom. Bisi and Biri were the sons of Peddo-Dobi. Thus the four boys were cousins. They lived at the source of the Siang River, in Tibet. For some reason or other, there was a quarrel and Bisi and Biri threw the hill on which the house of Namkir and Nomnang stood into the river. Namkir and Nomnang floated down the stream till they reached the plains. From them came the Bengalis and the Assamese. They had a dog with them and as it went down, it turned into a goat.

From Bisi and Biri was born the water-spirit, Ladang Laiyo.

12

MINYONG

Pangin, Siang F.D.

There was a man who had no water. He searched for it everywhere and daily grew more thirsty. Then he met a duck. 'If you will feed me on rice-flour,' said the duck, 'my droppings will be white and I will lead you to the place where you can find water.' The man fed the duck with rice-flour and its droppings became white. It flew away across the hills, and the man followed the track of the droppings until he came to a spring. He drank the water and gave it to the world.[4]

13

MOKLUM

Longke, Tirap F.D.

There was a great mass of water surrounded by hills. Human beings lived on the tops of two hills, one of which was called

[4] In a story recorded by Dunbar, man was led to the source of water, hidden in a rock, by a rat (Dunbar, op. cit., p. 65).

Rangokan (the Patkoi) and the other was Moklum. On the Moklum Peak was a great cock called Lang: on the Rangokan was the great snake Pu. One day the cock and the snake decided to let the water out and they dug through the hills in two different ways, and the water poured down towards the plains. One of the rivers was the Tirap, the other was the Namjin (Dihing).

14

NOCTE

Laju, Tirap F.D.

The chief thing in the body of man is water. When a man dies the water in his body goes up to the sky and falls to the earth as rain. Man drinks the rain-water and from his body it passes to his woman's body and she conceives and bears children.

15

SHERDUKPEN

Rupa, Kameng F.D.

There are four water-spirits: Lukarpo, a white spirit, Lunakpu, a black one, Lusirpu who is yellow, and Lumarpo who is red. They live in springs and wander across the sky for ever seeking wives as lovely as themselves. The rainbow is the path they make across the sky. When they cross it a little rain falls—this is the tea and rice-beer they drink to refresh themselves on their journey.

16

SINGPHO

(From J. Errol Gray, *Diary of a Journey to the Bor Khamti Country*, 1892-93, pp. 72f.)

Many ages ago the Dapha valley was inhabited by a race of Miris ; there were seven villages in all, and were situated on both banks of the stream. At that time there was no open grass plain as at present, but the forest came right up to the edge of the water. One day a party of Miris while out hunting came upon two strange beings seated on a large stone at the junction of the Dapha with the Dehing, these were two water spirits, father and son, who were sunning themselves in the open on the river's brink ; but the Miris were not aware of the nature of these beings, and one of their party putting arrow to bow drew string and pierced the elder sprite through the back, killing him instantly. The younger sprite dived into the water and disappeared. The Miris on coming up to the dead body saw that it was not an ordinary being they had killed, and guessing at its supernatural character, alarmed at what they had done, precipitately fled. The younger sprite who had dived into the water did not stay his course until he reached his mother's abode, when he at once related what had occurred to his remaining parent, who forthwith vowed vengeance. This vengeance she eked out by causing a heavy landslip to occur in a deep and narrow gorge in the hills through which the Dapha flowed, completely damming up its waters for several hours: then, suddenly breaking through the obstruction, the waters leaped and rushed down the valley in one broad wave sweeping away a whole forest in their course and leaving no vestige of the seven Miri villages that had lined the river's banks. At that time was formed the open grass plain on the site of the former forest, and certainly the appearance of the open plain studded with huge rocks and boulders of various sizes favours the idea of a formation such as would result from an excessively strong and swift rush of water down the valley.

17

SINGPHO

Wakitna, Tirap F.D.

Between heaven and earth lies the Land of Sawaka. To this Land go the souls of those who commit suicide, who are murdered, who are killed by tigers or elephants, who die in battle. There is a ladder from earth to Sawaka and this is the rainbow. Those who died of sickness go to the Land of Chulen.

18

SINGPHO

Imbu, Tirap F.D.

In the sky, in the Land of the Moon, which is called Sitamung, lived the god Jaukun-Tukung and his wife Nang-Susita. They engaged themselves in making a path from the Moon to the earth. This may be seen across the sky at night. But when he was making the road Jaukun-Tukung fell down to the earth and died. From time to time his soul climbs by a ladder to meet his wife in the sky and this is the rainbow.

19

TAGIN

Dasi, Subansiri F.D.

Long ago there was one in the water called Buru-Gudu. There was one in the sky called Doje-Karangu. Buru-Gudu had a daughter, and Doje-Karngu had a daughter. They had daughters but they wanted wives. They both sought everywhere but to no avail. Then Doje-Karngu went to Buru-Gudu and said, 'Let me marry your daughter and you can marry mine,' Buru-Gudu replied, 'How can such a thing be? You are in the sky: I am in the water.' Doje-Karngu said, 'I will make a path from the sky to the earth and in one day you will be able to fetch my daughter and I will fetch your's.' Having said this, Doje-Karngu returned to the sky and busied himself making the path to earth. This path is the rainbow.

By this path Doje-Karngu came down to the water and Buru-Gudu went to the sky. On the way back, each with his bride, they met in the space between earth and heaven. Doje-Karngu said, 'We must do no work, nor approach our wives, nor go hunting. If we fail in this, there will be disaster for us both.' Buru-Gudu agreed, and each went to his own home.

Each began faithfully to observe the taboo, but the Wiyus were frightened. 'If these two keep the taboo', they said, "the earth will always be as the sky is now, flat and without hills and valleys.

Then where will we live?' For the Wiyus love to dwell in the high mountains.

So the Wiyus called Tapeng the bat and said, 'Go to Doje-Karngu and tell him that Buru-Gudu has broken the taboo and is doing every kind of work.' Tapeng flew into the sky and said to Doje-Karngu, 'Look, you are observing the taboo, but Buru-Gudu has broken it and is doing every kind of work.' When Doje-Karngu heard this, he was angry and sent down rain in torrents. So heavy was the rain that it made great pits in the ground and flooded all the rivers and there were land-slides everywhere.

This is how rivers began to flow and the hills were piled up.

All the world came to Buru-Gudu's wedding: Wiyus and men, wild beasts of the forest, fish of the rivers, insects and reptiles, trees and grasses—they all came to it. But the plantain tree and the earthworm refused to go. Buru-Gudu was very angry at this and sent for them. 'You are too proud,' he said. He took the bones out of the plantain's stem and the worm's body. That is why today they are both without bones.

Dori-Sijji was the shaman at the wedding: he sacrificed mithuns and pigs.

Buru-Gudu became the Wiyu of water and Doje-Karngu is the Wiyu who sends down rain [5]

20

TARAON (DIGARU) MISHMI

Tetuliang, Lohit F.D.

There is a great snake whose name is Ka which lives sometimes in the water, sometimes in the ground. The rainbow comes from its head and climbs across the sky. When the snake is in the water, the rainbow is large and beautiful. When the snake is on the ground, the rainbow is small and you can hardly see it.

[5] The tradition in the Upper Tagin area, beyond Taliha, is also about a wedding, but the names are different. Dozing is the spirit of the sky and Buru the spirit of the water. They arrange for their sons and daughters to marry and when Dozing's daughter Yanyia is married to Tanya, Buru's son, a path of silver is made on which Yanyia is taken to join her husband. This was the first rainbow.

21

TARAON (DIGARU) MISHMI

Tushe, Lohit F.D.

There is a great snake living in the water from whose head the rainbow comes. When this snake gets hungry he wants to eat men and if he cannot get anyone, he climbs up into the sky to ask the gods to provide him with food. The path by which he goes is the rainbow.

22

WANCHO

Senua, Tirap F.D.

Rang, the god of the sky, is very fond of fish. Sometimes when he is hungry he comes down to earth by the rainbow to catch them.

23

WANCHO

Jaboka, Tirap F.D.

In the beginning there was no earth but only sky. Rang threw a star into the sky and this star after many many years turned into the earth. There was no water at first but it gradually oozed up from under the ground. As this stream flowed in different directions it cut through the ground and made hills in some places and plains in others.

24

WANCHO

Pomau, Tirap F.D.

Below the earth is a great lake of water and a snake lives in it. The earth rests on the snake's head. Sometimes the snake moves and then the whole earth quakes.

The rivers flow down across the world and collect in the great lake below and then rise up into the sky to Rang and he sends the water back to earth as rain. As in the Tea Gardens water is drawn up into a tank, so in the same way Rang draws the water into the sky and sends it down again.

Fog and mist also go up to Rang and form a thick layer across the sky, which sometimes turns into a pile of stones which fall to the earth as hail.

CHAPTER SIX

EARTHQUAKE

In view of the frequent seismic shocks that shape their country and in particular of the Great Earthquake of 1950, it is remarkable that the people of NEFA do not have more, and more vivid, ideas on the subject of earthquakes. On the whole, however, their traditions are rather conventional and resemble those found in other parts of India.

The traditional Hindu view of earthquakes is that Varaha, the boar incarnation of Vishnu who supports the earth, is shifting the burden of the world from one tusk to another. Another tradition changes the boar into a great bull or elephant. Bhattacharjee records that the Hindus of Sylhet say that below the earth there is a tortoise; upon this is a serpent and upon this an elephant. Should any one of the three creatures move its limbs there is an earthquake. The ordinary Mussalman of the same area is said to believe that the earth rests on the horns of the bull which has a mosquito at its side. Whenever the bull tries to shake its head the earth quakes, but the mosquito stings it by way of warning and the bull keeps quiet again.[1] The Kannikars also believe that the earth rests on one of the horns of an ox and an earthquake occurs when he shifts the weight.[2]

In Orissa, some tribes attribute earthquake, in the conventional manner, to a deity on whose head the world rests. The Gadabas associate it with the intercourse of Mother Earth and her husband. The Hill Saoras say a divine brother and sister share the weight, but when the sister goes to bathe the brother finds it difficult to hold it steady by himself.[3]

Among the tribal people of central India, the Birhors believe that an earthquake occurs when the giant who sleeps

[1] P. N. Bhattacharjee, 'Folk-Custom and Folklore of the Sylhet District', *Man in India*, Vol. X (1930), p. 122.

[2] L. A. K. Iyer, *The Travancore Tribes and Castes* (Trivandrum, 1937-41), Vol. I, p. 54.

[3] *Tribal Myths of Orissa*, pp. 91 ff.

in the bowels of the earth turns over.[4] The Bhuiyas say it is when the tortoise which supports the earth grows weary and turns from side to side.[5]

The Uraons have a similar notion. The earth rests on the back of a tortoise which is caught very firmly between the long legs of a crab. When the tortoise gets tired and wants to change her position an earthquake takes place, but the crab is always there attentive to her duty and saves the world from a catastrophe. She catches the tortoise firmly with her claws and never allows her to move too much.[6]

Some Lakhers say that an earthquake is due to sexual intercourse between the earth and the sky. Others say that when a chief dies, his spirit flies through the cords by which the earth is attached to the sky and as it passes it cuts through one of the cords with its dao thus causing an earthquake. There is an old Ao Naga tradition that the sky is supported by a post at the end of the world, which is held in position by a being called Ningtangr. Sometimes he feels hungry and lets go for a moment to pluck and eat leaves. The post shakes and there is an earthquake.[7]

Similarly in NEFA there is a common notion that the world rests on the head of a great creature, who may be a deity, a sort of mithun, a monster which is 'like an elephant yet not an elephant, like a mithun yet not a mithun', a mighty fish or a giant serpent. The earthquake is sometimes caused simply by the restlessness of this great creature; he wants his food, he turns over or he laughs and sings as in a Singpho tale. Sometimes, however, he is represented as being angered in some way with mankind; men have forgotten to give him sacrifice; a Chief or priest dies and this excites him. In a Hrusso story, an insect tells him falsely that all men have died and he weeps for sorrow. In a Wancho tale, the gods of heaven and earth go to war and the earth trembles at the impact of the mighty conflict.

In Bori and Shimong stories, the world is shaken when

[4] S. C. Roy, *The Birhors* (Ranchi, 1925), p. 498.
[5] S. C. Roy, *The Hill Bhuiyas of Orissa* (Ranchi, 1936), p. 280.
[6] P. Dehon, *Religion and Customs of the Uraons* (Calcutta, 1906), p. 168.
[7] *Census of India, 1931*, p. 128 and Mills, *The Ao Nagas*, p. 298.

the great creature, on whom it rests, goes to his wife: in a Dhammai tale the encounter of the earth with the sky her husband causes an earthquake. This tradition is also current in Orissa and central India.

A curious tale was recorded by T. K. Barua at Namsang. The souls of illegitimate children, so he was told by a Nocte informant, go below to a strange half-world of their own. From time to time in their boredom and frustration they join hands and dance, and it is this dance that shakes the world. The fact that the Noctes, at least in the past, have rarely allowed such children to be born, or if born to survive for long, touches the tradition with an appropriate sense of doom.

1

APA TANI

Duta, Subansiri F.D.

The great mithun Chango-Subbo lies beneath the earth and supports it on its body. Sometimes it twitches its ears and this causes a small earthquake. Occasionally it moves its whole body and this causes a great earthquake.[8]

2

BORI

Gameng, Siang F.D.

Below the earth lives the great Wiyu Neli-Gir-Gir who has the form of a great black creature rather like a mithun. When he goes to his wife he shakes the whole world.

[8] Recorded by B. K. Shukla.

3

DAFLA

Solo, Palin Valley, Subansiri F.D.

Chigo Ngirgo, who is like an enormous elephant made of stone, lives beneath the earth. He has eyes, a mouth and six legs but no ears or trunk. His head lies towards Nimme (Tibet) and his back towards the plains of Assam. The earth rests upon his body. Usually he lies still, but sometimes during the summer and winter he turns over and shakes the earth.[*]

4

DHAMMAI (MIJI)

Nakhu, Kameng F.D.

At first the Earth and Sky were far away from each other and the Sun and Moon lived separately. In those days the Sun and Moon did not move. It was the Earth and Sky that moved. For the Earth had many children whom she held in her lap. She was afraid that her husband the Sky would approach her and give her more babies and was always moving round to escape him.

But from time to time the Sky succeeds in going to the Earth and when this happens there is an earthquake. At such a time many new trees grow up and there are fine harvests.

5

GALLONG

Don, Subansiri F.D.

Below the land of men and above the land of Wiyus, in the space between, is an animal like a mithun though it is not a

[*] Recorded by B. K. Shukla.

mithun, called Sichi-Nide-Hargogi. There he lies asleep. Three times in the year he turns over and each time the seasons change, from hot to wet, from wet to cold, from cold to hot. Sometimes he shakes himself and there is an earthquake.

6

HILL MIRI

Chemir, Subansiri F.D.

Below the earth is an astonishing animal named Nide-Hargogi. It is like an elephant ; it is like a mithun: yet it is neither mithun nor elephant. It has four legs and four arms, two heads and two pairs of horns, two mouths, two tongues, four eyes but, strange to say, only one nose.

Nide-Hargogi spends his time sleeping and on his great body rests the world. When he breathes deeply there is a landslide in our hills and when, every two or three years, he turns over, there is a great earthquake.

7

HRUSSO (AKA)

Buragaon, Kameng F.D.

Below the earth there is a great creature called Phum-Badra and the world rests upon its back. Its head is turned towards the rising sun and its back towards the sunset.

There is an insect named Chunchi-Raba-Rubbu and from time to time it flies down to Phum-Badra and says, 'I have come from the face of the earth to tell you that all men and animals are dead.' This makes Phum-Badra very sad and he begins to weep and his whole body trembles and shakes the world.

When the earth quakes the birds and animals of the forest cry loudly and men shout in fear crying, 'We are here, we are here', and when he hears the noise Phum-Badra realizes that he has been deceived and stops shaking the earth.

8

MINYONG

Riu, Siang F.D.

At first all was water: the earth was below. Even the rocks were soft as wet mud. Kayum-Sedi-Nane-Wiyu looked on the water everywhere and tried to make the earth, but he could not. He found a spirit, Kayum-Polung-Sabbo-Wiyu, who had the form of a great mithun, and said to him, 'Make a pit with your horns that the water may flow into it.' The mithun-spirit dug such a pit and all the water drained away and the earth appeared.

There was a Wiyu, Sedi-Irping-Puing-Idum-Botte, who had lived always on the face of the waters. When they dried up, he had nowhere to live and he died. His corpse turned into a mountain. From his bones came every kind of tree, from his hair the thousand grasses, and they spread as forest over the earth.

Men went to cut trees and grass on the hills, at the beginning as they do now. If they do not sacrifice to Kayum-Polung-Sabbo and Sedi-Irping-Puing-Idum-Botte, these Wiyus get angry and try to turn the world again to water by shaking it.

9

NOCTE

Laju, Tirap F.D.

There is a god called Jovey who lives inside the earth. It is he who takes the souls of men after death. Sometimes very few people die and when Jovey gets hungry for souls, he shakes the earth so that more people will die and he will have enough to eat.

10

SHERDUKPEN

Rupa, Kameng F.D.

The earth is for ever revolving. There is a great ocean below us and in the middle of it a high mountain towers above the water.

Sometimes as the earth turns round it knocks against the mountain and this causes an earthquake. When this happens the earth begins to turn in the opposite direction and it continues to do so until it knocks against the mountain again.

11

SHIMONG

Shimong, Siang F.D.

Dine-Mane Wiyu lives in Ugom-Jegom, at the point where earth and heaven meet. At the beginning, he tied earth and heaven together with a rope. And now, when earth and heaven wish to come together as man and wife, Dine-Mane pulls the rope, and the two cry out and tremble.

12

SINGPHO

Imbu, Tirap F.D.

There is water below the earth and in the water lives a great fish called Palang-Ananda. From its back there grows a flower and the world rests on the flower. When a king is born above, the fish laughs for joy and this shakes the world. Similarly, when a king dies the fish weeps for sorrow and this also shakes the world.

13

TAGIN

Serra, Subansiri F.D.

There is a creature below the earth: no one can say whether it is an animal or a human being: but it has a great head with eyes and ears, but no horns, feet or tail. Its name is Modi-Mobe-ane and the world rests on its back. When a famous shaman dies, he has to go by Modi-Mobe-ane who tries to bar his passage. He strikes the great creature with his dao, and it shakes its back in anger, and this makes the whole world tremble.[10]

14

TARAON (DIGARU) MISHMI

Machima, Lohit F.D.

The earth rests on four pillars which stand in a great pool of water far below. In this water there is an enormous fish which lies most of the time quietly between the pillars. But now and then it wakes up and wants to go somewhere and so bumps against one or other of the pillars and this causes an earthquake.

15

TARAON (DIGARU) MISHMI

Tushe, Lohit F.D.

Below the earth lives the great serpent called Devibri. There is a pillar on which the earth rests. From time to time the serpent gets angry and wants to kill the people of the earth. It shakes the pillar and the earth quakes and many people die.

[10] A slightly different version has been reported from the Tagins of the area north of Taliha. Earthquakes are caused by the spirit Nido Hargo, who lives inside the earth. One of his tasks is to guard the path to the other world. When the soul of a dead man tries to pass he has to fight him and when he injures him with his arrows or dao, Nido Hargo shakes with the pain and this causes the earthquake. The dead then go on, first to Potailo and then to Chingterilo, their final and permanent home. It is said that the 1950 Earthquake was caused by the death of an important Tagin called Tengkio who died in Kodak village three days before and prophesied it just before his death.

PART TWO: MAN AND HIS HISTORY

CHAPTER SEVEN

THE FIRST MEN

TRADITIONS about the creation of man are confused and sometimes contradictory. We have exact information about the creation of the first elephant; there is a lot of material about the origin of the sun and moon, the mountains, rocks and rivers, but the picture of the emergence of the first man is less definite.

Nor is it clear whether the mysterious beings who appear even before the creation of the world are human or not. Indeed, in those early ages, there does not seem to have been any real distinction between man, animal and spirit. A woman gives birth to twins, of whom one is human and the other a tiger; animals talk and also often behave like men; of two brothers, one is the father of mankind and the other the father of the spirits.

However, it is possible to sort out certain main traditions. In one, man is described as born of the union of Earth and Sky; in another, men come direct down from the heavens; in a third, men and women are made by a divine being as an artist would model clay. In a fourth tradition, human beings emerge out of the ground or, more commonly, from a gourd or even the tusk of an elephant. Among some tribes there is a tradition that the original race of men was destroyed by fire and flood, and the world was repopulated, either from a surviving human couple or by the direct creation of a new race.

Thus a Dhammai story describes how men have descended from the union of the Earth and Sky who are regarded as wife and husband. A male and a female frog are born first and when they mate they have human children, though these are covered with hair. Brother and sister marry and have sons from whom the whole human race has come. Similarly, a Hrusso story describes how every kind of tree and grass and living creature came into being as a result of the love of the Earth and Sky. A Hill

Miri story derives the descent of Abo-Teni, who is father of all men, from the Earth Mother.

A variant on this idea is found in a Nocte story from a remote part of Tirap, which describes how first a woman and then a man fell down from the sky; they came together and had many children. Another Nocte story traces mankind to the marriage between the very pretty daughter of the Sky-God and a spirit on earth. These first men were the Noctes and their descendants, according to local tradition, were the Ahoms. The English, incidentally, have a less dignified ancestry in this story, for they are the children of a Nocte who married a monkey with a very long tail!

Then we have stories, which resemble those told in Central India and Orissa, of how the first men and women were modelled by the divine artist. In a Hill Miri story, the Sun takes clay and makes images of a man and woman and puts the breath of life into them. In a Kaman Mishmi story Matai, the Lord of the Sky, creates the earth but he is not satisfied with it, for it is desolate and lonely. He combines with the Lord of the Earth to make models of a man and woman and puts life into them.

In another type of myth, the first human beings are represented as emerging from various material things. The Moklums describe how the daughter of Rang, the Lord of the Sky, gives birth to a lump of flesh which is neither dead nor living. She dries it by the fire and presently it bursts open and bits of it scatter about the world and turn into human beings. A Khampti story recorded seventy years ago by Macgregor tells us that in the beginning there was a great tree, from the berry of which there grew a flower; out of this flower came a pair of human beings, the first man and woman. In much the same way, Bugun and Singpho stories describe how the first men and women come out of a gourd. In one Singpho story the great spirits who live at the dawn of the world have three children, one of whom is human, the second a rock and the third a gourd. As the children are playing together, the rock-child breaks open the gourd and many little people come out of it: these are the first human beings. In a Bugun story, a man marries a girl who is what the European tradition would call a fairy: she lives in a gourd but when she comes out to cook for him, he catches her and breaks the gourd to prevent her return. Her children are the ancestors of the Buguns. A Taraon Mishmi story also describes how many of the first men and women come out of the magic tusk of an elephant.

Finally, we may note the tradition that the first race of men was destroyed and a new race created. In a Singpho story, seven suns destroy mankind for its iniquity. And then, after the world has been washed clean by rain, it is repeopled with a new race. Similarly, an Idu Mishmi story tells how the first men were destroyed by fire and flood, and only one man and woman were saved: from them modern humanity has descended. In Wancho tales the world is destroyed by flood and the tribe is descended from a girl who was impregnated by the wind.

After the first man and woman have been created, there is the problem of providing them with children, for they are often represented as innocent of any knowledge about the facts of life. In a Hill Miri story, the Supreme Being sends two birds to teach the first man and woman how to people the world. In a Bugun story, after the first couple have come into being, a god excites them to intercourse. And in another version, a boy and girl are fertilized almost as flowers are fertilized by bees.

It was obvious that such traditions should raise the problem of incest, for the first man and woman are often represented as being brother and sister. The Tagin hero Abo-Teni, after trying to marry animals and leaves, has to marry his own sister and from her the first human children are born. Similarly, in a Dhammai story, at the beginning of the world the first brother and sister come together to produce the human race. In an Idu Mishmi story, the parents of the first boy and girl decide that, since there are no other people in the world, they will have to marry each other. The girl tries to escape, but in the end she is compelled to marry her brother and, in due course, gives birth to a tiger and a god in human form.

The shadow of incest, in fact, lies across many of these stories. In Bugun tradition, thunder and lightning is caused by the pursuit of a sister by her brother. To resist him, she beats him with a hair-pin which flashes across the sky as lightning and he runs away roaring as the thunder. The first bears, according to Mishmi tradition, came into being when a brother and sister came together and were so ashamed that they went to live in the forest; they drank some salt water and turned into bears. The first mithun, according to a Hrusso story, was a girl who, at the very beginning of the world, was forced by her parents to marry her brother because there was no man for her. Although two of her brothers married two of her sisters and seem to have lived very happily together, she herself refused to do this and, after some months of misery, turned herself into a mithun. In the widely distributed story of the holocaust of the monkeys, only one female monkey escaped. She was already pregnant and, after her son had grown up, mother and child came together and from them the whole tribe of monkeys has descended. But they were so ashamed of this that they went to live in the forest and lost the skill of using bows and arrows. The snake first began to bite mankind as a result of a Mishmi boy's attempt to seduce his sister.

Many stories in other parts of the world[1] about the first men show them as imperfect and even repulsive. Here too we have traditions that early man had no fingers (Kaman Mishmi), no eyes or teeth (Moklum), no idea of how to sing or weep (Wancho). They never laughed (Moklum); men menstruated instead of women (Tagin and Wancho); they had thick necks and enormous throats and only spoke

[1] 'A considerable part of all creation myths is concerned with the ordering of human life after the initial act of the creation of man. The newly created human being is often thought of as imperfectly formed, with only rudimentary limbs and features. In a widespread but rather pointless California tale it is said that at first people had solid hands, like the paws of a coyote, but that the lizard decreed that they should ever after have hands like hers. Far better known is the idea that original man was not properly provided with sexual organs. Many stories, most of them probably independent, account for the way in which this need was supplied, and for initiation into sexual intercourse.'—Stith Thompson, *The Folktale* (New York, 1946), p. 317

indecent and ugly words (Wancho). The stories, of course, describe how these defects were remedied.

A story that is known throughout NEFA attempts to explain how it is that the tribes are illiterate, while the plains people, though not such good talkers, can read and write. All wisdom was long ago written on pieces of skin and given both to the hill-people and the people of the plains. But the hungry tribesmen cooked and ate their piece of skin, with the result that they have always been ignorant. This story, in various versions, has been recorded here from Gallongs, Noctes, Panggi Adis, Taraon Mishmis and Wanchos, and is known to many other tribes.[2]

1

BORI

Gameng, Siang F.D.

There were five brothers, Yaiying, Nijo, Yebu, Nitan and Nigang. These five brothers came from beyond Gelling to Tuting and wanted to settle there. But the Membas fought against them and drove them away and they came to Janbo. Nijo liked the place and said, 'I shall stay in Janbo.' The others left him there and went on to Karko. They all liked Karko very much and built houses and settled down there.

While they were at Karko they performed the Dogin sacrifice. At this sacrifice the custom is to offer two male mithuns, after making them fight each other. As the mithuns were fighting, the foot of one of them went into the earth and water sprang up from the place. This made the people think that there must be some dangerous Wiyu living there, and for fear of the Wiyu they went away. But Yebu remained and became part of the Minyong tribe. The remaining three brothers went to Yuing-Kebe-Ronne. Yaiying said, 'I don't like this place. I am going on.' But Nitan and Nigang thought the place very good for cultivation and decided to stay.

[2] As, for example, to the Semas who believe that they once had the secret of writing, but that dogs ate the skin on which it was recorded.—Hutton, *The Sema Nagas*, p. 299.

Yaiying and his family went on and came to a place called Tulung and built their houses there, but the Gallongs of Kamking fought against them and drove them out and gradually they moved up the valley until they came to Gameng where they still remain.

After they had settled in Gameng they joined with the people of Payum and fought against the Tagins and drove them away from this part of the country.

2

BUGUN (KHOWA)

Kaspi, Kameng F.D.

Jan's brothers, Rei and Bai, went down towards the Assam plains in search of the other members of the family who had left their village. They reached Sissini, but when they saw in the distance the great plains with no mountains and no forest, they were afraid and turned back.

On their return they met three brothers and a sister, who had gone to the hills for trade and were now coming back to Assam. The brothers went ahead and the sister lagged behind picking flowers—she picked a flower and smelt it, picked another and put it in her hair. She spent so much time on this that she soon found herself alone. When the Bugun brothers saw the three men they were frightened and hid in the forest until they had gone by. But when they saw the girl by herself picking flowers and putting them in her hair, they were excited and decided to kidnap her and take her home as Rei's wife. When they caught hold of her, she screamed and struggled at first but soon became reconciled to her fate and went with them willingly enough.

When her brothers saw that the girl was not following them they turned back to find her. When the others heard them coming, the girl said to Rei and Bai, 'There is a big clump of plantains not far away. Let us go quickly and hide among them, for otherwise my brothers will certainly kill you.' Accordingly they ran quickly to the clump of plantains and hid there.

The three brothers came to the place and, suspecting that the fugitives were there, fired many arrows into the clump and the arrows stuck in the plantain stems. Then supposing that they had killed the kidnappers and their sister, they returned home.

When they had gone Rei and Bai took the girl to Sachidhah village and there Rei married her, and for the feast they killed two mithuns and a bullock and made a great quantity of rice-beer. But when the girl saw them eating the meat and drinking the beer she said, 'Don't give me any of this meat or beer, for if you do I shall die.' And they all agreed that she need not eat or drink. But in the party there was an old man who caught hold of the girl and said, 'You have married one of us and you have got to eat whatever we give you.' He forced her to drink a little of the beer and eat a piece of beef, but directly the forbidden things passed her lips she died.

Rei and his brother buried her and after a time bamboos, of the kind we call the 'lightning-bamboo', grew up out of the grave.[3]

3

BUGUN (KHOWA)

Kaspi, Kameng F.D.

Long ago there lived in the forest a man called Phoiphua and his wife Phoimua. He was a great hunter and every day used to go out to bring meat for supper. One day, as he was hunting, he found a wooden comb on the ground and he picked it up and

[3] The Hrussos tell this story in a somewhat different form. On the way from Assam one of the three brothers accompanying the girl fell ill. The Buguns came to the place and when they saw such a pretty girl, they offered to look after the sick man and, in order to get rid of the other two brothers, asked them to go and get a sheep to sacrifice for his recovery. When they asked where a sheep could be obtained, the Buguns said that they should go to Tibet for it. The two brothers, therefore, leaving their sister and the Buguns to look after the sick man, went to Tibet for a sheep.

Once they were well out of the way, Rei went and hid by the stream from which the girl would have to go and fetch water. When she came to the place, he caught hold of her, but she resisted and struggled violently. He caught her by the hand, but she bit him and when he caught hold of her clothes she threw them off. At last, when she was completely naked, Rei caught her by the hair and knocked her hair-pin to the ground, whereupon she turned into a stream of water, which flowed down to the plains as the Brahmaputra River. It was from the hair-pin, and not from the girl's body, that the 'lightning-bamboo' has grown.

brought it home for his wife. She was very pleased with it and immediately sat down and began to use it. In fact, she became so interested in dressing her hair that when she went anywhere she would sit down after every mile or so and comb it afresh

One day Phoimua said to her husband, 'I would like to go hunting with you.' So they went out together, but every time they covered a mile she sat down and did her hair. When she got up, her husband would say, 'Are you sure you have your comb?' They went on like this for many miles but at last while they were crossing a stream, the girl dropped her comb without noticing it and when she next sat down to do her hair, could not find it. Her husband said to her, 'Go back and look for it.' 'But I can't go alone,' she said. 'I am afraid of the spirits of the forest.' He replied, 'Then I'll go instead.' But even then she said, 'I'll be afraid to wait here all by myself.' At last after they had argued for some time, Phoiphua put the girl up in a tree and removed the bark so that no spirit could climb up to attack her, and then went off to find the comb.

Very soon a spirit came and sat below the tree. He called out in Phoiphua's voice, 'Phoimua, come down! I have found your comb and brought it back for you.' But Phoimua wondered how her husband could have got back so quickly and said, 'I won't come down, for you're not my husband.' The spirit replied in an angry voice, 'Of course, I am your husband. Come down at once, for it is already late for hunting.' At that the girl came down, and as she did so the spirit threw some black oil-seeds into her hair and said, 'Look, your head is covered with lice ; let me pick them out for you.' The girl sat down and the spirit picked out the seeds one by one from her hair and pretended to kill them with his nails. After he had done this for a little while, he broke the girl's head and killed her. Then he removed her skin and dressed himself in it and threw the bones and the flesh away. Having done this, he sat down below the tree.

Presently, Phoiphua returned with the comb and saw what appeared to be his wife sitting beneath the tree. 'Why did you come down?' he asked, 'For you know it is dangerous by yourself in the forest.' 'You were so late,' said the spirit, 'that I came down to find you.' But as Phoiphua came nearer, he realized that this was not his wife and ran away in fright.

He ran far far away and, as he went, he found two fine gourds. He picked them and took them home and put them away carefully in a corner. Now he was all alone in his house and he had to cook for himself and fetch his own water as well as go hunting. And then one day when he came home from the forest, he found the house had been cleaned and that there was food cooking on the hearth. This happened for several days and at last Phoiphua said to himself, 'This is a very extraordinary thing, for there is nobody else in the forest, so who can be getting me water and cooking me food?'

The next day Phoiphua hid behind the house and, after a little while, he saw a girl come out of one of the gourds and clean the house, fetch water and cook the food. When she had finished, and was about to return into the gourd, Phoiphua came out of his hiding-place and caught her by the hair. She struggled to escape but he held her tightly and at last broke the gourd and persuaded the girl to live with him as his wife.

The children of this couple were the ancestors of the Buguns and the Buguns even today tie their hair in a knot at the top of their heads, for this resembles the shape of the gourd from which they came.

4

BUGUN (KHOWA)

Senchong, Kameng F.D.

First of all, when there were no other people in the world, Apuphulwa and Muinini came into being. But when he saw that they were not living together, the great Lord Saja-Sange said to himself, 'Unless these two come together, how will the race of men be born?' So he sent a male-spirit called Phongma and a female-spirit called Duima and excited each of them with desire. Apuphulwa was soon longing for a woman,as a man is hungry for his food or thirsty for his beer or craves to smoke his pipe. And Muinini had the same desire for a man.

Apuphulwa and Muinini therefore came together, and from them the whole race of men was born.

And even today if there is a man who is not helped by

Phongma he is impotent, and if there is a woman who is not helped by Duima she is barren.

5

BUGUN (KHOWA)

Kaspi, Kameng F.D.

The human children of Apuphulwa and Muinini were called Assanga, who was the boy, and Arangma. When they grew up they wanted mates and went out to look for them. Though they travelled separately, they both went towards the East.

There was a great mountain: one side was called Kadampu, the other side was called Kadamlo. The girl went to live on the slopes of Kadampu and the boy lived on the slopes of Kadamlo. In those days everyone went about naked.

The boy made himself a shelter beneath a tree in which was a hive of bees. The bees flew over to Kadampu and when they saw the girl sitting there alone, they were filled with pity and discussed how to bring the two together. One of the bees went to the girl and settled on her body: it took a little scrap of her dirt and flew back to the boy. It put the dirt on the boy and he grew strong and was filled with desire.

Then the bee took a little of the boy's dirt to the girl and put it on her. It stung her and she was filled with desire. Presently, she found herself pregnant, and in due time a child was born.

The girl thought, 'There must be a man somewhere here, or how could I have become pregnant?' And she went out to find him. The boy thought, 'There must be a woman somewhere here, or how could I be so excited?' And he went out to find her. On the top of the mountain, between Kadampu and Kadamlo, they met ; they did not recognize each other and they came together.

Assanga and his sister lived as man and wife on the top of the mountain, but after a time the girl died. Assanga went to find another wife, this time towards the West. After he had journeyed for many days he met an old woman. She had only one eye, one nostril, half a mouth, one arm, one breast and one leg. But there was no one else and he married her.

From this woman a rock was born first, then a male child: this was Haklum, who makes thunder in the sky. Then she gave birth to Sakatung, the God of Death: when he grew up he went beneath the ground where he shakes the world from time to time. Then there was another boy called Khawai, who later became Abua, the god of water. Another son was Chakmao, who gives rain to the earth. And at last a girl was born ; she was the beautiful Halia, who is afraid of men and causes the lightning in the sky.

6

DHAMMAI (MIJI)

Nakhu, Kameng F.D.

Formerly Gunnu the Aka and Dhammai the Miji were brothers, Dhammai being the elder. Dhammai went towards Lhasa and Gunnu to Assam to tax the people. After a year, when they had brought home their dues, they met and Dhammai asked Gunnu what he had received. Gunnu showed him pieces of silk cloth, supari and cotton yarn. Dhammai produced sheepskin, salt and cows' tails. He said to his brother, 'You give me some yarn and cloth and I will give you salt and sheepskin.' In this way trade began between them and since then their descendents have intermarried.

7

DHAMMAI (MIJI)

Nakhu, Kameng F.D.

After the earth and sky were made, Abugupham-Bumo, who was human in form but covered with hair, lived with his three sons, Labukhanlung, Sangso-Dungso and Kimbu-Sangtung.

One day Abugupham-Bumo went to a stream and caught a great fish. He put it on the platform outside his house and his three sons ran to look at it. Soon they were quarrelling as to who should have it. When their father saw them fighting he cut the fish into three pieces and said, 'Each of you take which you like.' Labukhanlung chose the head, as it was the largest and he was the eldest. Sangso-Dungso took the middle part and Kimbu-Sangtung only got the tail, as he was the smallest.

But Kimbu-Sangtung was not satisfied and wanted to change his share, but the two other brothers ran away. He followed them and, as they were running, Sangso-Dungso threw the guts of the fish away and Kimbu-Sangtung picked them up.

After a time the three brothers met again and each of them cut open his share of the fish. Labukhanlung brought out of the head gold, silver, precious stones, sheep and cows. Sangso-Dungso hid his share, for it was fat and fleshy and he feared that the others would be jealous of him. 'Let Kimbu-Sangtung cut open his first,' he said.

So Kimbu-Sangtung cut open the tail and out of it came paper, iron, yarn and from the fish's guts came gold and silver. Then at last Sangso-Dungso cut his share, but nothing came out but the rich flesh.

When the eldest and youngest brothers saw Sangso-Dungso had nothing but the flesh, they were afraid that he would want to take part of their shares and so they ran away with them, Labukhanlung going to Lhasa and Kimbu-Sangtung to Assam.

As Labukhanlung was on his way, Sangso-Dungso followed to try and rob him of his share. He caught hold of the horns of one of the sheep and the horns of one of the cows and dragged them away, but Labukhanlung recovered them. Ever since the horns of these animals have been curved.

Sangso-Dungso was very angry and hit his brother's head with his dao and the marks may still be seen on the foreheads of the Lamas. Labukhanlung seized Sangso-Dungso's hair and twisted it into a knot and the Dhammais tie their hair like this even today. Sangso-Dungso was in such a temper that he cut off his brother's hair and this is why the Lamas have their hair very short.

Labukhanlung then said to Sangso-Dungso, 'Your hands and feet are very small' and he tied him up by the hands and feet. This is why our hands and feet are small and we tie cords round our wrists and ankles to strengthen them. In the end Labukhanlung said, 'You had the middle portion of the fish, which you thought would be the best, but you got nothing from it. That was your bad luck, and it's no use quarrelling about it. But never mind: instead of precious jewels you will have a great deal of land and when my children go to cultivate it, they will have to pay taxes to your children.'

Ever since then the Monpas living to the east of Tawang have paid taxes to the Dhammais.

Labukhanlung became Lord of Lhasa and was very rich. Kimbu-Sangtung became the Raja of Assam and was wealthy too. The Dhammais have plenty of land in the mountains and lots of meat to eat.

8

HILL MIRI

Meli, Subansiri F.D.

At the source of the Subansiri River, far to the north, is a place called Sipo-Rigo, where Abo-Teni used to live. Every year for seven years his wife bore him a son. The seven children were always crying, for there was no food for them. So one day, while they were sleeping, Abo-Teni and his wife fled away, down the valley of the Subansiri, all the way to the Assam plains.

The sons awoke one by one, each followed his parents, tracking them by their footprints. The eldest went to the plains this side of the great river ; the second lived in the foothills ; the third settled by the Panior River ; the fourth stayed in the Kamla Valley ; the fifth by the Simmi River, the sixth by the Singen, and the seventh, who did not care to travel far, was the ancestor of the Tagins in the north.

9

HRUSSO (AKA)

Buragaon, Kameng F.D.

Long ago there was a man called Awa. His body was like a bear's, covered with thick hair, yet in spite of this he managed to marry Jusam, the beautiful daughter of the Sun. At the wedding the Sun gave her a hen's feather and some pig's bristles. Awa took his bride home and in due time she gave birth to twins, a boy and a girl. They called the boy Sibji-Sao and the girl Sibjim-Sam.

When the children grew up a little, they both fell ill. The father sent for the Mugga-priest who said that if Awa sacrificed a fowl and a pig the children would recover, but he insisted that the fowl and the pig must be domestic animals and not caught in the jungle.

Unfortunately Awa had no pigs or fowls in the house and did not know where to get any. When his wife saw him looking so distracted she asked him what was the matter and he told her what the priest had said. Jusam replied, 'Don't worry. Make a bamboo cage and a trough.'

Awa accordingly made a bamboo cage and put a wooden trough beside it. When everything was ready, Jusam sat down in front of the cage and, taking one of the feathers she had from her father's house, blew on it and a cock and hen immediately appeared inside the cage. Then she sat in front of the trough and, taking some of the bristles that she had from her father's house, blew on them, and a pig and a sow immediately appeared before the trough.

But at once the pigs and the fowls began to weep. Jusam tried to console them by offering them milk from her own breast, but they would not take it and she said, 'Since you won't drink my milk, what are you crying about?' The pigs and fowls replied, 'Because we are very hungry.' Jusam said, 'I've got nothing else to give you, which is why I offered you my own milk.' The fowls and pigs said, 'No, whatever we do, we are not going to drink your milk, for then you will never want to kill us—and we have been made to be killed.' Jusam said, 'Well, that is all I've got to give you ; if you don't want to have it, eat anything you can find.'

At that moment the children relieved themselves and the pigs and fowls ran to eat the mess.

Soon afterwards the hen laid her eggs and hatched out chickens, and the pig had a litter. Awa took a chicken and a pig and sacrificed them for his children, who soon were well again.

In this way Awa and his wife got pigs and fowls in their house, but they had no seed. So Jusam said to her husband, 'Go to my father's house, for he has a great store of grain, and if you ask him nicely he will give you some of it.' Awa replied, 'But I don't know the way to your father's house.' Jusam, therefore, went with him part of the way as his guide. Then she said, 'Now you can follow the path, but presently you will come to a point where it divides in two. Be sure you take the right-hand path and not the left. If you go the left, you will find yourself in all sorts of trouble.' Jusam then returned home and Awa went on his way.

Presently Awa came to the point where the path divided in two and, remembering what his wife had said, went to the right, but there were so many thorns and pitfalls that he thought that she must have made a mistake, and turned back and went to the left.

He walked a long way until at last he came to a cave where a demon, Mithi-Chitjin, was sitting beside a great fire. When the demon saw him, he threw a burning bit of wood which burnt him and turned him into a dog.

Poor Awa slunk back to his house but did not dare go in ; he just lay down in front of the door, placing his front paws together on the threshold. Presently the two children Sibji-Sao and Sibjim-Sam came out ; they saw the dog lying there, and ran back to their mother and said, 'There is an extraordinary creature sitting at the door.' Their mother came hurriedly and when she saw the dog, she realized at once that it was her foolish husband who had taken the wrong path, and told her children, 'This is your father.' But they replied, 'How can this be our father, who is a great big man?' Jusam said, 'If you don't believe me, spit on your hands and offer them to this creature. If he licks them, it will mean he is your father ; if he doesn't, then he is something else.'[4] So the children spat on their hands and held them out to the dog who immediately licked them and Jusam said, 'There, don't you see? He really is your father.' The children said, 'Yes, you are right, he is our father.'

Jusam explained things to them saying, 'What happened was that your father was going to my father's house to get seed but he took the wrong path and has been turned into a dog. Now how I am to feed you both I really do not know. The only thing for me to do is to go myself to my father. I'll send you some seed and you'll be able to make fields and cultivate them and in that way get some food to eat.' But the children began to cry and would not let their mother go and she had to wait till evening. She put the children to sleep and then secretly went to her father.

[4] Compare the similar test in a Hill Miri story from Subansiri recorded in Chapter VIII.

When Jusam left the house, the evil spirits of the forest, seeing that the two children were alone, gathered round to devour them. But when the dog saw them coming he barked loudly and drove them away. In the morning when the children found their mother gone, they cried and said to each other, 'Come along, let's follow mother wherever she has gone.' The dog went ahead to guide them and the children followed him. He went as far as he knew the way, and then stood still. The children sat down to rest and the dog thought to himself, 'Let them sleep for a bit, while I go and try to find the right path.'

When the evil spirits of the forest saw the children alone, they gathered round to devour them and the children woke up and ran for their lives.

As they were running along they met a bear who asked them, 'What's the matter? Why are you running so fast?' They replied that the evil spirits of the forest were chasing them. The bear said, 'Don't be so frightened. I will save you.' He took them on his back and climbed up a high tree and, making them sit on a branch at the top, came down and scraped off the bark so that the spirits could not climb up. Having done this, he went away.

After the bear had gone, the evil spirits of the forest came to the tree. They tried to climb up, but the trunk was too smooth for them. So they began to cut down the tree with their teeth. When they saw what was happening, the children said to the tree, 'When you fall, fall towards the open country.' But the spirits of the forest cried, 'Fall towards the mountains.' At last when the tree did fall, it came down in the direction of the open country. It did this out of mercy for the children, for the evil spirits could not go towards the open country.

The children were safe for the moment and said to each other, 'Somehow or other we must find our mother.' As they were wondering what to do, a vulture flew down and asked them what the matter was. When they told him, he said, 'It is my duty to search every day for dead bodies and take their blood to the house of the Sun.' The children said, 'But that's just where we want to go ; our mother is the daughter of the Sun, so when you go take us with you.' The vulture replied, 'You are too heavy for me to take both of you at the same time. I can take only one of you.' So he took Sibjim-Sam on his back and flew to the house of the

Sun. When Jusam saw her daughter, she was very pleased and gave her a big basket of seed. She tied a rope to her hair and let her down to the earth, right in front of the house. When the girl reached home, she cooked some of the seed and made it into beer, and then sat outside watching the road until her brother should return.

Sibji-Sao remained standing where he was, for he did not know where to go, for a long time. But as he was wondering what he could do, the dog who had been searching everywhere for the two children found him. When he saw his son he jumped on him, licking his face, barking, and wagging his tail and then led him back home. When they reached the house Sibjim-Sam made supper for them and gave them lots of beer, for they were all very happy at meeting again.

After some time the two children came together as man and wife, and they were the parents of all mankind.

10

IDU MISHMI

Dibang Valley, Lohit F.D.

Long ago men and gods lived together on the earth. The gods, being more powerful than men, did what they liked and oppressed them mercilessly. But in the sky the supreme god Inni Taya became angry at what he saw of the evil done by gods and men on earth, and he and the god Anya sent many lesser gods from the sky to destroy them.

Mimanjam, the god of the wind, came down and swept everything before him. He snatched women from their husband's arms and dashed them against the rock. Then Leen, the god of earthquakes, shook the whole earth and caused the surface to break and the mountains to fall. The fire-god Inni Ala set fire to the earth and destroyed the granaries and houses and the crops in the fields. He burnt Adu Anuya, the place where men got their pigs and mithun and other animals. When the fire raged across the earth, the gods of this world took shelter on the top of a tall tree but the flames blazed all round it and leapt up until they devoured the gods also.

From this great devastation Anya saved only one man, Lyama-Meru, and one woman, Ani-Meru. He told them to live as husband and wife and in due time the woman gave birth to three children, Thralaru, Inni Anyamaru and Assamo. From the first of these came the Mishmis, from the second came the Tibetans and other races of man, and from the third came the tribe of monkeys.[5]

11

KAMAN MISHMI

Lohit Valley, Lohit F.D.

When men were first created they were not very attractive and were in many ways imperfect. Khrane gave them domestic animals and bows and arrows and taught them to talk. He made a great flat plain where they could live in comfort.

But in spite of this they preferred the hills and spent their time hunting in the forest. They neglected the chickens which Khrane had given them and let them run away to the plains. The pigs also left them and went to the forest.

When Khrane saw that men were doing nothing except hunt, he came and asked them why they were not using the gifts he had given them. They showed their hands to him and said, 'Since you have made our fingers all joined together, it is impossible for us to cultivate our fields or look after our animals.'

When Khrane saw this, he was filled with pity and took a dao and separated the fingers of the human hand so that each finger could move freely. After that men were able to use their hands for cultivation and look after their animals.[6]

12

KAMAN MISHMI

Lohit Valley, Lohit F.D.

The god of the earth was Khrane and the god of the sky was Matai. At the very beginning Matai created the Sun and the Moon

[5] Recorded by T. K. Barua.
[6] Recorded by T. K. Barua.

and fixed them in the heavens. Then he created the earth, but as it was heavier than the sky it fell below it. He then said to himself, 'We must have some living creatures on the earth or it will be a desolate and lonely place.'

But Matai did not know how to make men. So he went to Khrane who said to him, 'I will imitate what you do and you imitate what I do, and in this way we will make some splendid creatures.' They sat down together, and Khrane created a human form and to make it more attractive put some lumps of flesh on its chest. The creature was beautiful but rather fragile. Matai looked at the model and made a copy. But since the lumps on the chest of Khrane's model looked like small mountain peaks, Matai did not add them to his model but gave it more vigour and strength instead. They called Khrane's model a woman and Matai's a man. They put life into them and Matai send the man to Sangilang and told him to live there.

Once they had started making things they wanted to make more. Matai made a small model of the human hand, gave it life and threw it away. Khrane called it Sang-Khran the crab. Sang-Khran made a deep hole in the earth's surface and went down into it.

Below the earth there lay a great ocean of water. When Sang-Khran made the hole in the earth the waters came surging up to the surface. He then made another hole and more water poured out. Khrane and Matai told the two streams to take their own way across the world and they called one of them Talla (the Lohit river) and the other Kalam-Kamai.[1]

13

KHAMPTI

(From J. F. Needham, *Outline Grammar of the Khamti Language*, 1894)

A legend exists that a tree of iron grew in their country which yielded golden fruit ; that their enemies fearing they, the Bor Khamtis, would become inordinately rich by means of this tree, sent a demon to devour them ; that this took up his abode in the

[1] Recorded by T. K. Barua.

said gold-yielding tree and as he threatened to annihilate them they were compelled, in self-defence, to fell the tree in order to kill him, it being too high to admit of doing so in any other way. The legend says the tree was felled by fire and the demon was then destroyed.

14

MINYONG

Parong, Siang F.D.

Poini-Pollo had a flute and a jew's harp. One day he dropped them and they fell to earth, where they were picked up by Irki-Leni Wiyu. Presently the Wiyu died. No one buried him: his body lay on the ground, the flute in one hand, the harp in the other. Two men, Danni-Yasi and Liko-Yaman, came by and saw him. Danni-Yasi cut off the hand that held the flute and Liko-Yaman cut off the hand that held the harp. Danni-Yasi took the flute to the Padams and taught them the Sollung dance. From him arose the Sollung-Miris whose singing is sweet as the music of the flute. Liko-Yaman took the harp to the Minyongs, and from him came the Wiyu-Miris, and the Baris. For the Minyongs are great talkers, but the Padams are sweet singers.[8]

15

MINYONG

Pangin, Siang F.D.

There was a man who loved to hunt. He built a *dumbang* hut, the hut where you decide in which direction to go, where you give sacrifice to Bango-Paing, where you bring the game and cut it up in honour of the Wiyu-spirits. He set traps, noose-traps in the trees, fall-traps on the ground. Every few days he went to see whether he had caught anything. One evening when he went to the *dumbang*, he was surprised to find a meal of hot rice and meat

[8] The Abors have very few musical instruments. It is strange that a tribe so fond of dancing should not have developed some kind of drum. But they sometimes use a flute, a sort of *sarangi* made with a gourd, and a jew's harp. Baris are inspired orators at a village council.

ready for him by the hearth. He ate it greedily and was very pleased but wondering whoever could have cooked it. This happened again and again. Then he spoke to Doini-Pollo: 'Let me see the person who has done this for me.' Having spoken, he sat and waited.

Presently a Wiyu girl, an Epom-Wiyu, in bright and coloured clothes, with long hair and rich blue beads, slid down a rope from a tree above the hut. 'Who are you?' he asked. 'Just a girl,' she answered. 'Did you cook this food for me?' he said. 'Yes.' 'Good. I want to take you home and marry you.' He caught her in his arms, but she said, 'I too want to marry you, that's why I cooked for you, but I can't now. Come back after a few days and I will go with you.'

The hunter let her go and went home. After a few days he went again to the hut. As he went in, he found the girl cooking. He took her to his house and said, 'Let's get married tomorrow.'

'Not tomorrow,' said the girl. 'My brothers are coming with gifts of mithuns, pigs and ornaments. We must prepare a lot of rice-beer for them, or we will be shamed.' So the next day they were very busy, preparing mithun-flesh, pork, rice and beer—a great feast. When it was ready the clouds came down, thick dark clouds that filled the house and made everything dark. The girl threw the food and the beer into the rafters and her brothers came in the shadow and enjoyed it. Then the clouds cleared and the Epom said to her man, 'Go and see what there is outside.' He went and found mithuns tethered before the house, and fat pigs in the styes. On the drying-rack above the hearth was a pile of blue and white necklaces and beads.

This was how they married and began to live together. One day the girl said, 'My brothers are coming to work for us. We must have a feast ready for them.' So they prepared dried mithun-flesh and rice and a great deal of beer. When it was ready, the clouds came down, thick and heavy, and filled the house with darkness. The brothers came and made a great clearing on the hillside. They ate the feast and then the clouds lifted. When the man went out to see, he found his trees cut and everything ready.

Some time after this, the Wiyu-girl said to her husband, 'My brothers want to offer the Durrung sacrifice and they have invited us to join them.' So they made beer and went to the place. The girl said, 'When my brothers go hunting, you must go with them.

But here is a piece of ginger. Should you get hurt, put the ginger in your mouth and spit on the wound. For if my brothers were to lick the fresh blood they might find it so sweet they'd want to eat your whole body.'

They went to the village and were received by the girl's brothers, and ate and drank their fill. Then the Wiyu-brothers took the man to hunt. Presently a chameleon ran across the path and he stamped on it and killed it. The brothers ran to him crying, 'Have you seen the deer we were chasing?' He said, 'I saw no deer but I have killed this thing on the path.' 'That is our deer,' cried the brothers, and they sat down and cut up the meat. 'Make us a bamboo basket,' they said, 'so that we can carry it home.' The man sat down to make a basket but, as he was cutting the bamboos, he scratched his hand with his knife. One of the brothers, seeing the blood, licked it, and cried, 'Sweet, sweet!' Then another brother licked it and cried, 'Sweet, sweet!' Only then, as he saw them looking at him with hungry eyes, did the man remember his wife's warning. Hastily he put the ginger in his mouth and spat on his hand. Now when a third Wiyu came to lick the blood, he cried 'Nasty, nasty!' The first and second Wiyus, hearing this, came to lick the man's hand again and now they too cried, 'Nasty, nasty!'

They put the chameleon's flesh in the basket and took it home and everyone feasted on it as if it was venison. Then the man said, 'Let us go home.' But his wife's brothers said, 'No, you must stay one more day. Tomorrow we are slaughtering our younger sister and you must stay to enjoy the feast, for the meat will be good.' The man said to his wife, 'How can I eat this girl's flesh?' She replied, 'You must learn not to fuss so much. If we leave today my brothers will be offended and may do us evil. Stay on for the feast ; you needn't eat anything ; I will take your share.'

The next day, the Wiyus brought their younger sister, a lovely girl with the eyes of a deer and in gaily coloured clothes, so that the man's heart failed as he looked at her. But they killed her in front of him and made a great feast of the flesh. As they ate, the man dropped his share through the cracks in the floor. The next day he and his Wiyu-wife went home, and the brothers pressed a share of the meat that was left upon them. When the man saw his wife eating her own sister's flesh he was afraid.

In due time, the girl conceived and was delivered of a brood of children. But she ate all of them save one. This child lived and grew, and when the time came for him to die, he went into the forest and was never seen again.

16

MOKLUM

Longke, Tirap F.D.

Once, long ago, an old man was carrying a pig on his back. As he went along he met some friends and, quickening his pace to greet them, slipped and the pig fell from his back and escaped into the forest. His friends roared with laughter.

This was the very first time that people ever laughed.

17

MOKLUM

Longke, Tirap F.D.

At first men had no eyes and it was only when a woman who had gone fishing caught an eye and put it in her basket that they got them. They also had no teeth at first and it was very difficult for them to eat. Then one day they killed a pig, made teeth out of its bones and fixed them in their mouths. After that they were able to eat properly.

In the same way at first men had no clothes. Then Rang gave them cotton-seed and taught them to spin and weave. At first men wore a girdle of bamboo and women skirts of bamboo leaves instead of cloth.

18

NOCTE

Kothung, Tirap F.D.

At first there was only one man in the whole world. One day when he was cutting trees in his clearing on the hillside, the god Yang's daughter saw him and, as he was strong and handsome, she desired him and came down to earth. She asked him who he was and soon they were sitting and talking together.

Now this man had hair on his head, in his arm-pits and round his privates. The woman asked him what it was. He pulled out some of his hair and put it on her body and it grew there. Soon they came together and found such happiness that they continued night and day. The woman conceived, but when the time came to bear her child she did not know what to do. In the end, she gave birth to the child while she was standing in a stream and he fell into the water.

At that time all the water in the world was surrounded by high hills and there was no way for it to escape. In the water where the child, whose name was Teva, was born there lived a snake and when he saw the child he wanted to eat him. Teva was frightened and swam away and since he was very light managed to get to the opposite bank and escape onto the shore. But the snake followed him and burrowed into the hill so that there was a great landslide. The water at once rushed out and flowed down into the plains, carrying the child with it.

When Yang saw his grandson's plight he lit a torch and Teva followed its light to a village in the plains.

As time went by Yang's daughter had many children but they too went to the plains. Gradually the water flowed down from the hills and they became dry and barren but the plains were always full of great rivers. After many years, when Teva was grown up, he told his brothers that he would like to go to the hills and see his mother. 'As I go,' he said, 'I will whistle and you must reply.' After a long journey he found his mother and she asked why her other sons had not come to see her. He replied that they were too busy making love to their girls. She was angry with them and said that they should remain in the plains as the Assamese, but she kept the eldest son with her and his children were the first Noctes.

19

NOCTE

Laptang, Tirap F.D.

An old man had a deer-skin on which the history of his tribe was written. But it got burnt and he ate it. Since then the Noctes have not known how to read or write.

20

PADAM

Membu, Siang F.D.

(From E. T. Dalton, *Descriptive Ethnology of Bengal*, p. 26)

The Deodar gave me the following legend of the origin of the race:—The human family are all descended from one common mother. She had two sons, the elder a bold hunter, the younger a cunning craftsman ; the latter was the mother's favourite. With him she migrated to the west, taking with her all the household utensils, arms, implements of agriculture, and instruments of all sorts, so that the art of making most of them was lost in the land she deserted, but before quitting the old country she taught her first-born how to forge daos, to make musical instruments from the gourd, and she left him in possession of a great store of blue and white beads. These beads and the simple arts known to him he transmitted to his posterity, the Padam, and from him they received the injunction to mark themselves on the forehead with a cross.

The western nations, including the English, are descended from the younger brother, and inherited from him and the continued instructions of the mother their knowledge of science and art.

21

PANGGI

Geku, Siang F.D.

It was night. There was no day. There were Wiyus in the world, but not yet men. Kayum's son was Yumkang ; Yumkang's son was Kasi ; Kasi's son was Siang: Siang's son was Abo ; Abo's son was Bomuk: Bomuk's son was Mukseng: Mukseng's son was Sedi: Sedi's son was Dilling. Sedi also begot Dimen and Dikong.*

There was this Sedi-Dikong. When he died, his sons decided to

* Shri Jairamdas Daulatram has pointed out that the Adis and certain other tribes give a son a name which begins with the last syllable of the father's name (except that a concluding nasal syllable *-ng* is dropped), a practice which certainly makes the recital of genealogies, which may extend from thirty to forty generations, easier and by which their accuracy may be checked.

plant him in the ground. Each son said, 'He's my father ; I'm going to bury him.' There was a quarrel, but this ended, as quarrels end, in a Kebang (village council). At this they decided to co-operate and all joined together in burning the body. The whole body was burnt, all but the liver. They snatched it from the fire and, taking it aside, wrote on it, as if it was a book, the history of the world. Then they cut it up and divided it.

A deer lived on the mountains, and it said, 'Write on my skin whatever was written on the Adi's share of the liver, and when you need it, I'll give it to you.' But one day when the people were hunting, they accidentally killed the deer and ate it. This is why we Adis can talk well in Kebang, but cannot read and write, while the Membas and Assamese can read and write, but are not much good at talking.

Sedi-Dilling had a son, Litung, who in turn had a son Tuye. It was after the birth of Tuye that the light began. Litung and Tuye had no eyes and no arms. They said to Sedi-Dilling, 'You are our father: you must look after us.' So he made arms for them and gave them eyes. This is why, when our eyes are red and sore, we remember the name of Doini-Pollo in the day-time.

Tuye's was Yeppe: he had eyes, everyone had eyes by this time. Yeppe's daughter was Peddong-Nane. From her came a son, Doni. Peddong-Nane was a rock, but she was soft as flour. Her son had no milk from her. He ate the soft stones and earth and kept himself alive. He ate earth as if it was rice and stone as if it was meat. Then the rock, his mother, thought, 'I give birth to men, and they eat their mother.' In her anger she became hard. Ever since the rocks have been angry with men, and from time to time a great rock falls from the hills to destroy them.

22

SHERDUKPEN

Rupa, Kameng F.D.

The King Geporading-darje lived in Debolojari[10] with his queen,

[10] Sherdukpen tradition claims that the tribe originally came from Tibet. One of the Kings of Lhasa married an Ahom princess and had two sons by her and one son by a first, Tibetan, wife. To his eldest son, who was

by whom he had a son. But he heard that the Ahom King of Assam had a very beautiful daughter and his desire was kindled for her. He sent his Minister with a strong force to Sibsagar to ask for her in marriage. But the Ahom King refused to send his daughter to an unknown, distant land, and it took the Minister twelve years to persuade him to let the girl go.

At last they started on their journey home and came to the Brahmaputra and crossed to the far side. There sin entered the Minister's mind and he seduced the princess. When they arrived at Debolojari, the King of Lhasa was delighted with his bride and married her with great ceremony. But very soon, too soon, afterwards, he noticed that his wife was pregnant, and he asked his Minister how this could be. The Minister replied, 'How can I tell? I lived twelve years in exile and brought her to you with great pain and difficulty. The child must be your's.' The King said, 'Never mind.'

But when the child was born, although he had the body of a human being, he had the face of a dog and the horns of a goat. For the Minister, his father, was a man of low degree. When the King saw the child, he had him taken to the forest and left there to die.

But he loved his young wife and forgave her and in due time had two other sons from her. The elder was named Jabdung-Mawang-Namja and the younger Gyaptang-Bura.

When the boys grew up, the King gave his own kingdom to the son of his elder wife. He gave Bhutan to the prince Jabdung-Mawang-Namja and the country round Rupa and Shergaon to Gyaptang-Bura, who was the first Sherdukpen King.

When Gyaptang-Bura came to Rupa, the Ahom King heard of it at Sibsagar and invited his grandson to come and see him. He gave him all the land which lies between the Donsiri and Gabru rivers as they flow into the Brahmaputra and told him to tax the people living there.

Gyaptang-Bura was told by his father, the King of Lhasa, that his people should not pay taxes to the Tibetans or carry loads for them. But he should beware of the Hrussos, for they were

pure Tibetan, he gave the kingdom of Lhasa ; to his second son he gave Bhutan ; to his third he gave the country between Rupa and Shergaon extending south to the Brahmaputra.

demons at that time, and should give them cows and other tribute to satisfy them.

When King Gyaptang-Bura came from Lhasa to Rupa, he brought with him a great train of porters and servants. The King's descendents are now called Thongs and the descendents of the porters are called Chaos.

We were great in those days, but the power of our Kings was brought low by the British Government.

23

SHERDUKPEN

Rupa, Kameng F.D.

A King of Lhasa called Chajernurjan had two queens, Lama the senior and Luma the junior. One day the two women went to bathe in the Tongsin river. They were both very beautiful. That same day it happened that two demons, Nyapa and Nyaro, were going along the river-bank fishing, and when they saw the beauty of the queens they seized them and carried them off.

When the King found that his queens had disappeared, he was greatly disturbed and went to search for them. When he heard that they were imprisoned in Nyapa's house, he hurried to the place and, standing outside, sung to them in a language that the demons could not understand:

'Why did you leave me and come to this strange place?
Was it of your own accord, or did Nyapa bring you forcibly?
If you wanted to go with him, you should have told me.
I have sought everywhere, and with great trouble I have found you.
What is your desire—to stay with Nyapa or to come home with me?'

From inside the house the two women replied, also in a language that the demons would not understand:

'We went to bathe in the Tongsin river.
As we were in the water, Nyapa and Nyaro came fishing.
They caught hold of us.
We tried to escape but could not get free,

For they are men and we are but women.
Now you have come we would return home with you.'

Then the King went to Nyapa and said, 'Did you not know that these women are my royal wives? Why did you force them to go with you? If you wanted them, you should have asked me first. Now return them to me—or be prepared to fight.'

When they heard this, Nyapa and Nyaro were frightened and asked to be forgiven. 'We did not know who they were. We saw their beauty in the water and so we took them. Now you have come, you shall certainly take them home.'

The doors were opened, and the King and demons made friends, and they all danced together with the queens.[11]

24

SINGPHO

Lohit F.D.

(From J. B. Neufville, *On the Geography and Population of Assam*, 1828, p. 14)

In the beginning, the Great Gossein (the Supreme Being) created man, and regarded him with especial kindness and favour. He gave him the whole earth to dwell in and enjoy, but forbade him bathing or washing in the river called Ram Sita, under a threatened penalty of being devoured by the Rakhas (Demon) and totally destroyed as the forfeit of his disobedience. That if, on the contrary, he refrained, Rakhas should have no power over him, and he should inherit the earth eternally.

Mankind, however, soon disobeyed the injunction, and the whole race was devoured by Rakhas, with the exception of a man called Siri Jia and his wife Phaksat.

These were seated under a tree, when Gossein caused a parrot, perched on a bough, to speak, and give them warning to avoid the north and fly to the southward, by which they would escape from Rakhas's hands. The man Siri Jia obeyed, but Phaksat took the other road, and fell into the clutches of Rakhas. When Siri Jia

[11] This story is told in connection with the Ajilama Dance, in which two figures masked to represent demons with ferocious faces and flowing hair perform on one side, with a Raja and a Rani on the other.

saw Phaksat in the power of the Demon, he was divided from them by the river Ram Sita, the forbidden stream, and forgetting or disregarding the prohibition, he immediately crossed it to her rescue, and was also taken by Rakhas, who prepared to devour them. In the act, however, of lifting them to his mouth, a flame issued from all parts of his body, and consumed him on the spot, since which time no Rakhases have been on the earth, in a palpable shape.

The great Gossein having then fully instructed Siri Jia and Phaksat in all useful knowledge, placed them on the Mujia Singrabhum hill, and from them the present race of men are descended.

25

SINGPHO

(From J. B. Neufville, *On the Geography and Population of Assam*, 1828, p. 14)

The Singphos came originally from a place situated two months' journey from Satao Gaom, and peopled the earth.

The race of man having killed and roasted buffaloes and pigs, which they devoured, without offering up the prescribed portions in sacrifice to the gods, the Supreme Being, in his anger, sent an universal deluge, which covered the earth, and destroyed the whole race of man, with the exception of two men called Kung-litang and Kuliyang and their wives, whom he warned to take refuge on the top of the Singrabhum hill, which remained above the waters ; from them the present race is descended.

A brother and sister belonging to a race superior to man were also saved. The Supreme Being directed them to conceal themselves under a conical mound of earth, taking with them two cocks and nine spikes of bamboo, the latter they were to stick through the sides of the mound, and pull them out one by one daily. They did so for eight days, but the rocks took no notice. On drawing out the ninth, the light appeared through, and the cocks crew, by which they knew that the waters had subsided. They then went out, and as they were in search of fire, they encountered an old woman belonging to the Demon Rakhas, who endeavoured to seize them: they, however, effected their escape to the ninth heaven, where they were deified, and are sacrificed to by the Singphos with cocks and pigs.

26

SINGPHO

Lohit Frontier Division
(From E. T. Dalton, *Descriptive Ethnology of Bengal,* p. 13)

According to Bisa, one of the most influential and intelligent of the Singpho Gams (headmen) that settled in Assam, the Singphos believe they were originally created and established on a plateau called Majai-Singrabhum, situated at a distance of two months' journey from Sadiya, washed by a river flowing in a southerly direction to the Irawadi. During their sojourn there they were immortal, and held celestial intercourses with the planets and all heavenly intelligence, following the pure worship of one Supreme Being. Why they left this Eden is not stated in connection with this tradition ; but they have another, in which the fall is assigned to an act of disobedience on their part in bathing in interdicted water. On descending to the plains they became mortal ; and, having imbrued their hands in the blood of men and animals in self-defence and for subsistence, they soon adopted the idolatries and superstitions of the nations around them.

27

SINGPHO

(From C. R. Macgregor, *Military Report on the Khampti-Singpho Countries,* 1887, p. 69)

In the beginning there were only two people, one an old man Tingla and the other an old woman Gumgai ; in the skies dwelt two Nats, male and female, called respectively Mutum and Muta. The two terrestrial beings had a son and a daughter. The son left his home for some reason not known, and went to another place on the earth, and the Nats Mutum and Muta took the girl up to the skies. A Nat who dwelt on the earth, called Unga Du, adopted the son. The girl was brought down from above by the Nats, and was married to the boy. The result of this union was that two daughters were born, who intermarried, and hence sprang the race of Singphos. The word Singpho means a man. The name of the first man was Goiung and the name of the first woman was Gajam.

In the very beginning there was nothing but water, until Mutum and Muta came from the clouds, and taking a handful of earth from under the water caused it to remain at the top of the water.

28

SINGPHO

Imbu, Tirap F.D.

After the world was made, there were the gods Phan-Ningsang and Mathum-Matta. Phan-Ningsang is the greatest of all the gods and Mathum-Matta is his Minister. They looked at the world and, seeing there was no living creature on it, decided to explore and see what they could find. On their way they found a gourd in the shape of a man which was called Michang-Wakum. Wondering what it was they broke it open and many little people came out of it. But there was nothing to show which were men and which were women. Phan-Ningsang used his axe to carve breasts on the women and Mathum-Matta, finding that many of the creatures had two navels, made one of them into the male organ and so turned them into men. When they were ready, they put a charm into their ears by a golden pipe and the result of this was that they scattered across the world and began to love each other.

They came together and many children were born. When they had greatly increased in number, Mathum-Matta put them all in a place called Majoi-Singrabhum beyond the Himalaya Mountains. Soon, however, they found there were too many of them and Mathum-Matta decided to send some of them to the plains. But the people said, 'How can we go down from such high mountains?' Mathum-Matta made ladders of gold, of silver, of cane and of bamboo and wood. When they were ready, some of the men and women came down by the silver ladder and became the British and Assamese. Others came down by the golden ladder and they were the Burmese and Khamptis. When the Singphos saw the gold and silver ladders glittering in the sun they were afraid and when they touched the cane ladder it shook so much that they thought it would break. But they found the bamboo and wooden ladder strong and durable, and for this reason they have always made their houses out of these materials.

Since the Burmese and Khamptis came down by the golden ladder they have always been rich, and the British and Assamese who came down by the silver ladder learnt how to make silver coins and have always had plenty of them. The Adis and Nagas wear girdles made of cane and make cane bridges and houses.[12]

29

SINGPHO

Dumba, Tirap F.D.

A Raja and a Rani had a pearl-necklace which could speak like a human being. They were rich and had plenty to eat and drink.

One day the Rani said to the necklace, 'I hear that there are many people in the world who are poor and have not enough to eat and go naked. How can this be?'

The necklace replied, 'Those who live truthfully and do no harm to others but remain peaceful and gentle do not suffer, but

[12] According to R. S. Kennedy, the Medical Officer who accompanied the Aka Promenade of 1913-14, the Hrussos (Akas) have a somewhat similar legend. 'Long long ago all men descended from heaven to earth by means of ladders. The Assamese and Akas of the royal blood came down by a golden ladder; the remaining Akas had a silver ladder; the Tibetans and Monpas were given a ladder of iron; the Daflas and Abors had to be satisfied with a bamboo ladder; whilst the Cacharis and Khoas shared a plantain ladder.'

All these people came to earth on the Longkapur Hill in the Lohit Valley, whence they scattered in search of land. The Assamese were the first to start and chose the plains. The Akas spent so much time resting and drinking beer that the others got the best land and they had to accept what was left. They first settled near Bhalukpung, where, on the right bank of the Bhoreli River, their two chiefs, Natapura and Bayu, built their respective capitals. Bayu demanded Natapura's beautiful wife as a sort of tribute and, after a number of adventures the girl with a newly born child arrived at Bayu's court. The child Arima grew up to be a great warrior and finally killed his own father by mistake. Overcome with remorse he migrated to the present country of the Akas; it is from his children that the modern Akas are descended.—R. S. Kennedy, *Ethnological Report on the Akas, Khoas and Mijis and the Monbas of Tawang* (Shillong, 1914), pp. 1 ff.

the sinners, those who lie and steal and are violent, suffer from hunger and sorrow.'

The Rani said, 'But we too want to know what sorrow and poverty mean.' The necklace replied, 'You will repent for this desire.' But the Rani said, 'No, I shall never be sorry for it.' The necklace said, 'If you really wish to have sorrow and poverty, then when you get up tomorrow morning, be nasty to your husband.'

Thenceforward, every morning when the Rani got up, she beat her husband and insulted him. As a result the Raja would lose his temper and beat the Rani in return, and their life became one of constant quarrelling. The Raja did not go to his court and the Rani did not cook the food.

Gradually, since neither of them did any work, they became poor and because of their unhappiness and poverty they grew thin and old.

At last when her sorrow became more than she could bear, the Rani spoke to the necklace. 'I have had enough poverty and sorrow and I can bear no more. Now, somehow or other, make us as we were before.'

The necklace replied, 'Everyday, when you get up in the morning, touch your husband's feet and no matter what he tells you to do, obey him.'

Thenceforward, every morning when the Rani got up, she touched her husband's feet, and all day long did whatever he desired. As a result, the Raja gradually recovered his temper, lived happily with his wife and began to attend once more to his duties. The Rani took to cooking again. Gradually they became rich and happy as they were before.

30

SINGPHO

Dumba, Tirap F.D.

There was once a very great Raja who had seven wives. One year they all became pregnant at the same time. The six elder wives had human children but the seventh and youngest gave birth to a tortoise. When the Raja saw the tortoise-baby he was angry and drove the mother, though she was most beautiful, out of his house and made a little hut for her outside the village.

Gradually the six elder boys grew up and, when they were old enough, they prepared to go down river to trade. When the tortoise-boy heard about it he said to his mother, 'My brothers are going to trade ; let me go as well.' The mother said, 'Your brothers can walk about, for they have hands and feet, but you have none. What do you want to go trading for?' 'All the same,' said the tortoise-boy, 'even if I have no hands and feet, I'd like to go.'

So the mother prepared the tortoise-boy for his journey and put him in the boat with his brothers. When they came into mid-stream the tortoise-boy brought a flute from under his shell and played it. The trees of the forest heard the music and came to the bank to listen and this is why to this day there are many trees along the banks of rivers.

The boat went down the river and the tortoise played his flute. After a time he said to the six brothers, 'Leave me here ; you go on and when you return, call me and I will join you.'

He jumped into the water and sank to the bottom. There he found a great store of gold and silver and precious stones and hid them under his shell. He went on a little further and found many different musical instruments.

When the brothers had finished their trading they returned and called their tortoise-brother, and he came up from the bottom of the river and clambered into the boat. Then he brought out the instruments from beneath his shell and played them. He gave some of them to his brothers and they all played together very happily.

When the boat neared home and the Raja heard the music he supposed that his sons must have made a great deal of money and were celebrating their success. He went down to the bank to welcome them with honour and took them home. But he took no notice of the tortoise-boy and left him in the bottom of the boat. But soon his mother came for him.

Presently the Raja made arrangements for the marriage of his sons. The tortoise-boy said to his mother, 'My brothers are getting married ; find a wife for me too.' The mother said, 'But you are a tortoise, you are not a human being. What sort of girl will you get to marry you?' The tortoise-boy said, 'There is a Raja's daughter in a village not far away and I want to marry her.' The mother said, 'But she is the daughter of a Raja and you are a tortoise.' The tortoise-boy said, 'That may be so, but what does it matter? Go and ask the girl's father.' So the mother went to the Raja and said, 'Give your daughter to my son.' The Raja replied, 'Very well, I will give him my daughter on this condition, that within two days, before the sun rises for the second time, your son must make a boat of gold and diamonds and bring it to my palace.' The mother went home and told her son.

Now the tortoise had great wealth hidden beneath his shell and he brought it out and called a craftsman who made a boat of gold and diamonds and they took it to the Raja's palace before the sun rose for the second time. The Raja came down to see it and there the tortoise-boy was sitting in the boat shining like the sun. When the tortoise saw the Raja he changed his shape and became a handsome youth, and the Raja willingly gave him his daughter in marriage.

31

TARAON (DIGARU) MISHMI

Machima, Lohit F.D.

The Chins and Mishmis are children of the same parents. But the Chins are of older stock than the Mishmis. They are able to read and write, but the Mishmis have always been ignorant. The Chins worked very hard, but the Mishmis never did anything but wander about in the forest catching birds and rats.

Ultimately, the Chins got angry with the Mishmis for their laziness and said, 'Go away, we don't want to live with you any longer.' The Mishmis replied, 'Then give us a share of our parents' property.' The Chins divided everything carefully and gave the Mishmis half their books, their horses, their goats and their fowls. They wrote all the knowledge in the world on a buffalo's hide. The Mishmis went away, but they did not know what to do with the books and tore them up. They got hungry and cooked the buffalo's hide and ate it. Their horses had no bridles and tried to run away. The Mishmis caught them by their tails, but the tails broke and the horses escaped into the forest and turned into deer. The goats ran away and turned into barking-deer. The mithuns ran away and became the wild bison, the fowls disappeared into the forest and turned into jungle fowls.

This is why the Mishmis have nothing, not even wisdom.

32

TARAON (DIGARU) MISHMI

Machima, Lohit F.D.

There was a Khampti Raja who had the habit of rubbing his hands together. In time this caused a swelling which was very troublesome. Presently it broke open and a girl came out of it. Her name was Takeyanr and she grew up to be so beautiful that the demon Brase kidnapped her. He was very big with eight heads and eight enormous mouths full of teeth.

The Khampti Raja had a trusted sepoy called Sepu Langa and he sent him to find the girl and bring her back.

Sepu Langa made an iron arrow and went on a long long journey to find the girl. When at last he reached Brase's house, he said to him, 'Will you return Takeyanr to me or will you fight?' The demon said, 'I will fight. I'll never give her up.' There was a great battle in which Langa triumphed. He killed his enemy and brought Takeyanr home.

But the girl was so lovely that all the world desired her and she was kidnapped again, this time by the demon Piphiye who had great ears hanging down as low as his navel. Piphiye took her across the sea, and now the Khampti Raja himself followed them. He made a boat and for eight years he travelled by river and sea searching for the girl, but could not find her.

At last he went to the King of the Monkeys and asked his assistance. The Monkey King said, 'I know where she is, but I need your help if I am to reach her. Close your fist and let me sit on the thumb and then throw me up and I'll fly through the air to rescue her.'

The Khampti King did as he suggested and sent the Monkey King flying through the air to Piphiye's palace. Directly he arrived, the demon tried to kill him. But the Monkey King said, 'You cannot kill me with a spear or a knife, but only by setting fire to my tail.' So Piphiye set fire to his tail and the Monkey King ran round the village and set fire to all the houses. In the confusion he rescued Takeyanr and took her back to the Khampti country and its King.

The Khampti King was very happy at getting the girl back and said to the King of the Monkeys, 'Ask for anything in the world and I'll give it to you.' The Monkey King said, 'The only thing I want is a fine palace of gold and silver.' The Khampti Raja built one for him but directly the Monkey entered it, his hair dropped off, his skin turned white and he became the first Englishman.[13]

33

TARAON (DIGARU) MISHMI

Machima, Lohit F.D.

Tako-Kalla lived in a tree near the home of two brothers who had a lot of fowls. Tako-Kalla used to steal one of them every night until at last there was only one left. The brothers quarrelled about this, for each accused the other of stealing the fowls and eating them secretly, but in the end they discovered that the culprit was really Tako-Kalla.

So the two brothers went to see him. He himself was out somewhere, but his children were in the tree and the brothers took them away. When Tako-Kalla returned and found his children gone, he went to the brothers and asked for them back. They said, 'You are a thief and we have taken your children instead of the fowls you stole.' Tako-Kalla said, 'From today I promise that I'll never steal again.' But they had no faith in him and refused to return the children. Tako-Kalla then said, 'Give me my children back and I'll give you something very valuable.' They were still suspicious and said, 'Give us the thing first and then you'll get your children back.'

Tako-Kalla vomited up a round ball and gave it to them, but they said, 'What is the use of this?' Tako-Kalla spat on it and put it against two stones which at once began to fight each other: their blows sounded *drang-dring*. As they fought, they broke into

[13] In this story there are obvious echoes of the Ramayana: it was recorded in a village very near the plains.

pieces. Tako-Kalla put them in baskets and within a few moments the baskets began to fight. The brothers thought this was very extraordinary and decided to accept the gift and give Tako-Kalla his children back.

At this time in the Chin country there were two Rajas. They went to war with each other and one of them was defeated and killed and his kingdom was looted. The defeated Raja had two daughters who escaped into the jungle. They went on and on, day after day, until they came to the place where the two brothers lived. The brothers were very excited when they saw the girls and asked them to marry them. But the girls said, 'We are in mourning at present and can't marry you yet.' The brothers asked what had happened and when they heard, they promised to set things right. 'We'll go,' they said, 'and fight your enemy.' The girls at first did not think it possible but finally they all went together to the girls' home and sent word to the enemy that they had come to fight.

The Raja laughed when he heard the news but he led out his troops to kill the daring brothers. And when the soldiers came, the brothers threw bits of the ball at them and at once they began to fight each other and, in the confusion, the Raja himself was killed. The girls married the two brothers who themselves became kings of the Chin country.

34

TARAON (DIGARU) MISHMI

Machima, Lohit F.D.

There was a very young Khampti girl. One day when she was working in the forest, she felt thirsty and went to and fro on the hill-side searching for a spring but couldn't find a drop of water to drink anywhere. But in the end she found the footprints of an elephant and followed them. They led her to a place where the elephant had made water and the girl drank it.

As a result, she conceived and in fourteen months a baby boy was born. When he grew up, he kept on asking his mother where his father was. The girl did not like to tell him, but he made such a fuss that she had to say that his father was an elephant and tell him how it had happened.

The next day the boy went to see his father. They greeted each other and the elephant said, 'I have nothing to give you now. But when I die, take my tusks and give the one from the left side to any true friend who helps you but, whatever you do, keep the one from the right side for yourself.'

After a little while the elephant died and the boy removed the tusks and took the right-hand one home. He put it in his house, but presently he said to himself, 'This looks very fine but what is the use of it?' He broke it open and out came a girl. She was so beautiful that he at once decided to marry her. From the tusk there also came many soldiers armed with guns and carrying gold and silver. They kept on coming, more and more of them, until the boy thought he had enough, when he took the tusk to the Lohit River and threw it in. As it floated down, it was caught here and there against a tree or a rock and wherever it stopped, more people came out of it.

This was how the first Assamese, Bengalis, Ankas, Daflas, Miris and Mikirs came to the world.

35

WANCHO

Watnu, Tirap F.D.

In the old days men had very thick necks and their throats were wide. They used to speak vile and ugly things and had no sense of shame. When Paiyu saw this he made the human neck small and the throat narrow so that men could only utter sweet and good words. After that he taught them how to sing and how to weep.

36

WANCHO

Senua, Tirap F.D.

Two brothers once came together from the place called Uphannu to the Patkoi mountains. There they sacrificed a dog and agreed to divide the land between them. The elder brother remained in

Burma, the younger went on into India. On the Indian side there were the Noctes and Wanchos and many other people, even people in the plains. The Wancho was the eldest of all and the Assamese are his children.

At first there were no different clans or tribes, for all were one. Then at that time a great flood poured over the hills of Assam and levelled some of them and the land became flat. Since there was not enough water in the hills, some of the children of the Wanchos went down to the plains and became the Assamese.

The god Paiyu wrote all wisdom on two skins and gave one to the Wanchos and one to the Assamese. The Wanchos roasted and ate their skin, but the plains-people kept their's in a bambo tube. Paiyu came and asked the Wanchos where the skin was. They said, 'We have eaten it.' He turned to the Assamese and asked where their's was and they brought it out of the bamboo tube and showed it to him. Then Paiyu said, 'You will know how to read and write and will have wisdom, but these Wanchos will always be ignorant.'

37

WANCHO

Senua, Tirap F.D.

The Lord of Water is Namwang. One day, long ago, he took the form of a buffalo and went wandering through the forest, when a party of hunters killed him. They cut his body into pieces and divided up the meat and feasted on it. But there was a woman there named Khangthoak with a beautiful daughter, who was called Toizam. They had gone out somewhere and, by the time they returned, all the meat had been distributed and there was nothing left for them.

When Namwang saw these people eating the body of the buffalo in which he had taken form, he was angry and sent the great waters to flood the earth. Everyone was drowned except Khangthoak and her daughter who had not eaten the meat. These too then lived together, but there was no man to whom the girl could be married.

One day mother and daughter were sitting in the sun outside the house and discussing how the girl could ever have a child. They were naked, as all people were in those days, and the wind blew upon the daughter and entered her. She conceived by the wind and in nine months gave birth to a child. This was Uphannu, the ancestor of all the Wanchos. It was he who gave the goat and the dog to men.

CHAPTER EIGHT

THE TRICKSTERS

FEW myths, says Paul Radin, have had so wide a distribution as that of the Trickster and 'for few can we so confidently assert that they belong to the oldest expression of mankind.'[1] The myth is encountered among the ancient Greeks, the Chinese, the Japanese and in the Semitic world. Its popularity is 'the most characteristic feature of the tales of the North American Indians.'[2] Best known, as Stith Thompson points out, is the story of Coyote, while on the North Pacific Coast the Trickster is also the Transformer-Raven or Mink and Blue Jay. Among the Blackfoot and Crow Indians he appears as Old Man, among the Winnebago as Hare, among the Tlingit as Raven, and under a variety of names among all the major tribes. 'Many of the Trickster's traits were perpetuated in the figure of the medieval jester, and have survived right up to the present day in the Punch and Judy plays and in the clown.'

'Manifestly,' says Radin again, 'we are here in the presence of a figure and a theme or themes which have had a special and permanent appeal and an unusual attraction for mankind from the very beginnings of civilization. In what must be regarded as its earliest and most archaic form, as found among the North American Indians, Trickster is at one and the same time creator and destroyer, giver and negator, he who dupes others and who is always duped himself. He wills nothing consciously. At all times he is constrained to behave as he does from impulses over which he has no control. He knows neither good nor evil, yet he is responsible for both. He possesses no values, moral or social, is at the mercy of his passions and appetites, yet through his actions all values come into being.'[3]

This dual function of the Trickster has frequently been

[1] P. Radin, *The Trickster* (London, 1956), p. ix.
[2] Stith Thompson, *The Folktale* (New York, 1946), p. 319.
[3] Radin, op. cit., p. ix.

emphasized by scholars and noteably by Frank Boas.[4] He is at once benefactor and buffoon, Culture Hero and numskull, deceiver and deceived. In many of the North American stories he is actually the Creator of the world and arranges the pattern of human life. At the same time, he engages in every kind of folly and buffoonery and enjoys a series of Rabelasian sexual adventures. There is similarly a mixture of cleverness and stupidity, so that a Trickster like Coyote may appear 'in any one of three roles: the beneficent Culture Hero, the clever deceiver, or the numskull. As we look at these incidents, we find that this mixture of concept is continually present, so that any series of adventures is likely to be a succession of clever tricks and foolish mishaps.'[5]

Similar stories are found in the Assam plains (where they centre round a character called Tentan or Teton[6]), among the Mikirs and Meches, and frequently in the Naga Hills. He is known as Mache to the Angamis, as Iki to the Semas, as Apfuho to the Lhotas and as Che, Iki or Ichu to different groups of Rengmas.[7] Of the Lhota Apfuho, Mills says: 'He corresponds exactly to the Sema character Iki, and many of the stories told of the two are identical. He is always represented as getting in and out of scrapes, and as tricking his fellow-villagers or his friend the tiger, usually in the meanest possible way.'[8]

The NEFA stories, however, correspond more closely to the North American type, for their tricksters are usually 'serious Culture Heroes', an idea which does not appear in the Assamese and Naga tales. Another difference is that the NEFA tricksters are almost always in pairs, and the aim of most of the stories is to show how one of them gained the ascendency and thus acquired the best land, or how one became the ancestor of men and the other the ancestor of the spirits.

[4] See his introduction to J. Teit, *Traditions of the Thompson River Indians* (Boston, 1898), and Radin and Stith Thompson, *passim*.

[5] Stith Thompson, op. cit., p. 319.

[6] See P. Goswami, *Folk-Literature of Assam* (Gauhati, 1954), pp. 77 ff.

[7] J. P. Mills, *The Rengma Nagas* (London, 1937), p. 248.

[8] J. P. Mills, *The Lhota Nagas* (London, 1922), p. 176.

Thus we have the Apa Tani tale of Taniba and Baraba, which suggests the superiority of the Apa Tanis over the Daflas ; the Bori tale of Tani and Taki which describes how Taki became the first Wiyu (spirit) and Tani the ancestor of mankind; the Gallong tale of Tani and Taru, the two brothers who shared the Subansiri territory; the Minyong tale of Doini-Nibu and Derro-Rabbo who divided the spheres of influence of men and spirits; the Taraon Mishmi tale of Chinye and Karuwa which seems to have been a struggle for the personal ascendency of two rivals; the Hill Miri story of Abo-Teni and Dir-Pecha. By contrast there are a few, but only a few, stories of an individual trickster like the Lhota Apfuho or the Assamese Tentan, who plays his tricks and buffooneries by himself.

The NEFA Tricksters are in many ways devised on the classic pattern. Like their prototypes in other lands, they are at once clever and stupid. The Bori Reni-Tani cheats the daughter of the Sun into marrying him by some adept trickery with a bit of wood, but he has no idea of how to manage women, and his wives deceive him again and again. The Bugun Jan and Malong dress up blocks of wood to mislead their pursuers but show themselves singularly simple in their dealings with the Hrussos, to whom they agree to pay taxes in perpetuity. The Hrusso Awa cleverly tricks his brother Ossin into a bamboo swing and drops him into the river, but he has to be killed, and revived, four times before he learns that he will be safer living alone. The Gallong Tani is very smart in getting a supply of pork out of his brother Taro, yet he goes like a simpleton into a trap that is laid for him.

As in North America, the NEFA Tricksters are indefatigable in pursuit of sexual adventure. They marry fish, deer, bears, frogs, trees, dry leaves, snakes and even fire, and these are real, just what they appear to be, not beautiful damsels turned into animal or vegetable form. They seduce the wives of their dupes; the Hrusso Turu-Lebou carries off the beautiful Siksilia-sam; indeed it is from their sexual prowess that all mankind is born.

There are no very clear parallels to the interesting

sexual episodes such as occur, for example, in the Winnebago Trickster cycle of tales, but there is a general idea that, at least at first, the NEFA heroes had genitals of an enormous size, and there is some resemblance to the incident where the Winnebago Trickster has his penis nibbled down to normal size by a chipmunk in the oft-repeated tale of Tani's marriage to Fire. Seeing a blazing fire, Tani thinks it is a beautiful girl in a red garment and attempts to rape her (in a Tagin story he actually marries her) and his parts are burnt. In Tagin and Bori stories a worm comes from the wound and a cock devours it.

A striking feature of the NEFA tales is their cruelty. The Apa Tani Tariba tricks his brother Baraba into cutting off his elder wife's head and then killing his younger wife and children. The Bori Tani persuades Taki to pour boiling water over his wife and children and so destroy them; in revenge Taki obtains two of Tani's eyes, turns into a Wiyu and makes Tani's wife and children sick to death. In a number of stories the NEFA Trickster manages to get the monkeys into a hollow tree and burns them alive: their sufferings are sometimes realistically described. The Hrusso Ossin kills his own brother no fewer than four times and throws his body into the forest (where it is resuscitated by a friendly mongoose). In Hill Miri and Gallong stories there are incidents of the Trickster deceiving his dupe into killing a wife and child, boiling a whole family alive, cutting a mother to pieces, and there is a scene of great violence in a Gallong tale where Tani, finding his wife has injured her foot and thinking a thorn is in it, tries to cut it out with his dao. 'He could not find the thorn, so he cut again; then again, and again; madness seized him and he cut her till she died.' And in a Taraon Mishmi story, Chinye tricks his brother, ingeniously enough, into killing his own mother.

The NEFA Tricksters also have the power of transforming themselves into birds and animals. The Hill Miri Abo-Teni, for example, turns himself into a bird, the Gallong Tani becomes a worm and then a bird, Dir Pecha becomes a lizard.

This is one side of the picture. The Tricksters are shewn as irresponsible, cruel, alternately clever and stupid, without affection or loyalty, dominated by sexual urges and the desire for power. On the other side, there is evidence that they are regarded as serious Culture Heroes, even if none of them seem to be actually associated with the creation of the world. But although this greatest honour is not paid them, most of the Tricksters are regarded as the fathers of mankind or at least of their own tribe. Thus in the Apa Tani story at page 37, Chantu tells Abo-Tani to beget all mankind. All men are descended from the Bori Tani, and since Tani belongs to Doini the Sun, she cares for his descendents. The Hrusso Turu-Lebou is the ancestor of the Hrussos and Bangnis. The Dobang Nibu is the father of all flesh. The Gallong Tani is ancestor of all the people of Subansiri. The Bori Reni-Tani is the father of the Gallong, Bori and other tribes.

In Apa Tani tradition, Abo-Tani produces every kind of animal through his different wives, pigs, bears, birds, hornets and leeches. Snakes and elephants come from the Bori Reni-Tani, who also orders the life of monkeys and teaches men how to catch fish. The Gallong Abo-Tani gives the bat his black colour. The Hrusso Teru-Lebou passes through a fire which burns off his hair, and as a result men nowadays have only a little hair on their bodies. It was through Abo-Teni that men first got mithuns and his son was the first dog.

Most important of all, it is through the Trickster heroes that the land was divided, between tribe and tribe or man and spirits. It is not clear whether the two Tricksters are orginally men or spirits; they seem to exist in a mysterious primeval world where the normal laws do not exist; they have powers not shared by ordinary mortals. Often one of them becomes a spirit in the course of his adventures. One of them marries a daughter of the Sun, which implies something more than conventional human status.

The Bori Reni-Tani, for example, is described as having four eyes (in one story he has six) of which two are taken from him by the guile of his brother Taki. Taki now has four eyes and Tani only two. This is why the spirits can see men but men cannot see the spirits. The Dobang (Gallong) Nibu is the father of men and Robo is the father of spirits, and it is because Nibu was more adept at his tricks that the sons of Robo have always haunted the sons of men. In the Gallong tradition spirits are descended from Yapom, the elder brother and men from Abo-Tani the younger. Similarly the Minyongs believe that spirits come from Rabbo who lives in the hills, and men from Nibu who lives in the valleys. There are a number of ingenious tricks whereby the fathers of mankind got the best land from the ancestors of the spirits, for men are generally described as the more intelligent and certainly the more deceitful.*

As in similar stories all over the world, the NEFA Trickster is thus something more than a mere buffoon, a sadistic adventurer, a sexual athlete. He is on the side of mankind against the unseen world. Irresponsible and cruel he may be, yet he is at the mercy of forces far stronger than himself and in spite of this brings many blessings to mankind.

1

APA TANI

Reru, Subansiri F.D.

There were two brothers, Taniba the Apa Tani and Baraba the Dafla. One day Taniba went to the forest to trap rats. Later, when he returned with a fine catch, Baraba asked him how he had managed to get so many. 'I killed a fat pig,' said Taniba, 'and baited the traps with bits of the flesh. Many rats came to eat it and were caught.'

* A secondary trickster theme runs through the NEFA tradition, involving the trickery of animals by men and animals by other animals. In Nocte and Wancho stories the dog tricks the pig ; in a Dhammai story the monkey tricks the frog ; the bat appears as a Trickster in Tagin and Sherdukpen tales. In Dhammai, Gallong, Idu and Wancho stories men succeed in tricking tigers: in many cases the man and the tiger are brothers, sons of the same parents—one of them is born or becomes a tiger and is deceived by his more intelligent human brother.

Hearing this. Baraba also took a pig to the forest and baited his traps with bits of the flesh, and returned home. But Taniba turned into a bird and flew to the forest and stole all the bits of meat. When Baraba went the next day to see what he had caught, he found the meat gone and only one small mouse in the traps. He put it in his bag and started home. On the way Taniba, in the form of a bird, got into the bag. When Baraba reached home, he opened his bag and Taniba flew out with the mouse in his beak and perched on the head of Baraba's elder wife. Baraba lost his temper and tried to kill the bird Taniba with his dao. But he missed and cut off his wife's head instead.

Another day the two brothers went to hunt. On their way home, it grew dark, but presently they saw that there was a house not far away. 'That must be my house,' said Baraba. 'No,' said his brother, 'we have a long way to go still. But unless we destroy this building, we will never be able to get home tonight.' Baraba agreed and went to the back of the house and began to break it down, cutting at it with his dao. Taniba sat watching, but when the work of destruction was half done, he called out, 'You fool, why are you destroying your own house?' Baraba went round to the front and found his younger wife and children sitting terrified on the veranda. He was very angry with Taniba, but there was nothing he could do about it.

After this the brothers did not speak to each other for some time, but then at last Baraba went to Taniba's house and said, 'Let us go hunting today.' They took their bows and arrows and set out over the forest-covered hills. After a time they found two deer and Baraba killed them both. Each took one of them on his shoulders and carried it home. When Baraba arrived his younger wife had a hot meal ready for him, but Taniba's wife was sitting drinking beer and had done nothing. This made Taniba very jealous and he decided to kill Baraba's wife. He called Baraba and said, 'What is the use of having wives and children? We have to work all day and they sit at home doing nothing. I'm going to kill mine and get rid of them for good.'

Taniba went home and hid his wife and children. He killed a dog and scattered the blood all round the house. Then he sent for Baraba and said, 'Well, I have done it. You see the blood ; I have thrown the bodies into the forest.' 'But aren't you going to miss them?' asked Baraba. 'I have never been so happy,' said Taniba. 'Now there will be no quarrels, no trouble. Why don't you do the same?'

Baraba went home and killed his younger wife and children. But the next day when he saw Taniba's family alive and well, he was furious at the way he had been deceived.

2

BORI

Payum, Siang F.D.

There were two brothers, Tani and Taki ; Taki was the younger. They made clearings in the forest. One day Tani said to Taki, 'Brother, your field has a very bad Wiyu living in it ; you had better make a sacrifice to him and all will be well. But when you kill the pig, do not bury it ; throw the body down the hill.' Taki said, 'Good, I will do as you say.' He killed the pig at the top of the clearing and threw it down. But Tani was waiting for it at the bottom of the hill. He picked it up and carried it off to his house, and he and his children were richly fed for several days. In fact they ate so much that they began to look sleek and fat. When he saw them Taki said, 'How thin I and my children are! How is it that you have all got so fat?' They laughed at him and said, 'Because of your pig, the pig you sacrificed ; that's what has made us fat.'

Taki said nothing at the time, but he was naturally annoyed and decided to pay back Tani by playing the same kind of trick on him when he got the chance. After a few days, therefore, he went to him and said, 'Brother, there is a very bad Wiyu in your field ; sacrifice a pig for him and all will be well.' Tani pretended to agree, but when the day came he made a fire at the top of the hill and heated a large round stone. When it was very hot he threw it down the hill to where Taki was waiting. Taki, thinking it was a pig, caught it in his arms and was badly burnt.

Taki was very angry about this. So one day he went to the river and made a boat. Tani went down to see what he was doing and Taki said, 'It is very cold nowadays and I am making this boat to sleep in, because then I shall be warm.' Tani said, 'Brother, I too get very cold at night and I'd like to sleep in it too.' Taki said, 'Yes, certainly you may sleep in it for one night'.

When Tani was safely asleep, Taki shut him up inside and sent the boat floating down the stream. Presently Tani woke up and began to shout, 'Taki, *tain, tain* (stop, stop).' When nothing happened, he called to the forest creeper (*tari*), crying, 'Tari, *tain, tain.*' But the creeper did not help him. So he called on the reeds (*tapi*), crying, 'Tapi, *tain, tain,*' and the reeds helped him and stopped the boat. Then he called on all the birds of the air to come and rescue him. Two birds, Rodong and Tusing, came to help. They tried to cut a way into the boat with their beaks, but broke them.

But soon a bird called Randang came and rescued Tani and he went back to his house.

After this Tani and Taki lived together as friends. But Tani was always plotting to trick Taki in some way or other. One day he went to the forest and came to a pool where a lot of monkeys were busy fishing: they had put their bows and arrows down on the ground some distance away. Tani quietly collected them and tied them to a tree. When he had done this, he turned himself into a bird and flew onto a branch. He called to the monkeys saying, 'You are a poor and lazy crowd. You don't know how to catch fish properly.' When the monkeys heard this they were annoyed and wondered who could be speaking to them in such a place. They looked in every direction and at last saw the bird sitting on the top of the tree. They came running out of the pool and went for their bows and arrows: such a talkative and insulting bird, they said, must be killed. They caught hold of their bows and tried to pull them away but they were tied up together, and soon they were all struggling and quarrelling with one another. In the fight many of them were killed and only three or four were left alive and they ran away into the jungle. This is why the monkey has a flat nose and hollow eyes ; they are marks of the fight long ago. Because Tani tied up the bows and arrows, they no longer have these weapons.

Tani now came down from the tree and turned into a man again. He picked up as many of the dead monkeys and their bows and arrows as he could carry and took them home. He and his children ate the meat and soon became very strong. Taki asked him how he and his children had got their strength and Tani pointed to the great bin in which rice-beer was prepared. 'I put my wife and children into this,' he said, 'and poured boiling water on them and after three days they became strong as you see them now.' Taki therefore put his wife and children into the bin in his house and poured boiling water on them and killed them. When he went to look at them three days afterwards, he found that they had turned into worms.

Taki thought, 'What is the use of my staying here alone?' And he went away to Pedo-Siang-Among. On the way he found a great creeper tied across the path and began to swing on it. He could not stop, he continued playing on the creeper night and day. After a time Tani wondered where his brother was and went to look for him. When he found him swinging on the creeper, he asked if he might swing too and Taki came down and held the creeper on the ground for him. But when Tani got on to it, Taki released it and it sprang high into the air. Tani looked down and saw nothing but sharp rocks and stakes below him and was terrified of falling onto them. He begged his brother to help him down, but he refused.

Now Tani had four eyes—two in front and two behind—and Taki said, 'I will help you down if you give me two of your eyes.' Tani said, 'Very well, help me and I will give you two of my eyes.' Taki helped him down and Tani gave him the two eyes in the back of his head. Now Taki, who hitherto had only two eyes, had four and it was Tani who had two. Tani wanted to go hunting, but Taki said, 'I'm going home ; you can go hunting if you want to.' Tani said, 'No, we must go together.' But Taki made a sort of screen so that Tani could not see him and under cover of this he went back home.

When Taki got his four eyes he became a Wiyu. This is why the Wiyus can see men but men cannot see the Wiyus.

Now Taki Wiyu went to Tani's house and made his children ill. When Tani reached home and found them lying groaning on the ground, he wondered what the trouble was, but no one could tell him. After a little while his wife and children died. Then he himself also fell ill, and wondered who could save him but there was no one to help, so in the end he went to the place of Doini-Pollo. There were many Wiyus there and they said to him, 'Marry Doini-Pollo's daughter Doini Aiye and you will become well and have many children.' Tani said, 'How would such a great person as Doini-Pollo give me his daughter?' But the other Wiyus said, 'We will see if we can arrange it.' In the end Doini was persuaded to agree to the marriage and gave many presents with which Tani and his wife set up house together.

3

BORI

Bene, Siang F.D.

At the beginning there was Sichi ; his son was Chire ; his son was Rebuk ; his son was Bukre ; his son was Reni-Tani. Reni-Tani was the first who thought of getting married. There were no other men in the world and there was no woman anywhere. Searching for a woman he came one day to the bank of a river and saw many fish in the water. When he saw them he thought: 'If I turn into a fish, I can easily get a wife.' So he turned into a fish. But although he lived in the water, none of the female fish would come near him. He tried very hard to make friends with them, tried all his human tricks, but when every one of the pretty girl-fish swam away from him, he turned into a man again and came out of the water.

Some time afterwards he went to the forest and saw a whole lot of bears enjoying themselves and making love to each other. This excited him and he thought, 'If I turn into a bear, I will easily find a wife.' So he turned into a bear. But not one of the female bears would come near him. He tried very hard to make friends with them, tried all his human tricks, but when every one of the pretty girl-bears ran away from him, he became a man again.

Tani spent his entire time night and day, day and night, thinking about a wife and wandered over the mountains and through the forests in search of one. One day in the forest he saw many deer grazing and thought, 'If I were to become a deer, I could easily find a wife.' So he turned into a deer. But not one of the does would come near him. He tried very hard to make friends with them, tried all his human tricks, but when every one of the pretty does ran away from him, he became a man again.

At last realizing that neither the fish nor the bears nor the deer would accept him, he made a bow and arrow and went out to hunt. On the way he met a great many monkeys who were also hunting with their bows and arrows. When they saw him they said, 'Tani, have you also come hunting?' Tani said, 'Yes, I too have come to hunt.' The monkeys said, 'Is your aim better than our's or is our's better than your's?' They set up a target on a tree far away and in between hung up a necklace. The monkeys sent their arrows through the necklace and hit the mark beyond. But Tani could not do this, and the monkeys laughed at him and said, 'However will you succeed in this hunting of yours?' Tani went home feeling very cross.

Tani said to himself, 'Though these creatures are only monkeys they can hunt better than I. I am Tani and I desire to produce more men, but if the monkeys are so good at shooting they will destroy my children one of these days.' He made some thread from the bark of a tree, dyed it red and tied it round his thing. When the monkeys saw it they were very pleased and asked him to make their's red also. Tani said, 'You are not my friends and you won't do what I tell you. When you're ready to obey me, I'll make your things red also.' The monkeys said, 'No, no, we'll do whatever you tell us.' So Tani said, 'Go and fetch fire-wood.' Many of them went for fire-wood and to the others Tani said, 'Go and fetch dry plantain leaves.' There was one monkey left and Tani sent him to find fire.

Some of the monkeys got wood, others got leaves and the last got fire. Tani then made them dig a pit in the ground, and told them to go into it and they obeyed. Then he threw in the wood and leaves and set fire to them. He fanned the fire and it burnt fiercely. As the flames leapt up the monkeys in the pit cried, 'O Tani, our things are red now ; let us out.' But Tani pretended not to hear. After some time the flames died down and Tani, supposing that all the monkeys were dead, brushed away the ashes. He removed the bodies, and it was true, they were all dead, except one baby she-monkey who had somehow survived. He tried to catch her but she escaped and climbed up a tree.

The baby monkey lived alone in the forest eating leaves and fruits. In time she grew up and one day when she was sitting under a clump of bamboos, she thought, 'Here I am all alone and there is no one of my own tribe for me to marry.' So thinking she fell asleep. As she slept a bamboo leaf entered into her and from this she conceived and in due time a baby monkey was born. When the baby grew up, they became husband and wife and from them many monkeys were born.

To-day monkeys cannot use bows and arrows because they are descended from one who married his own mother, and because Tani once burnt their ancestors they have ever since been afraid of man.

But Tani still had not found a wife. One day, as he was searching for one in the forest, he met a frog and married her. Some time afterwards, when he went to his clearing, his frog-wife followed him. Tani thought that if they both worked they would get through a great deal, and he made a dozen hoes. But the frog broke them all in a single hour. When Tani saw this he was annoyed and said to himself, 'How many more shall I have to make for this woman?' But he did not say anything aloud.

Next day Tani said to the frog, 'You stay at home and cook and I'll go alone to work.' But he did not go to the field, instead he hid near the house to see how his wife did her cooking. He saw her prepare the rice and she did it well, but for vegetables she rubbed some of the dirt off her bottom. When Tani saw this he was furious, reflecting that he had been eating dirt all these days and he picked his wife up and threw her into the river. Since then the frog, who formerly made her home in the forest, has lived in the water.

Now Tani had thrown his wife away and had to live alone. One day as he was going through the forest he came to an *oniyor* tree heavily laden with fruits, and to him it looked like a lovely girl. He thought, 'If I marry her I will surely have many children.' He said to the tree, 'I would like to marry you.' The tree replied, 'I am a killer of fish ; if I marry you how can I get my fish? So I will not marry.' Tani said to the tree, 'But how do you go fishing?' The tree replied, 'Look at the fruits, my children. If you take them to the river bank and cut them into small pieces and throw them in the water, the fish will die.' In this way Tani learnt from the tree how to get fish.

Tani went on his way and met a snake. He married her, and she bore him many children, but they were all like snakes and not human beings. This upset Tani who said, 'Your children are like you but not like me ; I'm not going to keep you any longer.' He put the children in a basket and threw them away in the jungle and sent his wife after them. He thought that the snakes would die, but they lived on and became the parents of every kind of snake that is in the world to-day.

One day Tani went to the forest and met a wild rat whose name was Butte. He caught her and shut her up in a cage, thinking she would be good to eat. The next day, leaving her in the house, he went out to work. When he came back in the evening he found a fine meal ready for him and was astonished, for there was no one there to cook. The following morning he said loudly, 'Now I am going far away to work,' but in fact he only went behind the house and hid to see what would happen. The rat, thinking that Tani had gone away, came out of her cage and cooked food for him. When Tani saw what she was doing he was very pleased, and said, 'I brought you home to eat, but you're such a good cook that I'll marry you instead.' The rat said 'I am ready to marry you, but if you ever call me a wild rat I shall leave you.' Tani said, 'I will never call you that.'

The two married and lived together, but one day they had a quarrel, and Tani exclaimed, 'After all, you are only a wild rat,' and went off in a temper to his clearing. Directly he had gone, Butte turned the house into an elephant, making the walls into skin and the wooden posts into legs. When Tani came home in the evening he found his wife and his house had disappeared and a great creature that he had never seen before was standing there instead. This is how the elephant was made.

Tani went out to find another wife. On the way he saw a blazing fire and thought it was a beautiful girl in a red garment. He married her, but the fire was neither man nor woman. But he made love to it by force and his parts were burnt; From the jungle came a fly to see the wound. He asked Tani, 'O Tani, what has happened to you?' Tani said, 'You can see the wound I have.' The fly sat on the wound and turned into a worm.

Tani made a cage out of the hair of his head and put the worm in it and, carrying it in his hand, went to the Village of Fowls.[10]

One day Tani tied his mithun to a tree and prayed to Doini-Pollo, 'I have got a mithun, so I want great heat from the sun

[10] There now follows the story of Tani's visit to a number of villages populated by different animals on the same lines as in the Tagin story at pp. 177 ff.

and great darkness in the night and a great storm of wind and rain.' As he prayed, a great storm of wind and rain came and blew down many trees in the forest. The tree where the mithun was tied fell on him and killed him. Tani cut the tree into bits and took one of them to the village of Wiyus, Mumpu-Mumlu-Mumen-Mumlen.

Tani told the Wiyus all that had happened to him and challenged them to break the wood he had brought into small pieces. The Wiyus tried to break it with their hands, but it was too strong for them. Then Tani secretly put insects into the wood, and they burrowed inside and made holes. Tani picked it up and went to Mumi, one of the daughters of the Sun, and asked her if she could break it. She said, 'How can I break such a thick piece of wood?' But directly she touched it, it crumbled to pieces, for it had been eaten by the insects. Tani at once said, 'You have spoilt my wood, so you must marry me.' Mumi said, 'I am a daughter of the Sun and you are a human being ; how can I marry you?' But Tani took no heed and went on saying over and over again, 'You have got to marry me.'

Mumi therefore went to Doini and told him what had happened and Doini came to Tani and said, 'I will give you whatever you want.' Tani said, 'The only thing I want is to marry your daughter. If you don't let her marry me, I will cut the throat of Higgu-Doggu, and earth and heaven will become one, and no one will be left alive.' For Higgu-Doggu carries the sky on his head and if his throat is cut, the sky will fall to the earth and kill everyone upon it.

Doini, therefore, agreed and told Mumi to get ready for the marriage and go with Tani. Mumi said, 'I am ready to marry him, but what will you give me?' Doini said, 'I will cut off the nose of Jimmi Wiyu and turn it into an otter ; then you must make a trap, catch the otter and kill it, remove the skin and dry it in the place called Wikku-Garku-Idung. Dye the skin red. From this skin you will be able to get everything you need.'

This was how Mumi and Tani were married. They caught and killed the otter and from its skin they got everything they desired—dogs, mithuns, cows, pigs and all kinds of seed. They built a house and lived together. After some time Mumi gave birth to a daughter, and said to her husband, 'Go to my father's house and bring a nurse to look after the baby.' He went there, but did not return for a whole year. When he came back he found his daughter grown big and running about, but his wife was angry with him for being away so long. She said, 'Tani, you are not a good man and I will not live with you any longer. Here is the child, you may keep her, but I am going away.' So saying, Mumi went to her parents' house.

Now once again Reni-Tani was without a wife. He waited until his daughter had grown up and then he married her himself and in due course the girl conceived and bore a son, whose name was Nito and from whom the Gallongs are descended.

4

BORI

Payum, Siang F.D.

Doini-Pollo is the creator of men and all things. Below him is Doing-Angong who decides the fate of men, whether they will be rich or poor. Sitking-Kedeng is the earth-god who lives within the earth. Tani came out from him: he had six eyes, two in front, two behind and two in his backside. This meant that he could see all round and no one could ever catch him in an ambush and kill him. In all other ways he was like a human being.

Once he married a frog. But she was a bad woman, and when his friends came to see him she used to expose herself to them. Tani did not like this, and turned her out.

5

BUGUN (KHOWA)

Kaspi, Kameng F.D.

Long ago a Bugun and his wife, whose names were Apuphulwa and Muinini, were living at Miphu. They had four children, whom they called Jan, Malong, Rei and Bai. When the brothers grew up, they left Miphu and went to find a better site for their village. They journeyed for several days and, after a time came to a very great tree standing in the middle of the path ; it was so big that it completely filled the space between a cliff on one side and a river on the other: the only way to pass was to cut it down. A number of other people, Monpas, Dhammais, Hrussos and Bangnis had tried to fell it, but it was so big that they had become completely exhausted and were now cooking their food nearby.

The brothers said to each other, 'We ought to be able to cut this tree down quickly, and if we do so while these people are having their food, we will be able to go ahead and get the better land.' So they quickly cut down the tree and hurried on, but though they saw a lot of places, they did not like any of them. Presently the other people finished their food and came along behind. At last the Buguns came to a place called Kolai-Watong and liked it so much that they settled down there.

Later, the Hrussos and Dhammais also came to the place and settled down side by side with the four brothers.

The Buguns sacrificed a mithun and the Hrussos and Dhammais sacrificed a bullock. After the feast was finished the Bugun children played with the hoofs of the mithun and the Hrusso and Dhammai children played with the hoofs of the bullock. When the Hrusso and Dhammai children saw the mithun-hoofs in the hands of the Bugun children they began to cry, and the Buguns said, 'What's the matter? What are you crying for?' The Dhammais replied, 'It is because our children want those mithun-hoofs.' So the Buguns took two of the mithun-hoofs and gave one to the Dhammai and one to the Hrusso children and, though they kept the rest for their own children, this pleased the Dhammais and Hrussos. Presently they went on to a place called Bopha-Watong where they made a camp. The men went off to hunt and managed to kill a wild dog. When they returned to the camp bringing it with them, the Buguns and Bangnis arrived there and they all shared the meat. But although the hosts gave the Bangnis some of the flesh, they gave the Buguns only the feet, and said to them, 'Because you have only got the feet you will always rank lower than us. We will be the Rajas of this country and you will have to pay us taxes.'

Next day the Hrussos and Dhammais went on to find a proper place to live, and wherever they found suitable land they put up signs to show that no one else should settle there, and the unfortunate Buguns who came afterwards found everywhere they went that the land had already been occupied by the others.

Now the four Bugun brothers had a mithun. Presently they

came near a village called Sachidha and when they saw it they were frightened ; for they thought that the people there would kill them. They hid therefore in the jungle, and killed the mithun and ate the meat. When they had eaten, they felt more courageous and went to the village and, after talking to the people there, found that they also were Buguns and decided to stay with them.

Near Sachidha there was another village called Namphri. Here there lived one Khro, an old woman who had a pretty daughter called Abui-Liang who was still unmarried. In this village there also lived a man called Lao-Sujjo, who was anxious to marry the girl. He went to the mother and asked if he might do so and she said he might.

But after a time two of the brothers, Jan and Malong, both of whom were unmarried, heard about the girl and went to the old woman to ask for her and she liked them and said that her daughter could marry Jan. 'I won't give her to that fellow Lao-Sujjo,' she said. The two brothers were very happy about this and on their way back they ran into Lao-Sujjo and said to him, 'The old woman Khro has given us her daughter and isn't going to give her to you.' Lao-Sujjo was furious about this and quarrelled with them. They parted and the two brothers went home, but Lao-Sujjo was determined to marry Abui-Liang himself and somehow prevent Jan from getting her.

One day shortly afterwards Lao-Sujjo went hunting and killed a deer. He cleaned and dried the skin and when it was ready took it to Khro's house. He put it on the platform and sat on it, feeling very pleased with himself at being able to sit on such a fine skin. He began to sing:

'I am a great rock,
I am a great tree,
No one is greater,
No one can conquer me.'

It was dark now and the two brothers, Jan and Malong, came secretly and when they heard the song they said to each other, 'I wonder if this is true or not,' and hid underneath the house. Presently Khro came out and said to Lao-Sujjo, 'What a beautiful song you are singing! Come and eat some fruit.' Lao-Sujjo got up and went indoors.

From underneath the house Jan and Malong poked at the skin with their spears, and made holes in it. They said to themselves, 'This isn't a rock or a tree, but just an ordinary bit of skin. Why is this fellow so proud of himself?' Lao-Sujjo heard the noise and thought that a dog was eating his skin and shouted at it to go away. When the two brothers heard him they kept very quiet, but when he went back to drinking his beer and eating the fruit they continued making holes in the skin. Finally Lao-Sujjo finished what Khro had for him and came out again to sit on his deer-skin and sang:

'I am a great rock,
I am a great tree,
No one is greater,
No one can conquer me.'

But Jan and Malong thrust their spears up through the platform, and right through Lao-Sujjo's body until the points came out at the top of his head. So he died and the brothers came running out shouting, 'You were a tree, you were a rock, no one could defeat you, so how is it that you are now dead?' But when they realized what they had done, they ran away.

When the people of the village saw Lao-Sujjo had been murdered, they went to the Dhammais to report the matter and ask for their help. The Dhammais were more than willing and prepared to attack Jan and Malong. Before they could do this, however, the brothers escaped along the banks of the Dugakho river. After they had gone some distance they came to a great rock. They cut two pieces of wood, dressed them in their clothes and put them down as if they were men sleeping by the side of the path. They themselves climbed to the top of the rock and placed great stones on the edge. When their pursuers came to the place they thought that Jan and Malong were sleeping there, and struck the pieces of wood with their daos. The two brothers threw down the great stones from above and killed many of their enemies. Those who escaped ran away in fright.

After this Jan and Malong became fugitives, living in the forest, afraid to approach any village and getting what food they could by hunting.

At that time there were living in Jamiri two Hrusso brothers—

one was called Nisu and the other Nimu. One day, taking with them a basket of roots and vessels of beer, they went to the forest. They hid the things in a tree and went to hunt. In the meantime, Jan and Malong came to the tree and found the roots and beer and feasted on them. When they had finished, they put the vessels and basket back as they were before. It was a long time since they had a drink of beer or eaten such good roots and, greatly encouraged, went on their way.

Presently Nisu and Nimu, hungry and exhausted, came to the tree, looking forward to their refreshment and found there was nothing left. They were annoyed and rather anxious as to who could have stolen their food in such a lonely place, and they hurried home.

This went on for several days. Every day Nisu and Nimu went hunting, put their food and drink in the same place and every day Jan and Malong came and stole it. At last Nisu and Nimu could not stand it any longer and determined to discover the thieves. They brought four large dogs with them and hid behind bushes near the tree. When Jan and Malong removed the food from the tree and sat down to eat and drink, Nisu and Nimu released their dogs. When he saw them coming, Malong ran away, but Jan was a little drunk and could not get up in time. He was seized by the dogs and then Nisu and Nimu came and caught hold of him. They shouted to Malong, 'We're not going to hurt you ; come back and talk to us. We'll give all the help you need.' Hearing this, Malong came back. Then Nisu and Nimu asked the brothers a lot of questions and they explained how they were fugitives from their village because they had killed a man there. 'We have no Raja and have to live in this miserable state in the forest. If only we could get a Raja, we would settle down and build houses for ourselves.' Nisu and Nimu said, 'We ourselves are Rajas. You may make a village in our territory, but you will have to pay us taxes.' While they were considering the best site for the new village, a Kujing bird flew down and said, 'There is an excellent place for Jan and Malong at Kyang.'

So Jan and Malong made their houses at Kyang and when they were ready they fetched wives for themselves from Lichni village.

This is why the Bugun people for many years paid taxes to the Hrussos.

6

DOBANG (GALLONG)

Siang Frontier Division

(From G. D. S. Dunbar, *Abors and Galongs*, pp. 62f.)

At the beginning of time, the gods for seven generations dwelt alone on the earth, to which they came in the following order, father to son, as they are named by the Miri in his incantations. Jimi, Michek, Shegrum, Rombuk, Buksin, Sintu, Turi and, in the eighth generation, Riki and Rini. Riki, as was the custom of the gods, ate flesh raw, bůt Rini cooked it. Riki was renamed Taki and Rini, who burnt the flesh before he ate it, was called Tani.

Now the time came when Tani wanted a wife and he searched through all the world, but could find no woman with whom to mate. So he made a likeness of one, of leaves on a bamboo frame just as the images of the gods are made to this day. From this image was born the leech that gained its vitality only when the instinct came to it to suck the blood of the man ; but still Tani had no wife. In his despair he tried to find a mate amongst the creatures of the forest. But he could find no companion there and none bore him any children. Amongst other creatures Tani mated with the Pajak. But one day while they were preparing their food the bird fouled it. Tani got very angry and the bird flew away and he never saw her again. Then the search for a wife went on until at last Tani went to the Sun, who gave him a woman, Mumsi to be his wife.

The *killing-le-tung* stone of creation is hollowed like a cave. On this stone the footprints of men and all creation are to be seen, and about the rock are pebbles that the children bit and played with, and because the flinty rock was soft in those early days, you can see the marks of their teeth and the prints of their tiny fingers. The stone of creation is near the source of the Sisap, the river just beyond Koku (Karko).

After the creation, Nibu the father of all flesh and Robo the father of all spirits one day set their traps in the river. Robo set his up-stream, and Nibu down the current. After a little Nibu came back and saw that while his traps were (not unnaturally) quite empty, Robo's were already full of fish. So Nibu lifted Robo's traps and emptied them into his own, and went away. Next day when the two hunters came out to look at their traps Robo was very much surprised to find that his own were empty and Nibu's were full of fish. However, he said nothing. Then they went on and set their *egom* trap. Robo set his on the ground, Nibu on the branch of a tree. During the night Nibu went round the traps to see what luck had befallen them. And he found that Robo had caught a barking deer, but in his trap there was only a hornbill, so he changed the contents of the two traps. Next day, when Robo saw what was in his trap he exclaimed, 'How can a hornbill be caught in a trap on the ground?' And Nibu said, 'Quite easily, if he goes there to look for food.' Then Robo said angrily, 'Anyway a deer cannot be caught up in a tree,' to which Nibu replied, 'Oh yes, he can if he is looking for fruit.' At that Robo got very angry indeed and went away furious. And from that day to this the spirits of Robo have haunted the children of Nibu.

7

GALLONG

Dollum, Subansiri F.D.

Two brothers, Tani and Taro, lived near each other. One morning Tani set traps for birds and rats in the forest, baiting them with bits of raw plantain. Later that day he took a bunch of the ripe fruit to the Village of Rats, where the rats crowded round him and snatched the plantains from his hands. Tani said, 'These are not enough: would you like more?' 'Yes, we want much more,' said the rats. 'Then go to such and such a place: you can follow my footsteps: I left a lot of plantains there.' So saying, Tani went home.

The next morning Tani went to see his traps. On the way, he passed a small rat who was running in the same direction. 'Brother rat,' he said, 'where are all your friends this morning?' 'They went to eat plantains, but I hear they are lying flat under a lot of stones. I don't know what they think they are doing.' Tani hurried on when he heard this and collected a whole load of rats.

On his way home Tani met his brother Taro. 'However did you manage to catch such a lot of rats?' 'I killed a pig and put big lumps of the meat in my traps. It is no good being stingy. If you want rats, kill a pig and do the same.'

So Taro killed a pig and baited his traps with big lumps of flesh. But when he went home, Tani secretly removed the meat. Next morning, when Taro went to inspect his traps, there were no bits of meat— and no rats.

But in Tani's house there was feasting. Tani gave the fat to his wife and children and they rubbed it on their bodies and their skin was soon clean and shining. Taro saw them and asked, 'How did they get like this?' Tani said, 'I tied them by the hands and feet, and poured boiling water over them.'

Taro went home and tied his wife and children by their hands and feet. He poured boiling water over them, and they died.

Taro now began to realize that Tani was not altogether honest, and he decided to kill him in revenge for his tricks. He made a boat and a lid to put on it. While he was doing this Tani went down to the river-bank and asked him what he was making a boat for. 'I am going to keep my pig in it,' said Taro. 'But tell me, what do you think? Could a man get in as well?' 'I should think so,' said Tani. 'Then get in for a moment, brother,' said Taro, 'and let's see: personally I don't think it's big enough.' Tani got in, and Taro hastily shut down the lid, fixed it in place with nails, and pushed the boat out into the stream. As it floated down, many birds flew round it and Tani cried, 'O birds, open the door for me.' The woodpecker heard him and perched on the boat and pecking, pecking, gradually made a tiny hole in the lid. It was far too small for Tani as he was, so he took the form of a worm, wriggled out into the roof and there turned himself into a bird.

As he was flying home, he met his wife going to fetch water. 'I thought you were dead,' she said. 'Where is Taro?' asked Tani. 'Taro is with me: he has made me his woman.' Tani said, 'I will go secretly into the house and hide in the loft. Give me food and my long dao without Taro knowing it.' So Tani hid in the roof and his wife gave him food and water. As he was eating, he spilt some of the water and it fell on Taro's head who was sitting below by the hearth. Taro said, 'Can Tani have returned?' 'How can he?' said the woman. 'You told me he was dead.' 'Then why is water falling from the roof?' The woman climbed up to the loft and said, 'No, there's nothing here.' Then the children climbed up and said, 'No, there's nothing here.' Finally Taro himself climbed up, and Tani attacked him with his dao. But he escaped and ran out of the house with Tani in pursuit. As he ran, Taro cried to the earth, 'O earth, open and let me in.' The earth opened and he went down and the earth closed above his head. Tani was left standing stupidly with his long dao in his hand.

After some time Tani said to himself, 'After all we are brothers. How can I live without him? I must find the poor fellow.' He went down to Nipo-land below the ground. There he found Taro feeding a Wiyu's child. 'Brother Taro,' said Tani, 'we have quarrelled, but I cannot live without you. Come home.' 'No, I won't ; I can easily live without you.' 'No, you must come.' 'But how can I come?' said Taro, relenting. 'This is Nipo-land and I have to feed this child.' 'We must get the Wiyu here,' said Tani and he beat the child to make him cry. The mother was on the veranda weaving cloth of bark-fibre and when she heard the child crying she sent a rat to find out what was the matter. Tani gave the rat a bit of meat and it sat down to eat it, and did not return.

Then the mother sent a little bird and Tani caught it by the tail. But the bird escaped, leaving its tail in Tani's hand. It flew back to the Wiyu and said, 'There are two men beating your child.' The mother left her loom and ran to the rescue.

When she came in, Tani killed the child and cut the mother into three pieces. Then the brothers ran away, but the Wiyu's body came together again and she pursued them. Tani cut her up again, and again and again, but every time the severed pieces joined together.

A cock came by and laughed. 'You'll never kill her like that. Shoot an arrow into her breast and that will finish her.' So Tani shot the Wiyu in the breast and she died. She turned into a black hen and said, 'Tani beware—I shall put a *panji* (sharp bamboo stake) somewhere in your house.' Tani was all the time worried about this and went about very carefully.

Then one day, when Tani was out hunting, the plantain before his house blossomed into flower. His child cried for it and the mother went to pick it—and ran her foot on the *panji*. When Tani came home, she said, 'My foot is very painful.' Tani thought she must have got a thorn in it, so he cut it with his dao. He could not find the thorn, so he cut again ; then again, and again ; madness seized him and he cut her till she died.

Tani did not know how to bury his wife, but he made some sort of hole in the ground and sprinkled earth over her body. Then one day his two children said, 'Our mother is here and we have drunk her milk.' Tani wondered how this could be. He gave each child a bit of string and told them that, when they next drank their mother's milk, they should tie the string to her nipples.

The children went to their mother and tied her by the nipples. They ran to tell Tani who came and caught hold of her. She said, 'Let me go. You are still the man Tani, but I am changed. You didn't bury me properly ; that's why I have come back. Cover me with earth and I'll be able to go down to Wiyu-land.'

But Tani would not let her go. When night fell, she took the form of a rat and escaped into her grave. Tani followed her there, but could find nothing. He called a shaman and told him what had happened. The shaman said, 'She has become a Wiyu: you cannot have her now. Bury her properly: build a hut above the grave: put her things before it.'

So Tani buried his wife properly and she fled to the land of spirits.

Then Tani said to Taro, 'Brother, listen. Let us not quarrel any more. Here is the land: let us divide it.' Taro was agreeable to this, but Tani said, 'Let us first eat and then we'll attend to business.' He made dry flour of rice and millet, and took some in each hand. He put it into Taro's mouth, filling it so full that he could not speak. He took a little himself on the tip of his tongue. Then he said, 'Let each say what land is his.' Taro, his mouth full of dry flour, could not speak, so Tani declared: 'This is all mine: Sipi, Singen, Subansiri, Khru, Kamla, Siang, Yongbong. All this is mine.' At last Taro swallowed the flour and said, 'Very well. All this is yours. But everything beyond the Rute-Mette is mine.'

So Taro went to live beyond the Rute-Mette and those who are born there are his sons. But all the people of Subansiri are the sons of Tani.

8

ALLONG

Don, Subansiri F.D.

At the very beginning Sichi-Chitu-Tuni gave birth to two brothers, Yapom the elder and Abo-Tani the younger. The brothers lived near each other on the spur of a great hill. Yapom gave Abo-Tani mithuns, pigs, fowls and dogs, but in his own house he had only wild animals, tigers, deer, porcupines, bears. But Abo-Tani's animals often used to visit Yapom's house and this annoyed him. 'Why don't you look after your animals properly?' he said.

This led to a quarrel and the brothers decided to live separately. Abo-Tani said, 'Let us divide the land and each make his own house and live there.' Yapom said, 'Very well ; I will take the low land in the valleys.' But Abo-Tani said, 'No, I want that: you go to the hills.' Yapom said, 'Well, I will go to the hills.' When they divided the land, they killed a mithun and shared the meat between them. Yapom carried his share away, but it was too heavy for Abo-Tani. He was wondering what to do, when Tapeng the bat came out from beneath a stone. Abo-Tani asked him to be his porter, but Tapeng took the meat to his own cave. He also took the mithun-horns and set them over the door.

When Abo-Tani realized that he had been tricked, he went to find Tapeng. He reached the cave and recognized the horns above the door. He caught hold of them and Tapeng flew out. Abo-Tani seized him and was about to kill him with his dao. But Tapeng persuaded him to tie bits of wood to his wings and set fire to them. This is why the bat is black.

But Tapeng did not die. He flew to Yapom's village and burnt his house and granaries, and his wives and children perished in the flames. Yapom and his clan began to fight with Abo-Tani.

Dige-Wiyu was born from Sichi-Nido (earth and heaven) to bring the war to an end. This Wiyu was white in colour. He separated the enemies, and said, 'From Abo-Tani will come the race of men, from Yapom the race of Wiyus.'

Dige-Wiyu divided the land and wrote down his orders. For Abo-Tani he wrote on skin, for Yapom he wrote on stone. Abo-Tani took the skin home, but one day when he was hungry he roasted and ate it. This is why the children of Abo-Tani know nothing of reading and writing.

9

HILL MIRI

Godak, Subansiri F.D.

There are many versions of the legend of the Wives of Abo-Teni in Subansiri. The Sarak Miri story resembles the Tagin version, but there are a number of differences.

Abo-Teni marries a leaf in the forest and their child is the leech. He then marries a plantain-leaf and their child is the mosquito who sings in the night. But when he tries to bite his father, the latter leaves mother and child in the forest and goes away. He then marries Fire and goes on his pilgrimage through the villages of various animals, as described in the Tagin story at page 117.

The Miri tale then diverges. Abo-Teni does not marry Mumsi, the sister of the Sun: he marries Duinye the Sun herself. The story then proceeds as follows.

After their marriage Duinye said to Abo-Teni, 'What sort of house have you? What things have you got?' Abo-Teni declared boastfully, 'I have a very fine house and many mithuns, goats, pigs, fowls and dogs.' Duinye was pleased when she heard this and went gladly with her husband. But when she saw his miserable little hut with only one hearth and no animals at all, she was disappointed and angry. She forced Abo-Teni to make styes for pigs, baskets for fowls, halters for goats, ropes for mithuns, troughs for feeding dogs. When he had finished, he was so tired that he fell into a deep sleep.

While he slept, Duinye went out and collected many animals. She put pigs in the styes, fowls in the baskets, goats in their halters. She tied up mithuns with the rope and fed a score of dogs in Abo-Teni's troughs.

In the morning, when Abo-Teni awoke, he found himself a rich man and he and his wife lived happily together.

But there was one difficulty about Duinye as a wife. She would not cook, she would not work in the clearings. All day long she sat at her loom. Abo-Teni soon got tired of doing all the work himself and thought, 'I must get a second wife who will do the work of the house and help me to cultivate.' He sacrificed a mithun to Ilu, greatest of the Wiyus, and a pig to Ponjer and a dog to Kainye. Then he put a big load of the meat on his back and went out to find a second wife.

As he was leaving, Duinye said, 'Go: you are doing a good thing.' She gave him a fine piece of cloth she had made herself and a string of beads and said, 'Be careful to take the right path.'

Abo-Teni started out, but presently he lost his way and took a steep slippery track over the hills. He slipped in the mud and fell and all his things, the meat and the cloth and the beads, went tumbling down the hill

At the bottom of this hill there was a man called Dir-Pecha. He was a poor, dirty creature, with many sores, his skin diseased,[11] dressed in rags. Now, as he sat scratching himself with his dao, there suddenly fell from above meat and cloth and beads. He jumped up, dressed in the cloth, put the beads round his neck and the load of meat on his back and went straight away to the very same girl that Abo-Teni was after, and married her.

When Abo-Teni had scrambled down to the bottom of the hill, he found his own things gone and only Dir-Pecha's rags scattered on the ground. He put them on and went home. But he felt so ashamed of himself that he went round to the back of the house and sat down there all by himself.

Duinye knew that a man had come, but she was not sure whether it was her husband or not. She spat on her hand and said to him, 'If you are Abo-Teni, you will eat my spittle ; but if you are someone else, you won't.' Abo-Teni licked her hand and swallowed her spittle. But Duinye, instead of being pleased, exclaimed, 'What a disgusting creature you are! I'm not going to live with you any longer.'

And that very day Duinye left Abo-Teni's house. But she has never been able to settle down and as the Sun she wanders ceaselessly across the heavens.

The Miri story then proceeds to utilize the other very common motif of two rivals who constantly fight and trick each other. Abo-Teni, deprived of his wife, goes to Dir-Pecha's village, determined to revenge himself on the man who had brought so much trouble

[11] The people of northern Subangiri suffer abominably from *tinea imbricata* and may often be seen scratching off the scales with their daos.

upon him. He builds a house there, and we now have the familiar story of the rivals who set traps for birds and rats. But the Miri version has an interesting variant.

Abo-Teni turned himself into a bird and allowed himself to be caught in one of Dir-Pecha's traps. When Dir-Pecha, therefore, next went to examine his traps, he found this bird. But it was a pretty thing and so, instead of killing it, he took it home for his child to play with. But when the child took it in his hands the bird escaped and perched on his mother's head. The child cried for it, and Dir-Pecha, annoyed by the noise, picked up his bow and shot an arrow at the bird. But he missed it and killed his wife instead. The bird then perched on the child's head and Dir-Pecha shot at it again, and this time he killed the child.

Then the bird flew into the air and away, and Dir-Pecha knew that it was Abo-Teni.

To revenge himself, Dir-Pecha builds a boat (as in the Minyong and Tagin tales) and imprisons Abo-Teni in it.

Abo-Teni cried loudly for help, but no one heard him except his former wife Duinye, for there is nothing the Sun does not see and hear. She put her foot down into the water and pushed the boat to the bank and released the prisoner. Abo-Teni caught hold of her foot and said, 'I want to go with you. Let us live together again.' But Duinye refused and went away.

Abo-Teni returned to live near Dir-Pecha and they quarrelled again. Dir-Pecha turned into a lizard and ran into a hole. Abo-Teni dug into the hole to catch and kill him, but Dir-Pecha came out of the other end as a man.

At last they agreed to divide the land between them. Dir-Pecha took the hill country, and Abo-Teni went to the plains of Assam, where he still is. From time to time he sends sickness and death for men and animals to the hills.

10

HRUSSO (AKA)

Buragaon, Kameng F.D.

The two brothers, Ossin and Awa, were very fond of hunting. One day they met a girl in the forest. She was very pretty and Awa, the younger brother, declared that he would marry her. But Ossin said, 'No, I am the elder and she is for me.' There was a furious quarrel and Ossin killed Awa and threw the body into the forest. He took the girl as his wife and built her a house.

After a time a forest-fire burnt all Awa's flesh, leaving only the bones. Presently a mongoose came along the path and saw them. He said to himself, 'These surely are the bones of a human being ; I must restore life to them.' He covered the bones with clay, making them into the shape of a man. He tied it together with leaves and put life into the body.

When Awa found himself alive again he said, 'I wonder where my brother is. Somehow or other I must find him.' And he went searching among the hills until he at last came to Ossin's house. He stood before the door and said, 'You are my elder brother and you killed me, but life has come back to me and here I am. Now let us live together as friends.'

After this Ossin and Awa lived together and all went well for a time until one day they had a quarrel and once again Ossin killed his brother and threw his body into the forest.

Once again the mongoose saw the bones and covered them with clay, making them into the shape of a man. He tied the body together with leaves and put life into it.

When Awa found himself alive again he went back to his brother's house and all went well for a time.

One day Awa went with Ossin's wife to clear the forest for cultivation and Awa said to her, 'You know that it was I who wanted to marry you, but Ossin took you from me. Now I am going to kill him and have you as my wife.' But when the girl went home she told her husband what Awa was plotting to do. Ossin was frightened and, before Awa could do anything to him, killed him and threw his body into the forest.

After a time there was a fire in the forest and it burnt Awa's flesh leaving only the bones. Presently the mongoose came along the path and saw them. He covered the bones with clay in the form of a man and tied it with leaves and put life into it.

This time Awa thought to himself, 'Now my brother has killed me thrice and thrice thrown my body into the forest. I won't go to his house again, but somehow or other I'll have to kill him.' He went to the river and put great pillars on either bank and tied a cane-rope between them. To this he attached a box as a sort of swing and sat in it.

Meanwhile, Ossin was thinking to himself, 'I have thrice killed my brother and he has always come back to the house, but this time he has not returned. I wonder where he can be.' And he went out to find him. Presently he came to the place where the great swing was standing. When he saw Awa there he asked him what he was doing. Awa replied, 'I am looking at the fish, for there are many different kinds in this river and they are singing songs and dancing.' Ossin said, 'I too would like to see this wonderful sight.' So Awa brought the swing to the bank, and allowed Ossin to take his place, tying him firmly in the box. He allowed the box to slide down until it was in the middle of the river and then cut the rope. Ossin fell into the rushing water and was carried away.

Awa, thinking that this was the end of his brother, went back to the house where he took Ossin's wife and lived with her very happily.

But Ossin was carried down the river until he came to a place where the Moon had set a trap for fish and he was caught in it. When the Moon came to remove his trap he found it extremely heavy and thought it must have caught something really big. But when he opened the box he found a man inside. He was very pleased at this and said, 'For a long time I have been wanting to meet a human being. Now tell me, who gives the better light, the Sun or myself?' Ossin replied, 'You may kill me or throw me back into the river, but I must tell you the truth. The Sun gives the brighter light.' This naturally annoyed the Moon and he put Ossin into the box, tied it up and threw it back into the river.

Ossin was swept down the river until he came to a place where the Sun had set a trap for fish and he was caught in it. When the Sun took the trap from the water she found it very heavy and thought it must have caught something really big. But when she opened the box she found a man inside. The Sun was very pleased at this and said, 'For a long time I have been wanting to meet a human being. Now tell me, who gives the brighter light, the Moon or myself?' Ossin replied, 'You give the brighter light.' The Sun was delighted at this reply and said, 'Tomorrow morning when I come up into the sky, be standing here and I'll take you home.' So saying the Sun went away.

But next morning when the Sun rose Ossin had forgotten what he had to do and was still sound asleep. The Sun came and put down her hand to find him, but there was no one there and she went away.

When the Sun was high in the sky, Ossin awoke and remembered what he had been told to do. Next morning, therefore, he was up early and long before the Sun rose he was standing there. When the Sun came she caught Ossin by the hair and carried him home.

Ossin approached his house cautiously and found his wife busy making rice-beer and Awa away in the forest. When his wife saw him she was very happy and made him sit down and gave him beer to drink and said, 'Awa told me that he had killed you and he forced me to be his wife. But I never liked the fellow: it's wonderful to have you back.'

Presently Awa returned from the forest carrying a wild pig which he had shot. When he saw Ossin he said, 'So you have come back, my brother.' Ossin was very angry and killed him again and threw his body into the forest.

After a time there was a fire in the forest and it burnt Awa's flesh, leaving only the bones. Soon afterwards the mongoose came along the path and saw them. He covered the bones with clay in the shape of a man and tied it with leaves and put life in the body.[12]

And now Awa said to himself, 'I am not going to have anything more to do with Ossin. I will build my own house and live there by myself.' He went far away and made his own home in the middle of the forest. After a time he found a wife. His children were the Hrussos and Ossin's children were the Bangnis.

From time to time the Hrussos and Bangnis quarrel with each other and the Bangnis say, 'You are the children of Awa who was killed four times by our father Ossin.' When they say this the Hrussos have no reply.

[12] The role of the mongoose in restoring life to the dead appears in tales from Middle India. Thus in a Muria story from Baster, a mongoose gives the dead hero some medicine to drink and so revives him. In a Baiga story, the hero's father dies of snake-bite. A mongoose kills the snake but not before it has itself been bitten. It goes to a certain tree, sniffs at it and recovers. The hero follows the mongoose's example, gives some of the root of the tree to his father and so restores him to life. There is an old tradition that when a mongoose is bitten by a snake, it immediately seeks an antidote. See my *Folk-Tales of Mahakoshal* (Bombay, 1944), p. 68.

11

HRUSSO (AKA)

Buragaon, Kameng F.D.

Siksilia-ao, the Lord of the Rivers, had a daughter called Siksilia-Sam, who used to play with the fishes and frogs in the water. Though she was human in form she lived like a fish and had never seen any other human being. One day as she was playing with the fishes and frogs in the water, she came out onto the bank and went running, naked as she was, along the river-side.

At that moment a good-looking youth called Turu-Lebou came down to the river to fish. The girl saw him, and said to herself, 'I have never seen anything like this before.' She ran up close to get a better look and asked the boy, 'Who are you? Where do you live? What is your name?' Turu-Lebou told her his name and showed her where his house was. Then he in turn asked her whose daughter she was, where she lived and whether she was married or not. She replied, 'I am the daughter of the Lord of the Rivers, whose name is Siksilia-ao. I myself live in the water and I am not married, for you are the first human being I have ever seen.' Turu-Lebou exclaimed, 'Good. I'm not married either.' And he caught her by the hand and ran away with her to his house, where he married her without delay.

When Siksilia-ao heard of the marriage he sent a frog to Turu-Lebou with a message that if he did not send the girl back at once he would come and destroy him.

When Turu-Lebou heard the frog's message he replied, 'I am a human being and am not afraid of any Lord of the Rivers. I too know how to fight.' When the frog repeated this to Siksilia-ao, he was very angry and went himself to see Turu-Lebou.

When Turu-Lebou saw the Lord Siksilia-ao approaching, he hastily put his wife into a hollow bamboo, closed the lid and hid it in the loft. Siksilia-ao sat down on the threshhold of the house and cried, 'Return my daughter or I will kill you.' Turu-Lebou replied, 'Your daughter isn't here. If you don't believe me, come in and look.' Siksilia-ao went in and searched everywhere, but could not find the girl. He then said, 'You say that you are a man and I am only the Lord of the Rivers. Now prove what strength you have.'

Siksilia-ao cut some great bamboos, thick and strong, and said to Turu-Lebou, 'Carry these down to the valley below.' The boy picked them up and carried them easily from the top of the hill to the bottom. Siksilia-ao followed him to see that he did not cheat and when they got to the bottom Turu-Lebou said, 'Look, I have brought them down,' and Siksilia-ao said, 'Yes, you have.'

Then Turu-Lebou in his turn cut down a great tree and said to Siksilia-ao, 'If you are really the Lord of the Water, carry this tree to the top of the hill.' Siksilia-ao picked up the tree, but after he had carried it a little distance he put it down and said, 'It's too heavy: I can't carry it a step further.' Turu-Lebou said, 'Then I've defeated you.' But Siksilia-ao said, 'Not yet you haven't.' He made a big pile of dry grass and set fire to it and the boy easily went through the fire, but all the hair on his body was burnt off. Formerly this hair used to keep him warm, but now he felt cold and naked and made himself clothes of bark. This is why now-a-days men do not have a great deal of hair on their bodies.

Then Turu-Lebou said, 'Now you must admit that I am greater than you.' But Siksilia-ao replied, 'What is there in going through a little fire? I can do that myself.' This annoyed Turu-Lebou and he made a great pile of wood and set fire to it and told Siksilia-ao to pass through the flames. Siksilia-ao tried, but the heat and smoke was too much for him and he turned back. But even now he would not give up and said, 'Well, let's try once more. We will each take a stone and whoever can throw it further will be the greater.'

Turu-Lebou said to Siksilia-ao, 'I must go and relieve myself.' But all he did was to go a little distance away and catch a tiny bird which he hid in his hand. He came back to Siksilia-ao and said, 'You throw first and then I will.' Siksilia-ao threw his stone, but as it was only a stone it did not go very far. Then, pretending that he had a very heavy stone in his hand, Turu-Lebou threw the little bird as hard as he could and it flew away, away to a great distance.

Now at last Siksilia-ao admitted that he had been defeated and agreed that Turu-Lebou could marry his daughter and went so far as to say that he had a fine son-in-law. Then Turu-Lebou and Siksilia-ao returned home and Turu-Lebou brought his wife out of her hiding-place and they all began to live together.

But though they were apparently quite happy, Siksilia-ao was actually far from being pleased with the arrangement. He could not forget that he was a great Lord and that an ordinary peasant had defeated him and taken away his daughter.

One day Siksilia-ao and Turu-Lebou went together to fish, but when the fishes and frogs saw the Lord of the Rivers, they ran away in fright. Turu-Lebou tried very hard to catch some of them, but it was no good, and then Siksilia-ao said, 'Look, son-in-law, what the fish are afraid of is your beard. Take it off and you'll soon be able to get something.' Turu-Lebou accordingly took off his beard, put it on a stone and went into the river. When he was in the deep water Siksilia-ao picked up Turu-Lebou's beard and ate it, then followed him into the river. But directly Siksilia-ao ate the beard Turu-Lebou was attacked with fever and returned to the bank. He looked everywhere for his beard and for his father-in-law too, but could not find them anywhere. He felt very ill and went home as quickly as he could and said to his wife, 'I have got fever and must lie down.' When she saw him she was surprised and said, 'But where is your beard?' Turu-Lebou told her and she replied, 'I will tell you what really happened. My father has eaten your beard and gone down into the river. That is why you've got this fever.' Turu-Lebou said to her, 'Go and see your father and ask him what we should do about it.'

The girl went to her father and asked him what should be done and Siksilia-ao replied, 'Sacrifice a domestic pig and fowl and he will recover. But they must not be wild creatures.'

She returned home and told her husband what Siksilia-ao had said. Turu-Lebou went to get a pig and a fowl from Sibji-Sao and Sibjim-Sam who had plenty in their house. He brought them back with him and when they had sacrificed them, he recovered.

In due time Siksilia-Sam gave birth to a son whom they called Buslu-Ao; he was the father of Awa and Ossin from whom descended the Hrussos and Bangnis.

12

MINYONG

Riga, Siang F.D.

Doini-Nibu and Derro-Rabbo went down from the sky to live on earth. They were soon quarrelling for possession of the best land. Then Rabbo said, 'Let us each take a stone in his hand, and bury it in the ground. The *pengum* bird will be born from one of the stones: if it is your's, you will get the good land: if it is mine, I will get it. From the other stone will come the *peku-peru* bird and that will mean the bad land.' So they planted the stones, and the *peku-peru* bird was born from Rabbo's and he got the poor land. The bird flew there and it still weeps in barren places. But from Nibu's stone was born the *pengum* bird and it flew away to the good and fertile land, and Nibu followed it there. For this reason the Wiyus, who are the children of Rabbo, live in hard and lonely places.

Rabbo was angry with his bird and said to it, 'Why are you a *peku-peru* bird? You got me the bad land.' He spat on its head and its tuft of feathers turned white. No young man eats this bird, for fear his hair too will go white.

Rabbo was going to live on his poor land, but Nibu said, 'No, brother, come and live with me, and we will go fishing.' One evening they went to the river to set traps for fish. During the night Rabbo awoke and said to himself, 'I wonder if there's any fish in my trap.' So he crept out of the house and went down to the river to see. There was nothing but rubbish, dead leaves and bits of wood in his trap, but Nibu's was full of fish. Rabbo took the fish out of Nibu's trap, filled it with rubbish, and put the fish in his own. In the morning, the brothers went to the river and when Nibu found he had caught nothing but rubbish, he was annoyed.

Another day they went to the forest to set traps. Nibu made a stone fall-trap on the ground: Rabbo made a noose-trap in a tree. During the night Rabbo awoke and said to himself, 'I wonder if there's anything in my trap?' So he crept out of the house and went to the forest to see. There was a hornbill in his trap, but there was a barking-deer in Nibu's. Rabbo took the deer out of Nibu's trap and put the bird in it instead ; he put the deer in his own.

In the morning, the brothers went to the forest and when Nibu found he had caught nothing but a bird, he was very angry.

Then the two brothers made clearings on the hillside and each went to cultivate his own field. Rabbo said to Nibu, 'Do you hear that bird which is always calling in your clearing? I'm afraid it means that you will get a bad harvest. Kill a pig and take its flesh and some beer to the clearing, climb a tree, and throw the flesh and beer to the ground for the Wiyus to eat and then your crop will be good.'

Nibu considered this advice and found it good. He prepared rice-beer and killed a pig. He went to his clearing and climbed a tree. But Rabbo followed him secretly and when Nibu threw down the flesh and beer, he recovered it and took it away for himself.

Somehow Nibu discovered how he had been deceived. He said nothing about it, but presently he in his turn warned Rabbo that his harvest would be bad and that he should satisfy the Wiyus by taking beer and pig's flesh to his clearing and throwing it down from a tree. Rabbo pretended to agree to this. He caught a pig and made it scream loudly so that Nibu would think he was killing it. He made a great fuss of preparing beer. But all he did was to roast a stone instead of the pig and put water instead of beer in the gourds. Then he took the stone and the water to the tree. Nibu followed him and stood below expectantly. But Rabbo poured the water on his head and dropped the stone on his chest. Since then men have had pains in the chest.

In time Nibu and Rabbo had children. Nibu's son was beautiful and Rabbo's son was ugly. When Rabbo saw Nibu's son, he was pleased and said, 'Brother, your son is very beautiful. But why is he so much more beautiful than mine?' Nibu replied, 'Brother, I shut my son in a basket and poured a lot of boiling water on him.' Rabbo thought, 'I too will make my son beautiful.' He went home, found a basket, tied his son up in it and poured boiling water over him. As a result the hair came out of the child's head, and the skin came off his body. Rabbo was naturally very angry about this and quarrelled with Nibu for deceiving him. For a long time there was war between them, but neither prevailed.

One day, they were both down by the river making boats. Rabbo's boat was very fine, Nibu's was ordinary. Rabbo said to Nibu, 'My boat is much better than your's: why not sit in it?' Nibu got into Rabbo's boat and fell asleep as they went along. Rabbo drew into shore and lifted up Nibu's own boat, turned it upside down, and put it as a cover over the sleeping man and tied it there. Then he pushed the boats out into the river.

Rabbo went home and lay with Nibu's wife.

Presently Nibu awoke and found himself floating down stream. He was terrified and shouted for help. 'I want to go on living. I want to create the race of men.'

A bird called Siggo-Pareng heard his cries and flew to help. It drew the boat to shore and undid the ropes with its beak and Nibu escaped.

Nibu hurried home. On the way he met his daughter and asked her, 'Is your mother at home? Is anyone with her?' 'Yes, she is with your brother.' 'Go home and tell her that your father is coming.' When the girl reached the house, she found her mother weaving cloth. She said, 'My father is coming.' Her mother cried angrily, 'Your father is dead: where is he coming from?' She took the sword from the loom and hit the child in the belly. Since then men have suffered from pains in the belly.

But Nibu discovered Rabbo in his house and there was a violent quarrel as a result, Rabbo went away and found employment in the household of Nippong Wiyu. He had to look after the Wiyu's children. After a few days, however, Nibu went to call Rabbo home, for he remembered that he was his brother. But Nippong Wiyu said, 'I will not let him go: he has got to work for me.' And all the Wiyus there attacked Nibu.

When Rabbo heard of the battle, he came to help Nibu, and the brothers killed Nippong Wiyu and her relations and carried off the flesh to eat. Nibu went ahead, Rabbo behind, each with his load of flesh. As Rabbo went along, he ate and ate the flesh, uncooked as it was. When he had finished, he said to Nibu, 'You have a very heavy load: let me carry some of it for you.' Nibu gave him a part of his load, and then some more, until at last Rabbo had it all. Then Nibu said, 'But how can you carry all this?' He looked back and there was Rabbo with his face red, covered with blood, bits of meat in his mouth. At this Nibu was frightened of his brother, and said, 'You are not a human being. I'm not going to have you living with me any longer.' They began to fight, and in the war between them, they went to the high mountains, but neither prevailed.

Then Rabbo said, 'Brother, we are equal, what is the use of fighting longer? Let us blindfold ourselves and see which way we will go.' They agreed on this. Rabbo tied a leaf round his eyes, but there were holes and cracks in it. Nibu tied a broad strong leaf and could see nothing. This is why the spirits can see men, but men cannot see the spirits. Rabbo remained on the hills, but Nibu came to the valleys. From Rabbo were born the spirits, from Nibu came all the men in the Adi country.

13

TAGIN

Duni, Subansiri F.D.

Abo-Teni's first wife was the Luki-Pipi bird. She was very lazy and while Abo-Teni worked all day in his swidden and went to hunt and fish, she stayed at home doing nothing: she didn't even cook properly. After a time Abo-Teni said to himself, 'What is the use of a wife like this? I must get rid of her.' And he said to Luki-Pipi, 'Go away; get out of my house.' Luki-Pipi said, 'Well, I will go. But before I go, let me tell you one thing which you must remember. Sow your maize, and then your rice, when you hear me cry *Pipi-pipi*. Sow in that month, not before, nor after.' When she had said this, she went away. And still the Tagins wait to sow their seed till they hear her cry *Pipi-pipi*.

Then Abo-Teni married Pejek the blue jay. This bird used to cook excellent food and pleased her husband greatly. One day he asked, 'What do you put in your food that makes it taste so nice?' Pejek replied, 'Nothing special: I just cook in the ordinary way.' But Abo-Teni did not believe this, and one day he hid in the house to see what she did. He saw her prepare the food, then fly above it and let her droppings fall on it. For her droppings were very sweet. Then Abo-Teni came to her and said, 'So this is how you cook—you feed me on your droppings. Go away: get out of my house.' Pejek said, 'Well, I will go. But before I go, let me tell you one thing which you must remember.'

But no one has ever remembered what she said.

There was a tree called Yurne-Tami. At that time this tree had the form of a woman, and Abo-Teni married her. She did no work in the house but every day she went fishing and every day Abo-Teni had fish to eat. One day he asked, 'How do you manage to catch so many fish?' Yurne-Tami said, 'I don't do anything special. I just go to the river and catch them.' But Abo-Teni did not believe this and next time she went fishing, he followed her secretly. He saw her piss in the water, so much that the river was full of it, and the fish, drunk with it, came to her and she caught them. Then Abo-Teni came from his hiding-place and said, 'So this is how you fish. You feed me on your piss. Go away: get out of my house.' Yurne-Tami said, 'Well, I will go. But before I go, let me tell you one thing which you must remember. I will turn into a tree. If you cut my bark and pick my fruit and leaves, and throw them into the river, the fish will get drunk on them, and you can catch all you want.'

After that Abo-Teni went to the forest and married a dry leaf. Soon there was a child in the leaf's belly and in due time a son was born. This child cried all the time, for there was no blood and no milk in the dry leaf. Abo-Teni picked him up and nursed him, but he fastened his teeth on his father's hand and drank his blood, then fell to the ground.

After a time Abo-Teni thought, 'How long am I to feed this child on my blood? A wife without flesh or breasts is no use to me. I will leave them in the forest.' Ever since the leech has drunk the blood of men.

Abo-Teni said to himself, 'How many wives have I taken, birds, trees, leaves, and all to no purpose! Not a single human being has been born.'

Abo-Teni had a sister, Chine-Yapi. He thought the only thing to do was to marry her, even though she was his sister. 'If I do, there will surely be human children. But first I will ask Dori-Wiyu.' So he went to the space between earth and sky, and when Dori-Wiyu heard his story, he said, 'You can marry your sister, but first take an egg and put it in her parts. If it breaks, you can marry her; but if it does not break, you cannot.'

Abo-Teni went home and told Chine-Yapi what the Wiyu had said. He put an egg in her parts and it broke. So he married his own sister, and she bore him human children. Their names were Nije, Nittum, Niddin, Nima, Nikko and Nipo. From them came all mankind.

14

TAGIN

Serra, Subansiri F.D.

Abo-Teni married Fire, but when he went to her she burnt off his parts and there was a horrid wound. He lay on the ground and presently a worm was born from the wound. Abo-Teni thought, 'I've had my parts burnt off and have only a worm for my pains. This is no place for me.' He took the worm in his hand and went away.

After a time he came to the Village of Fowls, where only cocks and hens lived. He sat down and put the worm on the ground before him. A cock came to him and said, 'Brother Abo-Teni, where are you going?' 'I am searching for a wife.' As he spoke, the cock saw the worm and in a moment he had pecked at it and swallowed it. Abo-Teni said, 'Where is my worm? Who has eaten it?' 'I have.' said the cock. 'Then you must come with me instead,' said Abo-Teni. 'I brought forth this worm with great pain and you have eaten it. Come with me or I will kill you.' The cock was frightened and went with him.

Next they came to the Village of Dogs. Abo-Teni tied the cock to a tree and sat down. A dog came to him and said, 'Brother Abo-Teni, where are you going?' 'I am searching for a wife.' As he spoke, the dog saw the cock and sprang at him and killed him. Abo-Teni said, 'Where is my cock? Who has eaten it?' 'I have,' said the dog. Abo-Teni was angry and tried to kill him. 'Why are you so angry?' said the dog. 'With great pain I brought forth a worm,' said Abo-Teni. 'But the cock ate the worm, and now you have eaten the cock. So I'm going to kill you.' The dog said, 'Don't kill me. I will go with you and be your servant.'

Abo-Teni said, 'Don't come yourself: give me one of your puppies.' The dog gave him a small puppy who went with him as his servant.

They next came to the Village of Goats. Abo-Teni tied the puppy to a tree and sat down. A goat came to him and said, 'Brother Abo-Teni, where are you going?' 'I am searching for a wife.' As he spoke, the puppy barked at the goat and the goat killed it with its horns. Abo-Teni said, 'Where is my puppy? Who has killed it?' 'I have,' said the goat. Abo-Teni was angry and tried to kill him. 'Why are you so angry?' said the goat. 'With great pain I brought forth a worm,' said Abo-Teni. 'But the cock ate the worm, and the dog ate the cock, and now you have killed my puppy. So I'm going to kill you.' The goat said, 'Don't kill me, I will go with you and be your servant.'

Abo-Teni said, 'Don't come yourself: give me one of your kids.' The goat gave him a small kid and he went with him as his servant.

They next came to the Village of Cattle. Abo-Teni tied the kid to a tree and sat down. A bull came to him and said, 'Brother Abo-Teni, where are you going?' 'I am searching for a wife.' As he spoke, the kid bleated and the bull killed him with his horns. Abo-Teni said, 'Where is my kid? Who has killed him?' 'I have,' said the bull. Abo-Teni was angry and tried to kill him. 'Why are you so angry?' said the bull. 'With great pain I brought forth a worm,' said Abo-Teni. 'But the cock ate the worm, the dog ate the cock, the goat killed the puppy, and now you have killed my kid. So I'm going to kill you.' The bull said, 'Don't kill me ; I will go with you and be your servant.'

Abo-Teni said, 'Don't come yourself ; give me one of your calves.' The bull gave him a small calf and he went with him as his servant.

They next came to the Village of Mithuns. Abo-Teni tied the calf to a tree and sat down. A mithun came to him and said, 'Brother Abo-Teni, where are you going?' 'I am searching for a wife.' As he spoke, the calf made a noise and the mithun killed him with his horns. Abo-Teni said, 'Where is my calf? Who has killed him?' 'I have,' said the mithun. Abo-Teni was angry and tried to kill him. 'Why are you so angry?' said the mithun. 'With great pain I brought forth a worm,' said Abo-Teni. 'But the cock ate the worm, the dog ate the cock, the goat killed the puppy, the bull killed the kid, and now you have killed my calf. So I'm going to kill you.' The mithun said, 'Don't kill me. I will go with you and be your servant.'

Abo-Teni took the mithun with him and they made their way across the hills until they came to the tree Subomsire. It was a very great tree and it fell on the mithun and killed him. Abo-Teni was angry: he picked up the tree and carried it away.

Daini the Sun had a sister called Mumsi. Abo-Teni reached her village and when he saw her, decided to make her his wife. He put the tree down in the middle of the village, and many children climbed onto it. But for all their playing and jumping about, it did not break. But when Mumsi climbed onto the trunk, it broke in half. Abo-Teni was angry and said, 'Why have you broken my tree. You must marry me, or I will kill you.'

Mumsi said, 'Yes, but you have nothing. How will you feed me? Go first and make a house for me and prepare a field. Make two houses for our fowls and pigs. When you have everything ready, I'll come and marry you.'

Abo-Teni went home and built the house as Mumsi had said and cleared a field. When everything was ready, he went to fetch his wife. But she said, 'I will only marry you on one condition. Let us sit opposite each other, on either side of a fire. If the smoke goes towards you, I will not marry you, but if it comes towards me, I will.' They sat down on either side of a fire and the smoke went into Mumsi's eyes, so she agreed to the marriage.

Mumsi had every kind of seed—mithun-seed, cow-seed, goat-seed, fowl-seed, pig-seed, dog-seed, rice-seed, millet-seed. They went, laden with the seed, to Abo-Teni's house. They put the cow-seed in the cow-shed, the pig-seed in the stye, the fowl-seed in the hen-coop, and soon many creatures were born. Mumsi sowed seed of rice and millet in the clearing, and soon they had plenty to eat and lived happily together.

In due time Mumsi gave birth to a child, but it made her weak and thin. Abo-Teni tried to tempt her to eat: he caught fish for her, hunted and trapped for her: but she could eat nothing. He said, 'Then what do you want? Tell me, and I'll bring you anything in the world.' Mumsi said, "All I want is some food from my parents' house. Go to them and tell them that their daughter won't eat anything. Then bring me whatever they give you.'

Abo-Teni went to the house of Mumsi's parents and told them what their daughter had said. They made a basket and secretly put into it a fine boy and a long, sharp knife, and closed it with a lid. They said to Abo-Teni, 'Take this basket and put it in the forest near your house and tell our daughter that you have brought food for her from us. But you must not open the basket on the way.' They made him swear that he would not open it. Then he put the basket on his back and set out.

But as he went he began to wonder what was in the basket, for it was heavy and seemed alive. He had sworn not to look, yet he could not help wanting to, and at last put the basket down and opened it. There was the knife and the lovely boy. But the boy abused him, 'Why have you opened the basket after swearing you wouldn't? I'll tell Mumsi what you have done.' Abo-Teni hastily put the lid on again, and continued his journey. When he reached home, he left the basket in the forest and went in to see his wife. He told her that the food from her parents' house was in a basket outside. She went at once to see it, and Abo Teni followed her secretly.

He saw her open the basket, take out the beautiful child, kill him with the knife and eat the raw flesh. It was not until late at night that she came fat and satisfied. Abo-Teni said nothing, but he thought, 'How can I keep a cannibal wife? She will soon be eating our child or me myself.' Mumsi was very well now, strong and plump, but Abo-Teni was too frightened to eat much.

At last Abo-Teni said openly to her, 'I don't want a cannibal wife.' Mumsi was ashamed and took her child in her arms and went to her parents' house.

After this Abo-Teni married Chigo-Chuma. This woman had only one breast. In due time, she gave birth to a child. But the child would not drink from the single breast: he cried and cried and grew thin. Abo-Teni said to his son, 'Why won't you drink your mother's milk? What will you eat?' The child said, 'There is a tree called *cheni*: take me to it and I'll drink its juice.' Abo-Teni took him to the tree and the child said, 'Return after five days.' In five days he returned and found the child fat and well. 'Return after twelve days,' said the child. But when Abo-Teni returned he found that the child had gone away to live by himself in a cave on a great hill.

This child was Ninur, the craftsman, who first made daos and spears and precious dishes and vessels.

15

TARAON (DIGARU) MISHMI

Tushe, Lohit F.D.

There were two brothers, born of one father but of different mothers. The name of the elder was Chinye and that of the younger was Karuwa. Their father died and as the boys grew older, they quarrelled as to who should be the greater. Chinye was a rather clever and tricky boy and he said, 'Let us do this. We'll throw our mothers down from the top of a cliff and then there will only be two of us and you can be the greater.' Karuwa agreed to this and Chinye said, 'You throw your mother down first.' But Karuwa said, 'No, you throw your's first.'

Chinye hid his mother inside the house. He dressed a pestle in a woman's cloth, carried it to the edge of the cliff and threw it down. Karuwa saw what he thought was a woman falling down, so he took his mother to the top of the cliff and did actually throw her down and killed her. Now when the pestle fell down, it had made a lot of noise banging against the rocks and Karuwa said to Chinye, 'Your mother made a great deal of noise while she was falling, but my own mother went willingly.'

After a few days, Karuwa said, 'My mother knew how to weave cloth better than anyone in the village,' for her ghost was weeping as she wondered who would make cloth for her son now she was dead.

After a time, Chinye's mother came out of her hiding-place. Karuwa was very angry at having been deceived and swore to take revenge. Chinye was frightened, for his arrows were rather weak but his brother had iron arrow-heads. So Chinye said, 'There is a great stone on the other side of the Brahmaputra River. Let us both shoot at it. Whosever arrow sticks to it will be the greater.' Karuwa said, 'Very well.' But when his brother was not looking, Chinye put wax on the tip of his arrow and so when it hit the stone it stuck to it. But Karuwa's arrow-head being made of iron bounced off. Chinye said, 'Look, this proves that I am greater.'

And so, ever afterwards, he was.

CHAPTER NINE

THE LAND OF WOMEN

TRADITIONS of a Land of Women,[1] where men lose their customary position of dominance and live, when they live at all, as slaves or victims of magic are widespread and very old. Stories about the Amazons go back to Homer. Herodotus describes their capture by the Greeks and their settlements in Scythia. Strabo gives the tradition about their mutilation of the left breast so that they could throw the spear better. Diodorus says that in Libya a people lived under the rule of women; there were men in the country, but of an inferior position.

It is not until we come to the Middle Ages, however, that we find traditions of a real Land of Women. The Arab geographers describe a great town in an island of the western ocean, entirely free from the rule of men, where the women were visited by slaves at night, and male children were killed. Adam of Bremen describes an exclusively women's community on the shores of the Baltic. They became pregnant by drinking magic brews or through intercourse with monsters which were frequently born among them. The ancient Chinese also had the tradition and a Chinese chronicle of the seventeenth century is quoted as saying that the women conceived through the south wind, before which they placed themselves when naked. The Amazons of Venezuela and Brazil, about whom so much was written, probably do not belong to this tradition, but in recent times the missionary Chalmers found tales of a Land of Women current in New Guinea, and there is a Papuan tale of two Ginggala men in the Land of Women, where they cut a male child out of the mother's body and buried him. Similar legends are said to be current among the Polynesian Maoris and the Mentawei Islanders.

[1] Some paragraphs are quoted from my *Myths of Middle India*, pp.458 ff. A convenient summary of the classical traditions will be found in *Woman*, Vol. I, pp. 468 ff.

The earliest reference to this legend in India appears to be in the story of the fifth adventure of the horse released at the Aśwamedha rite in the Mahabharata. The horse enters the country inhabited only by women, whose Rani is named Paramita. The women become mothers as a result of chance contacts with visitors: male children are killed the moment they are born. Any man remaining in the country more than a month is put to death. When Arjun arrived in the country he said to his warriors, 'This is a marvellous country whither the horse has led us. If we conquer these women, we shall gain no credit; if we are conquered, our disgrace will be inconceivable.' But Arjuna was defeated by the women, though in the end he conquered them, for he married their Rani and took her away to Hastinapura.

In the Matsya Purana (Chap. XI) Siva and Parvati enjoy themselves in their Saravana, a pleasure-garden beautiful with every kind of tree. They ordain that any man approaching the garden will be transformed into a woman, a fate that befalls Raja Ila when he enters the enchanted area.

The tradition has persisted to modern times and is found in widely distributed parts of tribal India. The Santals associate the Land of Women with their great Guru Kamru and it bears his name. 'The country is very rich and fertile, and there are only women living there, or else the women predominate, and no one is able to go there and stay.' Bodding, who makes this report, says that men are not liked by the Kamru women for 'definite reasons that cannot be recorded'. He gives a story of a Santal who went to Kamru and was kept there by the women for five years, by day covered with a large bamboo basket and instructed in the magic arts at night. When he was initiated, he was turned into a kite and flew back to his own country. A Santal child was carried off to Kamru by a vulture. Here he grew up and ultimately married. But when he tried to get away, he found himself always coming back to the place he started from. At last a woman told him he must leave everything behind and not take anything of that country along with him; then he made his escape.

'The traditional Kamru country is a country of strange people with strange powers; the inhabitants can at will turn a man into a dog or any other animal....It is a land full of magic and witchcraft, but the stories seem to imply that it is the women who are so dangerous and powerful.'[2]

Bodding suggests that since Santals who go to Assam as labourers in the Tea Gardens pass through the Kamrup District, they have probably associated the two names and this is why they locate the land of magic to the east.

The Angami Nagas have a similar legend. 'There is in a certain place a village of women only, and if a man go there they drive him away by shooting at him with war bows, and they raise not any males save one only, and when other male babies are born they boil water and put them therein to kill them. These women, moreover, do no hard work, but eat great store of starch and oil to make them strong to battle. Others say that when a man goes there, the women that be there be so eager for him that in striving to possess him they tear him to pieces utterly.'[3]

In a similar Naga story recorded by Hutton in *Folk-Lore,* it is said that the women in this village become pregnant through hornets sucking their breasts.[4]

In central India the Land of Women is located to the east, to the sunrise, often in Bengal, and is a place of magic where male intruders are turned into cats, goats, or bullocks and where the best and strongest liquor in the world is distilled. A Baiga tale adds that the women wore men's clothes and terrorized the neighbourhood. In Baiga and Jhoria stories the absence of men is due to a curse.

The NEFA traditions do not have the motifs of magic and transformation nor is there any idea that the Land of Women is the best place to get rice-beer—not even the most credulous audience would swallow that! The stress is rather on the domination of women over men and on the desire of women for men. The old idea that women without men can

[2] P. O. Bodding, *Studies in Santal Medicine and Connected Folklore* (Calcutta, 1925), p. 126.

[3] Hutton, *The Angami Nagas,* pp. 263 f.

[4] *Folk-Lore,* June 1923.

conceive by the wind appears. A Taraon Mishmi story relates the tradition to the practice of polyandry. There is a general, if vague, notion that the Land of Women is somewhere in Tibet.

There have been many other attempts to locate this country. Hutton says that the Sema Nagas place it somewhere east of the Patkoi-Barail range.[5] Hiuen Tsiang speaks of a country Po-lo-hih-mo-pu-lo, the Country of the Eastern Women, where the men manage the wars and sow the land, but the women do everything else[6]—a country identified by Wilson with the Malabar Coast where the Nayar system of mother-right might well be supposed to have impressed a stranger.[7] Hiuen Tsiang also describes a Country of the Western Women, which is in Persia, the abode of demons who by intercourse with a girl of southern India 'engendered a clan of women children.'[8] This story is repeated by Marco Polo and his editor Yule discusses at length the possible position of the island.[9] Logan suggests that the Island of Women is Minicoy, in the Laccadive group. The men, who are Mussalmans, are absent on sea voyages for much of the time and the women go unveiled and manage the island. After marriage the girls remain for a time with their fathers, and leave the paternal home in order of seniority, the houses erected for them becoming their own property.[10] 'It is easy to understand,' says Crooke, 'how mariners visiting the island could find none to receive them but women, and everything arranged and managed by women. The men

[5] Hutton, *The Angami Nagas*, p. 263.

[6] S. Beal, *Buddhist Records of the Western World*, Vol. I, p. 198.

[7] H. H. Wilson, *The Vishnu Purana* (London, 1840), p. 481.

[8] Beal, op. cit., vol. ii, 240 Hiuen Tsiang continues, 'In the middle of a great iron city of this Tatnadripa (P'ao-chu) was the dwelling of the Rakshasi women (Lo-t'sa). On the towers of this city they erected two high flagstaffs with lucky or unlucky signals, which they exhibited according to circumstances, when merchants came to the island. Then they changed themselves into beautiful women, holding flowers and scents, and with the sound of music they went forth to meet them, and caressingly invited them to enter the iron city; then having shared with them all sorts of pleasure, they shut them up in an iron prison, and devoured them at their leisure.'

[9] H. Yule, *The Book of Ser Marco Polo* (London, 1871), Vol. II, pp. 337 f.

[10] W. Logan, *Malabar* (Madras, 1887), Vol. 1, p. 287 f.

who remained in the island would probably keep out of the way until the strangers left, as they were pirates, and it would have fared ill with them if they were discovered.'[11]

1

HILL MIRI

Bini, Subansiri F.D.

Far to the north, there is a place hidden among the mountains called Miyuman, where only women live. These women have ancient and sacred beads and bells, and old swords, very costly.

Should a man go by accident to Miyuman, the women struggle for him. In every village of that country there are two quarters: in one live the old women, in the other the young, and they fight bitterly over any man who comes there. When one or other quarter has triumphed they assemble and each woman claims him for the night. Whoever is strongest drags him to her bed.

Apart from this, the women treat the man with honour and feed him well ; only for this is he in torment, with the women pulling him in all directions and overwhelming him with passion.

When he can persuade them to let him go, the old women give him an ancient and valuable sword and beads, in the hope that if other men see them they will be tempted and come for them too. The young women give him a new sword and new beads.

If a child is born in that country, the people wait anxiously to know its sex. With a girl they are delighted. But if a boy is born, they torment him until he dies.

2

MOKLUM

Kimiyang, Tirap F.D.

At first there were no men on the earth which was entirely populated by woman. One day a woman went fishing and caught a human eye. She put it in her basket and when she went home and opened it, she found it had turned into a man. She told the

[11] W. Crooke, 'The Land and Island of Women', *Man in India*, Vol. II. pp. 1 ff.

other women and they came crowding round, all wanting to eat him. But he escaped and as he ran along he felled plantains across the path to stop the women following. They chased him but kept on falling and tripping over the plants. But one woman was stronger than the rest and she caught him up and made him her husband. It is from them that all the people in the world have come.

3

NOCTE

Laju, Tirap F.D.

At first there were only women living in the world. Then after a long time four men came. When the women saw them they all desired them. But there were so many that the men became utterly exhausted and three died. Only one managed to escape and though the woman chased him, as he ran away he felled plantain trees across his path and stopped the pursuit. But one woman who was more determined than the others caught him: they came together and were the parents of all mankind.

4

SHERDUKPEN

Rupa, Kameng F.D.

Beyond the Himalaya mountains is the country of the Sirinpus, which was inhabited by male and female ogres, and the country of the Sirinmus where only women lived. If a Sirinpu husband and wife had three daughters they used to keep one with them and send the other two to the land of the Sirinmus. No man could go to any of the villages of the Sirinmus ; they used to take the girls to the boundary and leave them there.

In the Sirinmus' country the women were very beautiful and very small. They were of two kinds, the young and the old. If a man went by accident to that country he was lucky if the young women caught him, for they would keep him only for a week and if he survived their passion they would send him home laden with rich gifts. For they possessed all the gold, silver, iron and beads in the world.

But if such a man fell into the hands of the old women, they would shut him up in a house of stone and close it with a stone door. They fed him with the best of food until he grew fat. When he was ready they filled a great pot with water and put a fire under it and when the water was boiling threw him in. When he was properly cooked, the old women ate him with loud cries of pleasure.

5

SINGPHO

Wakitna, Tirap F.D.

The Land of Dogs lies beyond the great Ocean. There, though the rest of his body is human, every man has a dog's head. When they talk to one another, the men bark like dogs.

But though the men have the appearance of dogs their womenfolk are very beautiful.

When any visitor comes from another country, the women are attracted by him and quarrel with one another to possess him. But the men, directly they hear about the visitor, attack him like dogs and tear him to pieces.

When children are born, provided the child has the head of a dog, he is allowed to live and the men are happy about it, but if anyone is born with a human face, the dog-men immediately kill him.

Whatever woman calls her husband a 'dog' goes to the Land of Dogs after her death.

6

SINGPHO

Dumba, Tirap F.D.

Once upon a time there was an old man who lived with his wife and one child. The boy's name was Choumoklang. The boy's father died and the boy said to his mother, 'Lots of people go trading. Let me too go and earn my living.' His mother replied, 'There is plenty to eat and drink in our house ; what do you want to go trading for?' They argued and argued until the boy lost his temper and kicked his mother. He put all his belongings in a boat and went down the river to trade.

There were many other people on the river but Choumoklang's boat went faster than them all. But after a time it came to a narrow channel and stopped there ; it was unable to go back or forward and the other boats could not pass it. The other people thought, 'This boy must be a sinner and that is why his boat has stopped.' 'We must do some thing about it,' they said, and threw Choumoklang into the river, removed his boat and proceeded on their way.

The boy floated down the river until he came to a place where a lot of sinful women were bathing, and when they saw him they dragged him to the bank. These women were very happy when they saw that Choumoklang was young and handsome, for there were no young men in their country, so they took him home and looked after him well.

These women were as they were because in another birth they had called their husbands dogs. Phara the Supreme God, therefore, sent them back after they had died to live in a place where there were no men at all. The women lived well during the day but at night they had to go to the place of sin. There they found many dogs who sprang upon them and tore them to pieces. In the morning a kite would fly over the place and drop the Water of Life upon their bodies, whereupon they would revive and return home. This happened every night and morning.

Choumoklang wondered where the women went every evening and one night he followed them secretly but, when he saw the terrible incidents of the night, he ran away.

He went on his way until he came to the Land of Sinful Men where all the men wore golden helmets. When he saw them, Choumoklang asked them to give him one. Somebody gave him one but when he put it on his head, it burnt like fire and he began to scream.

But when Phara heard his cries, he came to the place and removed the helmet. The boy was very grateful to Phara for saving his life and said, 'I sinned when I kicked my mother and it is for this that I have suffered. Let me live with you and whatever tasks you give me I will fulfil.' So Phara took the boy home with him and made him his Minister. As a result of living with Phara for many years, Choumoklang himself became a god.[12]

[12] The Singphos now worship Choumoklang along with Phara and offer him sacrifice.

7

TARAON MISHMI

Tetuliang, Lohit F.D.

Far away to the north is a land where only women live. Because so many women live in this country there are not enough of them in other places and the number of men is too great. This is why among the Lamas one woman sometimes has five or ten husbands. This is not because she wants to have them, but because all the women are living together in another land.

8

WANCHO

Pomau, Tirap F.D.

There was a village of Konyaks where only women lived ; there was no man there. Whenever there was a big storm the women conceived by the wind. If a girl was born they rejoiced, but at the birth of a boy they wept. They let the boy grow until he was ten or twelve years old and then killed and ate him.

One day an old potter went to this village to sell his pots. When the women saw him they were pleased, for they thought he would make a good meal, and they said to him, 'Put your pots down here by the village gate and we will give you rice for them.' But directly he came through the gate into the village, the women fell upon him and tied him hand and foot. Then they went to the forest to get herbs and vegetables to eat with his flesh.

When the women had gone away, a number of children came to look at the old man. One of them said, 'I will eat his hand.' Another said, 'I will have his ears.' A third said, 'The liver's for me.' The old man said to the children, 'If you will undo me, I will cut off my hands and my ears and take out my liver and you can eat them while the women are away. Once they come back you will get nothing.' So the children untied him and he ran for his life, leaving his pots behind. It was from the old man himself that we heard this tale, but no one knows where the village is.

PART THREE: THE DAILY LIFE OF MAN

CHAPTER TEN

THE DOMESTIC LIFE OF MAN

THROUGHOUT tribal India myths about the origins of human institutions sometimes come very near what is probably the historic truth. Thus, Singpho, Moklum and Mishmi stories describe how men originally lived in caves; a Wancho tale says that like birds they made their homes in nests high up in the trees. They gradually learnt how to tie bits of wood together to make a wall and to use suitable leaves to thatch a roof. There is an excellent Singpho story describing how the first men learnt how to make the pillars of a house from the legs of an elephant, the poles from the body of a snake, the roof from the skeleton of a buffalo and the thatch from a fish's scales.

Similar traditions may be found in Orissa, where the Binjhwars say that men originally lived in trees, the Konds that they were in caves and pits, and the Saoras that they made burrows in the ground and 'lived like hares'.[1]

There are also parallels to the Bori story in the text that the first weaver learnt how to make cloth in a dream. A Bhattra story describes how, at a time when all men lived naked, the Supreme Being came to a man in a dream and taught him how to weave. A Gadaba tale recounts how the first cotton plant was discovered through a dream. In Kond tales, the growing of cotton and the art of weaving was taught men by the gods.[2]

In the Wancho story at page 200 the origin of tattooing is attributed to the belief that it makes girls look pretty. More common, even in NEFA, is the widespread idea that it will enable a person to be recognized after death. The tattoo marks are the only possession one can take beyond the grave; by them the ghosts will know each other; by them the God of Death will be able to distinguish the sex of his unsubstantial subjects.

[1] *Tribal Myths of Orissa*, pp. 583 ff.
[2] ibid., pp. 595 ff.

Two of the NEFA stories about salt trace it to the transformation of a dead woman's body; Moklum and Wancho tales trace it to the tears of an old woman. Other stories do not give it a magical origin but describe how the first discovery was made on a visit to Tibet. A Singpho tale stresses the importance of salt as a gift to make people friends.

Cultivation and food

1

HILL MIRI

Chemir, Subansiri F.D.

At the beginning men had no food. There were no swiddens, no gardens, no granaries ; there was only the rain and the wind.

Wiyu Lukum lay with his wife Chikkum and she conceived, but not in the belly as human women conceive. Her whole body became covered with swellings. When the pain became too great, she sat down and broke each of them open with a thorny twig. From each swelling came a little worm. Chikkum was dismayed as she found scores of worms on her body, and brushed them off onto the ground. The worms lay there weeping, but what could their mother do? How could she nurse so many?

The bird Doko-Polo saw the worms crying and felt sorry for them. She picked them up and took them to an old woman named Dirri-on. This woman had four breasts, two in front and two behind, and she took the worms in her arms and suckled them.

One day Abo-Teni's dog was out hunting and came to the place. He saw the worms, some crying, some laughing and playing, some quarrelling, all struggling for a place at the nipples and he thought, 'If I can persuade this old woman to give me these worms, I'll take them to Abo-Teni and he will be very pleased, for there will be food for everyone.' So the dog stayed with the old woman hoping to get the worms.

When his dog did not return, Abo-Teni grew anxious and went to look for him. He came to Dirri-on's house and the dog ran out to greet him. 'What are you doing here?' cried Abo-Teni. The dog said, 'There's an old woman here with a great many small children, and I am watching her. Come and see.' Abo Teni went inside and asked Dirri-on, 'What are these creatures?' 'These,' she said, 'will be the food of men. If you put them in your clearings, more children will be born, and you can eat them.' 'Will you give them to me?' 'Certainly,' said the old woman. 'But you must take them home within three days. Otherwise they will return to me and I will not give them to you a second time.'

Abo-Teni thought, 'How can I carry all these back in three days, for there are no porters here?' He asked the dog, 'Can you carry them?' 'Yes,' said the dog. 'Cut off my ears and fill them with the worms and I will take them.'

Abo-Teni cut off the dog's ears and filled them with the worms and the dog carried them home in his mouth within three days. Abo-Teni had the worms sown in his clearings and from them grew every kind of grain and pulse.

2

MINYONG

Siang Frontier Division

(From G. D. S. Dunbar, *Abors and Galongs*, pp. 64 f.)

In these days there is only a plant called *kojam koja*, but once it was the name of a flourishing village. In Kojam Koja there lived a Gam, Kosam Luntong, and one day he proposed that the village should hold a festival to the spirits. So the people of the village went out, and turned a stream to get the fish in it. Now Nippong's son was in this stream and he, like everything else that the people of Kojam Koja found, was taken back to the village and eaten at the feast. A bat carried the news of this to Nippong, who called on all the powers of water to rise and destroy Kojam Koja. He also sent two huge snakes to undermine a cliff under which the village was built. So Kojam Koja was blotted out, and all the people that were in it were buried in its ruins. But the heads of the people have sprung up as the chestnut tree and their other members have sprung up as the different kinds of bamboo, and the plant known as *kojam koja*. The hearts of the people sprang up again as ginger and onion roots.

3

MINYONG

Riu, Siang F.D.

The burial-place of the Wiyus is called Sedi-Gaddum-Lumlum. One day a Wiyu in the form of a mithun, Kayum-Polung-Sabbo, went there and proudly squared his shoulders so vigorously that blood fell from them. This blood fell to the ground and mixed with the earth. Presently a plantain tree grew from the place. This is why the plantain has no bones. It is all flesh and weak, for it was born from blood.

4

MINYONG

Komkar, Siang F.D.

There were two Wiyus, brothers. The elder was Banji, the younger was Ban-Mang. Banji had the form of a man: he was strong, vigorous, hardworking, handsome. Ban-Mang had only one eye, one arm and one leg ; he was weak, ugly, dirty and could not work at all. Banji got tired of feeding his useless brother and went away one day and left him. Poor Ban-Mang now had nothing to eat and after a few days died of hunger. His corpse rotted where it lay ; there was no one to bury it.

From the gall-bladder came a chilli-plant: this is why the chilli is bitter as gall. From the nails came the tobacco-plant. From his organ grew the brinjal, which is the same shape and which swings in the wind as a man's organ swings as he walks along.

5

PANGGI

Geku, Siang F.D.

Engo-Takar made a clearing in the hills. Kojam-Koja saw it and made one too. But when he sowed his seed, a wild boar came and destroyed the harvest. Kojam-Koja was furious at this and killed the boar with an arrow. He cut up the carcass and removed a round ball of flesh from between its hind legs. He put it on a tree and the tree withered. He put it in the grass, and the grass withered. He put it on a stone, and there came from it two insects, the stink-beetle and the cricket.

Kojam-Koja made another clearing and sowed his seed. At harvest-time he wanted to sacrifice to Pineng-Nyageng, but he had no meat to offer. He went to the forest and made a stone fall-trap. Next day he found the pig Laddang-Angur-Potung killed in it. As he removed it to cut it up, the kite Kayum-Kaki-Middu cried to him, 'Cut off the head and give it to me. You can use the rest for your sacrifice.' Kojam-Koja gave the pig's head to the kite and he himself ate the rest after the sacrifice. Secretly a bat watched him.

That night the bat came flying towards the river. There it heard a great noise of weeping. It was the Wiyu of the waters, Ladang Laiyo, who was weeping. 'What is the matter?' asked the bat. The Wiyu replied: 'I had one son and someone has killed him.' 'I know who it was,' said the bat. 'It was Kojam-Koja, who killed him for sacrifice and, having stuffed himself with the meat, is now sleeping off it.' In rage and sorrow Ladang Laiyo went to Bidi-Bidak Wiyu and said, 'Brother, Kojam-Koja has killed my son. Now help me to kill him.' The two Wiyus went to find their enemy and Bidi-Bidak shot him with an arrow and killed him. Ladang Laiyo tried to kill the kite which had eaten his son's head, but it flew away. So he sent Kayum-Kumtekrebo Wiyu to kill it for him. When he had done so, the bird's feathers flew into the air and fell among the hills near Karko. From them came the cotton plant.

It was Kojam-Koja who taught men to cultivate their clearings and to sacrifice in them.

When Kojam-Koja died, a kind of wild ginger grew from his excrement. So now ginger is used in every sacrifice.

The Nippongs hate the small of ginger. So now if they make anyone ill, we rub his body with ginger[3] and they run away.

[3] It is interesting to find ginger recorded as a spirit-scarer. The Hill Saora shamans of Orissa put ginger to the same purpose. They carry it with them when they go about, clean their teeth with it at the time of trance, and generally use it to keep away any hostile spirit who may attack them. It has also been recorded that a man who has transformed himself into a tiger can be restored by being given green ginger to eat—See my *The Religion of an Indian Tribe* (Bombay, 1955), pp. 195 f. Ginger is also regarded by the Ao Nagas as a protection against evil influences; it is offered to the spirits and eaten by the shamans.—Mills, *The Ao Nagas*, pp. 113, 236, 281, 370 etc.

6

SINGPHO

Wakitna, Tirap F.D.

When the earth and sky were first made, the Raja of the sky was Mathum-Matta and the Raja of the earth was Lan-Ning-Nan. Mathum-Matta had a daughter called Chikim-Kainang and Lan-Ning-Nan had a son called Kumsan-Lasipang. The sky-girl and the earth-boy married and the girl's father gave them many wonderful presents. In fact, he gave them everything they could possibly want, except clothes and household animals.

When Mathum-Matta saw that the young couple had no clothes, he cut off a bit of his own navel and holding it in his hand said, 'I send you to my daughter's house, go there and make cloth for her.' He put the bit of skin into a small box along with a pumpkin-seed and gave it to his daughter. She asked what it was and he said, 'Take this home and open it and a weaver will come out to make you cloth. There is a seed there. Plant it in your garden and when it grows into a tree it will bear two fruits ; when these have grown big, break them open.'

Chikim-Kainang went down from the sky to her husband on earth, taking the box with her. When she opened it, she found that the bit of navel had turned into a spider, who brought thread out of his belly and began to weave it into cloth. Seeing what the spider did, the girl also learnt how to weave.

She planted the pumpkin seed and when it grew it bore two great fruits and they broke them open. From one of the fruits came out the seeds of every kind of grain. From the other came all the animals, domestic and wild. It was after this that food-grains and animals spread throughout the world.

7

WANCHO

Chating, Tirap F.D.

The first rat fell down from the sky. As it fell, it brought a paddy-seed in its mouth and dropped it on to the ground where it took root and grew. This was how men first got rice. Men watched the rat digging in the soil and from this they learnt how to cultivate.

The rat still takes the rice from the fields because it believes that it is his, for he brought it to the world.

We Wanchos do not speak while we are reaping the rice for fear that Rang will hear us and will send the rats to take away the harvest.

8

WANCHO

Watnu, Tirap F.D.

When Rang created men and animals he also gave them seed so that they could get their food. When the rats and sparrows saw what he had done they grew jealous and said to each other, 'We will see whether men got the whole of the crop or not.' So when men planted the seed and the harvest grew up, the rats and sparrows took revenge by coming to eat the grain.

CUSTOMS

9

DAFLA

Solo (Palin Valley), Subansiri F.D.

In the beginning monkeys used to tie their hair in a knot in the front of the head in the fashion that the Daflas call ***podum***. One day a man called Nima Teni killed a monkey and removed the ***podum*** and decorated his own head with it. This is why all the Daflas, who are descendants of Nima Teni, tie their hair in a knot in front of the head.[4]

10

SINGPHO

Imbu, Tirap F.D.

In the old days, before any such thing as marriage was known, there were a great many men and very few women. Just as today one man may have six or eight wives, so in those days one woman could have six or eight husbands.

[4] Recorded by B. K. Shukla.

There was a goddess Panirani who had a daughter named Numrongnang. When she grew up many gods came to marry her. But she was frightened and said to her mother, 'There is only one of me. How can I marry all these men? I would rather die first.' The gods came to take her but she went and hid in her mother's lap. Panirani said to the gods, 'Whoever can dam the rivers Tilanka, Tinaik and Malika can carry my daughter, but no other.' Many of the gods tried to stop the rivers but failed to do so.

But there was a king of the mountains called Ningun-Mangan who succeeded in damming up the three rivers. Panirani was pleased with him and gave him her daughter in marriage. When men saw this custom they decided to follow it. One Madumwa-Chinga was the first of all mankind to marry. His wife was called Nimrang-Kaipa. He gave the girl's parents two buffaloes, one hundred and forty sacred bells, two bits of Burmese cloth, two large gongs, a Burmese coat and a parcel of gold. It was after this that men and women began to marry.

11

WANCHO

Khassa, Tirap F.D.

There were two girls who were very great friends. One of them had her parents alive but the other's parents were dead. One day the orphan girl left her friend and went to live in another village. As there was no one to look after her, they put marks on her legs and when she grew up, everyone thought she looked very pretty. But her friend, who had stayed at home, did not look so beautiful. Ever since then parents have had their daughters tattooed.[5]

[5] Among the Wanchos both men and women are tattooed, and great store is set on the custom. For men heavy 'spectacles' are drawn round the eyes and over the face ; the neck and throat are heavily decorated ; there may be further patterns on the chest, the arms, the back and even the belly. It was formerly the custom for the operation to be performed on the third day after a successful raid. On such occasions everyone who needed tattooing was done and it was the privilege of the Wangham's wife to do the work in her own house. Sometimes it took her a fortnight to finish all the youths who had to be tattooed. At the end, there was a feast of a mithun, and the Wangham's wife was the recipient of customary gifts of rice, beer and meat. I was told, though I have not been able to confirm it, that at the first head taken she tattooed the chest ; at the

Clothing and houses

12

BORI

Gatte, Sike Valley, Siang F.D.

At first human beings did not know how to make cloth. The only person who had the art was Doini-Pollo. One day a Wiyu named Podi-Barbi went to his house to learn how to do it. She is the Wiyu to whom the Dongin sacrifice is offered. She is very kind and always anxious to help mankind.

One day Tani offered the Dongin sacrifice and Podi-Barbi came to receive it. It was a good sacrifice, with rich offerings of meat and beer, and the Wiyu was so pleased that in return she came in a dream to Tani's wife and showed her how to weave.

At first Tani's wife used bark-fibre and taught her daughters to use it also. But in time they got tired of bark-cloth and began to make yarn from the soft feathers of the kite. Later, after they started visiting Tibet to obtain salt, they learnt the use of wool.

13

HILL MIRI

Chemir, Subansiri F.D.

It was Abo-Teni's wife, Chittu-Tomi, who first made the belts of cane that Miri women wear. At first they used to wear leaves, but these broke and fell off.

Si-Duinye (Earth-Sun) saw the belts and said, 'How can you go to your wives when they wear so many belts?' Abo-Teni said,

second she did the throat ; at the third, the face ; and at the fourth and subsequent heads she did the arms, back and belly. The order may not always be the same, but it is probable that the amount of tattooing does represent the degree of prowess of a man or at least of a man's family or morung. Sometimes human figures are tattooed on the chest, and such a man is regarded as very formidable.

The tattooing of girls is more becoming. There may be a necklace tattooed between the breasts ; or a cross over the navel ; or pointers climbing up the thighs ; or elaborate designs on the shoulders. I watched a girl being tattooed by the Wangham's wife at Jaboka. The old lady first drew the pattern with black powder on the girl's legs ; then she made her lie flat on her face and with a sort of hammer (it was a long root with a stick inserted: at the end of the stick were three thorns), she tapped out the pattern. The victim was in honour bound to make no outcry.

'We push them up above the breasts, then if anyone comes by, we can pull them down quickly.' Si-Duinye said, 'That is very good.' So Miri women sleep in their belts and never take them off.*

14

MOKLUM

Longke, Tirap F.D.

All the trees in the world come from Rang. At the beginning, he made them into different tribes, some great and some small. The plantain belongs to a great and important tribe and this is why it has big leaves. The palm tree is another which belongs to an important tribe and its leaves too are large. Sengwa and Phengwa taught men to use its leaves to thatch their houses.

15

SINGPHO

Imbu, Tirap F.D.

In the days when men were living in caves and under trees, Kindru-Lalim and Kincha-Lali-Dam decided to build themselves houses. Unhappily they had no idea of what to do, so they went to the forest to consult the animals.

Dalton describes the costume of Hill Miri women as 'elaborate and peculiar'. 'A short petticoat extending from the loins to the knees is secured to a broad belt of leather, which is ornamented with brass bosses.' Outside this they wore a 'singular crinoline of cane-work' which Dalton describes as 'about a foot in breadth, and fastened so tight round the loins that it restrains the free use of the thighs, and causes the women to move with a short mincing motion chiefly from the knee. The women are often seen with nothing on but this singular garment.' 'The upper garment', he continues, 'consists of a band of plaited cane-work girding the body close under the arms, and from this in front a fragment of cloth depends and covers the breasts. This is their travelling and working dress, but at other times they wrap themselves in a large cloth of eri silk of Assamese manufacture, doubled over the shoulders and pinned in front like a shawl.'—Dalton, op. cit., p. 32.

There have been fewer changes than might have been expected during the eighty years since this was written. I have not seen the 'short petticoat' but the 'singular crinoline of cane-work' is still the most striking thing in the attire of a 'Miri' woman. In some cases these cane rings may number over two hundred, and the women are evidently greatly attached to them, for they spend much of their spare time manufacturing new rings for themselves or their daughters.

The first animal they met was the elephant and they said to him, 'We want to build a house ; can you tell us how to do it?' The elephant said, 'Cut wooden pillars strong and thick as my legs.' 'What should we do then?' they asked. The elephant replied, 'I don't know what else you should do.'

The two friends went on and met the snake and to him they said, 'We want to build a house, can you tell us how to do it? The elephant has told us to make pillars strong and thick as his own legs, but he could not say more than that.' The snake replied, 'Cut poles as long and thin as myself.' They asked, 'What should we do then?' The snake replied, 'I don't know what else you should do.'

They went on and found a she-buffalo standing by the carcass of her dead husband. Other animals had eaten all the skin and flesh and only the bones remained. The two men said to the she-buffalo, 'We want to build a house, can you tell us how to do it? The elephant has told us to make pillars strong and thick as his own legs ; the snake has told us to cut long poles thin as himself, but what should we do now?' The buffalo showed them her dead husband and said, 'Put cross-poles and make a roof like the bones of this skeleton.' 'What should we do then?' asked the men. The she-buffalo replied, 'I don't know what else you should do.'

They went on and met the fish and said to him, 'We want to build a house. The elephant has told us to make pillars strong and thick as his own legs ; the snake has told us to cut long poles thin as himself ; the she-buffalo has shown us how to arrange them. What should we do now?' The fish replied, 'Look at the scales on my back. Get plenty of leaves and put them on the roof, one above the other like my scales.'

When they heard this the friends went home and built the first house.

16

TARAON (DIGARU) MISHMI

Tetuliang, Lohit F.D.

At first men had no clothes and no houses and no fire. They lived like deer among the trees. But when it was cold, they longed for fire for warmth and to cook their food. One day a man prepared a cord of cane and rubbed it against a tree until fire came from it. The fire jumped into the forest and sat there. But very soon it died. At that the man thought, 'The fire dies, what can we do?' Then he went to a river and found a stone and struck it against a bit of iron until fire came from it. This time he gave the fire some cotton to sit on and now it did not die but lived and grew.

Now men had fire, but how were they to get cloth? At first they dressed in leaves. Then they went high up in the mountains and found a kind of nettle from which they took the fibre, dried it above the fire and span it into yarn. A clever woman taught the others to make this into cloth.

Then men learnt how to collect wood and make rope to tie the pieces of wood together and so build houses. There were good trees in the mountains, but there was nothing to cut them with. So they collected *Mishmi teeta* from the hills and took it down to the Marwaris in the plains and sold it for silver rupees. With the rupees they went to Tibet and bought daos and axes.

The first tree to be cut was the Ero tree. It fell in a very old place where the demon of dysentery lived. Even now if we cut this tree we get dysentery, for the disease lives in the tree. It is a very bad tree. The men, having cut other trees into pieces, put pillars for their houses and found small strong trees for the floors and covered them with mats to make them flat and smooth.

17

WANCHO

Wakka, Tirap F.D.

In the beginning men were like deer ; they had no daos, no houses, they did not cultivate their fields. They lived like birds in nests high up in the trees.

One day a man threw some grain onto the ground and after a time found plants coming up. When they had grown and ripened he realized what had happened, and in this way cultivation began.

Presently men came down from the trees and lived in caves. They rubbed stones together and made fire. Many years afterwards they began to make nests on the ground and gradually turned them into houses. Previously they had eaten their rice raw, but now they learnt to cook it. The first houses were not at all comfortable, then they learnt to thatch the roofs with the leaves of fig trees, and later began to use palm-leaves as they do today.

Implements

18

SINGPHO

Imbu, Tirap F.D.

There was a craftsman named Intupwa who tried to cut wood with sharp stones. This was not very successful and he went out to find something better.

He asked the trees where he could find iron. But the trees replied, 'If we tell you, you will make a dao and cut us down.' Then he asked the grass and the grass replied, 'If I tell you, you will make a dao and cut us down.' He asked the wild animals and they replied, 'If we tell you, you will make arrows and kill us.'

At last he asked the water and the water said, 'Go to Numrang-Ningpu and you will find iron there.'

Intupwa went to the place but could not find any iron. But there was a goddess living there named Lepchan and during the night following Intupwa's arrival, she gave birth to a child as she slept.

This child was red as fire when he was born, but as he cooled, he became black as iron. Intupwa saw him and broke off a small bit and took it home. The child then broke into a hundred pieces, and a stream carried them away and scattered them about the world.

But Intupwa did not know how to work the iron he had found. As he was sitting outside his house wondering what to do, an elephant came by. When he saw the elephant's feet crushing everything beneath them, he learnt to make a hammer of stone. Then he heated the iron, but he had no tongs with which to hold it. He was thirsty and went down to a stream to drink. As he was drinking, a crab caught him by the hand. When he saw this he learnt how to make tongs. Now he was able to make daos, knives and arrow-heads.

SALT

19

BORI

Gatte, Siang F.D.

Long ago the two brothers Tani and Taro had a quarrel and Taro went away to Mimet (Tibet). As he was on his way, wandering over the snow-mountains and passing through great forests, he met a woman with white skin. She had hair that hung down to the ground and a large nose and great sharp teeth, but in spite of this Taro married her. The years passed and she bore him children ; at last she died. Taro carried her to the forest and buried her.

Meanwhile Tani, left alone at home, began to miss his brother's company and after some time decided to go and find him. On his way to Mimet, he came to the very place where Taro had buried his wife. He was thirsty and there was no water on the mountain, but at the grave he found a little spring. He took some of the water, but found it had a curious taste. On either side of the stream he saw some white stuff piled up. He liked its salty flavour, so he collected a full load and, forgetting all about his brother, carried it back home. It is because the children of Taro are living in Tibet that the people there have salt.

20

BORI

Gasheng, Siang F.D.

Formerly the Boris could not get salt. During the rains when the Sike river was flooded it brought down pieces of wood that had obviously been cut by human hands and the Boris therefore decided that there must be some people living higher up to the north. So they went up stream and over the hills until they came to Mimet. The Mimet people first of all gave the Boris a little salt to taste, as you give it to a mithun. Then they showed them their wool and their vessels and the coats they had made, and to everyone who went there they gave a little salt. When the Boris came back everybody assembled in the Bango (men's house) and all, young and old, tasted the salt. They liked it and wanted more. So they collected cane, certain kinds of creepers and leaves and took them to Mimet and received salt in exchange. Next time they went they took the skins of animals and got long woollen coats for them. Later they took more skins and rice also. The rate of exchange was then three loads of rice for one load of salt.

The Boris also took their goods to exchange with the Minyongs of Riga and Kerang. The Minyongs were so anxious to get salt that at one time they used to give the Boris even mithuns in exchange for it.

On one occasion when the people of Gasheng and Payung went to Tibet with a large quantity of things for barter the Tibetans killed two of them and stole their goods. The Bori warriors organized an expedition and went up to threaten revenge. The Tibetans apologized for what they had done and urged that there should be no quarrel but that their trade should continue. They agreed to improve the rate and to give one load of salt for only two loads of rice, and this rate continues to the present time. Later the Boris heard that salt could be had in Pasighat and they began to go there to get it. But at first they did not like the taste of the salt obtained from the plains, and in fact they still consider that Tibetan salt is superior to all other kinds. Gradually, however, the Pasighat salt became popular and today the Boris get most of their salt from Along, sometimes from Minyong intermediaries.

21

DHAMMAI (MIJI)

Nakhu, Kameng F.D.

In the mountains beyond Lhasa there is a place called Phoroa where there is a great lake of water. For a long time no human beings were able to find the way there. But one day a sheep who was very thirsty went out in search of water. As he went along he met a she-goat who had been to the lake and was coming back with drops of water falling from her lips. The sheep said, 'I'm very thirsty ; where can I get some water?' He licked the goat's mouth and it tasted salty. He said, 'Whatever you have drunk is very good. Take me to the place and I will drink too.' But the goat said, 'I cannot show you where I got this water, for if I do you will tell our enemies.'

The sheep said, 'What enemies have creatures like us?' The goat said, 'Our great enemies are men.' To this the sheep replied, 'But surely it will be a good thing to give this water to men.' 'No,' said the goat, 'men are full of sin and all they will do is to eat us, making our flesh tasty with the salt.' At that the goat ran away and refused to come back for all the sheep's pleading.

So then the sheep went his way following the she-goat's footprints till he came to the lake and drank the water. On the bank he saw piles of salt crystals and took some of them in his mouth to the Lord of Lhasa. The Lamas in Lhasa gave the salt to the Dhammais, who still get their salt from there.

The British tried to go to Lhasa and get salt but couldn't and so they made imitation salt in Assam, but this is not so good as the Tibetan salt.

22

KAMAN MISHMI

Lohit Valley, Lohit F.D.

After creating human beings Matai sent them all over the world. Some went to Sangilang, some to Tailong and others to different places.

One day a brother and sister at Tailong quarrelled and the sister hit her brother on the head with a stone. So they separated, the brother going to a place called Howa-Ui and the sister to a place called Te-Eng. When they grew up the brother went to search for a girl to be his wife, and the girl for a man to be her husband.

After many days had passed the brother and sister met. Since it was a long time since they had separated they did not recognize each other but fell in love and came together.

One day the boy asked his wife to comb his hair. As she was doing so she noticed the mark of the old wound on his head and this showed her that she was in fact living with her own brother. Full of shame she left her home and went to the forest.

After a time she met another man and married him. But she was always thinking of the evil she had done with her brother and this caused her to make mistakes in her work about the house. One day she put excreta in her husband's food by accident and when he tasted it, he was furious and drove her from his home.

The girl went wandering through the forest and at last in her weariness sat down beneath the Hanab tree. Ever since its fruit has been very sweet. Then she came down from the hills into the plains and lived there until she died.

In the place she was buried salt was found and many people came to get it. As the girl died in the plains salt is plentiful there and not in the hills.[7]

23

MOKLUM

Khimiyang, Tirap F.D.

There was an old woman who used to put the droppings from her nose into the food she was cooking to give it a nice taste. One day her son, who was very fond of his meals, asked her how she managed to make such good food. When she told him, he was very upset and drove her out of the house.

The old woman went weeping down to the plains and, as she went, her tears fell on the ground and turned into salt. She had some chickens with her and they pecked at the ground wherever her tears had fallen. When people saw the chickens pecking at the ground they wondered what it was, and picked up the salt and tasted it. They liked it very much and ever after put the old woman's tears into their food.

24

NOCTE

Kothung, Tirap F.D.

The Noctes and the Assamese were born of the same parents, but as time went by they forgot this.

In the hills there were salt mines. One day three Noctes were collecting salt near a river and they filled a boat with it. They had

[7] Recorded by T. K. Barua.

no oars and when the boat was full they let it drift down the river to the plains. There the people drew it to the shore and the Noctes gave them salt which they were very glad to have. In return they gave the Noctes red, blue and yellow cloth and they became friends. The Assamese asked the Noctes to come to the plains whenever they needed anything.

But as a result of the Noctes giving salt to the people of the plains, the latter gained possession of all the salt in the world, and now the Noctes, to whom it once belonged, have to go and buy it from them.

25

SINGPHO

Imbu, Tirap F.D.

When the first people came down from the Himalaya Mountains by the gold and silver and other ladders, they proceeded on their way towards the low country. The frogs living there thought that men would take away their country and give them a lot of trouble. So they fought against the travellers, but they were defeated.

The travellers went on their way and after a time were met by an army of snakes and defeated them also.

They went on their way and next encountered an army of hornets, but defeated them also.

Then on their way they came to a place where the ground was rough and broken and out of the cracks in the earth many gods came out and fought against them. This time it was the men who were defeated and driven back. When Mathum-Matta heard what had happened, he gave them a bamboo tube full of salt. He told them not to open it on the way but to take it to the gods and offer to share it half and half. If both they and the gods ate it they would, he said, soon make friends.

So the men took the salt to the gods and said, 'Share this with us and let us be friends.' The gods accepted the bamboo tube and were very pleased at the thought of getting salt. When they opened the tube there came out a girl called Chum-Machan,[8] whose body

[8] *Chum* is the Singpho word for salt.

was entirely made of salt. Both men and gods got hold of her and tried to break off bits of salt from her body, but she was frightened and ran away. She came to a place called Yang and there she spat and blew her nose and from this came a pool full of salt water. She went on her way and came in turn to Malung, Pangta, Moga, Jammo and Namsak. In each of these places she made pools of salt water. Finally she came to a place called Ketu where there was a very deep lake. She went into the water and sank to the bottom with the result that here there has always been plenty of salt.

Now the girl is young and from time to time desires a man. Her desire makes the water so hot that the steam rises from the lake and turns into salt.

26

WANCHO

Watnu, Tirap F.D.

Long ago there was an old woman with one son. She was a good cook and whatever she made for her son was very tasty. One evening after supper the boy went to the dormitory for the night. There he told the boys how well his mother cooked. One of them laughed at him and said, 'Your mother puts the mucus from her nose into the food and that is why the taste is so good.'

The boy came home and asked his mother if this was true and she said it wasn't. But he did not believe her, got into a great temper and drove her from the house. The poor old woman went to the river called Lukling and sat on the bank weeping. Presently she died and the place where her tears had fallen became a pool of salt.

CHAPTER ELEVEN

THE COMFORTS OF MAN

LIFE, said Samuel Johnson, 'is a pill which few can take without gilding' and in NEFA, where life is often hard and unrewarding, the people have found some sweeteners of existence to cheer and comfort them. Many of the tribes are passionately fond of chewing a soft wood mixed with lime, a habit which discolours teeth and lips and encourages a universal habit of spitting. But the Mishmis, Khamptis and Singphos have not taken to this substitute for betel and their beautiful teeth add greatly to the charm of their appearance.

Tobacco is universally popular; it is grown in small patches near the house or purchased from the plains and administrative centres. It is one of the most highly appreciated of presents. It is traditionally smoked in pipes, of which there is a wide variety in NEFA, ranging from the Wancho pipes elaborately carved with symbols of head-hunting, to the long silver pipes popular among Mishmi women and the simple wooden stumps used by the wilder tribes of the north.

A Bori tale describes how tobacco came into the world to console the living, a Gallong tale how it grew from the grave of a dead girl. These stories do not, however, repeat the very common motif of 'The Girl whom Nobody Loved', which is common all over tribal India—I have found it among the Konds, Gadabas and Juangs of Orissa, the Murias of Bastar and the Gonds of Madhya Pradesh. The main outline of the motif occurs in a Santal tale recorded by Bompas:

> This is the way that the chewing of tobacco began. There was once a Brahmin girl whose relations did not give her in marriage and she died unmarried. After the body had been burned and the people had gone home, Chando thought, 'Alas, I sent this woman into the world and she found favour with no one; well, I will confer a

gift on her which will make men ask for her every day.' So he sowed tobacco at the burning-place and it grew up and flourished.[1]

Curiously, in NEFA this motif which, elsewhere, is always associated with tobacco, is connected with opium, and Khampti, Moklum, Taraon Mishmi and Singpho stories repeat it with interesting variants in detail. The Khampti tale is on the regular lines; an ugly girl dies and is sent back to the world as something which all men will love. In the Moklum tale, however, the poppy grows from the body of an angry wife who commits suicide to revenge herself on her husband. There is no suggestion, as in the previous tale, of the wife being compensated: if anything it is the husband who derives far more pleasure from the poppy after his wife's death than he had derived from his wife herself while she was living.

The Taraon Mishmi tale introduces another variant. Here the girl is not ugly but all too beautiful, and it is not frustration from lack of love but weariness at too many contending suitors that causes her to die. From her body grow the poppy and tobacco plants and her disappointed lovers, who could not enjoy her in life, decide to divide and use the fruits of her body after death.

The Singpho tale, however, is much nearer the classic model, but introduces the interesting motif that the reason for the girl's unpopularity was the smell of the dirt from which she had been made; a god had created her by rubbing his hands together and making a ball of dirt which he turned into a girl. This notion of an evil and ominous body-odour occurs also in a Mishmi story. A dead boy is revived by having a living earthworm put in his mouth, but the smell of the worm makes his whole body so offensive that he has to go into exile.

The use of opium is restricted to a few tribes, but some form of rice-beer or millet-beer is universal. It is called by different names and varies considerably in quality, but is everywhere regarded with the same esteem. It is an essential element in the tradition of hospitality which is one of

[1] C. H. Bompas, *Folklore of the Santal Parganas* (London, 1909), p. 407.

the most admired of tribal virtues; it is an important element in the price paid for a bride; it is used in fines; it is almost a medium of exchange; it has its share in most religious rituals; no tribal conference can succeed without it; it is the tie that binds together those who make a pact of peace.

In fact, what the Hill Miri story says is true. 'Before rice-beer was invented, life was very dull. Men sat about feeling bored; they had nothing to talk about; they did not hold councils or tell stories or laugh.'

It is curious that the stories about this drink, so precious to the people and so important for their social life, should attribute its origin to such chances as a few drops falling on a hero's leg, a girl tying up rice with a certain kind of creeper, and—in two Hill Miri tales—to a woman putting blood, dirt and hair into the fermenting rice to improve it. The stories are far from worthy of their subject.

Betel

1

MOKLUM

Longke, Tirap F.D.

The mosquito sucks blood from the bodies of men and when its belly is full of blood, it looks red. This is why men chew betel to make their lips red. They learnt to do so from watching the mosquito.

Rice-Beer

2

BORI

Gasheng, Siang F.D.

The Wiyu Biridebo carried off the wife of Wiyu Takar Yapur. When Takar Yapur knew of it he went to Abo-Tani, and said to him, 'This fellow has carried away my wife ; come with me and we will hold a Kebang about it.' So Abo-Tani went with him to

Biridebo's house and, sitting before the door, held a Kebang. Abo-Tani said to Biridebo, 'You have carried away Takar Yapur's wife and you must give so many mithuns, so many dishes, so many beads and whatever else is proper.'

They went into the house and sat by the fire under the rack on which were stored rice and other things. As they were discussing what present Abo-Tani should receive, as is the custom for anyone who holds a Kebang, a drop of liquid fell on Abo-Tani's thigh. He wiped it off with his fingers and touched it with his lips and found it tasted very good. He said to Biridebo, 'Don't give me anything else, all I want is some of the stuff which fell on my leg.' Biridebo said, 'I don't want to give you that, for if I do you'll make a great deal of noise and will soon be quarrelling.' But Tani said, 'No, I must have it: I won't have anything else.' So Biridebo put some of it in a bamboo and gave it to him to drink. When Abo-Tani drank it he felt warm and happy and asked Biridebo what it was and how he made it. Biridebo said, 'This is rice-beer' and told him how it was to be made and finally gave him the *epop* which is placed in the beer to make it ferment.

Abo-Tani took the ferment back to his house. As he was going, he dropped it and it fell into a hole in the ground. Tani tried to get it out, but it went down too deep and he could not reach it.

At that moment a rat came out of the forest and Abo-Tani said to it. 'My *epop* has fallen into that hole ; get it out for me.' The rat said, 'If I do, what will you give me?' Tani said, 'I have got nothing with me at the moment, but I will take you to my house and let you live with me.' The rat was pleased at this and got the *epop* out of the hole. Abo-Tani took the rat home and ever since rats have lived in people's houses. When he got back, Abo-Tani made beer according to the method that Biridebo had shown him.

3

HILL MIRI

Chemir, Subansiri F.D.

Before rice-beer was invented, life was very dull. Men sat about feeling bored ; they had nothing to talk about ; they did not hold councils or tell stories or laugh.

From the droppings of the mithun the first dog was born.

In the forest the woman Kane-Timme lived by herself, and the dog went to her. Now this woman had never seen a dog and did not know what it was. 'Who are you?' she said. 'And why have you come to see me, for I live alone?' The dog said, 'I was born from the mithun's droppings and I live among men. But it was so dull there that I have come to you.' 'Well, what can I do about it?' asked the woman. 'Make rice-beer for them,' said the dog, 'and their lives will be brighter and happier.' 'Yes,' said the woman.

So Kane-Timme prepared rice-flour and millet-flour and brought every kind of leaf and fruit from the forest and mixed everything together. But the beer did not taste right. 'There is something wrong,' said the woman. 'Take some of your hairs and dirt and mix it in the beer and it will become sweet.' The woman did as the dog suggested, and the beer was right.

4

HILL MIRI

Godak, Subansiri F.D.

Kane-Timme had a little daughter. One day, when she had put her to sleep and gone to fetch water Topuk the owl carried the child away. Kane-Timme returned and, looking up, saw the owl flying into the sky with her daughter. She ran after it, crying and screaming, but could not catch it.

Abo-Teni heard the sound of weeping and came to the woman. 'What is the matter?' 'Topuk the owl has carred off my baby,' cried the mother. 'Do you know where it has gone?' Abo-Teni said, 'On a tree there was an owl eating a child. Your child is dead.' 'Then will you kill the owl for me?' Abo-Tani took his bow and arrows and shot the owl. He took the body to Kane-Timme. She was very pleased and gave him rice-beer to drink. He had never tasted it before, and was delighted with it. She said, 'Will you have beads or sacred bells or what can I give you?'

Abo-Teni said, 'I don't want anything, but that stuff you gave me just now was excellent. Tell me how to make it.' Kane-Timme went into her house and there took some of her hairs and blood and dirt and made the 'medicine' for the beer. Abo-Teni watched her secretly. Kane-Timme gave him the medicine and told him to be careful of it, using only a little at a time, for it would grow stronger as it grew older.

In this way Abo-Teni learnt how to make rice-beer and taught his children.

But there was a bird in Kane-Timme's house. It saw what she did and flew away to Assam. There it became the first Brahmin. This is why Brahmins do not drink beer, for they know its horrid origin.

5
SHIMONG
Shimong, Siang F.D.

Peddong-Kebo was a Wiyu in the form of a yak. As he was grazing in the forest, he trod on an ant, and as a result his neck became small, his head large, and his hind-quarters enormous. Shortly afterwards Kojam-Koja met and killed him. His blood flowed in two directions: some went to the Assam plain and became salt ; some went to Tibet and became salt ; some went to the Mishmi Hills and became a shrub, the fibres of which are used for the best cloth. His bones went to Assam and turned into iron. They cut off the udders and made the 'medicine' for rice-beer from them.

This is how people of old first made beer. Doni-Botte was married to Takar-Kardu-Dudeng, but Engo-Ngudu-Dupir carried the girl away. One day as they were sitting together, Doni-Botte saw them and said, 'This fellow has taken away my wife, but I will not accept money or ornaments for her. He must give me that sweet stuff he is making and then I will let her go.' So Engo-Ngudu-Dupir gave Doni-Botte the secret of making beer in a leaf-bundle. He told him to go to the home of the Wiyu on his way back and open the bundle there. As Doni-Botte did so, a bee flew down and carried off some of it. This is why honey is so sweet.

The woman Pedo-Dode-Demung died in Engo-Ngudu-Dupir's village. The marrow of her bones turned into millet. They planted it but it had no husband so, although it grew, there was no grain in the harvest. The wasp became the millet's husband and then the crop was good.

They took the grain home, prepared the beer and mixed the 'medicine' in it. It was sweet in those days, and did not make men drunk. But when the wasp put its poison into the grain, the beer gained its intoxicating power.

6

TARAON (DIGARU) MISHMI

Machima, Lohit F.D.

Long ago, a young girl went to the forest to fetch wood. When she had got sufficient, she tied it up in a bundle with a creeper. Next day, she had to go to another village and before starting she cooked food for the journey. She tied it up in leaves, but there was no string in the house and she used the creeper instead. She went along carrying the bundle in the hot sun until mid-day and then, when she ate her food, she found it made her drunk. This was how the Mishmis learnt to make rice-beer.

Opium

7

KHAMPTI

Choukham, Lohit F.D.

There was once an ugly girl, very black in colour, whose name was Kani. She was so ugly that no one could love her, and she used to weep and pray that God would have pity on her. At last he promised to send her back to the world as something which all men would love. 'No one,' he said, 'will ever be able to begin his work without kissing you first.' So she died and turned into the poppy plant which gives the opium that is loved by all men.

8

MOKLUM

Longke, Tirap F.D.

One day a man quarrelled with his wife and beat her with his stick. The woman ran away, resolving that she would hang herself and thus make her husband realize what a wrong he had done her. Although women often say this kind of thing without meaning it, this woman actually did hang herself, and her husband and his relatives found her body hanging from a tree and brought it home and burnt it in front of the house. After a time a seedling sprang up from the ashes and when it was fully grown there came from it a lovely purple flower. Her husband cut it open and collected the white juice. He took it home and after a time found that it had turned red. He thought that since this flower had grown from his wife's ashes it must be something precious. So he soaked a bit of cloth in the juice and put it in his pipe and smoked it. It gave him so much pleasure that he found he could not stop smoking it, and gradually more and more people grew the poppy flowers and began to smoke opium.

9

SHIMONG

Shimong, Siang F.D.

Kebo-Akbo was a Wiyu in the form of a yak who lived in the high northern mountains, where the Sun and Moon were born. But when the Sun and Moon came from their house, Kebo-Akbo was terrified and fled away to Assam, and died there. As he lay dying, seed fell from him, and urine after the seed. From his seed grew the poppy, from his urine the tea-plant. This is why those who take opium always drink a lot of tea.

10

SINGPHO

Imbu, Tirap F.D.

The god Phan-Ningsan rubbed his hands together and made a ball of dirt. He felt that it would not be a good thing to throw it away and presently he turned it into a girl. At first there was no life in her, so he put a charm into her ear with a golden pipe and she became alive. She was very beautiful and dark in colour. But the smell of the dirt from which she had been made was so bad that gods and men turned aside from her in disgust. All her life she could find no one to marry her and when she was very old she said to Phan-Ningsan, 'All my life I have been without a man. What did you make me for?' He said, 'You may die now and, when they put you in the grave, there will grow from your navel a plant which will be so desirable that all men will love you.'

So when the woman died she was buried and from her navel came a plant which bore flowers and fruit. A party of men went by the place and thought that the fruit must be good to eat. They cut it open and tasted the milky sap and this was so agreeable that everywhere people began to take it. This is how opium came to the world.

11

TARAON (DIGARU) MISHMI

Machima, Lohit F.D.

There was once a very lovely Chin princess. When she was ready, eight princes came to marry her. But they quarrelled among themselves so much that at last the girl was ready to die of weariness. At the time of her death she said to the princes, 'I can't marry any of you, for I am dying. When I am dead, burn my body and on no account bury it. On the fifth day after you burn the body, come to my tomb and see what you will see.' As she said this, she died.

The eight princes carried her body to the pyre and burnt it. On the fifth day, they went to the tomb, and found two plants growing from it. One was the opium plant which had beautiful flowers and fruits. The other was the tobacco plant. When the princes saw them, they were very happy and said, 'We could not marry her, but we can at least divide the fruits of her body.' They cut up the opium seed, the sap flowed and they caught it with bits of cloth as it fell to the ground. They put the cloth in their pipes and smoked it. This is how we learnt to take opium.

TOBACCO

12

BORI

Yihu, Siang F.D.

Long ago Doini-Botte and his wife Peddong-Nane cleared the forest on the side of the Wiyu-Among hills. They did not sow any seed, for everything grew of its own accord, rice and millet, beans and tobacco. But when the crop was ready, the wild animals came in from the forest and spoilt the crop. The only things they spared were the tobacco plants. Doini-Botte and Peddong-Nane wondered why this was. One day they picked the leaves and took them home.

A few days afterwards one of their children died. They were very sad and had no heart to go anywhere, but stayed weeping in the house. There was nothing to eat and they got very hungry and presently thought that they might as well eat the tobacco leaves which even the animals had rejected. 'If we die we die,' they said, 'but if the leaves are good we shall live.' But when they ate the tobacco, they found it so good that they began to cultivate the plant and later learnt to chew and then to smoke it.

13

GALLONG

Kamking, Siang F.D.

Tani made a clearing on the hill-side, but he had no seed to sow in it. He went to the Wiyu Mopin and his wife Ampir and said to them, 'I have cleared the forest, but I have nothing to sow and I have come to you for help.' The Wiyus, therefore, gave him every kind of seed, so much that he was unable to carry the load and asked for help. The Wiyus had a daughter who was weak and sickly, but her parents told her to help carry the load. As Tani was leaving they asked him to send their daughter back as soon as possible. But Tani kept the girl in his house while he himself went to sow the seeds. He was so excited over his work that he forgot all about the girl and when he came back he found her dead.

Tani was frightened and at once went to tell the Wiyu what had happened. When they heard that their daughter was dead they began to weep loudly, and told Tani to go home and bury the body in his clearing.

Tani went home and carried the body of the girl to his clearing and buried her there. Some time afterwards, while he was looking after his crop, he came to the girl's grave and there he found that a beautiful plant had sprung up. He was astonished at seeing it and picked some of the leaves and ate them. They made him feel very good inside. He took some of the leaves home and dried them and when the time came, he carefully collected the seeds and sowed them. This is how tobacco came to the world.

CHAPTER TWELVE

THE DISCOVERY OF FIRE

THE danger of fire is constantly before all the frontier people, for the houses of wood, bamboo and thatch are generally built close together and fire quickly spreads throughout an entire village. Sufficient water is seldom available and in any case fires often occur when most of the villagers are away in their fields. Every year there are heavy losses from this cause throughout the area, although due to the fact that the granaries are built at some distance from the villages, the food supply is not usually affected.

To meet this danger some tribes employ regular fire-watchers; others rely on dreams and supernatural methods of preventing fire and even of extinguishing it.

For just as the tribal theory of disease is that it is normally caused by supernatural agencies, although certain illnesses or accidents may have a natural cause, so fire is, in the opinion of many tribes, the result of an attack by a dangerous spirit, even though at the same time it is recognized that it can be caused by an enemy or by some natural accident. The Adis of the Upper Siang speak of a Wiyu called Piang-Rongne who kindles disastrous fires in their villages. The Hill-Miris attribute fires to the spirits Churum-Pira and to Ler-Karom. The Sherdukpens attribute them to Mikam, the god of fire. The Mishmis have a fire-spirit who is the son of the Supreme God, Intaiya. His name is Erosu and his body is full of fire. He lives in the sky and wherever he sees evil he comes down and destroys it with his flames.

The Minyongs and other groups of northern Siang maintain regular fire-watchers, who remain at home when everyone else is in the fields and parade up and down with spears erect to frighten away the Fire-demons, Banjibangman and Piang-Rongne Wiyu. There do not now seem to be any ceremonies observed at an actual outbreak of fire, but a hundred years ago, Father Krick described what happened when fire broke out in the Padam village of Membo in 1853 which he was visiting at the time. 'On hastening to the spot,' he writes, 'what was my surprise to see standing on the top of each roof one or two men brandishing long swords, and endeavouring to kill the fire-demon. The next thing to do was to imprison the spirit of fire on the scene of the disaster. The burnt houses were hedged in and surrounded with devil-scaring emblems. In spite of these precautions, it was feared that the devil might escape and take refuge into some corner of the village, so the very next day all the men, armed to the teeth, with beating of drums, and fearful howls, set out in pursuit of the devil, far into the jungle. The two families, whose dwellings had been burnt down, were banished for one year, for if any of their members were to set foot in a house within those twelve months, the building would not escape from the flames.'[1]

Today precautions against fire are taken in the light of warning dreams. If anyone, even a child, dreams that snow is falling, a tiger has roared in the street or the sky is filled with clouds, he at once tells the elders and they observe taboo for one day. An old man, taking a plantain-root filled with water and a basket, goes from house to house. At each he is given a burning stick, which he extinguishes in the water and drops into his basket. Then waving his spear he goes down to the nearest stream. The boys of the *dere* (dormitory), who have collected a pile of bits of plantain-stem, follow him, throwing the bits after him to drive away the Fire-demon. Finally the old man throws his pot and basket into the stream, and returns home.

The Bori attitude to fire is similar. If a house catches fire the people put a charm in some rice-beer and throw it at the house along with earth hurriedly collected from a grave and the black dye which is used to colour their cloth. If there is an otter's skin in the village, they throw this also. It is believed that these objects drive away the Wiyu, Yasupiyang, who causes the fire.

[1] W. Krick, 'Account of an Expedition among the Abors in 1853', *Journal of the Asiatic Society of Bengal*, Vol. IX (1913).

The Boris also have a system of fire-watching. Young boys of twelve to fifteen years of age, called Lamkangs, are appointed for this purpose.

There are generally three of these Lamkangs, of whom one is the cook for the other two. Their main duty is to go round the village to protect it against fire. Early in the morning you may see them, marching round the houses and shouting 'Guard your fires.' They do this three times in a day and at night they go at irregular intervals to inspect the granaries and ensure there is no trouble in the village. In the old days when the country was unsettled there were more of these boys and they used to guard the villages against the approach of possible enemies as well as against fire.

These boys live entirely in the *bango* (dormitory); they cook their food and eat and sleep there—it is their real home. The villagers support them by gifts of rice which are kept tied up in baskets hanging from the roof. They do not function during the rains when the danger of fire, of course, is less and their heaviest duties come during the busy season of the cold weather.

The association of young boys with fire-protection probably accounts for the rule that the Lamkangs must never build a hearth in the *bango* or their homes, nor make the bamboo tongs used to lift vessels off a fire. Only older men may do this; if boys do it, it will stunt their growth.[1]

In Hill Miri opinion Churum-Pira Wiyu, who lives between earth and heaven and appears as a little child, is very mischievous and sets fire to houses and destroys a village's prosperity. Another Wiyu of Fire is Ler-Karom. But should a village catch fire, the Nibo-shamans do not sacrifice to these spirits, but to Niddo-Pumpo, the spirit of rain or water, who they hope will come down to quench the flames. If a house catches fire, the neighbours throw eggs at it and fan the air with their shields away from their own homes, crying to Ler-Karom to go away.

The Mishmis have a prophylactic sacrifice to prevent a second fire after one has occurred. Five days after the

[1] There is a similar organization among the Padams.

disaster a priest makes a hole in the ground near the site of the fire, fills it with water and covers it with a leaf. He calls upon Erosu, the god of fire, and 'catches' him in a plantain leaf, ties him up and pushes him into the water to drown him. It is said that steam rises from the water as a sign that the god is dead.

To the Sherdukpens, Mikam is the god of fire (*mi*). He is a restless spirit, always moving from place to place. He visits Rupa every year and if he is not quickly appeased he burns down a house, and indeed has caused several disasters both in Rupa and Shergaon. The orthodox method of appeasing him is for the Jiji-priest to take a cow or a pig to a place where two streams meet and let it go in Mikam's name. As Buddhists the Sherdukpens will not kill a sacrifical animal themselves, and the Buguns profit by this, for they have no such taboo and catch the animals for food. The idea is that as the animal goes into the water, so the god will become wet and cool. If they fail to do this, it is believed that small children in the village may go dumb —and in fact there is a certain percentage, about 4 per cent, of cases of deaf-mutism among the many sufferers (28 per cent of the whole tribe) from goitre in this region.

If the Sherdukpens hear that there has been a fire in another village, they offer a chicken to Mikam to prevent him coming to their's. The headmen give orders that all the fires must be put out and the Jijis go round the village and collect a little ash from the hearth of every house. They take the ash down to the confluence of two streams, throw it in and let the chicken go. The people collect at the village temple and the Jiji warns them to watch their fires. Then he makes new fire with bamboo and cane and some bombax cotton, and the people carry the new fire to their homes.

The stories recorded here about the origin of fire also reveal a dual attitude. Some of them attribute it to natural means and some to a gift or theft which takes us into the world of myth and magic.

For example, there is a general belief that fire, early in the history of the world, took refuge in a stone or a tree. A Dafla story describes how at the time of a great flood Fire fled away from the rising waters and as a last refuge darted into a stone and has remained there ever since to be the servant of man. Similarly, a Wancho story describes how once Fire and Water had a quarrel and in his fright Fire ran away and hid in the trunk of a tree.

On the basis of this there are stories which tell how men learnt long ago to make fire by forcing 'two stones to fight each other' or, as in a Wancho story, how fire was discovered when a man threw a stone at a bird and it struck a rock instead and sparks flashed from it. In this way men learnt how to use the steel and flint. A Minyong story describes how originally fire was in the possession of a Wiyu called Sedi-Botte. When he died, he was buried with his fire, but the corpse was dug up and the Wiyu's body was found still fresh and his heart beating. The blood turned into a flint and the flesh into a bit of iron.

Other stories recall how men had to get fire from various animals. The Moklum tradition is that it was originally in the possession of the owl who, in those days, was naked and used to feel very cold. Men, on the other hand, had wings and feathers but they exchanged these for the owl's flint and iron and henceforth it was they who had fire. Another Moklum story tells us that fire was originally possessed by the monkey and men had to get it away from him by sending red ants to bite him. A Nocte tradition places fire in the possession of a crow who gave it to men, though this tribe also knows the Moklum story of the monkey. A Panggi tale traces the origin of fire to the death of a great Wiyu. The Sherdukpens say fire was formerly in the country of the Sirinpu demons, whence it was brought for men by the bat. A Shimong tale says that fire comes from one of the eyes of a Wiyu.

1

BUGUN (KHOWA)

Senchong, Kameng F.D.

Formerly men had no fire. One day they sent the firefly to bring it from the Sun. At that time the firefly had long legs and great wings, but no light in its tail. When it came near the Sun its legs and wings were shrivelled by the heat and its tail caught fire and it was so frightened that it turned round and flew back to earth. It gave its fire to men, but kept a spark always in its tail.

2

DAFLA

Subansiri Frontier Division

(From G. D. S. Dunbar, *Abors and Galongs*, p.65)

Once upon a time fire fought water.[3] And all things growing in the jungle, green things to whom water was life, helped water. So water rose steadily out of its bed in the valley below and followed fire up and up the mountain side. And fire fled up to the top of the mountain and flickered there, for he could go no further. And water rose and rose and covered all the low hills and filled all the valleys and at last was lapping the topmost peak on which fire had taken refuge. Then, just as water began to break over the very top of the mountain, fire darted as a last refuge into a stone and has remained there ever since to be the servant of man. And then water sank and sank down into its bed once more.

3

HILL MIRI

Chemir, Subansiri F.D.

In the days before men knew the use of fire, they had a lot of trouble, for they were always cold and their raw food tasted horrid. So one day they went to Si-Duinye the Sun and asked him for something that would keep them warm and enable them to cook their food. Si-Duinye did not know what to do, so he sent Wiyu Tessi to call Wiyu Kujum-Dad. Wiyu Tessi went to the Land of the Wiyus and said to Kujum-Dad, 'Si-Duinye wants you to come

[3] A similar tradition has been recorded among the Ao Nagas. 'Long, long ago fire and water fought. Fire could not stand before water, and fled and hid in bamboos and stones, where it is to this day.' The grasshopper saw where it had gone and told the monkey, from whom man stole it.—Mills, *The Ao Nagas*, p. 100.

at once.' Kujum-Dad wondered what he had done wrong and went hurriedly to him and said, 'What is the matter? Why have you sent for me?'

'It is nothing,' said Si-Duinye. 'Men have need of warmth and light. Can you give it to them?' Kujum-Dad said, 'You must make two stones quarrel. When they strike each other, the fire inside will come out. And you must get cotton from the bombax tree to catch it.'

This is how fire came to men.

4

MINYONG

Parong, Siang F.D.

Sedi-Botte was a Wiyu in the form of a man. He alone had fire in his possession. When he died, they buried him in the ground and his fire with him. Doini-Pollo said, 'There is no fire in the world ; how can we give it to men?' He went to Sedi-Botte's grave and dug up the corpse. But everything had rotted away, everything except the heart which was still fresh and living. Doini-Pollo took it out and cut it open and the blood spurted out. The blood turned into a flint and the flesh turned into a bit of iron. Doini-Pollo put them together on the ground, and went to his own place.

Presently a Wiyu in human form called Missum-Botte came along the path. He picked up the flint and iron and played with them, striking them together. Sparks flew from them and thus fire came to the world.

5

MOKLUM

Khimiyang, Tirap F.D.

At first men had feathers and wings but they had no fire. There was an owl who had flint and iron and used to make fire with it. This was because he was quite naked and used to feel very cold. One day some men met the owl and gave him their feathers and wings in exchange for the flint and iron. After that men were able to make fire.

6

MOKLUM

Khimiyang, Tirap F.D.

Rang created men in the sky and sent them down to earth. But they were very wild and did not know how to build houses or cook their food. They lived like animals in the jungle on wild fruit and leaves. When he saw this Rang sent two spirits, Sengwa and Phengwa, to teach them how to build and cook. The two spirits gave them daos and showed them how to cultivate ; they gave them cooking-pots and taught them the use of fire and how to eat boiled rice.

7

MOKLUM

Longke, Tirap F.D.

Fire was brought from Rang by the monkey. He came down to earth from the sky, climbed up a tree and, sitting on one of the branches, shouted, 'I've got all sorts of things you haven't.' He danced among the branches, beating a drum and blowing a trumpet. Hearing the noise a lot of people collected and when they saw the strange bright thing in the monkey's hand they wanted it. They threw stones at him, but he climbed higher up the tree, right to the very top.

But men are cleverer than monkeys. They got a nest of red ants and put it at the foot of the tree. The ants climbed up the tree and bit the monkey all over and he was soon jumping about patting his body with his paws. This made him drop the fire to the ground and after that men had it instead.

8

NOCTE

Tut, Tirap F.D.

The tiger said, 'Fire will come from my ear.' But the elephant said, 'No, fire will come from *my* ear.' In the end the gods gave fire to the crow and the crow gave it to men.

9

NOCTE

Havi, Tirap F.D.

At first men had no fire and it was all owned by the monkey. But men felt the need of fire more and more and one day one of them dug out some insects from the earth and put them on the monkey's body. When they bit him, he jumped and threw the fire down and the men went off with it.

10

PANGGI

Geku, Siang F.D.

There was a man called Peddong-Doini-Ningkang-Kanga, whose brother, Peddong-Doini-Ninur-Botte, was the greatest man of his day. When Ningkang-Kanga died, his brother refused to bury his body in the ground.

He took a rib from it and made it into a sword. He made the fingers into ornaments, the skull into a bowl, his nails into a spear-head, his thumb into an arrow. The cord round the waist turned into a poisonous snake. The marrow of his bones became rice-grain.

Ninur-Botte threw the rain-hat into a stream and it became a duck. He pulled out the lower teeth and turned them into a flint ; he pulled out the upper and turned them into iron. The nose became the wild plantain, very large, whose leaves are used to thatch a house. The tongue became a fish.

From the fire kindled by Ningkang-Kanga's teeth all the forest was burnt and the fire spread throughout the world. The Wiyus saw the birds with their feathers burnt off and were very sad. So Peddong stood up and made water to quench the fire. All rivers flow from the stream of Peddong's urine.

11

SHERDUKPEN

Rupa, Kameng F.D.

Originally men used to eat their food raw, for they had no fire.

All the fire in the world was in the land of the Sirinpus.[4] The Sirinpus used to kill birds, roast them and put them aside for supper.

One day the bat flew over that country and stole one of the birds and carried it away to the land of men. He sat on a tree and let the roasted bird fall to the ground. A man happened to be resting beneath the tree ; he picked up the bird and ate it and found it delicious. He took a piece of the cooked meat home and said, 'How can we get fire to cook with? Our raw meat is horrid, but this cooked stuff is very good.' The bat had followed the man to his house and hearing what they said, he offered to bring them fire and they asked him to do so.

The bat flew away to the land of the Sirinpus. All the fire they had was the size of a little ball that you could hold in your hand. The bat stole it and as he was escaping the Sirinpus tried to kill him. But he said, 'Don't kill me ; I am your father-in-law.' When he said that, they let him go.

So the bat brought fire to men and since then there has been no fire in the land of the Sirinpus, but men have been able to cook their food.

12

SHIMONG

Shimong, Siang F.D.

Banji-Botte made the ear of the mithun-spirit Polung-Sabbo into a bamboo, which is hollow as an ear is. The tail became the tree whose poisonous bark is used for killing fish. The bones became a tree, whose leaves give a man itch when he touches them.

As Banji-Botte was thus employed in turning the body of Polung-Sabbo into so many things, the water-spirit Ladang-Laiyu and Epom-Wiyu, a spirit who lives in the forest, came and said, 'Don't throw away the eyes, but give us one each, for we have

[4] The Sirinpus and Sirinmus are the legendary demons, whose home was—and perhaps still is—beyond the Himalayas. Here is the Land of Women ; it was from here that fire was stolen by the bat and brought to men ; it was the Sirinpus who were the chief enemies of the Lamas in the early days ; from them come the mosquitoes who bother men and the rats which eat the sacred books.

no fire.' Ladang-Laiyu took one of the eyes down into the water where it lights the village of the water-spirits down below. He uses it to make the water flash and glitter when it rushes over rocks. Epom-Wiyu took the other eye to the hills and sometimes at night you may see him wandering with it and hear him crying 'Huey-huey'.

13

WANCHO

Pomau, Tirap F.D.

Formerly, Fire and Whirlwind were brothers just as Water and Mist were brothers. But Water and Fire have always been enemies. The Wind is the friend of Fire against Water and he fights the rain and drives it before him.

Fire is frightened of Water. Once upon a time, Fire and Water had a quarrel and, in his fright, Fire ran away and hid in the trunk of a tree. This is why it is possible to get fire by rubbing bits of wood together.

14

WANCHO

Senua, Tirap F.D.

When men had no fire they lived like animals in the forest. One day as a man was cutting the trees in his clearing, he threw a stone at a bird. The stone struck a rock and sparks flashed from it. The man threw another stone and there was another spark, which set fire to some dry bushes nearby. This was how fire came to men.

CHAPTER THIRTEEN

THE BEGINNINGS OF RELIGION

In this Chapter I have collected a number of stories which illustrate how certain religious institutions came into being. This is not the place for a general account of religion in NEFA, which is a large and complex subject; it will suffice to say that the people have a strong sense of the unseen world, which they people with an immense variety of gods, spirits and demons, and into which they themselves expect to enter after death. Every tribe, so far as our information goes, believes in a Supreme Being, who is just and benevolent, though ideas about his influence on human affairs vary greatly from place to place.

The Buddhist tribes—the Monpas and Sherdukpens, the Singphos and Khamptis—practise a religion that is an interesting blend of Buddhist and tribal ideas. By the Sherdukpens, for example, the Lord Buddha, whom they call Konchosum, does not seem to be regarded as a god in the ordinary sense. He is the teacher of righteousness; temples and shrines are erected in his name; there are festivals and sacrifices in his honour. But he is not the Supreme Creator of the world and he stands rather apart from the tribal pantheon.

At the head of this pantheon is Chungba-Sangyat and his two brothers Lopong-Rimbuche (sometimes Lopong-Chungba) and Chom-dande. All three live in the sky, whence the two brothers once looked down on the watery expanse of the primaeval ocean and wondered where mankind could live. They threw down a lotus flower which covered the face of the waters with its blooms and called to the four winds to bring the dust which mingled to make the world. Chungba-Sangyat created fish and was angry when they denied his creative power. He appointed a King to rule over the birds. He showed mercy on the young Tepagalu when he called upon him in his despair. He saved the magic deer threatened with poison and removed the evil from its body. Lopong-Chungba tried to protect mankind against the terrible cannibalistic birds who were preying upon them.

Chungba-Sangyat and his brothers, who are almost a committee of Supreme Beings, appear to be imagined as great, powerful and benevolent, but by no means omniscient or omnipotent. In fact at one point Lopong-Chungba admits himself defeated and Chungba-Sangyat is successfully defied by the fishes.

Khampti Buddhism is of a purer kind and the Khamptis tend to look down on their neighbours, the Singphos, who have admitted into their religion many ideas of lesser spirits (who have to be placated by sacrifice) and even of sorcery.

The stories recorded here deal in the main with three subjects—the origin of gods or spirits, the origin of the priests or shamans who were created to mediate between them and mankind, and the origin of certain sacrifices. They illustrate a strongly anthropomorphic notion of the unseen spirits, a belief in their power to harm or help humanity and the importance of sacrifice for their appeasement.

I hope to deal with this subject in greater detail in the second volume of this collection.

1

DHAMMAI (MIJI)

Nakhu, Kameng F.D.

The Lord Jumu-Nuchu was not at first known to the Dhammais. He used to live with the Nichangs (Monpas). Once when the Dhammais went to tax the Monpas they found a man in a village called Tembang who was not able to pay and they gave him a lot of trouble.

But this man had a goat which he had set aside for the Lord Jumu-Nuchu and when they pressed him so hard he gave it to them. They tried to sell it, but before they could do so, it died and after its death the children of the Dhammais fell ill. They sent for a priest but he said that it was the god of the Monpas who was troubling the children and he knew of no way of appeasing him. So they sent him to call a Lama and he built a stone shrine for them and worshipped Jumu-Nuchu. But he did not kill the goat they gave ; he only offered it before the shrine and let it go.[1]

2

HRUSSO (AKA)

Hussigaon, Kameng F.D.

Khabrou-Phogo-Sogo is the Lord of the Earth. Huphu-Liti is the Lord of the Mountains and Siksilia-ao is the Lord of the Waters. These are the three greatest of all the gods. Their father's name is Matti-Dau and he lives in the sky in Ban-Nebine which is the place the rain comes from.

When the boys grew up they said to their father, 'How can we live here, for we will get no wives in a place like this? Show us somewhere better where we can make our homes.' Matti-Dau said to Khabrou-Phogo-Sogo, 'Go down and be Lord of the Earth and look after everything that is born of earth, men, trees and grass.'

To Huphu-Liti he said, 'You will be Lord of the Mountains and you must look after the mountains and the animals that live on them.'

To Siksilia-ao he said, 'Go and be Lord of the Waters and care for whatever living creatures there are in the rivers and see to it that wherever you are there is plenty of water.'

Then these three brothers descended from the heavens and came down as Lords of the Earth, the Mountains and the Waters.

3

IDU MISHMI

Ichuli, Lohit F.D.

When the world was burnt and all the water dried up, Matomai, the god of rain, gave birth to Asoso-Aru and sent him with an iron stick to bring water out of the rocks and to make mountains.

When Asoso-Aru came back his hair was white and his iron stick broken. He said, 'I have been everywhere and have brought

[1] The Dhammais, although not Buddhists, worship the Lord Buddha under the name of Jumu-Nuchu—*nuchu* means a god.

water from the rocks for the sake of men.' But in the Diu country, which lies towards China, he left a bird to get water. After a time, the bird came back to the Mishmi land and made water flow from the mountains and down a long channel which he dug. The bird said, 'All those who are mad and sick and woman in childbirth should worship with this water and all will be well.'

And still today when people are sick or a woman has a difficult delivery we bring water in a bamboo from a mountain stream and give it to her to drink. We offer it in sacrifice and the child is born easily.

4

IDU MISHMI

Ichuli, Lohit F.D.

There was a woman who had a child every year but they always died, for the Atu spirits ate them, as they used to kill and eat so many of the children in those days. The poor woman wept and wept and presently one of the gods hearing her cries came to her and asked her what the matter was. When she told him, the god gave her a dao and said, 'When you put your child to sleep in his basket, lay the dao above it.'

So the next time the woman gave birth to a baby boy, she laid him in a basket and placed the dao above him. Then when late at night, the Atu spirit came to devour him, the mother cut him into pieces with her dao.

The name of this child was Atungi-Aru. When he grew up, he married and had a son called Aru-Pe who became the first Igu-priest. Aru-Pe used to go with his dao whenever he heard that a child had been born and would sit by it until the Atu came. Then he would spring up and kill him with many blows.

So still today, when we offer sacrifice at the birth of a child, we place a dao beside him and recite this story.

5

IDU MISHMI

Ichuli, Lohit F.D.

The goddess Malumai was so beautiful that everyone wanted to marry her. But she did not want to marry anyone, for she said to herself, 'If I conceive and have to bear a child, it will give me a great deal of pain, so it will be better not to marry at all.' But one day when she went to work in the clearing the wind blew into her and she conceived. When the people saw that she was big with child they asked her who the father was. She said, 'I have never been to a man and I do not know how I have got a child.' But there was a man there called Anzoru who said, 'This is my child.' And he put aside a cock and a hen to sacrifice when the child was born.

Eight months passed, but the child was not born. In the ninth month they prepared rice-beer, but still the child was not born. In the tenth month Anzoru went to catch fish and the child was born.

Directly after the birth, Anzoru went to get a priest called Arupa to perform sacrifice. When Arupa came, he found tall grass growing round the house on this side, this side, and that side and he could not see the dangerous spirits for the grass. So he cut down the grass first and stored it in the house. Then he put some beer in a bamboo and the blood of a fowl and offered it to Nani-Intaiya. After the sacrifice Anzoru ate the fowl, the priest Arupa drank the rice-beer and the mother ate the fish. The house was taboo for ten days. Then they sacrificed again, bringing water from a mountain stream. The priest said to the god, 'Are we now clean of the taboo? Is there anything more we need do? Will the child be well?'

We still offer water in sacrifice so that a child shall be clean as water, and for ten days after the birth of a baby the parents cannot go to the forest.

6

IDU MISHMI

Ichuli, Lohit F.D.

In the old days when the Mishmis were always fighting one another, a man called Alyomi was born to bring peace. When he was old enough to do anything there were two men, Yutute and Potonye, fighting each other. Alyomi went to make peace between them, taking his cat with him. The cat went ahead of him and on the way he caught and ate many rats and as a result left his droppings all along the path. Then, very tired, he lay down to sleep. When Alyomi came to the spot he found him lying among his droppings. There was a horrid smell and he stopped up his vent with a leaf.

Alyomi went on and made peace between Yutute and Potonye. He gave an egg to the priest to sacrifice to ensure lasting peace between them and for his own safety. The priest cried, 'Let the man who brought peace live well and be in health.' He put the egg on the ground and Alyomi broke it with its foot and went home.

Ever since we have sacrificed an egg whenever there is a meeting of the tribe, in order to free the chief man present of any blame.

7

IDU MISHMI

Ichuli, Lohit F.D.

There was a priest called Sineru who lived towards the sunset He used to go to help people whenever they felt sick. When he went to a house where a man had died he would purify it so that the ghost would not come again. The only difficulty was that in those days there were no leaves in the world which could be used for such ceremonies.

So Sineru went to Kandibro, where the stars are, and brought tree-seed down through Mitumembro, which lies between the earth and sky. On the way he passed through many sky and earth villages—Adu-Embro, Yuyua, Ipussi, Satilo, Lemo, Iduba, Idunzo, Abola, Adega, Milomidro, Epe-Embro, Metta-Embro, Alombro and Assimbro. He planted the seed in Assimbro and it was from here that trees spread all over the world.

Ghosts are very fond of the fruit of this tree which is offered whenever the unseen beings are worshipped, for in the leaf there is a fire and when the spirits see it they go away. This is why the priests use the leaves to free mourners of their taboos. All the taboos run away when they see the leaves.

8

MOKLUM

Longke, Tirap F.D.

Two brothers lived on the hill called Mochoi-Singrabhum. One day they left their house and travelled down to a great river. Tired and hungry they prepared their food on the bank. The elder brother heated water in a hollow bamboo and peeled and cooked some roots. The younger brother also heated water in a bamboo, but he put the roots in to cook with their skins. The result was that the elder brother's food was ready first and he ate it quickly and crossed the river. Immediately after he had crossed, the water came down in a flood and the younger brother could not get over.

The elder brother climbed up the opposite bank and shouted to his brother to follow him, but the water was too strong. So the elder brother remained in the hills and became a Moklum and the younger went down to the plains and became a Singpho.

When the water subsided, the elder brother came to find his younger brother, but could not find a trace of him. The next year the elder brother again came and this time he found the younger boy and his mother and asked them to come to his house. The younger boy refused, but later he sent his mother and the elder brother kept her in his house by force.

Then a year later, the elder brother asked the younger for some seed. The younger boy was angry at the loss of his mother and so instead of seed he gave a parcel of boiled rice and when the elder brother planted it there was no harvest. When he asked why this was, the younger brother said that it was because he had taken away his mother. So the elder brother said, 'What shall I do with my mother?' The younger brother said, 'Cut her into two pieces as sacrifice and you will always have a good harvest.' So saying the younger brother gave the elder some fresh seeds.

The elder brother went to his house and sacrificed his mother. Then he planted the fresh seeds and got a good harvest and this is why the people of this tribe used to sacrifice human beings.

9

NOCTE

Tut, Tirap F.D.

Once long ago two men had a quarrel. One of them escaped into the sky and fired at his enemy on earth. The man on the earth fired back. After a time they both became gods.

10

PASI

Siang Frontier Division

(From G. D. S. Dunbar, *Abors and Galongs*, pp. 66 f.)

Now in those days, when gods and men lived together, a quarrel arose for the possession of the rich plain country. The gods said it belonged to them, but this the men disputed. At last it was agreed that the decision should rest on the proof of a sign ; the rich country should belong to whoever could cook a stone. So mortals and immortals took stones and earth in their hands. First of all the gods tried to cook the stones, but fierce though they made the fire the stones remained stones still. But the men cheated the gods and obtained the sign by a trick, for they hid an egg amidst the earth and stones ; and this they roasted and showed to the gods. So the gods went away from the pleasant smiling lands of the plains to dwell for ever in the high hills and deep forests of the uplands.

It is told that when gods and men lived no longer together, but dwelt as immortals on the high hills and men in the plain below, that a mortal was seized by the gods and held by them a prisoner. To buy back his liberty the men offered the gods fowls and pigs and mithun taking their offerings to the mountains, the dwelling-places of the gods. These offerings the gods said they would accept for the man and the people returned to their homes. But in the evening, instead of the man who had been a prisoner, the fowls and pigs and mithun came wandering back to the homesteads. Again the offerings were taken up to the gods and again their gifts returned to them ; and the gods remained angry and held the man a prisoner. So the man went up a third time and said to the gods, 'We have given you, twice, those that you asked, but each time you have driven them back to us, and still you will not release our brother.' And the gods said, 'How can we give you back your brother, your offerings do not come to us—they go straight back to you. So we cannot set our prisoner free.' Then the men said to the gods, 'If what we give to you we give with life, then of a truth it returns to us, so we will kill the offerings that the spirit may go to you and return to us no more.' So the first sacrifices were made, and the captive was restored. And from that day the spirit of the creature sacrificed has, in death, gone out to the gods.

11

SHERDUKPEN

Shergaon, Kameng F.D.

In the old days when we wanted to sacrifice to our gods we had nothing to offer them. So one day our ancestors went hunting and caught a red deer. They took it to their god and let it go. They did not kill it but the god ate the deer.

After this they always sacrificed in this manner. But one day when they offered a deer it escaped before the god could eat it. The priests followed it into the forest and came to a place where there were many ant-hills of every sort of colour. They broke a black ant-hill and a black cow came out of it. They broke a red ant-hill and a red cow came out of it. They broke a white ant-hill and a white cow came out of it.

Ever since we have kept cows in our villages and offer them to the gods. But we do not kill them: we give them to the gods and when the gods have accepted them, the Buguns kill them.[2]

[2] The Lamas are regarded as set apart from other men by their greater love of living creatures. A Lama at Shergaon told me that he must never use a plough for fear of killing a worm in the soil. He should not eat a fish until it had been dead for twenty-four hours, so that any 'warmth of life' would have time to leave its body. Strictly speaking, a Lama should not eat any meat, but in practice and especially in view of the rule that compels a Buddhist monk to accept anything he is offered, the Lamas do eat fish, venison and other game, but only if the killing is done by other persons.

This, of course, adds a complication to the business of sacrificing animals to the forest and water spirits. For even the Jijis (priests) ought not to kill the domestic animals who are the suitable offerings for this purpose. The above story represents one of several attempts to solve the problem.

12
SHERDUKPEN
Rupa, Kameng F.D.

When the world was made and men first created, the great God Lopung-Chungba made Jumu-Wang-Sing, the god of the forests. After his son had gone away deep into the jungle Lopung wondered how people would know of him. For he was afraid that he might injure people. So he created the Jiji-Priest whose name was Bonsarap and sent him to serve and help mankind.

On his way the Jiji met Konchosum [the Lord Buddha] who asked him, 'Who are you and why have you come here?' 'I am a priest,' replied the Jiji, 'and I have come to sacrifice to the gods and spirits and so save mankind from distress.' But Konchosum said, 'You cannot stay here, for you are a sinner. I am righteous and I teach righteousness. I take the life of no living thing, I injure no living thing. But you kill every kind of creature. You must go away.'

As they were talking Jumu-Wang-Sing came to the place and said to Konchosum, 'It is true that you are righteous and a teacher of righteousness. You take the life of no living thing. But I am not like you. I am a spirit of the forest and I eat meat and drink blood. If you are not willing to give me my food, at least allow the Jiji to give it to me.'

Konchosum was wise and merciful and he said, 'Very well, you may do as you wish.' Then he said to the Jiji, 'Have you a book of sacrifice?' 'No,' said the Jiji. 'Then how can you sacrifice? How can you know what to do? I know every kind of goodness because I have the sacred books.'

The Jiji went to Junia-Wang-Sing and told him what Konchosum had said. The god of the forest replied, 'It is not too difficult to live a good life. Follow the laws of goodness: do not eat onions or the flesh of deer or pig or fowl. There are certain kinds of fish you must avoid. Do this and I will come to you in dreams and tell you what to do.'[3]

[3] The Jijis, like the Lamas, observe (though less strictly) a certain number of food taboos, and they avoid the sin of killing animals for the forest-gods, who so eagerly demand blood and meat, by taking the animals to the altar and there releasing them in the name of the god. The Buguns or Hrussos then come and kill the animals, so the god is satisfied and nothing is wasted.

13

SHERDUKPEN

Rupa, Kameng F.D.

At the beginning, before the world was created, the spirits, good and evil, lived with Chungba-Sangyat. But when the world was made, he sent them to live on earth and they became a great nuisance to mankind. No one knew who they were until the Jijis were created. The Jijis then discovered their names and were able to say what was to be done to keep them quiet.

14

SINGPHO

Imbu, Tirap F.D.

Men were first born in Majoi-Sigrabhum and later, as their numbers increased, they went to Chaiku-Majoi. On a hill nearby called Numrang-Ningpu lived the goddess Lepchan with her two sons Limum-Nan and Sowa-Sapot-Nan.[4] These two boys lived on human flesh. The elder ate it cooked and the younger ate it raw. Every day Lepchan used to turn herself into a kite and fly to Chaiku-Majoi in order to catch human children for her sons. In this way many babies and young children were destroyed.

At last men went in despair to Mathum-Matta and when he heard their story he himself went home with them and next time the kite came shot it with his bow and arrow.

The goddess fell on her hill and died there. When her sons saw what had happened they cried loudly and, collecting wood, burnt their mother's body. Presently a party of hunters came to the place. There three of them found a large round mushroom which had grown from the ashes of the dead goddess, and said to one another, 'This will be good to eat.' The first ate the skin covering the top and cried, 'This is very tasty.' A second ate the middle part of the mushroom and said, 'You are right, it is very tasty indeed.' The third man ate the stalk. Directly they had eaten they were filled with magic power and as they went home, they used

[4] *Nan* is the Singpho word for god.

it to destroy things. They saw a beautiful tree and one of them said, 'That is a very fine tree' and immediately it withered away. A little later they saw a deer and the second man, who had more power than the others said, 'That is a beautiful animal,' and the poor creature died immediately.

When the two gods saw what had happened they followed the three men and caught hold of them saying, 'This mushroom was our own mother. Why have you eaten her? We used to eat raw and cooked meat every day, but now who will feed us? We will have to eat you instead.' The men were frightened and said, 'Don't eat us but live with us and help us, and we will always feed you with raw and cooked meat.' This is how sorcery came into the world.[5]

15

SINGPHO

Imbu, Tirap F.D.

In the old days when there were no houses but only jungle and hills,[6] there was a Raja whose name was Kiru-Kumyung-Mukam-Mintong. He had a brother whose name was Kaitu-Liwang and a sister Sibi-Jatai. The brothers said to their sister, 'Go into the forest, cut down the trees and make a field which we can cultivate.' The girl replied, 'You cut the trees and when it is time to burn them, I will come and join you.' The brothers went to the forest and cleared it and when the wood was dry they burnt it. Then they said to their sister, 'We have done the heavy work of the field. Now you go and clear it.' The sister said, 'I won't go now, but when everything is ready and you have sown your seed and it has grown up a little, I will go and weed it.'

When the crop had grown up a little, the brothers asked their sister to go and weed it, but she again refused saying, 'I will come

[5] There do not appear to be any charms or initiation ceremonies in Singpho sorcery. It is generally supposed that the powers of the Singpho sorcerers have decreased in the course of time, although they can still kill people. It is believed that it is the Noctes, and the Singphos living in Burma, who have the greatest power. They can turn themselves into tigers even today. The Khamptis and Singphos of NEFA used to be able to do this, but contact with civilization has deprived them of their powers.

[6] The Singphos refer to this ancient time as 'the time of Kindru-Kinchha'.

when the harvest is ready.' When the harvest was ready, the brothers asked their sister to go and see to it, but she refused saying, 'Make a platform in the trees near the field and I will come.' When they had done this they again called her to go, but she said, 'First of all make me a jews-harp.' The brothers made her a harp and the girl took it with her and went to guard the crops. She used to stay all night in the field and come home in the morning.

One evening as Sibi-Jatai was playing her jews-harp on her platform in the trees, a monkey heard the sound and came and sat on the ground at the foot of the tree. Presently he climbed onto the platform and danced before the girl as she played, and when she saw him she burst out laughing.

The monkey said, 'Why are you laughing? I am only enjoying your music.' The girl said, 'If you dance so well to my music, what will you do if I sing?' And so they began—the girl sang and the monkey danced, then the monkey sang and the girl danced. They sang and danced until love came between them.

This went on for many days. Every morning Sibi-Jatai would go home and in the evening she would go to meet the monkey and they would dance and sing together. But the girl's clothes used to get torn and when she came home in the morning, her brothers would say, 'What have you been doing that you have got your clothes in such a mess?' The girl would reply, 'A wild pig came into the fields and while I was chasing him away, I got caught in some thorn bushes which tore my clothes.'

But at last the elder brother, the Raja, grew suspicious and one evening he said, 'You had better not go to the field today ; I will go instead.' So that day the girl did not go and her brother went in her place. He hid himself behind the platform and when the monkey came as usual to meet his lover, he shot him dead.

In the morning when the brother came home, Sibi-Jatai asked him, 'Did any animal come to rob the field last night?' The brother replied, 'Yes, there was a monkey who came to steal the crops but I shot him dead and cut his body into pieces and threw them into the field.' When she heard this the girl began to weep loudly and said, 'He was my husband, why have you killed him? I have his child in my belly. When the child is born, who will look after him?' When he heard this, Kiru-Kumyung-Mukam-Mintong was offended and said, 'I am a Raja and you are a Raja's sister. How could you marry a monkey? Get out of my house.'

So Sibi-Jatai left the house to live in the forest. When it was time for her to be delivered, she went to a wild pig and said, 'My child is about to be born ; give me a place in your house where I can live.' The pig said, 'You did not marry a pig but only a monkey ; how can I let you stay in my house?'

She then went to a wild dog and said, 'My child is about to be born ; give me a place in your house where I can live.' The dog said, 'You did not marry a dog but only a monkey ; how can I let you stay in my house?'

She then went to a wild cow and said, 'My child is about to be born ; give me a place in your house where I can live.' The cow said, 'You did not marry a cow but only a monkey ; how can I let you stay in my house?'

She then went to a wild buffalo and said, 'My child is about to be born ; give me a place in your house where I can live.' The buffalo said, 'You did not marry a buffalo but only a monkey ; how can I let you stay in my house?'

She then went to a deer and said, 'My child is about to be born ; give me a place in your house where I can live.' The deer said, 'You did not marry a deer but only a monkey ; how can I let you stay in my house?'

At last Sibi-Jatai came to a barren place which had no owner, where there was no grass or a single tree and there she was delivered of her child. When he was born, he had the body of a man but a monkey's head. The girl had been weaving a piece of cloth, but after the child was born he was always crying and demanding her breast and she could not finish it. So she employed a squirrel as nurse. The girl would sit down to work on her unfinished cloth, but every now and then the squirrel would bring the child to her, for he was always crying for his mother. This made her angry with the squirrel and she said to her, 'Don't keep the child near me, but take him somewhere far away.' The squirrel was annoyed at this and took the child a very long way indeed. As she went along, she had to cross the Liju-Luang river and, as she jumped across, she dropped the child and he fell into the water. The stream swept him far down until he came to a place where some men had set traps for fish. He was caught in a trap and when the fishermen came they took him out and killed and ate him.

When Sibi-Jatai saw that the nurse and the child did not come back, she went out to look for them and followed the nurse's footsteps to the river-bank. Then she went down the river until she came to the very place where the fishermen had eaten her child. She found a few bones lying on the ground and knew that her child had been killed and eaten. She went weeping to Mathum-Matta and said to him, 'Show me my son.' Mathum-Matta said, 'I cannot show you your child myself ; you must go to Muphung-Tingnu-Nan.' So the girl went weeping to him and told him all that had happened saying, 'I beg you to show me my son.'

The god put a coloured feather before her eyes and she became the goddess Sisam-Nan. He gave her a black cloth and said, 'Go and wash it.' She went to the river to wash it and as she did so, it changed its colour and became yellow. Then the god gave her a white cloth to wash and the cloth turned black. In this way the god knew that Sibi-Jatai really had become Sisam-Nan. She herself realized that her son would be in the place where he had been killed and eaten. So she went there and found that a woman had been the first to eat the flesh of the child. This woman became pregnant and Sisam-Nan realized that her own child was in her belly. She went into the woman's belly and tried to remove the child, and this made the woman ill. The neighbours called for a shaman and he told them what was happening. They offered sacrifice to Sisam-Nan, and said, 'We sinned in eating your child ; now forgive us and we will always offer you sacrifice.' When they did this the woman was cured and ever since we have offered sacrifice to Sisam-Nan.[7]

16

SINGPHO

Imbu, Tirap F.D.

The Great Lord Sangthu-Phara was called Chousithat as a boy. His father, Raja Parasi, was a great and wealthy king and named after his own country, Parasi. When his son was born the Raja

[7] Now-a-days when sacrifice is offered to Sisam-Nan, this story is repeated by the priest.

was very happy, for he had no other child, and took such care of him that he never allowed him to go outside the house.

When Chousithat was still a baby at his mother's breast, the god Phanningsang-Phara came one night when all were asleep to see him in the form of a Lama. He took him in his lap and said, 'You too will be a Lama and you must even now begin to learn the Path of Dharma.' He gave him the sacred robe, but the child replied, 'I will not wear your robe, for I have no desire to be a Lama. I am the son of a great king and I shall rule over my kingdom.'

This happened many times and every time the Lama tried to dress him in his own robe, the boy refused to wear it. But he kept his own counsel and did not tell his mother or father or anyone about what was happening.

When he grew up, Chousithat was married and his wife bore him a child. Gratified by this, his father wished to hand over control of the kingdom to him. But one day when Chousithat was walking in his great flower-garden with his Mantri, he noticed thousands of people going to and fro outside and the sight pleased him. But presently he saw a very old man with bowed head hobbling along with the help of a stick ; the throng of people pressed against him and knocked him down. Chousithat asked why this should be. The Mantri replied, 'This is old age.' And the boy asked, 'Will this also happen to me?' The Mantri replied, 'You too will grow old.'

Then as they went along, they passed a sick man lying by the roadside with many flies sitting on his wounds. Chousithat asked why this should be. The Mantri said, 'This is a sick man.' And the boy asked, 'Will this also happen to me?' The Mantri replied, 'You too will fall sick.'

Soon afterwards Chousithat saw a corpse carried by four men and many following them in tears. He asked why this should be. The Mantri replied, 'The man is dead.' The boy asked, 'Will this also happen to me?' The Mantri replied, 'You too will die.'

Chousithat continued to walk among the flowers, but now his face was sad. He came home and pondered on what he had seen. When his wife offered him his food, he refused it. She asked him what was the matter, but he did not say a word ; she pressed him and at last to satisfy her, he ate a little.

That night Chousithat decided to leave his home and go into the world, but as he was getting up his child awoke and cried and he returned to bed. But as soon as the child went to sleep, he got up again and this time escaped from the house unnoticed and went far away. As he went it began to rain, and he took shelter beneath the Likatphun tree. The rain poured down and drenched him, but he remained sitting in meditation, and so passed into a deep trance. Many people went by, but no one could see him. Day followed day and gradually as he sat there, white ants built a nest around him.

Chousithat's wife searched everywhere and when she could find no news of her husband, she rubbed dirt from her hands and made it into two pigeons. She painted them with gold and told them to go and find him. They flew away and came to the tree beneath which Chousithat was sitting, and as they hovered above the tree his breath came up to them and they realized that he was there, covered with earth brought up by the white ants.

The pigeons returned to the palace, and Chousithat's wife said, 'Tell me where he is, so that I may go and bring him back.' The birds said to her, 'He is no longer a man ; he has become a god.' But the woman said, 'If he is a god, why is he still sitting beneath the tree?' The birds replied, 'We ourselves will go to the tree and take him to Phanningsang-Phara.' She replied, 'If you can take him to Phanningsang-Phara, I will bless you and you will become husband and wife.'

The birds flew to Likpan, heavenly home of the gods. When the Supreme Lord saw them he said, 'Why have you come here?' The birds told him all that had happened to Chousithat and that his wife had sent them to him. When he heard the story the Lord at first laughed loudly when he remembered that as a boy Chousithat had refused to become a Lama but now had become one of his own accord, but afterwards he was sad because he had suffered so greatly.

Then the Lord sent five beautiful girls from Likpan to Chousithat and they threw water over him and gradually made him clean of the dirt and earth that had covered him. But even when he was free of it, he did not speak a word.

Then the Lord took the form of a Lama and himself came to see Chousithat. He sent for five hundred cows, milked them and gave all the milk to one hundred of them to drink. He milked the one hundred and gave all the milk to ten of them to drink. He milked the ten cows and gave all the milk to one. He milked this cow, boiled the milk, removed the cream and gave it to Chousithat to eat, and at last Chousithat opened his eyes and folded his hands in greeting to the Lord. The Lord said, 'From today your name will be Godma-Phara,' and so saying returned to Likpan.

When the people heard that Godma-Phara had become a great god they came in thousands to visit him and he preached to them the Path of Dharma.

Now at that time there was a Raja called Khochra, who in a single night had sixteen dreams. He asked many Lamas their meaning, but no one could tell him. But when he heard that Godma-Phara had great wisdom, he went to consult him. He sat before him among the trees and told him all he had seen.

The Raja said, 'In my first dream I saw a man tie a cow with a rope and as she dragged it along behind her, a god ate it. What does this mean?'

Godma-Phara replied, 'The meaning of this is that a time will come when the rulers will try to govern their countries well, but for all their efforts things will go ill.'

'In my second dream,' continued the Raja, 'there was a horse which ate the grass in front and behind. What does this mean?'

Godma-Phara replied, 'The meaning of this is that the day will come when the officers of Government will not only eat their own pay, but will also eat the money of the people.'

The Raja said, 'In my third dream I saw a calf, but one year old, dragging a cart.'

Godma-Phara replied, 'The meaning of this is that however young a boy may be, provided he is educated, he will be able to drag the cart of Government.'

'In my fourth dream,' said the Raja, 'I saw a stone and a leaf fall into the water—the leaf sank to the bottom but the stone floated on the surface.'

Godma-Phara replied, 'A day will come when the rulers will sink down and the ruled will rise up to take their place.'

The Raja said, 'In my fifth dream I saw a great sheet of water. In the middle of it was a dry place from which clouds of dust arose, but all round was water.'

Godma-Phara replied, 'The meaning of this is that Dharma is to be found on the frontiers of the world, but in the great towns it is betrayed.'

The Raja said, 'In my sixth dream I saw a pig climbing on the back of a cow.'

Godma-Phara replied, 'This means that a time will come when men and women will no longer observe the rules of their caste, but will marry one another at will. Therefore until a woman has borne seven children by a man, he should not put faith in her.'

'In my seventh dream,' said the Raja, 'I saw a frog swallowing the Sun and there was darkness everywhere.'

Godma-Phara replied, 'A time will come when all men will forget the laws of Dharma. Sin will increase, the earth will be destroyed and everything will be in darkness.'

The Raja said, 'In my eighth dream, I saw a man holding a golden flower in his left hand and fire in his right. What does this mean?'

Godma-Phara replied, 'A time will come when men will forget the true Dharma and will follow lies. This is why the man held the fire of falsehood in his right hand where he should have had the golden flower of Dharma.'

'In my ninth dream,' said the Raja, 'many children were born of one father and mother. And these children were bathing in blood and drinking it.'

Godma-Phara replied, 'The meaning of this is that a day will come when, although the Lord will remain one, there will be many spirits, good and evil, to whom men will have to offer all manner of sacrifices.'

The Raja said, 'In my tenth dream there was a man who changed his appearance many times.'

Godma-Phara replied, 'The meaning of this is that a day will come when all kinds of disease will spread through the earth.'

'In my eleventh dream,' said the Raja, 'I saw a dish from which many people were eating together.

Godma-Phara replied, 'A time will come when there will be no caste in the earth, none will be regarded as high, low or untouchable and all men will eat together.'

The Raja said, 'In my twelfth dream I saw a man who had

one foot on the ground and the other in the sky. What is the meaning of this?'

Godma-Phara replied, 'This means that a time will come when ordinary men will learn a little and think that they have become kings and will try to dominate over others.' And in truth, this day has already come when our boys and girls, after a little schooling, think they are fit to rule the country as servants of Government.

'In my thirteenth dream,' the Raja said, 'I saw a man eating human flesh.'

'The meaning of this,' said Godma-Phara, 'is that a time will come when there will be great wars, man will kill man and brother will kill brother.'

The Raja said, 'In my fourteenth dream, a man was carrying two baskets on a pole across his shoulders. In one was a seer of sweet things and in the other two seers of sour things. The sweet things were behind and the sour things in front. As he went along the man wanted to change them and have the sweet things in front and the sour things behind. But all his attempts to do this failed and the sour things always remained in front.'

Godma-Phara replied, 'Many Lamas will say, "Give up sin and follow the Path of Dharma." But man will always forget the Path of Dharma and follow the Path of Unrighteousness.'

'In my fifteenth dream,' said the Raja, 'I saw a dead man whose corpse remained erect and did not decay.'

Godma-Phara said, 'This means that when great Lamas go to Likpan, their images will remain on earth.'

Finally the Raja said, 'In my sixteenth dream I saw a pillar on which many houses were built. What does this mean?'

Godma-Phara said, 'The meaning of this is that a day will come when there will only be one ruler over all the world.'

So saying Godma-Phara went to Likpan, but his image remained on earth. Men call this image Sangthu-Phara and worship it.[8]

[8] The story of the sixteen dreams is an obvious echo of the Mahasupina-Jataka, in which the King of Kosala (the Kochra of our text) comes to the Master for the interpretation of sixteen dreams which he has had in a single night. Although, with two exceptions, the Singhpho dreams are entirely different from those recorded in the Jataka story, they are of the same general pattern and reveal the same gloomy apprehensions about the future of the world. Kings will be unrighteous; the young and inexperienced will rise to power; noble families will be brought low; 'women

17

SINGPHO

Imbu, Tirap F.D.

When sorcery began and as a result people fell sick and died, they went to Mathum-Matta for help and he said, 'Go to Madainan and he will help you.' When they met Madainan he at once said, 'I know what is the matter and of course I will help you. I have with me three other gods—Singlapnan, Munnunnan and Mingsenan. We will all go to see what we can do.' So the great god and the three small gods went with the men to their village.

Near the village there was a hill and the three lesser gods made their home there and Madainan went to live in the sky. These four are the gods who help the Tumsawa priest who fights against evil spirits. Madainan watches over them from the sky while the three other gods go about the world making men priests and teaching them what to do.

18

TAGIN

Sigga, Subansiri F.D.

Abo-Teni lost a mithun in the forest, and it died. After a long search, he found the carcass and cut it up, but there was no one to help him carry the meat home. Presently Tapeng the bat flew by, and Abo-Teni said to him, 'O brother bat, if you will help me to carry this meat home, I will give you a share of it.' 'Of course I will help you,' said the bat. So Abo-Teni cut the meat up into small pieces and the bat picked them up one by one and flew away.

will lust after men and strong drink and finery and the joys of this world'. Religious teachers, and even the gods themselves, will leave the path of righteousness.

In only two cases do the actual dreams even partly coincide. The Singhpho second dream is paralleled by the Jataka fifth, of a horse with a mouth on either side, to which fodder is given on both sides, so that it eats with both its mouths. The Jataka tale interprets this as foreshadowing the rise of corrupt judges who will take bribes from both sides as they sit in the seat of judgement. The Singpho fourth dream bears a slight resemblance to the Jataka twelfth, of empty pumpkins sinking in the water, which prophesies a day when 'the low-born shall become great lords while the nobles sink into poverty.'

Tapeng did not take the meat to Abo-Teni's house but to a secret place of his own far away on a high mountain. Gradually he stole it all, bit by bit.

When Abo-Teni went home, he looked for the meat, but there was nothing there, no meat, no Tapeng. He was very angry and went out to search for the deceitful bat. He climbed the high mountains, but Tapeng's place was well hidden and he could find no trace of it. He got very thirsty and went to a stream to drink. As he bent down to the water, a crab came out of his hole and said, 'Brother Abo-Teni, I have not seen you for a very long time. What are you looking for?' So Abo-Teni told him. The crab said, 'Well, Tapeng comes here every day for water.' 'Then will you catch him for me?' 'Certainly I will: you hide somewhere and I'll catch him.'

By and by Tapeng flew down to drink. The crab said, 'How is it you're always drinking such a lot of water nowadays?' The bat said, 'I got thirsty eating all that mithun-flesh of Abo-Teni's.' At that the crab caught Tapeng's foot in his claws. As he was struggling to get away, Abo-Teni came and took out his dao to kill him. But Tapeng said, 'Brother Abo-Teni, we are brothers. If you kill me with your dao, people will think ill of you for killing your brother. Why not tie bits of wood and grass to my wings and set fire to them? I will fly up and die and everyone will think it was an accident.' So Abo-Teni tied grass and bits of wood to Tapeng's wings and set fire to them. The bat flew into the air and in the flames his body turned black. But he did not die. He flew away to the great hill where the Wiyus' houses are, and set fire to them. In this way, he burnt all the village of the Wiyus and the fire went from him.

The Wiyus were angry, and went to Abo-Teni and abused him for not killing Tapeng with his dao. 'Through your stupidity our houses are burnt, so we will punish you.' After that the Wiyus gave him a lot of trouble. And they still trouble his children and we have to give them sacrifices.

CHAPTER FOURTEEN

THE THREAT OF DISEASE

THROUGHOUT Tribal India disease is generally attributed to supernatural causes. Sometimes it is due to the attacks of the unsatisfied dead or to the anger or jealousy of gods and demons. Sometimes the gods feel that they are receiving insufficient attention from men and make them ill to remind them of their existence. There is a common idea that the gods and spirits, and the dead too, get hungry and in order to extract food from men they make them ill and feed on the sacrifices that are offered for their recovery. Disease also may be due to breach of certain taboos and a feeling of guilt, and in some tribes is regarded as the result of bad dreams.

The general pattern of ideas about the cause and cure of sickness is very similar throughout NEFA and since it would be impossible here to give a complete account of all the tribes, I will give, as an example, a brief summary of the ideas of the Adi groups on the left bank of the Upper Siang; a similar attitude, with different names and small divergences in detail will be found almost everywhere.

Perhaps the greatest single fact in the life of all tribal people is the threat of sickness and death. The Adis suffer atrociously from every kind of disease and their theory of its causation is not calculated to relieve it, for it discourages them from turning to scientific medicine. Sickness is caused by dreams, by sorcery, by breach of taboo, but above all by the Wiyus, and even where there may be some other immediate cause, a Wiyu is often its active agent. Let us consider the less common causes first.

Dreams not only warn of sickness to come : they actually cause such infections as leprosy and goitre.

Breaches of taboo make one ill or liable to an unpleasant accident. A headman at Riu described how he once brought home the harvest without offering the prescribed sacrifices, and Taleng Wiyu made him cut his foot with his dao. He twice broke the taboos on going in and out of his house, and Ratte Rameng Wiyu and Patpum-Palleng Wiyu were angry with him and made him cut himself again. His wife died of a similar neglect.

An expectant mother who is careless of the rules during her pregnancy may cause much trouble later to her child. If she or her husband drink water from a stream that dries up in the hot weather, their child will be deaf. If she eats the flesh of the *perek* bird, the child will have red and inflamed eyes. If she eats monkey's flesh, the child will have sunken eyes like a monkey. If she kills a snake, her child will be born dumb, 'for a snake's tongue shoots in and out.'

A man who carries out a corpse to burial must not eat a gourd for a year: if he does, he will get goitre. Nor must he eat a pumpkin, or his body will be covered with sores.

Sickness may be caused by witchcraft. The Miri-shamans may put their great powers to the wrong use: then 'they devour men secretly and so destroy them'. Certain women can send their Wiyus to drink the blood of their enemies.

The chief danger to human beings comes, however, from the Wiyus. This great company of unseen spirits surrounds man on earth and, while some Wiyus are benevolent, the majority are touchy, jealous and naturally hostile to him. It was the trickster and cannibal Rabbo who was their ancestor and his descendents are worthy of him: there is no evil to which they will not stoop.

So Sitking-Uness Wiyu causes eye-trouble of every kind, Yenne Wiyu wanders about the world, giving dysentery wherever he goes. Dorum-Lissam Wiyu, who lives in the village of the same name between earth and heaven, 'looks on a man and drives him mad'. Doing-Ero causes epilepsy.

Venereal disease is caused by Sikkom Wiyu. Sacrifice is offered to him at night and the house is taboo to strangers for several days and the whole village for one day, 'for all men fear this disease'.

Malaria was, according to Adi tradition, unknown

before the Military Expedition of 1911. 'It is caused by Doli-Tameng Wiyu, for it comes from outside.'

Sterility in women is caused by a female Wiyu called Daini-Api. Long ago, this girl, daughter of a Wiyu, lived in human form on earth. At her first menstruation, she went unwittingly to the stream where Doini-Pollo used to bathe. There she washed her clothes and body, and drank a little of the water. By doing this, she offended Doini-Pollo and she never bore a child. After her death, she lived on as a Wiyu in certain streams and pools. Sometimes, a girl is unfortunate enough to meet her when she goes to wash her clothes at the end of her first period, and then Daini-Api makes her barren.

Two Wiyus devote themselves to troubling women in child-birth: they are Nite-Wiyu and Nippong-Wiyu, and the Adis have many ways of checkmating their activities.

When delivery is delayed, the attendants place an egg on the floor and make the mother break it with her knee and then drink some cold water. As the water of the egg is thus released, the aminiotic fluid will begin to flow.

The husband makes a bracelet of grass, puts it before his wife and says, 'If I have forgotten anything; if I have left anything shut up anywhere: if there is a vessel closed or basket unopened, it is my fault: I admit my mistake.' Then he cuts the bracelet with his dao.

At Riu I watched a score of men with spears range themselves round a house where a young mother was wearily struggling for delivery. At a given sign they raised their spears and drove them at the walls, again and again, shouting to drive away the obstructive Wiyu.

If, in spite of all this effort, the child is not born, the Miri is called and he sacrifices a hen on the mother's head, letting the blood pour over her and saying to the Wiyu, 'Take this, but let the woman alone.' They do not eat this fowl, but throw it away: 'all the flesh is for the Wiyu'. If this fails, they kill a dog above the mother's head.

Another method is to dress the mother in the best and oldest ornaments they have, put on her a fine Mishmi coat and a new skirt, and cry: 'Come out quickly: don't stay inside. Whether you are a boy or girl, come out and get the lovely things we will give you.'

The Adis have some idea of the spread of infection, and it is interesting that this applies not only to material but to moral sickness also. Thus, if anyone is guilty of incest, always a very grave matter in tribal society, no visitor will enter his house for at least three months for fear of catching the infection and committing the same crime. So too, if a man kills a mithun by accident, he is not fined, but his house is avoided for some time, for such a man is spiritually infectious: he has been driven to his deed by some hostile spirit, who may also attack his friends.

Once, on entering Komsing village, I was greeted with a ceremonial arch and a large crowd of people, who shouted loudly as my party approached and pelted us with chunks of plantain stalk. The same thing happened in the Bori country, where a sort of fence had been erected and long white strips of bark hung from it. I have sometimes had to pass through several gates before being regarded as spiritually aseptic.

A hundred years ago Father Krick had the same experience. 'Eighteen young men,' he writes, 'met me at the foot of the mountain. No sooner did I move on, than the two youngest of the band proceeded to cover my body with leaves. They meant of course to purify me and deliver my body from all diabolical influence. This exorcism was soon to be followed by a second performance more weird and threatening. As I emerged from the forest, I was made to pass under an arch bristling with bows and arrows, and decorated with all sorts of devilries and monsters pierced with arrows, and in striking attitudes that baffle description. This piece of architecture was fearful to behold, as well it might be, for it was to expel from my body the more stubborn devils who had been daring enough to cross the first obstacle.'[1]

The fearsome architecture today has lost some of its picturesqueness, but many villages still have elaborate

[1] Krick, op. cit., p.109.

defences against those who might bring sickness-giving Wiyus from outside. Spiked fences and gates, with imitation arrows, are erected and the head or body of a fowl, dog or monkey is hung up to deter the mischievous spirits.

The NEFA stories illustrate this general attitude towards disease. In an Idu Mishmi tale a frustrated spirit falls from the sky and is attacked by a swarm of ants. He gets fever as a result and in his rage and disappointment sends this sickness to all men and excites the tree-spirits to torment them. Similarly in a Kaman Mishmi story, two disloyal and quarrelsome spirits are condemned by a greater god to live, one in a cave, the other in the dirty corners of the houses of men and in the cremation-grounds. All he now gets to eat are the sick and aged. Yet again a Minyong tradition tells how the ghosts of spirits killed in war turned in despair to attack mankind and so brought disease to the world. Only one tradition attributes sickness to a 'natural' cause. In the old days, according to the Wanchos, men's skins were very thin and fragile, and bad air came up from the earth and passed into their bodies through their skins, thus making them ill.

There is an interesting Hrusso tradition that goitre originated among trees and came (it still comes) to men by their contagion. Similarly, leprosy can be contracted by touching a certain kind of deer.

Some of the stories describe how fowls, pigs, mithuns and buffaloes were established as sacrificial animals to be offered to the spirits at a time of crisis.

1

HRUSSO (AKA)

Buragaon, Kameng F.D.

Originally it was only the trees that suffered from goitre.

Buslu-Ao[2] had many children and when they grew up, he found wives for them and sent them to live separately in their own homes. Now none of these children knew how to eat meat, so one day their father sent them a message that he proposed to teach them

[2] Buslu-Ao is the ancestor of the entire human race.

its use and that they should bring wood to his house in order to cook it.

Buslu-Ao made a large enclosure, in which he collected every kind of wild animal and bird. The birds and animals were greatly disturbed at this and said to one another, 'This has never happened before. Why has Buslu-Ao caught us and shut us up like this?' The cock said, 'As you know, Buslu-Ao has a great many children and none of them know how to eat meat. Now he wants to teach them to do so and he has caught us and, when the children come, he will kill us for their dinner.' Then the cock said again, 'You can all stay here if you like, but personally I am getting out.' And he flew into the air and escaped.

Then the mithun said, 'The cock is a small creature and I am great and strong. If he can escape, why shouldn't I escape too?' And he broke down the wall of the enclosure and escaped. The wild pig followed him and then all the other animals and birds.

And now when the enclosure was empty, Buslu-Ao's children arrived carrying loads of wood on their heads. They did not put the loads down, but stood there waiting until their father said, 'I had collected a great deal of food for you but you have come too late and all the animals and birds have run away.'

The children were very angry and threw their bundles of wood at Buslu-Ao. Now among the wood were some pieces that had been cut from trees that suffered from goitre and when these struck Buslu-Ao he fell down unconscious and his throat swelled up.

The children thought that they had killed their father and ran to him and lifted him up and began to weep loudly. When they touched him, their throats also became swollen, and this is how goitre first came to men.

Trees and animals still suffer from goitre, but we never cut a tree that has it or eat the flesh of a goitrous animal, for fear of catching it.

2

HRUSSO (AKA)

Buragaon, Kameng F.D.

At first men and animals lived happily without sickness. Now the Lord of the Waters, Siksilia-ao, had two sons Mumogro and

Mumugi. When they were born the crocodile heard of it and said to himself, 'These two are going to bring disease to men and animals', and decided to kill them both. So he took his bow and his arrows in a quiver and came out of the water to hunt them.

As the crocodile went along he fired his arrows in all directions, but quite uselessly. At one moment he thought that his enemies were hiding in a tree ; at another that they were hiding in a rock. All that happened was that his arrows hit, now a man, now an animal and killed them. After he had done this for some time men and animals gathered together and said to one another, 'The crocodile has always been our friend. How has it happened that he is killing us like this?' So they decided to steal his arrows to prevent him from doing further damage. As the crocodile was returning to his river, therefore, men and animals made a great outcry and the crocodile said to himself, 'I was only trying to help them ; now why are they trying to destroy me?' And he began to run as quickly as he could towards the water. Mumogro and Mumugi put a trap in the river to catch him, but when they came to the bank the crocodile caught them instead and put them into his quiver with the arrows and then plunged beneath the water.

Men and animals, not knowing what had happened, pursued the crocodile into the deep water, but he left his quiver floating on the surface and they seized it and took it to the bank. When they saw the trap that the two brothers had thrown into the water they decided to try and catch the crocodile with it. They collected lots of sweet fruit from the forest and put them in the trap and then hid on the bank. The crocodile came up to the surface of the river to see whether the men and animals were still there or not. He saw the sweet fruit and ate them, but caught his mouth in the thorns of the trap. The men and animals immediately rushed into the water and dragged him to the bank. They took the bow and the quiver with its arrows from him and, freeing him from the trap (for after all he was their friend), let him go back into the water and then returned home, taking the bow and quiver with them.

But as they went along they found that the quiver, due to the fact that the two brothers were inside it, grew heavier and heavier. They soon got tired of carrying it and decided to put it down somewhere and come back for it the following day.

When they had gone away, the two gods, Mumogro and

Mumugi, came out of the quiver. They removed the arrows and picked up the bow but set fire to the quiver itself. When the hornet saw the smoke from the fire, he went to warn men that the quiver had been burnt. But the smoke had so confused him that he could not speak and all he could do was to sting them on the back of their necks. They looked round to see what had bitten them and noticed the smoke rising to the sky. They went to put out the fire and as they came running back the two gods shot them with their arrows. Thorns pierced their feet ; they stumbled over logs of wood ; they ran into trees ; everyone who was shot fell ill.

Ever since, Mumugro and Mumugi have shot people with their arrows and this is how diseases have come to men, animals and trees.

3

HRUSSO (AKA)

Buragaon, Kameng F.D.

There is a kind of black deer which we call *wophu*. You get leprosy by eating its skin or legs. Even if you touch a tree against which it has rubbed its back you will get leprosy. For this reason, although we eat the flesh of this deer, we do not touch the skin or legs.[3]

4

IDU MISHMI

Ichuli, Lohit F.D.

Anyo badly wanted a wife but no one would marry him. He went up the great river into the mountains searching for a girl who would be his wife. On the way he saw the marks of a fowl. 'What is this?' he wanted to know, so he cut bamboos and made a trap. When he went to it the next morning, he found he had caught the star-girl Andicru. She was very pretty and bright as a star. He took her home and married her and after a time they had a son.

[3] The Hrussos segregate the leper to some extent, and do not eat or drink with him. For they fear that when he dies, his ghost will affect them with his disease. They burn his corpse separately and, if he has no relatives, the others carry it to the forest and throw it away, performing special ceremonies to prevent the ghost's return.

One day Andicru said to her husband, 'I don't like to be seen by day, but I am very happy to see and be seen by night.' Anyo said, 'Don't be silly. Come along and drink rice-beer.' But his wife did not leave the inner room, so her husband went out for the beer and while he was away, she went back into the sky.

Some days after this, their little son was sitting on the veranda cleaning his hair. There was a spirit who lived near the house called Asa and when he saw the child's hair undone, he said to Anyo, 'Why has your child undone his hair?' Anyo said, 'He wanted to clean it and has burnt it off as we burn the feathers off a fowl.' When Asa heard this he went home and burnt his own child's hair, but in doing so he burnt the whole head and the child died. In revenge Asa kidnapped Anyo's child, intending to kill him for sacrifice. He hid the boy in his house and sent for an Igu priest called Iphu.

When Anyo heard what had happened, he went down to a river over which Iphu would have to pass and made a bridge of plantain trees, arranging it so that it looked strong but would actually collapse directly anyone went on it. Having done this he hid in some bushes nearby. Iphu came to the place, but while he was crossing the bridge it collapsed under him and he fell into the water and was drowned. Anyo pulled the body to the bank and took off the special priest's dress and put it on himself. Then he came to Asa's house as if he himself was the priest. Asa, hearing that the priest had come, sent one of his servants to see if it was really Iphu and the man returned to say that it was not. But Asa would not believe him and said, 'No, it must be,' and killed him for telling lies. The servant turned into a squirrel.

Anyo, in the form of the priest Iphu, went to sacrifice outside the house. Asa put the little boy in a basket and brought him to be killed. But directly he took the child out of the basket Anyo picked him up and ran away. Asa followed him and Anyo climbed to the top of a bamboo and clung to it. Asa cut it down but Anyo, with the child in his arms, jumped onto a tree. Asa then cut down the tree, but Anyo escaped into a rat's hole. Asa put a cat at the entrance to the hole and began to dig, but the cat said, 'There's no man in there ; it was a crane who went in.' Hearing this, Asa went away.

Presently Anyo came out in the shape of a crane and drove

away the cat ; then he flew away to join his star-wife and he and Andicru were very happy together in the sky.

But when Asa heard what had happened, he made a great ladder of wood and bamboo: it took him ten years. When it was ready, he climbed up, but the ladder could not quite reach the sky, and Andicru called to him saying, 'Asa, it is good to see you and we are glad you have come. Here is a rope by which you can reach us.' Now Andicru had made a rope with real rope at the lower end, but tied with the guts of a fowl at the top.

She let the rope down to Asa and he caught it and began to climb up. But directly his weight came on it, it broke and he fell down, far down, onto the stump of a tree, where a swarm of ants attacked him and bit him all over. This gave him high fever and in his rage and disappointment he sent this sickness to all mankind. Then in madness he cut the tree in which the spirits lived and they attacked him, but he sent them too to torment mankind. This is how disease came to man.

5

KAMAN MISHMI

Lohit Valley, Lohit F.D.

The god Matai first created the earth and then men and animals. He gave them many gifts such as fire, water, food and weapons so that they might live in comfort. But he was so busy making things that he had no time to visit the people and see how they were getting on and so he sent two other gods, Cupa and Kasamfan, to see whether they were happy or not.

Accordingly Cupa and Kasamfan came to earth, but instead of enquiring into the joys and sorrows of mankind, they went about enjoying themselves. One day they met and Kasamfan asked the other how many places he had seen. Cupa replied that he had seen very little, whereupon Kasamfan boasted that he had seen half the world. Cupa was angry at this and said that to see half the world was nothing. Kasamfan would only be great if he could defeat him in battle. And at that the two spirits began to fight.

When Matai saw this he was angry with them and said to Kasamfan, 'You have been disloyal to me and so henceforth you will have to live in the dirty corners of the houses of men and in the cremation grounds, and all you will have to eat will be the sick and the old men of the earth.' He then summoned Cupa and banished him to a great cave in the mountains.

Since then Kasamfan has lived on the sick and the old. Whenever he finds anyone falling ill, he goes to him and makes him worse.

We, Kaman Mishmis, fear Kasamfan and Cupa greatly and whenever anyone falls sick we offer sacrifice to Kasamfan so that he may not trouble them, and whenever we cross the mountains we walk very quietly so that the noise we make may not disturb Cupa.[4]

6

MINYONG

Riu, Siang F.D.

Engo Wiyu lives deep in the earth, Takar Wiyu is in the sky. Takar had a brother named Liujong: Engo had a daughter, Podam. Takar married Podam, but she betrayed him and went to his brother Liujong. Takar came down to Engo and said, 'Your daughter is bad. She has been to my brother. Why did you give me such a girl?' They both lost their tempers and a great war began. Takar killed very many of Engo's men and Engo killed very many of Takar's men. The ghosts of those killed turned in despair to attack men and so brought disease to the world.

7

SINGPHO

Imbu, Tirap F.D.

On their way down from the Himalaya Mountains the first travellers rested at a place called Chaiku-Majoe. Mathum-Matta had given them buffaloes to show them the way. He also gave them a

[4] Recorded by T. K. Barua.

medicine which would save them from disease and death and would also make the old people young. They collected all the medicine in one place and built a stone wall round it. But the buffaloes broke down the wall and ate the medicine.

Soon afterwards the travellers began to fall ill and had nothing for it, so they went to Mathum-Matta and told him how the buffaloes had eaten up all their medicine. But Mathum-Matta said, 'There is no more medicine for you now. When you fall ill, sacrifice these buffaloes and you will become well.' They went back and said to the buffaloes, 'You have eaten up our medicine and now Mathum-Matta has told us that we are to sacrifice you and that will make us well.' The buffaloes replied, 'Don't sacrifice us. We ourselves will get you medicine.'

But when Mathum-Matta heard that the buffaloes were going to get medicine for men, he himself came to the place and twisted their tongues so that they could not talk any longer. And then since it was not possible for the buffaloes to explain things, the people decided to sacrifice them, and when they did so they found that the sick recovered. Ever since we have offered buffaloes to the gods in time of sickness.

8

WANCHO

Wakka, Tirap F.D.

In the days when men were able to change their form, just as a caterpillar appears, at one time, to be one thing and at another time to be another, their skins were very thin and fragile. Wind used to blow up from the ground and go into their bodies through their skins, and this was the main cause of disease, for as breath comes out of the mouth so bad air used to come from the earth.

9

WANCHO

Pomau, Tirap F.D.

The thunderbolt is Rang's bullet. Rang is a great hunter, but sometimes when he fires his gun he misses his mark and the bullet falls to the earth. It goes deep down into the ground and remains there for four years. In the fifth year it grows up as the plantain tree.

Sometimes, however, it does not go into the earth but strikes a tree. Then if a man touches the leaves of this tree he turns into a leper, for leprosy does not come like other diseases out of the earth but from Rang-Bau in the sky.[5]

[5] The Wanchos (among whom the disease is rather common) realize that leprosy is contagious and do not normally allow lepers to live inside a village. People refuse to eat with a leper and he is not allowed to go to the *jhum* or to sit in the village council. It is said that when a man becomes a leper he has no more authority over his wife, who may go to anyone she chooses. If she wishes, she may stay with him and indeed often does, but she will not sleep with him and whenever she gives him his food, she puts it on the ground without touching him.

Leprosy may be caused in two ways. One is a natural way: if (as described above) you touch the leaves of a tree struck by lightning, you will begin to suffer from agonizing itch and this develops into the graver disease. In the old days, if a commoner (Wangpan) knowingly took the head of a Chief, he became a leper. If he did it in ignorance, he had to observe certain taboos; if he broke them, he became a leper.

The cure was to bathe in the hot blood of a man whose head had been taken. For this reason, lepers were always taken on head-hunting expeditions. Such lepers were safe enough, for it was held to be very risky to take a leper's head: if even a drop of his blood fell on you, you would be infected.

CHAPTER FIFTEEN

THE COMING OF DEATH

THERE is a great diversity of customs in the disposal of the dead by the tribes of the north-east frontier. Cremation, burial and exposure are all common, and in the areas bordering on Tibet there is the custom of cutting up a corpse and either throwing it into a river or offering it to the birds. The Wanchos place a dead body in a coffin and expose it outside a village. Some of the Tangsa groups burn the dead inside the village, others take it outside for the same purpose. The Yoglis bury a corpse in a sort of coffin underneath the house itself, hanging food for the ghost under the eaves. Mishmis either burn or bury according to the season and the inspiration of the shamans. Most of the Adi groups bury their dead in cemeteries outside the village, but the wilder Tagins and Gallongs bury immediately in front of the house, raising a special altar or tomb above the grave.

Despite this diversity in practice, however, there is a general similarity in the pattern of beliefs about the after-life all over NEFA. The people everywhere believe in the continued existence after death of what, for want of a better word, we must call the soul; they believe in a Land of the Dead, in some cases in several such Lands, which is reached by a difficult path and often guarded by some Spirit of the other-world who examines the soul's credentials before he admits them. It is commonly supposed that the soul can leave the body during life to visit this shadowy country; indeed the Tagins are said to believe that part of a man's personality called the Yalo should normally go and make arrangements for his ultimately permanent residence there while he is still alive. It is on the basis of such visits and the experiences of the shamans during trance that the NEFA tribesmen, like the Saoras of Orissa, have built up their picture of the Land of the Dead.

Details, of course, vary greatly, even from village to

village within the same tribe, but the following notes will give a general idea of theology and custom within the area.[1]

APA TANI ESCHATOLOGY

The eschatological beliefs of the Apa Tanis of Subansiri have been conveniently summarized by Dr C. von Furer-Haimendorf,

'The Apa Tanis believe that the souls, Yalo, of all those who die a natural death go to Neli, the place of the dead, which looks like an Apa Tani village with long rows of houses. At the entrance of Neli, they are met by Nelkiri, the guardian spirit who questions all newcomers about the exploits of their earthly life. He inquires how many enemies and wild animals they have slain, how many slaves they have bought, and how much land they have owned. As an Apa Tani lived on this earth so will he live in Neli: a rich man will find the cattle he has sacrificed during his lifetime, but those animals which have passed to his heirs are for ever lost to him. Every woman returns to her first husband, but those who died unmarried may there marry and beget children. Life in Neli is similar to life on this earth: people cultivate and work, and ultimately they die once more and go to another Land of the Dead.

'When a man is ill and loses consciousness, his soul or Yalo may leave his body and stray to Neli. A shaman priest, called to minister to the sick man, may trace the errant soul to the house of one of the many gods and spirits

[1] In his Frazer Lecture, Dr C. von Furer-Haimendorf says that 'the eschatological concepts of the hill-people of Assam follow on the whole a consistent pattern, which differs fundamentally from that prevailing in Middle India'. I find it difficult to agree with this. It is true that there does not seem to be anything comparable to certain Gond ideas, which to my mind are in any case rather doubtful, but in the main it seems to me that the pattern is closely similar. As Furer-Haimendorf says, the most characteristic features of the Assam tribes are 'a very detailed picture of the Land of the Dead' which is provided by the shamans who visit it in trance or dream, and 'the belief in a soul of the psyche type which can leave the material body already in a man's lifetime, and, if straying to the Land of the Dead, can be recovered by the shaman. This soul is clearly a separate entity and not merely the personality which after the death of the body appears as "the Departed" in the sense of the Gond *sanal*'. With this I agree, but most of the central Indian tribes hold the same view. See C. von Furer-Haimendorf, 'The After-Life in Indian Belief', *Journal of the Royal Anthropological Institute*, Vol. LXXIII (1953), pp. 37 ff.

who dwell in Neli, and are ever avid to draw unsuspicious souls into their sphere. Once the shaman has located the Yalo, he offers to ransom it with the sacrifice of an animal; if the spirits accept the ransom, the Yalo returns to its earthly body, and the patient regains consciousness.

'Neli is believed to be under the earth, a real underworld, but without any gloomy associations. Another Land of the Dead is situated somewhere in the sky, and to this abode, known as Talimoko, repair all those who died an unnatural or inauspicious death. Men who were killed by enemies and women who died in childbirth go to this Land in the Sky and are henceforth referred to as Igi. Both the departed in the underworld and those in Talimoko are believed to return at times to the dwellings of the living, but their visits are not welcomed and are thought to result in little good.'[2]

Bori Ideas and Customs

To the Boris, as to many other Indian tribes, death is a thing alien and unnatural; it was not part of the original order as planned by the first Maker of the World. And possibly because death has no business here, it is not regarded as having the last word. The soul, the Aith, is stronger than death and survives the dissolution of its bodily integument.

The soul has the power of leaving the body in sleep and experiencing what we call dreams. After death it goes, as a general rule, to whatever Wiyu has brought its earthly life to an end. If, for example, someone is drowned, the Aith goes to the Wiyu of the river. If a man dies in battle, however, he goes to a place called Taleng in the Sky. Small children are said to go to Doli-Tamong, which is situated in the foot-hills towards Assam. There is a belief that if a man is killed by a snake, he becomes a snake, but this is not apparently a belief in reincarnation, for the snake does not appear in this world but is a snake in the World of the

[2] ibid., p. 44.

Dead. So a man killed by a tiger or bear will be a spirit-tiger or bear in the other world. Awing-Kare, in an important story recorded in this Chapter, died as a result of an injury received from his pig. As a result his ghost went to the Village of Pigs in the other world, turned into a pig and lived among the other ghostly pigs.

When a poor man or a child dies, his relatives carry him to burial the same day. For a rich man, however, at whose funeral many guests will be expected, the Boris usually wait till the following day. Directly after the death they kill a dog near the house, and the family and clansmen feast on it. In the evening the hosts kill a pig and the next morning very early a mithun, and the visitors present rice and beer to the people of the house.

The most important and remarkable aspect of a Bori funeral is that the corpse is carried on the back of a single individual. Even old women fulfil this duty, but a young unmarried girl cannot, for if she did she could not get married, and a widow too, if she is young, must not carry her husband's body, for if she does she will not be able to marry again. If she is old and strong enough for the task, however, she may do so. If there is no suitable person available, a fellow-member of the same clan carries the body. If he carries the body of a married man, he thereby obtains the right to receive the customary marriage gifts if the widow marries again.

The Boris dig the grave about five feet deep and line it with planks so that it becomes a real coffin. They place the corpse on its side, as if it were sitting, with hands together under the head and they put beer, rice and meat by it. They close the coffin with planks and fill in the earth. Above the grave they build a little hut, three or four feet high, with a thatched roof, and inside this a fire is kept burning, in the case of ordinary people for a month and in the case of a rich man for as long as a year. On a pole outside they hang the trophies of the hunt and a rack of arrows. Hats, ornaments, daos, baskets and other possessions of the deceased are also hung on the tomb and gifts of beer, tobacco and rice are placed before it.

Minyong Eschatological Beliefs

To the Minyongs of the Upper Siang area, it is the Wiyus who bring death to men. There does not seem to be any god of the dead (although Dalton noted one among the Hinduized Abors bordering on the plains). The Nippong Wiyus kill women in childbirth. The Epom Wiyus attack men in the forest, taking them away and hiding them in great trees. Pomtum Yasang Wiyu kills men suddenly. Niling Poling Wiyu kills women in spite of any sacrifices offered for their safety: 'he devours sacrifice and human being together.' Taleng Wiyu causes fatal accidents.

After death, the Wiyu responsible takes the spirit of the deceased to his village and keeps him there as a slave for a year or two. Then the ghosts of his forefathers come to rescue him and take him to their own place. This is on earth, and though human beings cannot go there, mithuns may wonder through it. The dead have their homes in steep and rocky places: they plant roots, and build houses: the cock crows for them. In the end, they die again.

Hill Miri Beliefs and Customs

The eschatology of the Hill Miris, which to some extent resembles that of the other Subansiri tribes—the Apa Tanis, Dalflas and Tagins—is of considerable interest. When a man dies, his 'soul', the Yalo, is carried away by the Wiyu who has caused his death and is kept by him as a slave in his house for a certain period. The Yalo escapes from the body through the shoulder and in a form about which there is some difference of opinion. One tradition declares that it retains the human shape, but that everything is the wrong way round: the eyes are in the back of the head, the hands and feet are back to front. Others say that the Yalo only reassumes human form after it has left the Wiyu's house and made its way to Neli, the Land of the Dead, when it becomes an Orum or ghost.[3] While the Yalo does not normally return to trouble the living, the Orum often revisits its earthly haunts and has to be appeased by offerings of food. At the sowing of the crops, a little grain is specially sown for the Orums and it is supposed that the satisfied ghosts will help the crops to grow.

The journey to the Land of Orums passes through the Land of Wiyus, for the country of the dead is far below the earth, lowest of all habitable places. This country is not unlike the earth, with many steep hills and angry rivers, and the ghosts live in villages and continue to cultivate as in life. Husbands and wives meet again there; they live together and have children. But after ten children have been born, the ghost-parents die and turn into the small butterflies that may sometimes be seen hovering above a spot where one has urinated.

These beliefs underlie Hill Miri funerary custom. When someone is at the point of death, the relatives place an egg in his hand, and this goes with the corpse into the grave, so that when the ghost goes to Orum Land it will be able to test the omens on the way. After death relatives and friends put the personal possessions and small bamboo tubes filled with rice-beer by the head of the corpse, which they keep for one full day in the house. During this period they offer a sacrifice, which in some villages is called the Nintan. A rich family may offer a mithun, a poorer one a pig or even a fowl. The Nibo-priest calls on the senior ghost connected with the family and says: 'We tried in every way to make this dead man well. But the Wiyus were not satisfied with our offerings. They did not want the flesh of animals; they wanted to devour his human flesh. And so he has left us to go to Orum-Land. You know that country well. Care for him there.' He then addresses the ghost: 'Go carefully as you go to Orum-land. There are great hills to climb and deep rivers to ford. The way is hard, but there

[3] Furer-Haimendorf tentatively suggests that the Orum is a separate element in man to the Yalo, but B. K. Shukla considers that the Orum is simply the Yalo at a later stage of its existence. The people themselves do not seem to be very clear about it.

are camps from stage to stage where you can rest. But be careful as you pass through the country of the Wiyus, for they may try to catch you.'

The next day, the mourners dig a fairly deep grave in front of the house, put a mat in it and place the body upon it. If the deceased is a woman, men perform this last rite; if it is a man, women do so. They put food, rice-beer and personal possessions in the grave with the body, and then pile wood, stones and finally earth above it.

When the grave is filled in, they place a small stone menhir above the chest; this is associated with the incident in one of the Gallong stories, which is also known to the Hill Miris, and is intended to restrict the movements of the ghost. Above the stone, they build a rough shed or enclosure. In front of the shed a platform is erected and on this either now, or as soon as possible, two, three or even five stuffed monkeys are made to stand with their arms outstretched; each has a small basket on its back filled with little leaf-packets of food and bamboo tubes for rice-beer; each has a pipe in its mouth. In one village I saw a stuffed otter with the monkeys.

These are the ghost's permanent porters. The Hill Miri thinks of the other world in logical and realistic fashion, and since he knows that the road is long and lonely, he is careful to provide the dead with porters, firewood, food, drink and tobacco. Monkeys are chosen because they are so clever at climbing over obstacles.

When the funeral is done, those villagers who have come under some sort of Assamese influence go to bathe. The members of the dead man's family sit down on one side and visitors sit on another and the Nibo offers a fowl for each group separately. He breaks an egg, mixes the contents with water and sprinkles it with a bunch of bamboo leaves over the whole party. At this time he tells the legend of how death came to the world and cries, 'Let not the tears of Abo-Teni come to our eyes; let not the earth of Abo-Teni cover our bodies.'

For some time after this, the mourners maintain a small hearth inside the enclosure above the grave and a symbolic meal is prepared there. Small birds and rats or squirrels are killed and hung from the roof. A year later there is a great sacrifice, if possible of a mithun, and an altar, which may be twenty feet high and very elaborate, is built near by.

Not all ghosts become ordinary Orums. Those who are killed in battle or suffer accidental deaths, become Gir-Girom-Orums. For if, I was told, you die in the ordinary way, you are resigned; you are not frightened. 'But if you are drowned or fall from a tree, you die in terror.' Such ghosts are dangerous; they trouble the living; the ghost of a murdered man is said to torment his murderer. When a pregnant woman dies she becomes a Chittu-Rumru and does not live with the other dead, but in a place called Pis-Muri, which is on the side of a hill away from Orum-land. 'She lives apart, for she is for ever taboo.'

Should any of these ghosts desire to revisit the earth, they cannot come unattended. They have to pass through Wiyu-land and a Wiyu escorts them and is often the cause of trouble to the living.

The Taraon Mishmi Tradition

In Taraon Mishmi tradition, a man's ghost goes to Tagramiya, the Land of the Dead, and until the proper funerary rites are performed it lives there as a slave; its hands have no fingers but are described as being like fish-nets, unable to hold anything. As soon as possible after a man dies, the Mishmis make a sort of altar called the Brun near the house and within a week a ceremony is held before it. The Goak-priest summons the ghost and begs it to sit in its house, the Brun, which has been so carefully prepared for it, saying, 'You were very happy with us, but you have now taken a new life in another world. We did not send you away; you went there of your own accord and now we call you to us. Come and sit with us.' The priest then shows his possessions one by one to the ghost and names all the relations who have already gone to the Land of the Dead. 'Live in peace with all of them,' he says. 'Take these things with you. Cultivate your clearings in the other world, bear children, build a house; as you did here so do there. Never try to do injury to the living.' Then the priest places the various possessions of the dead on the tomb and kindles the fire within it, for on earth men all eat by a fire. The usual sacrifices are made and the priest performs a remarkable dance. The main elements of the ceremony are the feeding of the ghost; the flattering of the ghost to persuade him to leave the living alone; the presenting of his property to the dead; a feast for the living in which the dead are believed to share; the dance of the priest; and the worship of all the other gods who may be expected to be irritated by neglect.

In the case of important persons, another and much more expensive ceremony called Tagra-Talo is performed in the course of which Jebmallu is worshipped, for 'it is he who causes men to be born.'

The Mishmis practise both cremation and burial. If a man dies in the period between sowing the seed and the early ripening of the harvest his body is cremated, for it is expected that the smoke will go to the field and improve the crop. But when the harvest is about to be cut the Mishmis bury the dead, for it is supposed that if the smell of burning goes to the ripened crop it will spoil it and 'dry its milk'. Sometimes it is not possible to decide which method should be followed and there is a custom of temporary burial—the corpse is exhumed after two months and may then be burnt if the priest so orders. If a body is buried when it should be burnt, it is expected that heavy rain will spoil the crops.

Wancho Funerary Rites

Wancho funerary custom varies from village to village, but in the main resembles that of the Konyaks. Eschatological beliefs also vary greatly: indeed I doubt very much if we can say that 'the Konyaks' or 'the Wanchos' believe a certain thing—all we can say is that some of the Wanchos of some villages believe such and such a thing.

When a man dies, his Lumpu (his soul or ghost) goes down to the World of the Dead, which is here called Hapunglumpu, and maintains an uneasy and precarious existence there until certain rites are completed on earth. The older dead will not give him a place to cook and will not let him sit with them. But when his skull is put into its cist and a great feast is given in his name, then he can live with the other dead. If the feast is not given, the ghost may come and make relations and close friends (but not others) ill.

When a Chief dies, his body is bathed, wrapped in cloth, and laid on a mat. A special kind of basket is placed by his head. His relatives and subjects come one by one and each puts a little bark, betel and tobacco in it, saying, 'This is for you, to save you from trouble.' Sometimes a friend may add a piece of cloth and says, 'This is for you; this is for you to wear.' All the dead man's possessions, his dao, gun, spear, ornaments, bags are put by him, and later are hung on the tomb, which quickly becomes a most desirable museum. For the deceased must take these things below; in the Land of the Dead he will have to build a house, so he will need his dao; he will go head-hunting, so he will need his gun; there will be swiddens to cultivate. At Longkhao, I was told that if these things are not given, the ghost says, 'I have no cloth, I shiver with cold; I have no gun, how can I hunt? I have no dao, how can I clear the path? They won't give me anything, so I will not give them good crops.' If the dead man had owned a tree, a little of the bark or a twig is brought, for otherwise he might worry about it. Then the mourners kill an animal, a pig or fowl, and place its head by the corpse saying 'We give you this so that you will not be hungry.' The head is later hung by the tomb.

For a Chief a wooden coffin is made; commoners are wrapped in cloth and matting. The corpse is kept in the house for only a few hours while relatives are assembling; then men and women go together to the cemetery, which is generally by some path leading out of the village, and they place the coffin or wrapped corpse on a platform some six feet above the ground. They hang the possessions of the dead man on or in front of it.

In the meantime wooden images have been prepared. There is much diversity of custom in the disposal of these. Sometimes, the images are placed in pairs in front of the tomb; sometimes three or four figures are set in a small shed; occasionally, the image is made, not of wood, but of bamboo and cloth; if the deceased was a great warrior, there may be a block of wood with a number of human heads carved on it.

Where the images are made in pairs, the figure on the left is called Chasa, or 'man', and stands for the dead person; that on the right is Chapa and stands for his shadow. 'For the shadow goes with a man.' Where there is a third, or a fourth and fifth figure, this stands for someone whose head he has taken. I was told emphatically that no part of the soul lives in the image; but when the ghost comes from the under-world it sees the figure and is pleased and flattered.

In a few villages, there is a rule that relatives of the dead must keep guard before the tomb for ten to fifteen days in order to prevent any bird or animal desecrating it.

Some time later falls the 'skull-placing day'. Before the ceremony, a number of people go to catch fish; they cook the fish with rice and take the food to the cemetery. They make a wooden dao (for the iron dao is 'a brave thing; it cannot be used to cut a corpse') and with this someone removes the skull and cleans it. They put ornaments in the ears; sometimes they fill the eyes with blocks of wood. They tie a bundle of fish and rice to the skull saying, 'We give this to you; eat and go away, O Lumpu. Go and do not return; do not let us see you again.' Then they put the head into a stone-walled pit and lay a stone cover on the top. In the end, the ghost dies again in the other world.

The journey to the other world is by a path called Lumpu-Lam, which is guarded by an old man and an old woman. When they have greeted the soul they inquire whether it has done good or evil during its earthly life. If it has done ill it is sent to the sky by a winding difficult path, steep, overgrown with grass, and set with slippery stones. When the bad man reaches the Land of the Dead he gets no shelter there; he has to live among great rocks and the only tree is a plantain whose leaves are red instead of the familiar green, and its fruit is all that he will get to eat.

Attached to the skull of the dead man is a mysterious substance, known by a variety of names according to the local village dialect. This is of the greatest value and importance, for it protects the village and improves its crops and brings good luck in the hunt. It provided in the past a powerful motive for head-hunting, for the bringing of a skull to a village meant at the same time the import of the additional energy attached to it. Furer-Haimendorf has an interesting account of an incident at Wakching, which illustrates the nature of the *mio* substance, as it is called in this Konyak village.

'A men's house was being rebuilt and the villagers had been pursued by ill-luck in the ritual hunt which forms part of the building-ceremonies. They therefore decided to sacrifice a cock on the skull-cist of a prominent member of the men's house who had died that year. They cast a fishing-net over the skull-cist in order to catch the *mio* or soul-matter attracted by the sacrifice, and carried the net together with the captive soul-substance to the men's house. When next day the chase was resumed an antelope fell to the spears of the hunters and it was supposed that this success was due to the beneficial influence exerted by their clansman's *mio*.'[4]

To the Yoglis and Moklums the Land of the Dead is called Wulimha, where the houses are very small and can even now be seen by the living in dreams. Those who die in war by the blow of a dao or a shot from a gun must go along a path to a cross-road where they will meet the old woman who sends them forward by a very bad road. Those who die of sickness, however, are sent by a good road. But murderers, thieves and adulterers have to cross a bridge over a stream of boiling water into which they fall.

This moralization of the fate of the soul is rare in the

[4] Furer-Haimendorf, op. cit., p. 48.

tribal theology of other parts of India, but seems fairly generally accepted in NEFA. For example, it is believed that when a Wancho dies his soul or Lumpu must carry on his back to the other world all the things he has stolen, with any other evidence of the evil deeds he has committed. He has to fight all the enemies and wild animals he killed during his lifetime. A Kaman Mishmi story recorded in this Chapter regards the coming of death to the world as a punishment for the sins of mankind.

Among the Buddhist tribes a strong traditional belief in future rewards and punishments has its influence on life in this world. Many Monpa and Sherdukpen dances stress the fate of the sinner after death at the hands of the sombre figure of the God of Death, whom the Sherdukpens call variously Sinchegepu and Sangothung. This tribe believes in rebirth: a good man goes to Chungba-Sangyat: 'he sees the Sun and Moon and is feasted on splendid food.' Then he is sent back to earth as a human being.

But a bad man goes to Sinchegepu, King of the Dead, who punishes him in ways that are vividly illustrated in the dances, and sends him back to earth as an animal.

The punishments inflicted by Sinchegepu are similar to those depicted in Buddhist temples in Ceylon and Siam. The King of the Dead orders his servants to cut up a murderer as the latter cut up his victim. A liar has his tongue, the organ with which he offended, pulled out: a pin is put through it so that he cannot take it back. A thief has his hands tied together and dipped in boiling oil. An adulterer is punished by being chained to a pillar. His organ is tied to another chain and is stretched till the agony is unbearable. A woman guilty of the same offence is tied with arms and legs outstretched against a frame, her head is pulled upward and a fire is lighted beneath her. A mean woman is offered food but, as she is about to eat it, Sinchegepu ties a cord round her throat so that she cannot swallow.

The Singphos believe that there are three 'heavens', of varying degrees of comfort, to which admission is granted according to a man's conduct during life.

The above notes will provide sufficient background for the following stories about the origin of death. In some traditions, men were doomed to live for ever, and as they grew older and older life became more and more intolerable. Death here appears as an act of mercy, freeing men from the burden of an existence which has lost the savour of youth. In a Hill Miri tale, this boon is conferred by a good King upon his subjects. He sees the distress of those who in old age become 'dry as sticks with no blood in them and with nothing to do', and commits suicide in order to bring death to the world. In the northern Siang and Subansiri regions, death in fact is deliberately brought to men by Abo-Teni for their benefit.

In a Pasi story recorded by Dunbar, death is associated with the Sun, as it is in the Dhammai story at p. 284 and the Hrusso story at p. 288. It was after the first human being was sacrificed to persuade the offended Sun to shine that death came to men. The Tagins say that the Sun devours a human being every morning before he rises.

In only one story is there any hint of the idea, so common in central India and Orissa, that death came to relieve the pressure of a growing population. A Wancho tale describes how at first men did not die but changed their form, just as the caterpillar and silkworm do, with the result that the world got too full of human beings who gave a lot of trouble to the birds and animals. Death came to the world, not in this case as an act of mercy to men (who did not grow old and miserable, but constantly renewed their youth) but out of pity for the animals and birds.

1

APA TANI

Duta, Subansiri F.D.

At first the Wiyu Ditu Popi lived between heaven and earth. He decided that people should not die and called the monkey Bupo Ruku and the ant-eater Ami Pimi and asked them to tell this to all living men. But Bupo Ruku and Ami Pimi told the people that the Wiyu had decided that they must die.

Nigi Talo was the first of all men to die. When Ditu Popi heard about this he was very angry and sent for the monkey and the ant-eater and killed them. This is why people still kill these animals whenever they can.

The next man to die was Prokuan and when he died he said that everyone should die in the same way.[5]

2

BORI

Gasheng, Siang F.D.

Awing-Kare had two wives. He used to keep all kinds of animals as pets, and among them was a pig. One day, though he gave him lots of good food, the pig refused to eat anything. Awing-Kare was angry at this and let him out of his stye and he ran away into the jungle. Awing-Kare went after him but could not catch him.

As he was going along, a hornet flew down and laughed at him and said, 'You are such a great man and yet you cannot catch a pig.' Awing-Kare said, 'Well, can you catch him for me?' 'Certainly,' replied the hornet, 'if you want me to.' Awing-Kare said, 'Then by all means catch it for me.' The hornet caught and killed the pig. Awing-Kare went to pick up the carcass to take it home, but it was too heavy for him.

A bat came by and said to Awing-Kare, 'Cut a creeper and tie the pig's body on your back, then you will be able to carry it home.' Awing-Kare tied the pig on his back but it was too heavy, the creeper broke, the pig fell down and one of its long tusks pierced Awing-Kare's foot. The injury was so bad that he only managed to get to his house with great difficulty and soon afterwards he died. His relatives dug a grave and buried him.

Awing-Kare's ghost went to the village of pigs, turned into a pig and lived among the other pigs.

After Awing-Kare's death his two wives wept bitterly and went to search for his ghost. When they heard that he had gone to the Village of Pigs they turned into birds, flew to a tree near the village and sat on the branches weeping. When the pigs heard the

[5] Recorded by B. K. Shukla.

noise they were annoyed and tried to shoot the birds but missed them every time. Then they said to Awing-Kare, 'You used to be a human being and knew how to use a bow and arrow. Why don't you shoot these horrid creatures?' Awing-Kare made a bow and arrow and shot at the birds. He did not hit them, but they fell down and were lost in the grass. The pigs went snorting about trying to find them but there was not a sign of them. At last they said to Awing-Kare, 'It is you who killed the birds, you'd better go and find them.' As Awing-Kare went to find them he took the form of a human being.

We have forgotten what happened after that.

3

DHAMMAI (MIJI)

Nakhu, Kameng F.D.

At first men did not die, but the children of the Sun and Moon always died young and the Sun wept for them so that her face was covered with clouds and there was no sunshine. But men were pleased that her children died, for had they lived they would have made the world unbearably hot.

One day the Sun thought, 'My sorrow is the joy of men.' She said to her husband the Moon, 'Every day hide a little more of your face and I will weep, pretending that you are dying, and when you are completely hidden I will cry out that you are dead.' So the Moon hid his face and then began to hide a little more each day until after fifteen days he disappeared and men thought that he had died.

Down on earth a man tied up a dog by his four feet and wrapped it in a cloth. He put him in a basket in the corner of his house. That day one of the children of the Sun died and the Sun wept for him and the people in the house also wept, pretending that somebody had died. The Sun wondered why they were crying and sent a bird to see whether anybody had really died or not. The bird went to the house and flew about inside but could not discover anything. He went back to the Sun and told her.

Then the Sun sent a snake to the house, but he too could not find out anything. She sent a hen, but she too could not find out anything. She sent a pig, but he too could not find out anything. She sent a fly, but he too could not find out anything. She sent a bee, but he too could not find out anything. At last she sent a hornet, and with his great teeth he cut a hole in the cloth that was hiding the dog's body and pulled out some of the dog's hair. He took this to the Sun and showed it to her and the Sun was angry at men's deceitfulness.

Just then another of her children died and in her rage the Sun threw the body down to earth. As it fell to the ground it turned into the carcass of a deer. Presently a party of men went out to hunt and they found the deer's body and took it home and ate it. Everybody who took a piece of the flesh died and after this death came to men.

4

GALLONG

Kamking, Siang F.D.

The Wiyu Diddu-Kubbo married a girl called Jaye-Buneka. But soon afterwards another Wiyu, one Britapu, carried off the bride and took her down below the surface of a great river. In high rage Diddu-Kubbo pursued them, but could do nothing since they were hiding under the water. He tried to find poison to throw into the river, but failed to get any until at last he met a wild cat who was very sick, just able to crawl along and asked him, 'What has made you so weak?' The cat replied, 'In such and such a place I ate poison and this has made me weak.' Diddu-Kubbo said, 'Show me,' and the cat took him there and he collected the poison and took it to the river where his wife and her lover were hiding. He offered sacrifice in the name of the water-spirit Yebo and threw the poison into the water.

When they drank the poisoned water Britapu and Jaye-Buneka became unconscious and floated to the surface where Diddu-Kubbo cut them to pieces with his dao.

As he was cutting them up, a great storm broke and many trees in the forest fell and Tani's own house collapsed.

The next morning Tani said to himself, 'Many of the animals in my forest must have been killed by the storm. I must go and see how they are.' On his way he came to a place where a great tree had fallen across the path and, as he was looking at it, he heard the bird Lingo-Tongo weeping. He was pleased at the sound and said to the bird, 'Your weeping is most beautiful. Give me some of your spittle and I will put it in my mouth and be able to sing as you do.' The bird said, 'Tani, don't take my spittle, for later you will repent.' But Tani said, 'No, you really must give it to me.' The bird said, 'First of all listen to my story. Long ago, I made a nest in this tree and my children were living here. In yesterday's storm my house was destroyed and all my children killed. I was weeping for my children and my home. If you take my spittle your children will die and you will weep.'

But Tani said, 'I don't care. If you don't give me your spittle, I'll kill you.' The bird was frightened at that and spat on a leaf and gave it to Tani. Tani took the leaf and made two necklaces out of it. When he got home he called his two sons Niddum and Niggum, and put the necklaces round their necks. The following day both of them died and now Tani discovered how to weep.

Since that day dying and weeping have come to the world.[*]

5

HILL MIRI

Chemir, Subansiri F.D.

Before death came, the world was so full of people that there was not enough land to give them food, and they were hungry and unhappy. Most miserable of all were the old: they became dry as sticks, there was no blood in them, they had nothing to do For they got older and older and could not die.

In those days the world was ruled by Raja Kachu. He was a good man and when he saw the distress of his people he was sad. One day he said to himself, 'If I die, I won't have to see this misery and hunger any longer.' He went away secretly to the forest and dug a deep pit. He went into it and pulled the earth down with his own hands. Tei-Pakupi the hornet helped him. In this way he buried himself alive and died.

[*] Today, when anybody dies, the Gallongs tell this story to show the universality of death and 'so prevent too much sorrow'.

After a time, the Raja's subjects began to wonder what had happened and they deputed Abo-Teni to go and find him. Abo-Teni travelled over the hills and through dense forest. One day, as he went, he heard the sound of weeping. It was the bird Echi-Tongu mourning for the Raja's death. 'Why are you making such a noise?' asked Abo-Teni. 'Because the Raja is dead,' replied the bird. 'How can he be dead?' said Abo-Teni. 'There is no such thing as death.' 'No,' said the bird. 'All the same, the Raja really is dead.'

When Abo-Teni realized this, he also wept.

Now when the bird wept, tears fell from her eyes, but when Abo-Teni wept he shed no tears and his weeping was like laughter rather than mourning, and the bird said to him, 'This is no time for laughter. Why aren't you weeping for the Raja?' 'But I am weeping,' said Abo-Teni. 'Look at your eyes,' said the bird, 'and then look at mine.' 'It is true,' said Abo-Teni, 'that your eyes are wet and mine are dry. Put the water from your eyes into mine.'

Then they went to the grave and found Tei-Pakupi the hornet smoothing the soil above it and weeping. He gave Abo-Teni some of the earth to take home and show the Raja's subjects.

Abo-Teni returned and told the people what had happened. He gave them the gift of tears and shared with them the earth of the Raja's grave. After that the old began to die and the young buried them with tears.

6
HILL MIRI
Godak, Subansiri F.D.

In the early days of Abo-Teni and his children, people did not die: they lived on and on.

Echi-Tongu and Techi were winged creatures: they lived and talked like men, but they flew about like birds. Techi made her nest among creepers: she laid her eggs and her children were born. Echi-Tongu found a hollow in a great tree: she laid her eggs and her children were born. Then they both flew away to Assam to buy cloth and salt.

On their way back, while they were still a day's journey from home, there was a storm of wind and rain, and they felt anxious about their children.

The following day, when they reached home, Techi found her

children well and gave them cloth and beads. But the tree where Echi-Tongu had made her nest was blown down by the storm and her children were dead. When she saw what had happened, she began to weep loudly. Abo-Teni heard her, and was interested, for he had never heard a noise like that before. He prepared rice-beer and took it to Echi-Tongu and said, 'What is the matter? Why are you making such a noise?' Echi-Tongu did not reply. Abo-Teni gave her some beer to drink and said, 'Don't be afraid: I was very pleased at the noise you were making.' Echi-Tongu said, 'I was weeping for my dead children. Why should that please you?' 'Why not?' said Abo-Teni. 'Children ought to die.' Echi-Tongu said, 'That may be, but now what can I give you in return for your beer?' 'All I want,' said Abo-Teni, 'is the water falling from your eyes.' 'No, I won't give you that,' said Echi-Tongu. 'If I do, your children will also die.' 'Children ought to die,' said Abo-Teni again. 'I have far too many. If they all live, how will I be able to feed them?' So Echi-Tongu put the water from her eyes into the eyes of Abo-Teni.

As Abo-Teni was going home, he met Tei-Pakupi the hornet. That day the hornet's children had died, and he was digging them a grave. Abo-Teni said, 'What are you doing?' 'My children have died and I am digging their grave.' 'That is very good: you must drink some beer.' And he gave Tei-Pakupi some beer. Then Tei-Pakupi said, 'What can I give you in return for your beer?' 'Give me some of the earth you have dug.' 'No, I won't give you that,' said Tei-Pakupi. 'If I do, you too will have to dig earth to bury your children.' 'Children ought to be buried,' said Abo-Teni. 'I beg you to give me the earth.' So Tei-Pakupi gave him some of the earth from the grave and Abo-Teni went home highly pleased with himself.

On his return, his children began to die. Ever since men have had cause to weep, and have dug graves for their children.

7

HRUSSO (AKA)

Buragaon, Kameng F.D.

At the beginning there were two Suns who were man and wife and two Moons who were also man and wife. The heat of these four was so great that on earth the grass and trees withered away and men and animals died.

But then the Sun's wife and the Moon's husband began to make love to one another secretly. For this they used to come down to earth and when they met there everything caught fire around them and that is why today the earth is sometimes red and sometimes yellow ; when we see this we know that the Sun and Moon made love to one another there.

When the Sun and Moon came to the earth, men and animals ran away and hid for fear of being burnt to death. They gathered together in a secret place and said, 'Who can destroy these evil-doers?' But none of them was strong enough to kill a Sun and Moon, so they went to search for someone who could.

Now there were two mighty brothers, Chou-Siphu and Khrao-Libji. When they saw the men and animals going through the forest, they stopped them and said, 'Where are you all going?' Men and animals told the two brothers what had happened and the unhappy state in which they were living. Hearing this the two brothers said, 'We will certainly kill these evil-doers. You all hide somewhere and we will wait for them to come here and then we'll kill them.'

Men and animals hid and after a little while the Sun's wife and the Moon's husband came to earth, and Chou-Siphu and Khrao-Libji shot at them with their bows. Khrao-Libji's arrow pierced the Sun's wife and she died there on the ground ; Chou-Siphu's arrow struck the Moon's husband, but did not kill him immediately and he rose into the air and fled away with the arrow in his body to his wife in the sky and when he reached her he died in her arms. When his wife saw him pierced by the arrow she wept bitterly.

The Sun said, 'My wife has died down on earth, but the husband of my sister the Moon has died here. If now she gives his body to men and animals they too will die.' So he went to warn men and animals. 'When my sister the Moon calls to you,' he said, 'make no reply, but when I call you may reply.' He returned to his place and darkness fell.

With the coming of night the Moon came out of her house with her husband in her arms and weeping bitterly. Everyone was asleep except the barking-deer and the peacock in the forest. When these two heard the weeping of the Moon they cried, 'What is the matter?' When she heard them the Moon let the body of her husband fall to the earth and cried, 'As you killed my husband so may you all—men, animals and birds—die too.' This is how death came to the world.

But when the cock heard what had happened he roused the Sun, calling to him to come and help. The Sun came out of his house and saw that men and animals were weeping. He said, 'There is nothing I can do now. I warned you not to answer if the Moon cried to you. Now it is too late and you all must die.'

8

IDU MISHMI

Ichuli, Lohit F.D.

Long ago there was a priest called Si-Aneru who had living with him in his house his wife, his sister and his mother.[7]

One day he went far away to offer sacrifice and did not come back for a long time. The women grew anxious and his sister went with a bird to fetch him. Still he did not come straight home, but went from place to place while his sister followed weeping. On the road to Tibet there was a great bare rock and the sister sat weeping on it and her tears still flow from the place.

[7] There is an interesting variant on this story recorded by T. K. Barua in the Dibang Valley. In this case, Si-Aneru had a handsome son who died a natural death when his father was away from home. A bird brought the news to Si-Aneru who hastened home and attempted to revive the child by every means known to him. When these were unsuccessful, he put an earthworm into his mouth and slowly the body came back to life.

Although very young, the boy was already married and his girl-wife, though delighted at her husband's recovery, was repelled by the smell of the worm in his body. This led to many quarrels, for she would have nothing to do with him on account of this unpleasant smell, and at last he went away and hid in the forest.

Si-Aneru, anxious to remedy the matter, called on the spirit Ephatha and begged him to remove the smell from his son's body. Ephatha found the boy in the forest, treacherously killed and ate him and told the father that the boy had lost his way and was dead. Si-Aneru, who was a very powerful priest, brought his son out of Ephatha's stomach but since the body had been there for some time it had become very small and was stinking horribly. Si-Aneru, therefore, decided not to take the boy home, but dug a pit and buried him alive in it, covering him with large boulders, with the idea that the boulders would remove the smell.

After this Si-Aneru used to offer rice-beer and pork regularly to the ghost of his dead son and this has become a common custom among the Mishmis.

When Si-Aneru finally approached his village he climbed to a nearby hill and turned into a kite and flew over his house to see how things were. He saw that his mother was dead and the forest round the house had dried up, letting the red earth appear. His wife whom he had left as a young girl now looked old.

He flew back to the hill and became a man again and then went down to his house. After a few days he began to perform the rites for his dead mother. As he sang, his sister sat beside him and sang and wept at the same time. Soon his mother's ghost appeared in human form and sat on the veranda of their house. In her eyes, ears, mouth and nostrils worms were crawling. Inside the house the wife of Si-Aneru's son was weaving at her loom but when she saw the ghost she was terrified and threw the stick of the loom at her and drove her away.

Then from under a rock on the hill above the house an old priest called Iputo came down and said to Si-Aneru, 'Your mother is not clean, her whole body is full of worms but I have a plantain tree and I will make her clean with its leaves.' When he had said this he went away to get the leaves. But in the meantime they heard that the ghost had fallen down from the mountain.

When Si-Aneru heard this, he sent a bird to see whether she had been killed. The bird searched everywhere and came back and said, 'It is not true, no one has fallen down and no one has been killed. But I saw Iputo there and mosquitoes are flying out of his mouth. It looks as if he himself has devoured your mother's ghost.'

Si-Aneru was naturally angry at this and went to see Iputo. He tied him up and danced and sang before him. Then with his dao he cut his mouth open and a swarm of mosquitoes flew out. Si-Aneru sang, 'My mother's ghost was eaten by Iputo and has turned into a swarm of mosquitoes. O mosquitoes, don't come into my house, live in the jungle nearby and I will bring you food and drink, I will dig a hole in the ground and put it there.'

But as all the trees and grasses had been burnt the mosquitoes settled on the root of a bamboo. Si-Aneru took them rice-beer and food in a bamboo for them, but he did not pour the beer out properly and most of it fell to the ground. He put the bamboo upside down to prevent it growing, for he believed that so long as it did not take root no more mosquitoes would be born and come into his house.

Then he buried rice and pork in a leaf for the mosquitoes and said, 'If leaves shaped like a boar's teeth grow from this leaf, then more mosquitoes will be born. But if they do not grow, there will be no more mosquitoes.'

Then he buried a piece of fish saying, 'If no fish comes alive from this, then no fish will ever be able to climb to the top of a mountain.' This is why there are no fish on the tops of hills.

Then he buried the feather of a quail and said, 'If this feather does not come out and fly of its own accord, this bird will not be able to fly.' This is why the quail cannot fly.

When Si-Aneru had done all these things, his sister went to the place and wept, crying, 'From today you are no longer my mother. Once you were her ghost, but you were eaten by Iputo and turned into a swarm of mosquitoes. Don't come to see us any more but go to the Land of the Dead and remain there.'

Since that day ghosts have not walked about the world in human form.

9

KAMAN MISHMI

Lohit Valley, Lohit F.D.

After men had been created they soon turned to evil ways and, since the earth produced abundant crops, they neglected their cultivation and spent their time in pleasure.

When Matai saw this he was angry and sent two spirits, Anjao Kaca and Glang Kaca, to punish them. Anjao Kaca was the god of sickness and Glang Kaca was the god of diarrhoea and jaundice, and they tormented the people mercilessly with these diseases.

At last the people of the earth realized the folly of their ways and an old man called Affa declared that the only way to save themselves from disease was to offer sacrifice to Matai. So the people brought fowls and pigs and offered them to him.

Then Matai came to them and said, 'Since you have taken to evil ways, you and your children will have to die. You will not come back again to earth till the small stones grow into great rocks and the feathers of the crow turn grey.'

And still today the small stones have not grown into great rocks, nor have the feathers of the crow turned grey. So too no man has returned to earth after his death.[1]

[1] Recorded by T. K. Barua.

10

MINYONG

Parong, Siang F.D.

Ninur-Botte made an earthen vessel, and when it was ready, he picked it up to examine it, but he dropped it and it broke into pieces. He did all he could to put it together but to no avail. He said, 'Why can't I mend it? I took so much trouble to make it.' Doini-Pollo said, 'You did well to make it: you did ill to break it.' Ninur-Botte said, 'How was it that I did ill?' Doini-Pollo said, 'Because from today men will die.' This is why men die. Had it been possible to put together what was broken, men would have lived for ever.

11

MOKLUM

Longke, Tirap F.D.

Before death came to the world not only men but animals lived for ever. Rang did not like this and decided that the animals should die. So he gave death to Utokoo, the cock. The cock brought it to earth and gave it to the snake. The snake accepted it and died. The python saw it and said, 'If we keep it with us, we will die.' So he quickly gave death to men and they began to die instead, for the snake never dies, but only changes its skin.

12

SINGPHO

Imbu, Tirap F.D.

Long ago there was a Raja called Sitte-Charka, whose Rani shone in beauty like the light. When he went anywhere at night he used to take her with him so that her beauty could lighten the path by which he had to go. Not only light but a lovely scent came from her body.

After a time the Rani died and the Raja, who loved her greatly, had her body put in a box which he placed on a platform in front of the house. Even though she had died, the beautiful scent did not leave her body and the Raja would go four or five times every day to the coffin to delight in the sweet smell.

Many days passed in this way until the Supreme God Phara thought it was wrong that so beautiful a lady should lie unburnt, and came to see the Raja. 'Why have you kept your wife's body like this?' he asked. The Raja replied, 'Because she shone as the light and smelt as a flower I could not burn her hody, but when I die her body and mine shall be burnt together.' Phara said to him, 'Since you loved your wife so much, don't you want to talk to her?' The Raja replied, 'Of course I do.' Phara said, 'Dig a pit in the ground beneath the platform where the coffin rests and there you will meet your Rani.'

The Raja dug a pit in the ground beneath the platform and presently a worm came out of the ground and said to him, 'I am your wife. Because you did not burn my body, I have turned into a worm and am living in the ground. But if you burn my body, I will be able to live happily in my proper place.' When the Raja heard this he was very sorry and immediately had his wife's body burnt and her soul went to the Land of the Dead.

It is for this reason that the Singphos nowadays do not keep the bodies of the dead for more than one or two days before burning them.[9]

13

SINGPHO

Dumba, Tirap F.D.

At the beginning people did not die and did not know how to weep. They grew very old and as they got older and older their misery increased. They could not walk, they had very little to eat and there was no joy or comfort in their lives.

[9] The Singpho rule is that a corpse must be cremated during the actual Hindu month in which the death has occurred. If, for example, someone dies in the middle of the month the body can be kept for a day or two; but if death occurs on the last day of the month it must be burnt within a few hours. There is a tradition that formerly the Singphos used to dispose of the dead in a manner similar to that still followed by the Wanchos and Konyaks; they placed the body in a coffin and exposed it on a platform until it decomposed.

In the forest there was a squirrel living in a tall tree. One day a kite flew over the tree and the squirrel chattered in fright. The kite was angry and flew down and killed him with his claws, throwing the body down to the ground. A man called Singra-Phang-Magam passed by and when he saw the squirrel lying on the ground he was astonished, for never in his life had he seen a dead creature. 'How is it,' he thought, 'that our own people do not get like that, lying still and unable to use their arms and legs?' He picked up the squirrel and put it in a corner of his house, covering it with a piece of cloth.

Then he called the Moon and the Stars saying, 'A man has died, come and see him.' The Moon and the Stars came weeping with all the spirits of hill and forest, and Singra-Phang-Magam and his wife wept with them. But when the Moon and the Stars asked where the dead man was and Singra-Phang-Magam showed them the squirrel, they were angry and said, 'This is not a man, it is only an animal.' Singra-Phang-Magam told them, 'But how has this squirrel died and why don't men die in the same way?' The Moon and the Stars asked, 'Do men also want to die?' 'Certainly they do,' he said. 'As one grows old, life become intolerable.' Then the Moon and the Stars and all the spirits said, 'If you eat the squirrel's flesh, you will all die.' Singra-Phang-Magam cut the body up into tiny pieces and distributed it to all the men and women in the world, and as a result death came to them and they learnt how to weep.

14

TAGIN

Serra, Subanhiri F.D.

Two brothers went together to hunt. They came to a valley between three hills. The elder brother said to the younger, 'You go on this side and I will go on that, and we will meet where the hills join a third. Whoever gets there first will make a sign and go forward.' The younger brother said, 'How can we go separately through such thick forest?' But the elder brother insisted and they parted, hunting on separate hills.

The younger brother was the first to reach the place where the two hills met the third. But he found no sign there and was frightened, for he thought that surely his elder brother would have got there before him.

Suddenly there was a cry among the hills: 'Soon I shall go into the jaws of a wild beast.' The boy thought it must be his brother calling and ran to find him.

Soon in an open space he saw his brother. He had thrown his clothes and weapons on the ground and was going slowly into the mouth of an enormous snake. The boy shot the snake with an arrow and cut its body into pieces. So he rescued his brother. He put his clothes on him and said, 'Henceforth let us hunt together.'

But the elder brother said, 'There's nothing to worry about. Let us go on hunting separately.' So they parted again. After a while, there was another cry among the hills: 'I am dead. A tiger has killed me.' And in truth a tiger had killed the elder brother and dragged his body to a cave, where he shared the flesh with his tigress and two cubs.

The younger boy found traces of his brother's blood and followed them to the cave. By the time he got there, the tiger and his wife had gone out again to hunt, but they had left their children behind. The boy went into the cave and killed them. Then he sat by the threshold with drawn bow, and as the tigress came in he shot her. Then the tiger came and he killed him also.

After this the boy searched for his brother's bones, took them home and buried them. This is why we bury the dead in front of our houses.[10]

15

WANCHO

Wakka, Tirap F.D.

At first men did not die, but changed their form just as the caterpillar and silkworm do. The result was that before long the world got very full of human beings who caused a lot of trouble to the birds and animals, for they not only killed them but took

[10] The Tagins and Gallongs of Subansiri bury their dead in front of, or near, their dwellings and erect shrines above them.

away their food. Whatever the birds could collect was stolen by the human beings.

One day a crane caught a fish and was about to eat it, when a man came by and snatched it from its beak and ate it instead. The crane lost its temper and cursed him, saying that he would soon die. But the man caught hold of the crane and hit it on its head with the result that it became bald.

Another day a crow got a mouthful of meat and was about to eat it when a man snatched it from its beak and ate it instead. The crow exclaimed: 'If men live for ever, we birds will surely die.' The god Tatchak Namlong heard the crow and declared that men should henceforth begin to die.

16

WANCHO

Longkhao, Tirap F.D.

When the first man in the world died, he felt lonely and unhappy without company in the other world and longed to return to earth.

The souls of the dead are afraid of light and can only come in darkness. The first man therefore caught a firefly and carried it in his hands as a torch to light him across the dark mountains. He came to his clearing on the hill-side and danced there and then went on to the village to see his friends.

Since then the souls of the dead have always done this but because people shed tears at funerals, the fireflies refuse to go to the place of the dead, for they are afraid that their light will be quenched by the tears. So the newly-dead, after dancing in their clearings, have to go on in darkness to see the bodies of the old dead.

PART FOUR: THE WORLD OF ANIMALS

CHAPTER SIXTEEN

ARTHROPODS

STORIES about the arthropods generally show them as kindly and helpful to man. Ants, crabs and prawns assist in creating the world ; hornets heal the sick and bring warnings of danger ; in Singpho tales it is the spider who teaches the first woman how to weave and the crab who shows the first blacksmith how to make tongs: in a Moklum tale men learn to chew betel by watching the mosquito reddening its lips with blood. In a Bugun story a bee impregnates a lonely girl as if it was impregnating flowers. The Apa Tani story in this Chapter describes a very serviceable crab, and the Tagins also describe how the crab assists Abo-Teni to capture his enemy the bat.[1]

There are a number of stories about fireflies recorded here, for the tribal people all over India are fascinated by them; Gond songs flatter a girl's sparkling eyes—'your eyes are fireflies'. In Orissa, the Gadabas say they are the eyes of gods, the Kamars say that the first firefly was the eye of a youth which was accidently plucked out by the branch of a tree. The Binjhwar tradition is that God sent fire to earth by rubbing it off his own body and putting it on a little insect; after it had been given to mankind some was left and the creature became the first firefly. The Singpho story at page 304 is based on the same idea.

In the Minyong story given in this Chapter the bee was born from the dung of a Wiyu in the form of a mithun and its honey is sweet because it drank the Wiyu's urine. The Shimong tradition is less undignified; honey gets its sweetness because a bee stole rice-beer long ago.

[1] For a detailed account of the crab in Indian folklore, see my *Folk-Tales of Mahakoshal*, pp. 153 ff.

[2] See my *Tribal Myths of Orissa*, pp. 685 f.

1

APA TANI

Reru, Subansiri F.D.

Long ago there were two sisters ; they used to go together every day to work in the fields. The elder sister always drank a great deal of water, and one day the younger one asked her why. The elder girl said, 'I love eating grass and this makes me thirsty.'

The girl continued to graze on the grass by the banks of the stream and to drink deeply of the water, until presently she turned into a mithun. The younger girl wandered from place to place in sorrow.

One day, as she went weeping home, she met an old woman who asked her why she was crying. When the girl told her, the old woman gave her a crab and a fish, telling her to hang them up above the hearth. This she did and went next morning to the fields.

When she was out of the house, the crab came down to the ground. He prepared rice, fetched water and cooked food. When the girl came home she found everything ready and wondered who could have done it.

This happened for several days and then the girl told her dog to find out who was doing all these things. Next time she went to the fields, the dog hid in the house and saw the crab prepare rice, fetch water and cook the food. At this he barked so loudly that the neighbours came to see what was the matter.

At the same moment the girl returned with a load of paddy. The crab said that it was he who had been helping her, but the fish said that he too had helped. They argued about this for a long time, and finally the fish said that he wanted to marry the girl, for she was very beautiful. The girl agreed and the fish took her to his home in the stream.

2

BORI

Gatte, Siang F.D.

Taru-Tase is a Wiyu who takes the form sometimes of a hawk and sometimes of a firefly. In former times when the tribes were at war with one another he would take the form of a hawk and fight for the people who gave him sacrifice. The enemy also would offer sacrifice to him and he would take the form of another hawk on their side. Then the two hawks would fight and victory or defeat for those on earth would depend on who won in the sky.

Sometimes, however, Taru-Tase would take the form of a firefly and fly into the eyes of the enemy and blind them.

3

MINYONG

Parong, Siang F.D.

Limir-Sabbo was a Wiyu in the form of a mithun. When the Sun and Moon first gave light to the world, he began to wander in the hills. He passed dung and urine, and from his dung came the first bees: they flew above it and drank the urine. They liked it so much that they would not go away. So Dolling-Botte Wiyu picked them up and put them on a tree, but they fell off. He put his belt on the tree, and they sat on it and made their home there. The honey of bees is sweet, sweet as the urine of a Wiyu.

4

MINYONG

Komkar, Siang F.D.

Polung-Sabbo was a Wiyu, who had the form of a great four-footed animal like a mithun. Banji-Botte was a Wiyu in the form of a man. These two lived far from each other ; they never met.

But one day Banji-Botte went hunting and came to the forest where Polung-Sabbo lived. When the mithun-spirit saw the man-spirit, he was angry and shouted, as a Gam shouts in the Kebang, 'I am the greatest of all. I can make all things. What are you doing here?' He tried to kill Banji-Botte, but the man-spirit dodged him and broke his horn, so that the outer covering fell off. It turned into a firefly, for as it fell to the ground, it struck a rock and sparks flashed from it.

5

SINGPHO

Wakitna, Tirap F.D.

At the beginning, when men were first made, Mathum-Matta rubbed some dirt from his hands and blew into it from his golden pipe, whereupon it turned into a firefly.

Mathum-Matta said to it, 'Fly round the earth and see how many people there are.' The firefly said, 'But it is very dark, how can I see my way about?' Mathum-Matta was annoyed and spat on the firefly's backside and it immediately burst into flame.

By the light in its own tail the firefly came down to earth. It saw the state of mankind and flew back to Mathum-Matta.

As it was going along a kite attacked it and the firefly could not make its way to Mathum-Matta but returned to earth and lived there. This is why the firefly does not come out by day but only appears at night.

CHAPTER SEVENTEEN

FROGS, LEECHES AND FISHES

THE leech has a peculiar fascination for the tribal people in all the areas where it is found; the supposed difficulty of killing it, its singular shape and habits and its association with blood combine to make it an object of perennial interest. Hutton points out that 'the word for leech is one of the comparatively few words that are very patently traceable to a common root among most of the Naga tribes.'[1] Among the Kacharis, there is (or was) actually a sub-tribe named after the leech, and its members held the creature in high regard and could not under ordinary circumstances kill it; 'though on occasions of certain religious ceremonials, as for example purification after a death in the family, its members were required to chew a leech with vegetables for a certain limited period, though apparently only once in a life-time.'[2] There is a widely distributed belief that the leech is immortal, and several Naga tribes (such as the Semas, Lhotas, Aos, Changs and Phoms) have a belief that, although if a leech is cut in half, it dies, if cut in three pieces a little bird takes the middle part as his share and joins the two end-parts together by way of return.[3]

The Ao Nagas think it unlucky to be bitten by a leech on the knuckle of the index finger of the right hand, for you will soon use that knuckle to rub your eyes while you weep for the death of a near relation.[4] The Lhotas apply a leech to a sprain to suck out the blood and so relieve the swelling.[5]

Stories about the leech, both in NEFA and in other parts of India, have two main motifs—one sexual, the other based on revenge.

[1] J. H. Hutton, *The Sema Nagas* (London, 1921), p. 258.
[2] S. Endle, *The Kacharis* (London, 1911), p. 25.
[3] Hutton, op. cit., p. 258.
[4] J. P. Mills, *The Ao Nagas* (London, 1926), p. 295.
[5] J. P. Mills, *The Lhota Nagas* (London, 1922), p. 81.

In Baiga, Saora and Juang tales the leech is related, by a natural association of ideas, to the woman's period.[6] A Juang tale describes how some of the flesh protecting a woman's parts was torn off, thrown into a stream and there turned into a leech.[7] Similarly, in a Singpho tale recorded in this Chapter, the female organ, which at first was very long, was cut off and became a leech. A singular Dhammai story describes the leech as being born of the union of two women: there is an old Indian tradition that such a child will have no bones, and this child has no arms or legs or even a face. The mother puts it to the breast, but instead it catches her hand and drinks her blood.

Other stories are associated with the idea of revenge; the leech is a person or creature who has been frustrated or injured, and now takes its revenge on man by sucking his blood. Thus in a Koya story from Orissa, two parties of villagers quarrel over the use of a tank: the losers throw bits of wood into the water and these turn into leeches and attack the victors. In a Saora story, some thoughtless boys drown a young girl. She is reborn in the water and her children are leeches who take revenge by biting all who go to bathe in the stream. A Pengu tale describes how men were at first eyeless and blind, but the eyes of the leech were taken from it and given to them, and ever since it has sought revenge.[8]

So also, in the Singpho tale already quoted, the leech is asked by men to get them seed, and it agrees to do so on condition that it is allowed to return to the place whence it came. It obtains the seed but, when it claims its reward, men laugh at it and throw it away in the forest. It still remembers its injury and seeks revenge. There are a number ot stories about the wives of Abo-Tani told bv the Apa Tanis, Tagins, Hill Miris and Daflas. They all agree in describing how the ancient tribal hero marries a dry leaf or reed and, since his child can get no milk from so barren a mother, he fastens on his father's hand or knee

[6] *Myths of Middle India*, p. 175 and *Tribal Myths of Orissa*, p. 216.
[7] *Myths of Middle India*, p. 265.
[8] *Tribal Myths of Orissa*, pp. 217.

and takes his blood. The father shakes him off into the forest where he has lived, angry and frustrated, ever since. In a Singpho story, a baby is buried alive and reborn as a leech to torment his parents. In a Dhammai story, the leech is born from the blood dripping from the hand of a god, which is bitten by a girl whom he is trying to seduce.

A few other stories simply associate the origin of the leech with blood. 'It was born of blood, so it must live on blood,' as a Minyong tale puts it. Here the leech comes from the blood of an archetypal mithun at the beginning of the world. In one Bori story, the leech comes from the powdered bones of a sinister old man who wishes to eat human flesh and in another from the broken body of a cannibalistic Wiyu. These stories may be compared with Binjhwar and Kamar tales from Orissa which describe a lustful and dangerous demon who is killed and from whose ashes the leech is born.[1]

1

BORI

Gameng, Siang F.D.

Tani married Doini-Aiye, the daughter of the Sun, and had two sons by her. When the boys were old enough they used to go together to fetch water. One day when they returned home they found their mother sitting on the rack above the fire and asked her what she was doing. She replied, 'Your father has never mended this rack, so I am doing it instead.'

The next day when the boys came back after fetching water they found their mother sitting up in the loft and asked her what she was doing. She replied, 'Your father has never mended this loft, so I am doing it instead.'

The third day when the boys came home they found their mother sitting on the roof and asked her what she was doing. She replied, 'Your father has never mended the roof, so I am doing it instead.'

The boys went into the house to put the water down, but when

[1] *Tribal Myths of Orissa*, p. 215.

they came out, they found their mother had disappeared. She had gone away to her father's house. The boys set out to find her.

Their search took them through the forest and first to the Village of Fowls, where they found many cocks and hens working in the fields. The boys asked them if they had seen their mother. The fowls said, 'We have seen your mother ; but if you want us to tell you where she is, you must help us in our fields.' The boys worked for a time in the fields and then the fowls said, 'Go on your way, and where the path branches in two, go to the left.'

The boys did as they were told and after a time came to the Village of Wild Cats, where they found many cats clearing the forest and tilling the soil. The boys asked the cats if they had seen their mother. The cats said, 'We have seen your mother ; but if you want to know where she is, you must help us in our fields.' The boys worked for some time in the fields and then the cats said, 'Go on your way, and where the path branches in two, go to the left.'

The boys went on their way until they came to the Village of Boars, where they found many boars clearing the forest and tilling the soil. The boys asked them if they had seen their mother. The boars said, 'We have seen your mother ; but if you want us to tell you where she is, you must help us in our fields.' The boys worked there and then the boars said, 'Go on your way, and where the path branches in two, go to the left.'

The boys did as they were told and after taking the left hand turn met an old man sitting by the path and making a basket. They asked him where their mother was and he said, 'Sit down and help me for some time and I will tell you.' The boys did so and the old man said, 'Go on your way and where the path branches in two, go to the left.'

The boys went on their way, and after they had gone some distance, looked round and saw the old man following them. They said, 'Why are you following us?' At that the old man took out his dao and came forward to strike them, but the boys climbed up a tree and escaped. The old man began to cut down the tree so that the boys would fall and he would be able to kill them. They began to cry loudly, begging the other trees to help and send their branches so that they could escape. At once a strong wind blew a branch from a neighbouring tree towards them and they were able to climb onto it, and in this way, the wind helping them, they climbed from tree to tree until they came to the Village of Squirrels. The boys said, 'Hide us, for an old man is following and wants to kill us.' One of the squirrels had a quiver and he removed the arrows and told the boys to hide inside.

After a time the old man arrived. There was a bridge there across the river and he asked the squirrels if it was safe. They replied that it was. When he got half-way across, the squirrels called to him and said, 'Jump up and down and see how strong it is.' The old man jumped to test the wood, but it broke under his weight, and he fell into the river and was drowned.

After a little while the old man's wife came looking for her husband and asked the squirrels if they had seen him. They replied, 'Your old man has been drowned in the river.' She went down the river bank searching for her husband's body. When she found it, the flesh had rotted away and only the bones remained. She took the bones home and ground them into powder. She threw this powder into the forest and from it came the first leeches and all kinds of insects.

2

DAFLA

Solo (Palin Valley), Subansiri F.D.

Abo-Teni's son was Jingi Tani. He searched everywhere in the forest for a wife but could not find one, and at last in despair he went to the leaf called Ok. In due time the leaf conceived and bore a son called Tape. But she had no milk in her breasts and Tape cried and cried until his father took him and fed him with blood from his knee. This is why Tape, the leech, still feeds on human blood.[10]

3

DHAMMAI (MIJI)

Sachung, Kameng F.D.

There were two sisters, Riang-Mo and Nining-Mo, who could not find husbands. Presently they came together and Nining-Mo

[10] Recorded by B. K. Shukla.

conceived and after a time gave birth to a child. This child had no arms or legs, or even a face for that matter but he cried continually. Nining-Mo thought that he was hungry for her milk and took him on her lap but he caught hold of her hand and drank the blood. She tried to put him to her breast, but he would not leave the hand, so in the end she went to the veranda and shook him off into the grass outside.

When she saw the blood flowing from her hand and her child down in the grass, she said to him, 'You have no hands or feet, so you must live by drinking blood.' This was the first leech.

Some time afterwards Nining-Mo had another child. He too had no arms or legs or even a face, but he cried continually. The mother thought that he wanted her milk and took him on her lap and gave him her breast. The child did not take the milk but bit the breast and his mother in her anger threw him out into the forest. She said to him, 'You have no hands or feet, so you must live by biting people.' This was the first snake.

Because the snake bit his mother's breast, one breast of a woman is often smaller than the other.

4

HILL MIRI

Chemir, Subansiri F.D.

In the beginning when all the world was soft and there was a little water on the surface, the three Wiyus Chuch-Barji, Chakam-Pau and Titik-Kuluk made the rivers by heaping up the mud in some places and digging channels in others. When the rivers were ready, the Wiyus asked each other, 'What can live in these rivers? Men cannot, nor can dogs or pigs or mithuns: none of the creatures which have noses can live in water.' As they were speaking, Wiyu Nitpor and Wiyu Korala came by: they were carrying fish-traps made of cane.

When the three Wiyus saw them, they said, 'What are those things you are carrying?' Wiyu Nitpor said, 'They are traps: put them into the water and then lift them out.' The Wiyus put the traps into the water and lifted them out with their right hands: they were full of fish. They put them in again and lifted them out with their left hands ; and they were full of prawns, crabs, swimming creatures of every kind. But there were no frogs, for the frogs fell from the sky: they were not born on earth.

5

HRUSSO (AKA)

Hussigaon, Kameng F.D.

A tiger and a frog were friends. The frog used to go to visit the tiger's house and the tiger always gave him a good meal of meat. One day the frog said, 'Friend, you always give me very good food when I visit you. Now you must come and pay me a return visit.' The tiger replied, 'Friend, I am a meat-eater. If you can give me some meat I will certainly come to your house.' The frog said, 'Of course, you will have what you like ; come tomorrow to my house.'

The frog went away rather worried how to feed the tiger properly and went all over the place to try and find some meat for him. Presently, as he was going along the bank of a river he came across a horse which had come down to drink water. The frog hopped on to the horse's back and tried to bite off some of his flesh, but the horse kicked him and broke his legs. This is why even today the frog cannot walk straight.

The frog made his way slowly and painfully back to his house and a little later the tiger arrived for his visit. The frog received him with honour and made him sit down. But he felt very ashamed that he had no meat to offer him. So he crept slowly up to the loft and there began to remove the flesh from his own legs. This hurt him very much and he cried, 'O mother, I am going to die.' The tiger heard him and climbed up to see what was the matter. When he saw that the frog had cut off his own flesh for him, he felt very bad about it and said, 'Friend, there was no need for you to do this. In any case, I wouldn't eat your flesh.'

He comforted him as well as he could and went away. But the frog felt so ashamed that he left his house for good and went to live in the river.

This is why the frog always lives in the water and why his legs are so thin.

6

IDU MISHMI

Dibang Valley, Lohit F.D.

Nettles were growing all along the paths in the hills. One day when Anya was going somewhere, he brushed his feet against them and was badly stung. He called the leaves to him and said, 'I will destroy you for giving me this pain.' The leaves replied, 'Our hearts are as pure as the fragrance of a flower. We have been made as we are by the snake who poured his venom over us and this made our little stings so poisonous.'

Anya summoned the snake and the snake said, 'One day I was frightened when I saw a deer rushing towards me and I hid beneath the nettle.'

Anya summoned the deer and the deer said, 'All I did was to go to a tree to get some fruits. I had no idea of frightening the snake'.

Anya summoned the fruits and the fruits said, 'We had our home in the branches of the tree, but the squirrel cut our branches and we fell to the ground.'

Anya summoned the squirrel and the squirrel said, 'A bird asked me to bring the fruits for his chicks who were crying for food.'

Anya summoned the bird and the bird said, 'The humming of the mosquitoes made my chicks restless and they cried for food, so I asked the squirrel to bring them some fruit.'

Anya called the mosquitoes and the mosquitoes said, 'We are not to be blamed, for the toad disturbed us by croaking so loudly.'

Anya and the others summoned the toad. They found him in the middle of a pond happily croaking away at the top of his voice. Anya went into the water and gave him such a good beating that he became hump-backed, which he has been ever since.[11]

[11] Recorded by T. K. Barua. Anya is one of the greatest of the Idu gods, second only to Inni Taya himself. Stack and Lyall record a rather similar cumulative Mikir tale, which describes why the frog is spotty. The details are different, but it is interesting to find one of the comparatively rare cumulative tales associated in one case with the humped back of the toad, in the other with the spots of the frog. See E. Stack and C. Lyall, *The Mikirs* (London, 1908), pp. 46 ff.

7

MINYONG

Siang Frontier Division

(From G.D.S. Dunbar, *Abors and Galongs*, p. 64)

There were two stars Dupuir and Dudengu, brother and sister, who married and had a son Puirshem. He died and fell from the sky—a shooting star—into the water and was carried down with the stream. Now Tapu Talar, one of the water spirits, had set a trap for fish and in it the star was caught. And Tapu Talar took it out and ate it. Then the bat, who seems to have been the tale-bearer, both in Minyong and Galong stories, told the stars what had befallen Puirshem. So there was war between the stars and the dwellers in the water. And the fishes and the frogs came out of the water and began to climb up the rocks towards the stars, very slowly for they kept sliding and falling back into the water. Presently the stars began to shoot their arrows at them, and the frogs and fishes tried to shelter behind the rocks and stones as the arrows went by. But they could not cover themselves altogether, and the arrows speeding past them gashed and grazed them on either side, and gave to the fish the gills they have to this day.

8

MINYONG

Siang Frontier Division

(From G. D. S. Dunbar, *Abors and Galongs*, pp. 63f.)

Once upon a time there was a great flood in the Siang river (Dihang), that covered all the earth. And when it subsided, all the fish were found stranded on the ground. So Shile Shido (Shedi Melo, the omnipotent spirit) took the hills and piled them up on either side of the river, to shut it in for all time, and the fish fell back into the water and regained life.

9

MONPA

Themband, Kameng F.D.

An old man and woman grew old together. When she was old, the woman refused to work because, she said, she had a lot of pain in her knee. This naturally was very troublesome for her old husband and one day in a fit of temper he struck her with a stone pestle. When he did this a frog hopped out of her knee.

When they saw this they were astonished, especially when the frog asked them to get him a bride. They told him that the best thing would be for him to go round the village and find a girl for himself.

The frog went straight to the house of Chhatpa-Khochi, an old man living at the end of the village. He stood before the house and cried in a hoarse voice, 'Father-in-law, please come out, please come out, please come out.' Chhatpa-Khochi came out with his eldest daughter, but could see nothing but a frog sitting on a hollow log which contained water for the horses and cattle. Thinking he was mistaken, he went back into the house, but directly he went indoors the frog again cried, 'Father-in-law, please come out, please come out, please come out.' So Chhatpa-Khochi came out again, this time with his second daughter, but could see nothing but a frog sitting on a hollow log which contained water for the horses and cattle. Thinking he was mistaken, he went back into the house, but directly he went indoors the frog cried again, 'Father-in-law, please come out, please come out, please come out.'

This time Chhatpa-Khochi came out with his youngest daughter, who was the most beautiful of the three. Now the frog called to the old man and asked him to give him the girl as his wife. This made Chhatpa-Khochi laugh very much.

But it made the frog very unhappy and he began to cry. As his tears fell, clouds covered the sky and a strong wind came up. Then came the rain with thunder and lightning. It rained so hard and for so long that the people could not come out of their houses to get fuel and water, and everyone was in such great trouble that at last Chhatpa-Khochi agreed to give his daughter to the frog.

The frog then started to dance for joy and at once the rain

stopped and the sun came out. The people, now full of happiness, went to the Gompa to worship, but as the story of the frog was passed from one to another they began to laugh, and they laughed and laughed so much that the noise nearly caused the Gompa to fall down.[12]

10

SHERDUKPEN

Rupa, Kameng F.D.

Long ago Chungba-Sangyat looked down upon the world and saw that the rivers, lakes and seas were empty of living creatures. So he made fishes out of something or other and scattered them in the water. Presently he went to the fishes and asked who had created them. The fishes replied, 'No one made us ; we were born from the water of our own accord.' Chungba-Sangyat said, 'You were not born of water: I myself created you.' At this there was a great quarrel between God and the fishes.

Chungba-Sangyat summoned all men and animals and said, 'I created the fishes, but in their pride they will not admit the fact. Since I created them I cannot punish them myself, but you may eat them.'

Then he asked the horse, 'Will you eat the fishes?' And he replied, 'No.' He asked the deer and he replied, 'No.' He asked the tigress and she replied, 'No.' Then he asked men and they agreed to eat the fishes. He asked the cow and the pig and the birds and they all agreed to eat them. 'You must eat every fish in the water,' said Chungba-Sangyat. 'They are too proud to live ; not one of them should remain.'

In those days fishes did not lay eggs, but bore one baby fish at a time. God's brother knew that all the fishes were doomed to be eaten and realized that this would mean that once more there would be no creatures living in the lakes and rivers. So he went to the fishes and said, 'You know perfectly well that Chungba-Sangyat created you ; why be so proud as to deny it? Because of your pride he has ordered that all of you should be devoured.' The fishes said, 'We are ignorant creatures and our eyes and ears are ever

[12] Recorded by R. S. Sharma.

full of water. We did not know that God had created us, and now we beg you to save us.'

When he heard this, the brother went to Chungba-Sangyat and said, 'So long as fishes live in the water they keep it clean and beautiful. If they are destroyed the water will quickly get dirty. Have these guilty ones eaten if you wish, but devise some means of preserving their race.'

God had compassion upon the fishes, and gave them sand to eat with the result that they began to lay eggs. They laid so many eggs and there were so many baby fishes that you could not see the water and when people went to bathe the fishes bit their feet. Then everybody started eating them, but even so there were still far too many. So at last Chungba-Sangyat went to the male fishes and pointed to the baby fishes which were lying in thousands on the banks of lakes and rivers with their mouths open in hunger and said, 'Why don't you eat these baby fishes and the eggs?' The male fishes then started to eat both eggs and babies with the result that soon there was enough room in the water. But ever since female fishes have had to hide their eggs.

11

SINGPHO

Imbu, Tirap F.D.

In the old days there were no leeches but the female organs were very long. Husbands found them very inconvenient and cut them off and threw them away, whereupon they turned into leeches. Because of their origin neither men nor women would ever kill them.

In the middle of the ocean there was an island of fine rice, but no one could obtain the seed, because of the water all round. People asked the frog to fetch it for them, but he could not. They asked the birds to bring it for them, but they could not. The leech, however, said, 'You have been to so many others and they have not helped you. I alone will be able to help you. If you will obey my orders, I will go and get it.' Men said that they were ready to do whatever the leech wanted and he agreed to go on condition that they put him back in the place where he was before. Men said,

"Very well. First of all bring us the seed of the rice and then we will put you where you were before.'

The leech went into the ocean and brought the seed and gave it to men. But when he said, 'Put me back where I was before,' the men laughed at him and said, 'How can we do that?' And they threw him away into the forest. This is why the leech is always angry with men and steals their blood whenever he can.

12

WANCHO

Longkhao, Tirap F.D.

Once there was a girl who had very beautiful ornaments and beads on her body. Her younger brother wanted them but she refused to give them to him. He was annoyed about this, but said nothing at the time. Then one day they went together to the forest. The boy found a creeper hanging from a tree above the river and asked his sister to swing on it. She sat on the creeper and was swinging to and fro when suddenly the boy gave her a great push so that she lost her hold and fell into the river. There she turned into a fish.

This is the fish which the Wanchos call Yami and neither they nor the Assamese eat it because it was once a girl. It has a head which looks rather like a cow's.

13

WANCHO

Watnu, Tirap F.D.

An old man and his son went to the forest and caught a bird. They hung it up on a bamboo and went to work in their clearing, but Rang's daughter removed it. The next day the boy again caught the bird, hung it on the bamboo and went away, but again Rang's daughter removed it.

The boy told his father what had happened and so on the third day the old man came to help him. After hanging the bird on the bamboo they hid behind some bushes and now when Rang's daughter came to steal the father caught her and took her home. She was very beautiful and he married her to his son.

At this time there was no water on earth and people used the juice of the plantain tree instead. But Rang's daughter used to bring clean fresh water to the house everyday. The boy boasted to his friends of what his wife could do and they, wanting to know the secret, followed her. They saw how she went along into the forest and presently fetched water from a hole in the ground. Directly she had gone home they ran to the spot and dug all round the hole to make it bigger. Suddenly water gushed out from the earth and with it came many fishes. This is how water and fishes first came to the world.

14

WANCHO

Senua, Tirap F.D.

There was a man who was always very thirsty ; but he could never get water to drink. He used to say, 'If only I could find some water I would never leave it.' At last he found a stream and went into it, and so drinking drinking turned into a fish.[13]

[13] The bones of this fish, which is called *niami* by the Wanchos and *garu-mach* by the Assamese, are preserved and hung up in the house, for 'the fish was once a man'.

CHAPTER EIGHTEEN

REPTILES

THE tribal story-teller is primarily interested in three things about snakes: how they originally came into being, how they got their poison and became the enemies of men, and how some of them have succeeded in marrying human girls.

The origin of snakes is generally slightly disreputable. The Boris trace them along with leeches, hornets and other such creatures, to the body of a cannibalistic Wiyu. A Minyong story describes how snakes and all kinds of poisonous insects were born from the womb of a girl who had illicit relations with a snake (a real snake, for there is no hint that it was a prince in disguise). Another Minyong story tells how the first snake was created from the virile organ of a mithun-Wiyu.

In this story the snake got its poison where a sliver of bamboo was dipped in the highly toxic gall-bladder of the dead Wiyu. The Kaman Mishmis say that it was when a snake drank the blood of an incestuous youth, who was killed in the course of his ignoble quest, that it developed a taste for human blood. In Taraon Mishmi, as well as Wancho, tradition, all other snakes, as well as scorpions and hornets derived their poison from the python. In a Phom tale, which clearly reflects missionary teaching about the Garden of Eden, God himself gave poison to the snake in order to foster its enmity to man.

There are many stories about marriages with human girls, and it is interesting that some of these turn out very happily. In the Minyong tale already quoted, the girl's jealous and rather puritan brother kills the snake and the girl is left with a litter of illegitimate snakes and insects. But in a Sherdukpen story, a water-snake comes out of a river, turns into a handsome youth and seduces the heroine. But the snake is only a man by night; every day he resumes his snake-form and returns to his home beneath the water. After a time he decides to regularize the relationship, and thereafter the couple live as man and wife down in the river. There is a romantic Bugun story of a girl who is loved by the King of the Snakes and finally leaves her home to live with him in the deep waters of a stream. In a Taraon Mishmi story, it is a boy who marries a snake-girl; she abandons her snake-form altogether and goes to live with her human husband in his village. After many vicissitudes the couple settle down happily to a normal life. The Bori hero Reni-Tani had a less enviable experience. He married a snake-girl, but none of the children were human, and the marriage broke up.

1

BORI

Yiyu, Siang F.D.

Abu-Tani married Doini-Aiye, the daughter of the Sun and lived happily with her. But they had one great trouble: the Wiyus devoured nearly all their children and only two boys were left. Now the younger of the two boys was very clever but the elder boy was stupid. When they grew up Doini-Aiye said to her husband, 'I want to go to my parents' house.' Abu-Tani said, 'That is a very good idea, I will go too: the boys are now quite old enough to stay behind and look after the house.' So husband and wife went away to the home of Doini-Pollo.

There was a Wiyu called Mikam-Purbo. One day he felt a desire to eat some human flesh and thought that the best place to get it would be in Abu-Tani's house, where the two brothers were living alone.

The Wiyu took the form of an old man and came to the house. When the younger son saw him he shut the door, but his elder brother opened it and invited the old man in. He entered and sat down in the part of the house called *kodang*. When it was night he asked the boys where he should sleep. They replied, 'Sleep where you are sitting.' But the old man said, 'If I sleep there you'll hear a strange noise like this—*dang-dang*'. So the boys said, 'Then sleep in the *bango*'. But the old man said, 'If I sleep in the *bango* you'll hear a strange noise like this—*bo-bo*'. So the boys said, 'Then if these places don't suit you, come and sleep with us in the *pudeng*.'[1] The old man accordingly lay down there beside the two brothers.

The elder brother fell asleep at once but the younger brother lay awake, for he suspected that their visitor was not a man but a Wiyu who intended to do them harm. So he pretended to be asleep and soon began to snore to see what would happen. The old man, thinking that the brothers were both asleep, heated two large knives in the fire. Presently he went outside to urinate.

When the younger brother saw what the Wiyu was doing, he roused his brother and they put two bundles of leaves where they had been sleeping and covered them with bits of cloth. They themselves went to hide in the pig-stye. The Wiyu returned and taking up the knives plunged one of them into the first bundle of leaves, and it went in easily. He then drove the other knife into the second bundle and it went through into the wooden floor beneath. The Wiyu thought that the flesh of the first boy must be good and tender, but that the other boy must be full of bones. But when he removed the cloth, he only found leaves.

There was nothing the Wiyu could do, angry though he was, so he lay down to sleep, but in the morning when he got up he saw the boys creeping out of the pig-stye and went after them.

[1] The Bori house is something more than an ordinary dwelling-place. It is also in a sense the Boris' temple and different parts of the building are known by special names. Each of the four sides of the hearth of the main sitting-room, for example, has its special name and significance.

On the wall farthest from the door and facing it are kept the trophies of the hunt, and the side of the hearth nearest to it, and facing the door is called the *bango*. This is the most sacred part of the building and no woman is allowed to sit here, probably because it is associated with hunting.

To the right of the *bango*, that is to say, to the left of the hut as you enter from the door, is the *pudeng*. This is the sitting and sleeping place of the head of the household and other people are not allowed to sit there. The side of the hearth nearest to the door is the *nyerolu*, and the fourth side, to the right as you enter by the door, is the *kodang*. In these two seats anybody may sit, either members of the household or visitors.

When the people make rice-beer they must not do it on either side of the *bango* : the proper place is by the *nyerolu*.

Behind the *pudeng* is the traditional place for storing rice-beer, which is called *kabang*.

If there is more than one hearth these rules do not apply for the others. The main hearth is called Romdang and the subsidiary hearths are called Rompan and Romke. There are no taboos in connection with the two latter.

They managed to elude him however, and ran to Komki Wiyu's house and begged him to tell them where their parents were. The Wiyu said, 'I know your parents well but they are not here. However, here is a cock, give it to Dongkong Wiyu, and he'll tell you where they are.'

The boys went accordingly to Dongkong and gave him the cock saying, 'Eat this cock and tell us where our mother and father have gone.' The Wiyu ate the cock and then went to the place of Doini-Pollo and told Abu-Tani that his sons were in trouble. Abu-Tani tied a long rope to a basket and lowered it down to the earth. The younger boy got into the basket and was pulled up safely, but when it came to the turn of the stupid elder brother, he got into the basket and began to swing it as if it was a swing, until he fell out and was killed.

The old man had by then reached the spot and when he saw the basket in the sky he shouted, 'Take me up too.' Abu-Tani lowered the basket down for him, pulled him up a certain distance and then dropped him, pulled him up again and let him fall again, so as to give him all the trouble he could. But finally when the Wiyu got near the top, he managed to catch hold of Abu-Tani's foot and tore a piece of flesh from it. The shock made Abu-Tani drop the basket altogether. As the Wiyu was falling down, down, down from the sky he cried, 'I shall die now and who can say what my body will become? If I fall on a stone it will be very good.' But Tani said, 'Let him not fall on a stone but on the earth.' In the end, however, the Wiyu did fall on a stone and was broken into tiny pieces. From these pieces came all the poisonous animals that are in the world—snakes, leeches, hornets and all other such creatures.

The reason why these creatures try to bite men and get their blood is that their father had a desire to eat human flesh. And the reason why men have insteps in their feet is because the Wiyu tore away a piece of Abu-Tani's foot in that place.

2

BUGUN (KHOWA)

Sengchong, Kameng F.D.

There was an old woman and her daughter. One day the girl went down to a stream and, removing her clothes, went into the water to bathe. Now the King of the Snakes was living in the stream and when he saw the girl he was very pleased and said to himself, 'If I could get this girl as my wife, it would be wonderful.'

This girl used to go with her mother every day to work in the fields. But one day she stayed at home and presently went down to the stream to fetch water. As she went she sang a little song:

'My mother has gone to work in the field,
I am left at home to do all the work,
But there is far too much for me to do.'

She fetched the water and brought it home.

The King of the Snakes heard what the girl was singing and said to himself, 'She will be all by herself at home. This is a real chance for me to meet her.' He came out of the water, took the form of a man dressed in the finest Monpa clothes, and started off for the girl's house.

When the girl saw what she thought was a rich Monpa coming towards the house she was excited and said to herself, 'I haven't seen such a fine-looking man for a long time.' The King of the Snakes reached the house and sat down on the front platform. The girl came out and received him with honour, spreading a mat for him to sit on, and brought some beer and roots for him to eat. They sat for a long time talking and the girl felt greatly attracted by her visitor. When the King of the Snakes saw what she was feeling he decided to test her love and said, 'Now it is time for me to go.' But the girl said, 'Don't go away. Why don't you stay here? If you go away how will I live without you?' The King of the Snakes said, 'You love me and I too love you, but if you were to see me in my proper form you would be afraid.' The girl replied, 'I could never be afraid of you, no matter what you looked like.' When she said that, the King of the Snakes took his proper shape as a great snake and she screamed with fright. He immediately turned back again into a man and said, 'What were you afraid of?' The girl said, 'I saw a great snake.' But he said, 'That was not a snake, that was me.'

The girl laughed at this and said, 'But tell me where you live; why not show me your home?' He replied, 'I live in the water, for I am the King of the Water and I live there in the shape of a snake.' It was now evening and time for the girl's mother to come home from the fields, so the snake said, 'I had better go now, for if your mother were to see me as a snake she would kill me. But whenever your mother is away I will come and see you.' So saying he turned into a snake in front of the girl and went away.

After this the girl always found some excuse for not going to the fields and her mother used to go alone. Directly she had left the house the King of the Snakes would come, drink his rice-beer, eat his roots and spend the day with the girl until it was time for the old woman to return. The result was that the girl not only did no work in the fields, but did not do any work in the house either and her mother got more and more annoyed.

After this had been going on for two or three months the girl found herself pregnant. One day when her time was approaching, she went down to the stream to fetch water and as she was filling her bamboo-tubes she suddenly laid two eggs, which fell into the water. She snatched at them but was only able to save one, the other egg falling down into the deep water. She took the egg home and wrapped it carefully in a cloth and hid it in a wooden box.

Now the mother was so upset by her daughter's refusal to do any proper work that she told her to get out of the house. When she heard that, the girl said to her mother, 'You stay in the house today and I will go to the field.' As she was leaving the house she turned back and said, 'Whatever you do, don't open that wooden box.'

Naturally the mother immediately opened the box and found the egg wrapped up carefully in a bit of cloth. She took it out and cooked and ate it. In the evening the girl came home carrying a great load of wood. She put it down and went indoors to see whether her egg was all right, but found that it had disappeared. She said to her mother, 'Did you open my box?' The mother replied, 'Yes, I did and I found an egg inside.' 'What did you do with it?' asked the daughter. 'I cooked and ate it,' said the mother. The girl cried, 'But that was my child. Why did you eat it? Tomorrow your son-in-law will come here and kill me.' And she burst into tears. The mother felt very sorry and begged her to forgive her.

The following morning when the sun was well up, the King of the Snakes came out of the water, took the form of a man and dressed in his Monpa clothes. As he was approaching the house the girl saw him and ran to her mother crying, 'Look mother, here comes your son-in-law.' The mother was delighted to see such a fine personage and hastily cleaned the house, spread a mat and prepared beer and roots.

Her visitor changed back into a snake as he entered the house and, going to the central pillar of the building, curled round it and climbed up. There was a fire burning on which the old mother was heating rice-beer and she snatched up a log of blazing wood and struck the snake with it and at once he left the house and the girl cried, 'Mother, that was your son-in-law. Why did you beat him?' And she wept bitterly.

The snake was so angry that for many days he stopped the rain from falling and the harvest was withered by the heat and there was nothing to eat in the house.

Now a great many fish were hatched out from the egg that had fallen into the river. The girl went to fetch water and when the fish saw her they all gathered together crying, 'Here is our mother.' When they saw her face thin and sad, they said, 'Mother, what is the matter? Why are you so sad? We are all ready to help you.' The girl replied, 'For many days no rain has fallen ; the crops are ruined and we have no food in the house. But if you can send some water to the field, all will be well.' The fish replied, 'Tomorrow we will bring water to your fieid.' The girl went home and said to her mother, 'Tomorrow go quickly to the field and sow seed there, for your grandchildren are going to bring you water.'

Next morning the mother got up early and took plenty of seed to sow, and presently the fish came flowing like a stream into the field and filled it with water. When it was thoroughly watered the fish return home, but a few of them could not get out of a little hole which had retained the water. When the mother saw them, she caught them and cooked and ate them.

When the old woman returned home her daughter asked her whether the water had come and the mother said it had. She added that the water had come like a small river and when it had filled the field it went away, where she did not know. The girl then said, 'But where are your grandchildren?' The old lady replied, 'I did not see any grandchildren, but there were some fish in a little pond and I caught them and cooked and ate them.'

When the girl heard that she did not speak a word, but ran to the stream and jumped into deep water and went down to live with the King of the Snakes.

3

HILL MIRI

Godak, Subansiri F.D.

The three great creepers Tere, Rime and Mursu were born of Sichi the earth. Tebe the snake was the son of the creeper Mursu.

One day, when Abo-Teni was working in the forest, he injured his hand. Tebe the snake asked his uncle Tere the creeper what was the matter with Abo-Teni's hand. For some reason they began to quarrel and presently to fight. Snake and creeper twined round each other. Tere was very strong and Tebe shouted for help: 'He is killing me. Help, I am dying.' Abo-Teni heard him and ran to the place. He cut Tere to pieces with his dao and so saved Tebe. After that Abo-Teni and the snakes were friends.

4

HILL MIRI

Bini, Subansiri F.D.

Long ago, Si-Duinye the Sun took earth and made an image of a man. Then he made an image of a woman. He put breath into them and went away.

The man saw the breasts and parts of the woman and said, 'Why have you those strange things? Why aren't you made the same as me?' The woman replied, 'What can I do? I am as Si-Duinye made me.'

The woman saw the parts of the man and said, 'Why have you that thing hanging there? Why aren't you made the same as me?' The man replied, 'What can I do? I am as Si-Duinye made me.'

Then they agreed and said, 'Let us go to Si-Duinye and ask him why he made us different.' They went and asked what was the purpose of this, and this, and that. Si-Duinye said, 'What is the use of silly questions? Go and live together and you'll soon find out.'

Then the man said, 'But what shall we eat?' Si-Duinye said, 'I will send you food. I will arrange to drop rations for you. There will be no need for you to work so long as you only eat what I drop for you: don't touch anything else.'

The man and woman returned home and lived happily, except that they did not know how to come together. They did no work, had plenty of food, and went to bathe daily.

One day when the man went to bathe, the woman said, 'You go ahead, I'll come presently.' She sat down beneath a tree laden with fruit. A snake in the form of a man came to her. He picked one of the fruits and asked her to eat it. 'How can I? Si-Duinye has told us not to.' The snake said, 'But Si-Duinye himself made this, as he made me and all things. Of course you can eat it. Take it ; it is very sweet.'

The woman took a little bite of the fruit, liked the taste, and ate it all. The snake went away. Suddenly the woman realized she was naked. When the man returned from bathing, she covered herself with her hands. 'What's the matter?' asked the man. 'Has something bitten you?' 'No, but I am ashamed.' 'What is this "ashamed"? I don't know what you are talking about.' The woman told him about the snake and said, 'The fruit is delicious: you too try it.' The man did so and he too began to feel ashamed. They picked leaves and dressed themselves.

Si-Duinye came to the place and when he saw them dressed in leaves, he was very angry. 'Now as a punishment,' he said, 'you must work in the fields ; you must make fire and cook your food: you must weave ; you will have children and you will die.' Si-Duinye cut off the hands and feet of the snake and ever since it has had to wriggle on the ground.

The man and the woman desired each other, but they did not know what to do. Si-Duinye called the birds Apu-Todu and Tarem-Podem, and Apu-Todu covered his wife before them. They watched, but did not understand.

Then one day the woman was lying on her back asleep. The man sat in the shade of a tree near by. Apu-Todu flew down and perched on her and put his beak into her parts. The man saw it and said to himself, 'That must be the way to do it.' After this they came together and in time there were children.

The names of these two, the man and the woman whom Si-Duinye made, were Abo-Teni and Chittu-Temi.[2]

5

IDU MISHMI

Taraon, Lohit F.D.

The snake-god Baika went to live in a spring high in the mountains, the common source of the Siang and the Lohit rivers. This god is of many colours—white, red and black—and many snakes are born from him. He goes about the world and stays wherever there is water.

Two men once had a quarrel and in the fight one of them had his eye damaged. He went to the stream where Baika was living and bathed the eye. Baika came and drank the water mixed with blood and found it sweet. By this he learnt that human flesh was good to eat. Soon afterwards, a woman came along the bank with her little son in a basket and Baika said to her, 'You go and work in your field and I will look after the child.' But directly her back was turned Baika devoured the child, and when the woman returned she found her basket empty and no sign of her son.

6

IDU MISHMI

Koronu, Lohit F.D.

The people were keeping the Re Festival. There was a pretty girl named Jomba who watched it for three days and three nights. Then feeling very sleepy she went to her parents' house and lay down to rest. She was so exhausted that when her mother tried to wake her she couldn't. The mother got angry and put fire in her parts so that they closed up and she could not urinate.

Jomba had a brother and, when he saw what had happened, he turned her out of the house. She went to her husband and he also turned her out, for now she was no use to him. Then she went to her father and he said, 'You will never get a husband now, so who

[2] See also the Phom story and note at p. 333.

will feed you? Get out of my house.' Finally she went to her mother, but she too drove her away. At this the poor girl resolved to drown herself in the river.

Jomba had a little sister and when the child saw her going to the river, she said, 'What is the matter?' 'I am going to drown myself,' said Jomba. 'Don't do that,' said the child, 'come and live with me and I'll feed you and we'll live together.' Now Jomba had sixteen pigs, sixteen fowls and sixteen bundles of yarn, and she gave half of them to her sister. Unhappily, they did not get on very well and after a few days Jomba took her share of the things and went away. Her little sister followed weeping and begging her not to leave her, but she took no notice.

Jomba went down to the river and sitting on the bank sang a sad story of her wrongs. She called on the great river-snake as her father and the little river-snake as her mother and said, 'Take me home.'

There was a flower growing in the middle of the river. Jomba made a cane bridge and went to sit on it. Her little sister tried to pull her back but Jomba said, 'Look at that queer bird in the sky.' As the girl looked up, Jomba jumped into the river and was drowned.

The little girl wandered about weeping for her sister until at last a tiger ate her.

7

KAMAN MISHMI

Lohit Valley, Lohit F.D.

A man called Jane had a fair young daughter whom he loved greatly. The girl knew how to sing beautiful songs and when she sang, Khrane and the water-god Brue used to come and listen to her. When she was ready for marriage, Jane married her to Brue and after a time she gave birth to a fine child.

When the boy grew up he desired to see other countries and do great deeds. One day he made eight bamboo *chungas* and, filling them with water, left his home and wandered along until he reached a village inhabited by members of the Manin clan.

When the Manin people saw him they gathered round to ask

who he was and where he came from. But when the boy told them about himself they decided he was a foreigner and arrested him, demanding a high price for his release. The boy had nothing to give them, except the eight bamboo *chungas* full of water.

The people did not know what to do with these. So they put them together and poured the water into the earth. Immediately, where before there had been a village with many houses, there was now a great river. Many people were drowned and those who did escape were full of terror. But the boy was unwilling to spare any of them. He changed the rice-huskers in the village into great water-snakes who attacked the people and killed them all.

This is how the water-snakes came into being and the Glang river began to flow.[3]

8

KAMAN MISHMI

Lohit Valley, Lohit F.D.

After the Glang river had destroyed everyone except one Maninsa[4] boy and a Maninsa girl, who were brother and sister and who escaped death by grasping a bamboo *chunga*, they were carried down the river and, when they escaped onto the bank, went to different places ; the girl went to live on the Sambrai hill and the boy was left alone.

As the days went by the Maninsa felt very lonely, but one day as he was going along the bank of the Glang river he saw some insects of a kind which damage the crops. As he approached them they were frightened and flew away. The Maninsa, knowing that such insects are usually to be found in cultivated fields, ran after them as he supposed there must be some village in the neighbourhood. The insects led him to the place where his sister lived.

He did not recognize her and thought that she would make him a good wife. But she knew who he was and told him that she was his sister, which upset him very much. But in spite of the fact that they were so closely related, he had been alone so long and had found no other woman, that he urged the girl to marry him. But

[3] Recorded by T. K. Barua.

[4] A Maninsa is a member of the Manin clan.

she was terrified and repelled by the suggestion and ran away from him into the forest. The Maninsa followed her but she climbed up a tall tree and sat on a branch at the top.

The Maninsa did not know how to climb trees, so he set to preparing a ladder which would take him to the girl. It took him eight years to complete it, but when it was ready he put it against the tree and began to climb up.

Now the god Matai was watching this and felt pity for the sufferings of the girl as well as anger at the boy's evil desires. So he commanded the white ants to cut the ladder with their teeth and when the Maninsa had almost reached the top of the tree the ladder broke and he fell down to the ground and was killed. Where he fell there was a great snake and he licked up the blood of the dead boy and, liking the taste, ate the body bit by bit.

Ever since the snake has bitten human beings and tasted human blood.[5]

9

MINYONG

Pangin, Siang F.D.

A brother and sister lived together in the hills. The girl grew up but could not find a husband. One day her brother saw her going to the forest with beer, meat and rice. Wondering where she could be going, he followed her secretly. Presently she came to the bank of the Siang River, where she put the food on the ground and took a stick in her hand. She went down to the river and beat the water. Presently a great snake came out and coiled himself around her body. He rested his head on her shoulder and thrust his tail into her. Afterwards the girl and the snake sat together lovingly and the girl fed the snake with meat and beer and after a time she went away. The brother saw everything that happened and went home by another path.

The next day the boy went to the place and he too beat on the water with his stick. The snake appeared and the boy cut him into pieces with his dao and threw them into the river. Soon afterwards the girl came and beat on the water, but now no snake appeared.

[5] Recorded by T. K. Barua.

Soon there was a swelling of the girl's belly and in due season she was delivered, but not of a human child. Instead scores of little snakes and every kind of poisonous insect poured from her womb until there was a great basketful of them. She left them in the forest and went home to live alone with her brother.[6]

10

MINYONG

Komkar, Siang F.D.

When Banji-Botte killed Polung-Sabbo, the great mithun, he wondered what to do with the body. 'I must put every bit of it to some use,' he thought. He removed the mighty organ and put it on a stone. 'I'll make a snake of it,' he said. He gave it a head, but he had nothing for its fangs.

In those days, people used slivers of bamboo as needles if they wanted to sew anything. Banji-Botte put one of these as a fang in the snake's mouth. But even then the fang was harmless. So Banji-Botte dipped it in the gall-bladder of the dead mithun. The snake was now very dangerous, so Banji-Botte put it in a place where men would not easily come across it—and even today no one knows where the home of the snake is.

Then Banji-Botte threw Polung-Sabbo's head into the Siang River: it broke and turned into the rocks that now litter the banks. The vertebrae turned into cranes. What was left of the gall-bladder became the aconite which is now used to poison arrows. The blood became every kind of poisonous insect, all kinds of crawling and flying things, but only those which have no bones.

The leech was born from this blood. When Banji-Botte saw it, he said, 'You were born of blood: you shall live by sucking blood.'

[6] Dunbar gives a debased version of this story, which he thinks (and perhaps rightly) may represent an echo of missionary teaching. 'In the beginning a man and a woman lived alone on the earth. And a snake came and tempted the woman with a brew of *apong* that he had made. She drank it and under the influence of the wine, consented to have intercourse with him. Afterwards she gave birth to an immense number of little snakes that all slipped away among the trees. Then the man hunted out the snake and killed it. And the snake since then has been a deadly enemy of mankind.'

11

PHOM

Yangam, Tuensang

God shut the first man and woman up in a house but told them that they must not approach one another: he told them this by making signs to them with his fingers. They were both naked and the door was shut. But somehow a great snake, walking on his feet, managed to enter. He asked, 'What are you two doing here?' They said that God had put them in that place and had shown them that they must not do anything. The snake made signs to them that they should come together. The man said, 'No, we cannot disobey God's orders.' The snake replied, 'That is absurd. Unless you come together, there will be no children. But if you do, there will soon be men all over the world.'

When the snake said this, the woman pulled the man to her. But at that moment God came by and said, 'What are you doing?' 'We are peopling the world with men,' replied the man. 'But I told you not to,' said God. 'What new orders have you received and who gave them to you ?' 'It was the snake's order.' 'Then who obeyed him first?' 'It was the woman.'

At this God was angry and he said, 'I gave you everything man could desire—a good house, good food and no work to do. But from today you will have to live in the jungle and cut clearings with your daos, and only by hard work will you get food.' And he said to the woman, 'Because you forced the man to it, blood will flow from you, and your belly will swell and children will be born from you in pain.' And so it was. God cut off the legs of the snake, so that he had to crawl on his belly, and he gave him a fang and put poison on it. Ever since men and snakes have been enemies.[1]

[1] This, like the Hill Miri tale on page 326, is an obvious echo of missionary teaching. The story of the Garden of Eden is, of course, perfectly at home in a tribal setting: it has everything to appeal to the tribal mind —the rural background, the talking snake, the fruit that is 'genna' or taboo, the punishment for breaking a taboo which gives deep satisfaction to one and all. But both Phoms and 'Miris' alter the entire tone of the tale by introducing a strong sexual motive. But I find it hard to believe that the idea that it was the act of sex which brought 'death into the world and all our woe' is truly tribal, for everywhere the unsophisticated tribesman

12

SHERDUKPEN

Rupa, Kameng F.D.

There was once an old woman who had two daughters. The elder daughter was very beautiful but nobody thought anything of her because she could not weave properly. The other girl made cloth with beautiful patterns but this girl could only weave plain cloth, and the other girls used to laugh at her.

Once, when she was feeling very miserable about this, she did not eat all day and in the evening went down to bathe in the river. As she was bathing a great snake came out of the water and she started to run away. But when the snake saw how beautiful she was, he turned into a handsome youth and said, 'Why are you frightened?' The girl replied, 'Because I thought you were a snake.' 'No! I'm not really a snake,' said the youth. 'I live beneath the water and I can take the form of a snake or a man as I please.' Then the girl, seeing the boy's beauty, came near him and they fell in love with one another. After that, every evening when the girl had eaten her supper she used to go down secretly to the river and spend the night with her lover on the bank. Every morning the youth would turn into a snake and go down to his house beneath the water.

One evening when they met as usual, the girl refused to speak, for she was very sad because she could not weave properly. After a lot of persuasion she told her lover about it and he said, 'Don't worry about this. In the morning I will come in my beautiful skin ; you can take me to your house and when you sit at your loom you can hold me in your lap and copy the patterns on my body.'

The boy turned again into a snake and went into the water and the girl sat all night on the river-bank. At dawn he came back as a snake in his beautiful skin. The girl took him home and sat down to her loom with him on her lap. The other girls came to watch but when they saw the snake they ran away in fright. But soon she was making the finest cloth in the whole village.

regards sex as something natural, decent and innocent: it is possible that to excite the interest of a tribal audience the Garden of Eden story has been intensified to make it more attractive. It is equally possible that these stories represent a genuine tribal version of the old myth.

That evening the girl carried the snake down to the river-bank and he turned into a man again. In a few days the girl had made three beautiful pieces of cloth. She gave one to her sister, one to the other girls so that they could imitate it, and kept one for herself.

After a little while, the snake said, 'This is no way to live. The right thing will be for me to marry you and take you to my house.' 'But how can I live under the water?' asked the girl. 'Don't worry about that,' he replied, 'I will come to you with a great party and many instruments of music and you will be able to live in the river quite happily.' So next morning the girl said to her mother, 'I am going to my husband.' 'What husband is this?' asked the mother. 'It is my snake-husband who taught me to weave.' 'But how can you do such a thing? He will kill you. The mother alternatively abused and cajoled her, but she refused to listen.

After two days the boy came with a great procession and playing many instruments of music. To the eyes of the villagers the visitors looked like snakes, but to the girl they looked like human beings. As her husband was taking her away, she said to her mother, 'I'm going now, but if ever you are in trouble come to the bank of the river and call me.' So the girl went into the river and deep down below the water there was a palace of gold and the two lived there happily and had many children.

Then one day her younger sister said, 'Why shouldn't I too marry a snake?' She went down to the river and found a hole where a black snake lived. She lay down beside it hoping that this snake also would turn into a handsome youth and marry her. But when he came out of his hole, he was just a snake and killed her.

Now the girl's mother had no one to look after her and she was very old ; she could only hobble about and there was no food in the house. So one day she went weeping to the river-bank and cried, 'My daughter, my daughter!' Night fell and the girl came out of the water and said, 'Come with me.' Her mother refused, but her daugher tied a cloth round her face and dragged her down. There the old woman saw the palace of gold and a crowd of children crying, 'Granny.' They surrounded her, played with her dress and climbed into her lap. Suddenly they turned into snakes and coiled themselves round her. She threw them off in fright and they became human again.

After this the old woman said to her daughter, 'Send me home, this is too much for me.' Her son-in-law said, 'Very well, but I will give you something to take back with you.' He tied some sand in one piece of cloth and a little grain in another piece. He found a scrap of rope and a bit of wood each as long as his little finger. He tied these things up in a bundle and gave them to the old woman saying, 'Don't look at them on the way ; take them home and put eac' of them in a separate basket as big as you can find. Then after a week open the baskets and see what you have.' Then he took her out of the water.

When she was left alone on the bank the old woman thought, 'I have been on a visit to the house of my daughter and son-in-law and they have given me no money but only these wretched things.' She felt so upset that she threw the bundle on the ground. But later she thought, 'Perhaps I had better do what my son-in-law said,' and she picked up all the things she could find and put them in little baskets. After a week she opened the baskets and found the bit of wood had turned into dried fish, the rope had turned into dried meat, the sand had become rice and the grain had become rice-seed. But since she had thrown away most of what her son-in-law had given her and had only put what was left in small baskets, there was not very much. But even then there was now something for her to eat and she lived on what she had until she died.

13

TARAON (DIGARU) MISHMI

Machima, Lohit F.D.

There was an orphan boy, a Mishmi, who one day took his net to fish in a stream. He threw it in the water and the first thing he caught was a river-snake. He tried to pull it out, but it was too heavy for him.

The snake's daughter lived in that river ; she was a snake as long as she was in the water but turned into a girl when she came onto dry land. When she saw her father caught in the net, she turned into a girl and came up on the bank and said to the boy, 'Let my father go and I'll marry you.' She was so beautiful that the boy at once agreed and went down into the stream and gradually pulled the net away until the snake was free.

The girl said to her father, 'I am going to marry this boy, for he has let you go.' But her father was angry and said, 'You and I belong to the snake-tribe. How can you marry someone from the human-tribe?' The girl did her best to persuade him, but he would not agree and dragged her back into the water and she became a snake again and the boy went home.

After some days, the boy went again to fish higher up the stream. He cast his net and again caught the same river-snake. The girl came out as before to plead for her father and this time she said, 'I really will marry you.' But the boy said, 'You deceived me once and now I cannot trust you. I'll not let your father go.' The girl said, 'No, this time I really will marry you.' And in fact when the boy did let the snake go, there was no difficulty and he was able to take the girl home and make her his wife.

When the other villagers knew that the boy had married a snake, they were angry and reported the matter to their Raja. He too was angry and called the boy to his house, and said to him, 'Look, your cock and my cock will fight. Whichever wins can kill the loser or exile him'. The boy was frightened at this, for he had no cock. When his wife asked him what was the matter and he told her, she said, 'Don't be afraid. I'll get a cock for you from my father.' The snake brought a fine cock up from the bottom of the river and the boy took it to the Raja's house. It was so strong that it easily defeated the Raja's cock.

But the Raja said, 'Your cock has defeated mine, but there must be a further test. Your buffalo must fight my buffalo.' The boy was frightened at this, for he had no buffalo. When his wife asked him what was the matter and he told her, she said, 'Don't be afraid. I'll get a buffalo for you from my father.' The snake brought a fine buffalo up from the bottom of the river and the boy took it to the Raja's house. It was so strong that it easily defeated the Raja's buffalo.

Yet again the Raja said, 'This does not settle the matter ; there must be one more test. Whoever can dam the Lohit river and divert the stream will be the victor and can kill the loser.' This really did frighten the boy, but the wife said, 'Don't be afraid. My father will help you.'

Now the snake had a golden basket and the girl put it in the stream and it diverted the water, making it flow towards the Raja's house. The boy said, 'Now at last I have conquered you and I shall kill you.'

But the Raja said, 'No, now we must fight hand to hand.' The Raja had many soldiers but the boy had none. His wife went down into the river and brought up a golden drum and a golden drum-stick. The Raja prepared his troops and they came to attack but as they approached, led by the Raja himself, the girl began to beat the drum and at the noise all the grasses, trees and houses began to dance. The Raja and his soldiers threw down their weapons and danced as well.

When they were exhausted, the boy threw his fishing-net over them and so caught and killed them all.

13

TARAON (DIGARU) MISHMI

Tushe, Lohit F.D.

Jebmallu had a wife who wove very beautiful cloth. One day while he was out hunting, she made a bag and prepared a cord to hang it up by. In the evening when Jebmallu came home he saw the cord lying on the ground and thought it was something dangerous. He kicked it into the forest outside the house. There it turned into a python.

At that time the python was very poisonous and he bit many people and they died. The news went round and no one knew what it was except that some great danger was near and they wept for fear. But the crow said to men, 'Don't be afraid, I'll find a way to save you.' He went to the python and said, 'You are always biting people and killing them, but it will be no use, for in the end they will become stronger than before.' The python was so angry when he heard this that he vomited up all his poison and since then has had to kill creatures by squeezing them to death.

From the python's vomit there were born scorpions and hornets. It was also eaten by the other snakes and they themselves became filled with poison.

15

WANCHO

Longkhao, Tirap F.D.

The god Punnu sent two snakes to the earth, one big and one small. One day the bigger snake bit an old man and he died and his friends carried him home. The big snake said to the little snake, 'Go and see how he is.' The little snake went to the place and could not find the dead man's body but saw a lot of people blowing trumpets, firing guns and weeping. He thought that the people were rejoicing because the old man who had been bitten had come alive again.

When he returned and told the big snake what he had seen, the latter was very angry and declared that he would never bite anyone again. 'In future,' he said, 'I will swallow them and then they will never recover.' He spat out his venom and some of it fell on the leaves of the nettle and made them sting. The rest fell on the ground and the ant, the wasp and the small snakes ate it and they became poisonous.

CHAPTER NINETEEN

BIRDS

STORIES about birds may be classified around four principal motifs. First are stories about the relations of birds with the Sun. Then there are stories about the creation of birds for sacrifice. Thirdly, there are stories about helpful birds and particularly about birds who act as messengers and go-betweens for human beings. And finally, there are stories about dangerous birds.

The crowing of the cock has appealed to story-tellers all over the world and not least in NEFA. In a Minyong tale, the cock is one of the animals who goes to find the Sun who has hidden in fear and sorrow. He acts as a messenger to tell mankind what must be done to persuade her to return and crows triumphantly when she appears. In Nocte tradition, the cock claims to be the Chief of men and animals because even the Sun and Moon come into the Sky at his command.[1] In a Singpho tale the cock crows to tell men when the first waters have subsided and they can come to occupy the earth.

There are a number of stories explaining how it is that fowls are specially suitable for sacrifice to the gods. An Idu tale describes in detail the process of transforming a small round stone into a fowl for this purpose. A Hrusso story explains the dilemma of a man who is told to sacrifice a domestic fowl and pig for the relief of his sick children, and how he manages to create them.

Birds in fact are nearly always helpful and useful to men. In a Moklum tale it is the owl who originally possessed fire, while men were dressed in feathers. Men bartered their feathers for the bird's fire. In a Nocte tale men obtained fire through the crow. In Idu, Minyong and Hrusso stories it is a bird who brings water to mankind. Men learn from birds, in Hill Miri tales, how to weep and

[1] So also, in Angami tradition, the Sun, who is afraid of going out in the dark, comes when the cock crows.—Hutton, *The Angami Nagas*, p. 260.

how to come together to people the earth. In a Wancho story the boon of death comes to the world through birds.

Birds are specially helpful as messengers. In classical Indian folklore the parrot is the most popular go-between of lovers. Here, in a Kaman Mishmi tale, a bird, seeing great gods levelling the mountains, becomes frightened that his nest will be destroyed, and brings them a message that their wives are sick and their parents dead, thus saving the hills and mountains for the world. In a Singpho tale a parrot warns men to escape from the power of a dangerous demon. In Tagin tradition a little bird persuades men and animals to act in a way that saves them. The Kamans tell how at the beginning of the world the birds came to tell men when it was time to cultivate their land. In a Bugun tale a bird shows two fugitives where to find land. In the Singpho tale based on the *Mahasupina-Jataka*, a pair of pigeons act as messengers of the Lord Buddha's wife. They find her husband and tell her where he is; the Singphos carve images of these birds and gild them.

Finally, there are stories about dangerous birds. The Khamptis have an enormous bird who preys on children and lives on a golden tree. The Sherdukpen tale, which is illustrated in the Jachungacham dance, describes two terrible birds which carried off human beings in the days when men were very small.

The most venerated of all the birds is the Great Indian Hornbill, whose beak and feathers are prized for decoration and who is carved in symbolic form in Naga morungs, but I have not yet found any stories about it.

1

IDU MISHMI

Dibang Valley, Lohit F.D.

At first there was no rice growing on earth and men lived like wild animals on roots and leaves in the forest. They passed their days in misery, for there were storms of rain ; the Sun was too hot, and they had to live in the forest without any roof over their heads.

But the gods were very kind to the birds and animals. The god of the mountains was Gallan who cared especially for them. He gave the sparrow rice and taught him how to cultivate it. When they saw this, all the men on earth assembled and decided to send a messenger to Gallan to ask him to give them rice also. The sparrow heard the discussion from the top of a tree and said to himself, 'As I am a small bird it is going to be very difficult for me to cultivate the soil in order to grow this rice. On the other hand, if I teach men how to do it, I will have no trouble and will get all I want free.' So the sparrow came to the meeting and said that he would reveal the secret of cultivation provided they gave him one gift in return.

Men agreed and the sparrow asked them to follow him to the top of a hill nearby. He told them to clear the jungle and ask Gallan for help. Gallan was pleased and sent rain pouring down on the earth. Ever since, it has been the custom for the Mishmis to offer beer and a piece of silver in their fields before they sow their seed.

Men were pleased at what the sparrow had done and told him that he could take such rice as he needed from their fields. This is why you will always see the paddy fields covered with sparrows feeding on the young crops.[1]

2

IDU MISHMI

Ichuli, Lohit F.D.

Long ago an Igu priest made it his business to look at every bird that flew in the sky in order to see which could be offered in sacrifice to please the gods. He saw hundreds of them but decided that not a single one would do. And then one day he found a round stone shaped like an egg. He held it in his hands and wondered if anything could be hatched from it. After warming it in his hands he put it in a safe place and fifteen days later a chick came out. But the little creature had no wings, no nails on its feet, and no crest on its head.

The priest looked at it and put it on a thorny tree. Directly the chick sat on a branch the thorns fixed themselves in its toes

[1] Recorded by T. K. Barua.

and the leaves of the tree fixed themselves as its wings. But it had no blood. It went flying to a place where there was a pond of blood ; it drank some and the blood filled its veins. Then as a fowl it flew down to Assam. There a girl called Mamili saw it and thought it would make a good pet ; she offered it food and it went to her. She kept it in her house and in time there were many fowls and people offered them to the gods.

Still today when we sacrifice a fowl, we tell this story to the gods.

3

KHAMPTI

(From J. Errol Gray, *Diary of a Journey to the Bor Khamti Country*, 1892-93, p. 54f.)

The legend says that in olden days an enormous bird used to haunt this part of the country, preying on children ; and that on one occasion it perched on this stone to devour a child it had seized, when certain marks were left. The legend goes on to say that this bird at last grew so rapacious that the whole country took up arms against it, but the more it was hunted the more wary it got, and whenever it seized a child would go off with it to a high hill in the Nam Yun valley called Noi Kham (the golden hill) on which grew an enormous tree whose branches were of silver and gold and which was held sacred by the Khamtis, and there perched on the topmost branches it would devour its prey in safety. No other trees in the country were strong enough to bear the weight of this bird on their branches, so a general consultation being held it was determined to sacrifice the sacred golden tree and cut it down, when the bird finding no resting-place would either quit the country or perching on some stone or rock would afford an opportunity to destroy it. So the tree was cut down and things turned out just as had been calculated: the bird in vain tried to rest on the branches of other trees ; they all gave way under its weight until at last in desperation it perched on a huge slat of rock at the mouth of the Sada stream where it was killed by four slaves who pierced it through and through with their arrows. The tree of gold disappeared after it was cut down in a small lake which had formed around it. This lake is now overgrown with weeds, and in the cold season when the water dries up these weeds are said annually to take fire by spontaneous combustion.

4

LUNGCHANG (TANGSA)

Chungling, Tirap F.D.

The snake asked the cock not to bathe in his pond. But the cock took no notice and went to bathe there. He broke the banks of the pond with his wings, and the snake was angry. He challenged the cock to fight, and accordingly the cock with his friends came out to do battle with the snake and his friends. The cocks won, and ever since there has been enmity between the two tribes.

5

MINYONG

Komsing, Siang F.D.

Doini the Sun and Pollo the Moon both made water in the same place. The jackfruit tree grew from their urine. It grew and grew until it bore its great fruits.

One day Doiying Botte Wiyu took his dao and cut the tree. A piece of the bark fell to the earth and went down to the home of Kine-Dene where he lives far below the ground. He found it and sat on it as a hen sits on its eggs. For five days and five nights he sat there and then a chick was hatched from the bark. He fed and cared for it and it grew into a fine cock.

During all this time, the Sun did not once appear and everything was dark. So the cock went to the home of the Sun and Moon and cried, *'Kokokoko'* and after half an hour the Sun came out of his house.

6

NOCTE

Khamua, Tirap F.D.

There was once a man called Rasa who had no parents. One day walking across the hills he met the wife of Rang-Bau in a lonely place and lay with her, and she had a child by him. When Rang-Bau knew about it, he made the child the first Wangham (Chief) and said, 'You shall rule over the land.' But the people did not like this and they rebelled.

The boy went to his father Rasa and told him about it but as there was nothing he could do, he sent the boy to his mother in the sky. She gave him a basket and told him to take it down to earth but not to open it on the way. As he went along he became more and more curious and at last could not help opening it and looking inside.

Out of the basket came the mighty spirit, Jang-Kiang, and he attacked the rebels and cut them into little pieces. He imprisoned those who survived and forced them to promise to obey Rasa's son and his descendants as their Chiefs.

It was to Rasa that Rang-Bau gave the first cock. Since the cock has come down from the sky, it knows the time when the Sun rises. This is why whenever it crows the Sun comes up into the sky.

7

SHERDUKPEN

Shergaon, Kameng F.D.

There were two birds, male and female, who were called Jachung.[3] In those days, human beings were very small and just as a kite carries off chickens these birds used to catch men and women and eat them. After many people had been killed, Lopong-Chungba thought: 'If this goes on any longer, there will be no human beings left in the world. Somehow or other I must save them from these birds.'

So he called the birds to him and said, 'I have got the heads of five men here. If you can eat them, you can go on killing and eating human beings. But if you cannot eat them, you will have to stop.' The birds agreed to this, for they were proud of their strength and appetite.

[3] In the Jachungacham, a Bird Dance, two 'birds' called Jachung, male and female, appear with brilliantly coloured bird's heads on their shoulders, and gay clothes covering their bodies. Presently an old woman, who represents the god Lopong-Chungba, appears with a fish-trap and tries to catch them.

The two birds flew high into the sky and Lopong-Chungba quickly hid the human heads and put five stones in their place. The birds swooped down and seized the stones, but they were too hard for them and they fell senseless and with broken teeth to the ground. Lopong-Chungba quickly put the heads back where they had been before.

When the birds recovered, he said, 'Why don't you eat the heads as you promised?' The birds replied, 'But we have eaten them.' 'Then what are these heads doing here?' asked Lopong-Chungba. The birds said, 'Let us try again and this time we certainly will eat them.'

The birds again flew into the sky and Lopong-Chungba quickly substituted stones for the heads with the result that once again the birds broke their teeth and fell senseless to the ground. But this time they realized that Lopong-Chungba was tricking them, so when they tried for the third and last time they watched carefully and now they saw where Lopong-Chungba hid the heads and were able to pick them up and eat them.

They said proudly, 'Now we shall always be able to kill and eat men.' 'Yes,' said Lopong-Chungba. 'You have defeated me,' and he went home.

But soon he grew worried again and tried to think what sort of creature could destroy the birds. 'Perhaps an elephant will be able to do it ; I must create one.' Even as he thought, an elephant came out of his body, and he sent it to kill the birds. But the birds fought against it and killed it.

Then Lopong-Chungba thought, 'Perhaps the snake will be able to kill the birds with its poison.' And as he thought, a snake came from his body and he sent it to kill the birds. But the birds fought against it and killed it.

Now Lopong-Chungba had two brothers Esaribo and Yonmiyonga and he said to them, 'Go to the birds and dance with them, and while they are dancing I will come secretly and catch them.' The two brothers went and persuaded the birds to dance.

Lopong-Chungba thought, 'If I go in my own form, the birds will recognize me and I won't be able to catch them.' So he took the shape of an old woman and went, carrying a bird-trap, as if to watch the dance. The birds were so excited at dancing with his brothers that they never saw him and he was able to catch and kill them.

Lopong-Chungba himself refused to eat their flesh and his brothers ate it instead. Then he thought, 'My brothers have eaten these birds and we must see that nothing evil is born from their excrement.' So he called the dog to eat it. But then again he thought, 'Suppose something evil is born from the dog's excrement,' and he called the cock to eat it. This is why these two animals eat excrement.

8

SHERDUKPEN

Shergaon, Kameng F.D.

In the old days, the birds had no king. But after a time Chungba-Sangyat said to the birds, 'You have no king and there is no discipline or order amongst you. You must decide whom you will choose.'

The crane said, 'I am the tallest of all and my neck is so long that I can see everything. So I should be king.'

The kite said, 'I am the cleverest of all and I can pick up other birds in my claws. So I should be king.'

The cock said, 'I know when the sun is going to rise and I warn men and animals. So I should be king.'

The crow said, 'I myself am as clever as the kite and I can see much further. So I should be king.'

In this way every bird made its claim and there was a great noise of quarrelling.

Then Chungba-Sangyat said, 'Do not quarrel. I myself will decide who will be king.'

He filled a great pot with oil and made it warm over a fire. He tied a rope above it and declared, 'Whoever can fly under the rope and then perch upon it without soiling its wings or feet will be king.'

The crane tried to do this but its long legs went into the oil and were burnt. It ran away to cool its feet in a stream and has stood in water ever since.

All the other birds tried, but not one of them could pass the test. At last a little bird called Bichakhu, which takes taxes from even the biggest birds by pulling feathers out of their tails, managed to fly above the pot without getting dirty, and it became the king of the birds. Ever since all the other birds have been afraid of it.

9

SHERDUKPEN

Rupa, Kameng F.D.

Long ago, the bird Gymau-Lala-Pipi lived on the bank of a river. This bird was a woman-bird and very beautiful. But she was also very particular. Every kind of man-bird visited her to make her his wife but not one of them pleased her. Then one day the bat came flying by and when he saw her, he said to himself, 'What a wonderful thing it would be if I could get such a beautiful wife as this! But how would she ever marry an ugly creature like me?'

Then the bat thought, 'I'll visit her in the dark, for if she can't see me, she might agree to marry me.' So one night he went to her and said, 'Look! I'm very happy that you have refused all these other birds, for they were only deceiving you. What they would have done was to marry you and then not give you proper food. But if you marry me I'll give you the best food in the world both day and night. Don't be put off by my appearance, I'm only like this at night, but in the day I'm the king of all the birds.' When she heard this Gyamu-Lala-Pipi agreed to marry the bat and they spent the night together.

When dawn approached, the bat made haste to leave for fear his wife would discover how he had deceived her. As he was going, she said to him, 'There's going to be a meeting today to settle the matter of my marriage and all the birds are coming. You must also be there.' 'Yes, of course,' replied the bat. 'I shall be sitting in the middle and you will see me shining like the sun.' 'But how will I be able to recognize you?' asked his wife. 'You must give me some kind of sign.' 'That will not be necessary,' said the bat. But secretly Gyamu-Lala-Pipi tied a red thread round one of the bat's claws, and let him fly away while it was still dark.

Later that morning a great company of birds assembled to decide who should be Gyamu-Lala-Pipi's husband. In the middle was the peacock shining in his glory, but the bat took his seat on the far edge of the crowd.

When Gyamu-Lala-Pipi came out to meet her suitors, she saw the bat with the red thread round his claw. She was very angry when she saw how she had been deceived by such a black and ugly creature. She told everybody about it and they roared with laughter, and the bat ran away, for he could not face them. Ever since he has hung his head in shame.

Gyamu-Lala-Pipi had a chick from the bat, but when she saw it she abandoned it by the river saying, 'You're the child of an evil husband ; I'm not going to look after you.' She herself went to live in the forest and her chick still lives as a black duck by the river.

10

SHERDUKPEN

Rupa, Kameng F.D.

An old man who had a very beautiful daughter, brought a boy to his house to serve for her as her husband. This boy used to go daily to work in his father-in-law's fields and came home in the evening. The boy and girl fell in love with each other and thought of nothing in the world but their love.

The old man was a great lover of birds, and used to go to the forest and talk to them. But he was sad whenever he thought there was no such thing in the world as a peacock. One day he decided to make one and prepared a cloth with patches of many different colours. When his daughter saw it, she said, 'What are you making this cloth for?' Her father replied, 'It's not for anyone special, but just for whoever can wear it.' The girl said, 'Then let me wear it.' But her father replied, 'No. I would rather give it to my son-in-law.'

The old man put the cloth out in the sun to dry and that evening when the boy came home from work, told him to pick it up and bring it to the house. The boy thought what a lovely cloth it was, and instead of bringing it back put it round his shoulders. As he did so he turned into a peacock.

When he saw his changed shape, he began to weep for love of his wife, and his father-in-law beat him and drove him away to the bank of the stream.

That evening when it got late and the boy had not come home, the girl asked where he was. When her father told her what had happened, she abused him as a sorcerer and ran weeping after her peacock-husband. She cried to him, 'I am a human being and you have become a bird, so how can we be husband and wife? Tomorrow morning leave your droppings on the bank of the stream and when I come to bathe I will eat them. Then I myself will become a bird and we can live together as before.'

The girl went home. Next morning when she went to bathe, she ate the peacock's droppings and became a peahen. At that time she was wearing a dirty cloth and that is why the wife of the peacock looks less beautiful than her husband.

11

TARAON (DIGARU) MISHMI

Machima, Lohit F.D.

A number of people cut clearings in the forest on the top of a high mountain. When they had nearly finished their work, a star-girl came flying down on her wings. A boy saw her and liked her so much that he decided to keep her on earth. He cut off her wings and put them inside a drum, closing both its ends, so that the girl could not get at them and escape. But he was so pleased with himself that he picked up the drum and began to dance with it. He drummed so vigorously in his excitement that the ends broke and the wings came fluttering out. The girl caught them and flew with them back into the sky.

There was a Chin. He said to the boy, 'Why did you let those wings escape? They are very valuable. We must go and get them back.' So they cut bamboos and made a great ladder right up to the sky. The Chin went up first and when the star-girl saw him she let down a thin creeper, thin as the entrails of a fowl, and the Chin, thinking the girl wanted to help, caught hold of it. But she let it go and the Chin fell down, down, down to the ground and turned into a cock.

But this cock had no wings, and no crest on his head. The boy took it to a tree and fixed a red flower on his head which turned into a crest. The next day he took it to another tree and tied leaves to its body and they turned into wings.

CHAPTER TWENTY

MAMMALS

STORIES about the larger animals are as popular in NEFA as they are among tribal people in all parts of the world and the NEFA stories follow to some extent the usual pattern and are perhaps less original than many of the other stories recorded in this book.

An important motif, which is very popular in NEFA, and is illustrated here and in the Trickster stories, is the Animal Marriage. 'In folktales everywhere,' says Stith Thompson, 'the human world and the animal world lie close together, and we easily move from one to the other, hardly noticing when the transition is made. In the European nursery tales, the wolf talks to Red Riding-hood, the cat and dog help the hero recover magic objects, or the frog marries the princess. To be sure, in the latter case, the frog is really an enchanted prince, and in this way the European tale recognizes that the animal actor is not really an animal. In tales of American Indians, however, and, indeed, of primitive peoples everywhere, the marriage of human beings to actual animals is of very frequent occurrence.

'An interesting Eskimo tale of animal marriages is the Fox-Woman. It has not been reported often, but its presence in various parts of the Eskimo area, as well as in Siberia, is clear enough. A tale almost identical is known in Japan. A man finds his house put in order by a mysterious housekeeper. He discovers that the housekeeper is sometimes a woman and sometimes a fox. They marry and are happy until one day he makes mention of her origin as a fox, and she leaves him in anger.'[1]

The NEFA story-tellers give full measure on this subject. For each of the great heroes—in the Apa Tani, Bori, Hill Miri and Tagin tales—marries a whole succession of animals (and they are real animals, not human beings in

[1] Stith Thompson, op. cit., p. 358.

disguise or under enchantment) as well as leaves, trees and even fire. There are many other stories of marriages, or at least liasons, with snakes, bears and other animals.

There are parallels to the Fox-Woman story of Japan and the Eskimos. A Sherdukpen tale, for example, gives us the mysterious housekeeper, a beautiful girl who has been born from a store of dry meat. The hero marries her, and they are happy until one day in a temper he reproaches her for her origin; she leaves him and turns into an elephant.

There are also stories of the miraculous birth of animals. There is a curious Sherdukpen tale describing how the yak was originally born from the egg of a great bird. Human beings give birth to snakes, monkeys, tigers, cows and dogs.

In a few cases, animals seem to have originated through an act of incest. For example, a Mishmi story attributes the origin of the bear to this and Dhammai, Bori and Minyong stories, which are widely distributed, similarly attribute the first monkeys to the same breach of a fundamental taboo. In a Hrusso tale, the first mithun was an unhappy wife who transformed herself into an animal to avoid incest with her brother to whom she had been forcibly married. The idea of a human being being turned into a monkey because he has committed incest is common in Burmese folktales and it is said that a King who lived some centuries before 1044 was turned into a monkey for attempting it.[2]

Nearly all the tribal people are greatly attached to dogs. This is specially true of the Adis. You may see puppies with necklaces of valuable blue beads round their necks. A man will carry his dog across a stream to save it getting wet. Small children, and sometimes older people too tie dogs to their backs in a sling as if they were children. They fondle their dogs and let them lick their faces. Nobody seems to mind eating from a plate from which a dog has shared the food.

The Gallongs eat dogs, but this is condemned by the Minyongs and allied groups. For the latter, however, a dog-

[2] M. H. Aung, *Burmese Folks Tales* (Calcutta, 1948), p. xxvii.

sacrifice has special potency. Dogs are sacrificed when a mother's delivery is delayed—the dog is killed above her head and the blood allowed to fall over her body. They are sacrificed at the gates of villages to avert disease and the head may be set up by the path. They are also sacrificed when a mithun is suffering from foot-and-mouth or some other disease, when the crops fail and at any other time when the Miri (shaman) so commands.

In the stories, however, the position of the dog is somewhat ambiguous. In Minyong and Bori tales, he brings to mankind the seed, hitherto unknown, which is put into his ear by a benevolent deity. The Kameng stories about dogs are even more favourable. There is a loyal and helpful puppy in a Bugun tale, and there is a Hrusso story of a father who is turned into a dog and looks after his children with courage and devotion. On the other hand, in Nocte and Wancho tales the dog appears as a clever cheat who tricks the pig and thereby gains an honoured place as a domestic pet. In other stories from the same two tribes, however, the dog appears as a simpleton from whom the goat is easily able to steal his horns. There are also Hill Miri and Kaman Mishmi stories as to how the dog lost the art of speech, neither of which are particularly creditable to him. With these may be compared a Rengma Naga tale recorded by Mills.

At the beginning of time men never died, and all living creatures and plants could talk and understand each other. Men went on increasing till food became very scarce. Things were worse because whenever a man trapped an animal it protested and he let it go, and whenever a man went to cut anything in the jungle the plant asked for mercy and the man went home again. God saw that the world would soon be full and there would be nothing to eat, so he took away the power of speech from all living things except dogs and men.

Then men began to hunt persistently. Their dogs, being able to speak, were able to call out exactly the line taken by the game they were chasing and the hunters were able to cut it off and kill it. Soon there was grave danger of all animals being exterminated. So God sent Hasung, and he stretched the dogs' tongues. And from that day dogs cannot speak.[3]

Stories about the elephant follow the usual lines. There is a very old tradition going back to the early *Hastya-yurveda* that formerly elephants used to fly and this is repeated in a number of tales in Central India and Orissa. Moklum and Nocte stories also speak of flying elephants.

As in the stories elsewhere the creation of the elephant is described in some detail. A house or granary may be transformed into the great creature, and there is a Sherdukpen story in which a girl is so changed; this is why the elephant obeys man, for formerly it was his wife. Fans and rice-pounders are fixed to the elephant's body as its ears and legs; sometimes plantain trees are put for legs and a pestle is often used as the trunk. In a Khampti story a tortoise turns itself into an elephant, using daos for tusks.

In other parts of Tribal India there are many stories which suggest that monkeys were originally men; the tradition, in fact, reverses modern ideas of evolution. Such stories will be found among the Gonds, Juangs and Saoras, and a few examples have been found in NEFA.

One set of stories describes how monkeys originally lived with men but were intolerably lazy and were driven out to live in the jungle. In a Nocte story a lazy boy is driven from the house by his step-mother and turns into a monkey. Another type of story describes the monkey as being actually human in the first instance.

There is a Lhota Naga story on the same lines.

Once upon a time a man called Kimongthang called his sisters' husbands' relations together and gave them rice beer to drink and said to them, 'I have cut a *chentung* tree ready for a sacrificial post. Go and drag it in for me, but do not let a single leaf fall to the ground.' So they went and began to drag the tree, but the leaves were half withered and they kept letting them fall. Then, determined not to let the leaves fall, they tied them onto the twigs and set to work to drag the tree again. In spite of this all the leaves fell off. Then they were ashamed to go back to the village

[3] J. P. Mills, *The Rengma Nagas*, p. 268.

and meet Kimongthang. So they fled away into the jungle, and the men became mynas and called '*Kyon, kyon.*' But the women ground up rice-flour to make rice-beer and smeared it on their foreheads and called out '*Woka, woka*' and became gibbons. That is why the gibbon now has a white forehead.[4]

The motif of a monkey being tricked to sit on a hot stone, as a result of which the skin is burnt off his backside thus turning it red, occurs in Gadaba and Jhoria stories;[5] it seems to be fairly widely distributed in NEFA. Equally well known are the stories of how men tricked the monkeys by mixing up their bows and arrows and by persuading them to go into a hollow tree where they are burnt to death. The former theme, of the bows and arrows, is found in Bori, Minyong, Idu and Taraon versions, which suggests a distribution over a very wide area which has had little or no inter-communication. The theme of the monkey massacre is known to the Dhammais of Kameng and to the Boris and Minyongs of Siang. From the holocaust one pregnant she-monkey escapes; her son is born and when he grows up they come together to produce a new race of monkeys. A Taraon tale describes the descent of the Mishmis from a human brother and sister who are born of a monkey, but the central massacre motif does not seem to be known in Lohit.

In stories about the mithun, the buffalo and the pig there is emphasis on the use of these animals in sacrifice and it is suggested that they were specially created for this purpose. In the case of the pig, Hill-Miri and Moklum stories are concerned to explain why it is that it lives on excreta.

The tiger in NEFA, as elsewhere, has a special fascination for the story-teller. Sometimes a man turns into a tiger, sometimes a woman gives birth to twins, one being human and the other a tiger. There is Minyong story of two brothers, one of whom turns into a cat and the other into a tiger. A Wancho story describes how men and tigers

[4] J. P. Mills, *The Lhota Nagas*, pp. 184 f.
[5] See my *Tribal Myths of Orissa*, pp. 388 and 391.

exchange their teeth and how men get control of all the guns in the world and thus gain ascendency over the tigers.

The marks on the tiger's body are naturally of great interest. The Buguns say they are due to a beating which the animal received.

A Nocte story describing how the tiger sends the cat to steal fire, whereon the cat decides to stay in human habitations where it is warmer and more comfortable, is paralleled by a Parenga story from Orissa.[*] There is probably a literary source for both tales.

1

BORI

Gameng, Siang F.D.

There was a brother with four sisters who made a clearing in the forest. One day the four sisters went to fish in the river, but before they could catch any a great snake came out of the water. When they saw him three of the sisters ran away, but in the eyes of the eldest sister the snake appeared to be a man and she stayed behind. She said to him, 'We came here to catch fish, but we haven't got any.' The snake replied, 'If you will bring me rice and beer you will be able to get as many as you want.' So saying the snake went down into the water again.

The eldest girl called her three sisters to come back and continue searching for fish, but they were frightened and refused. So in the end the eldest girl also went home with them.

One day a little while afterwards the brother said to his eldest sister, 'We will go to work in our field. You will cook rice for us and bring it to us with some beer ' The brother and his three sisters went away. When the food was ready the girl set out for the field. Now the path went by the river and when she came there she remembered that the snake had told her that if she brought rice and beer to the place, she would catch many fish. So she put the rice and beer down on the bank and went into the river and splashed the water about. When the snake heard it he came onto the bank in the form of a man. He ate the rice and drank the beer and the

[*] *Tribal Myths of Orissa*, p. 357.

girl and the snake-man made love to one another .It grew late and it was not possible for the girl to reach the field. The snake gave her a lot of fish and told her to go back to her house, and she did as he said.

When the brother and the three other sisters came home, the brother said to the girl, 'I asked you to bring our food to the field ; why didn't you?' She replied, 'I was taking it to you, but when I reached the river I saw a great many fish and stopped to catch them. As I was doing so some animal or other took the food away.' She showed the fish that she had caught and they were all very pleased, and the brother said, 'There must be a great many fish in that river.' He decided that on the following day they should all go to the river and catch fish instead of working in the field.

Accordingly the next day the brother and his four sisters went to the river to fish. But the girl did not take them to the place where the snake was, but higher up the river. As the brother was fishing, he worked his way down stream to the place where the snake lived and when he got there the snake came out, and he and the three younger girls ran away in fright. The eldest girl stayed behind and the snake took the form of a man and said to her, 'I told you to come alone. Why did you bring the others with you? To-day I won't give you any fish.'

The next day, therefore, the girl came alone with rice and beer and after they had made love, she caught a lot of fish. This went on for many days until the brother got suspicious and wondered how it was that when his sister went alone to the river they always got plenty of fish to eat, but when they went together they caught nothing. So he hid among the trees on the bank and presently he saw his sister arrive and then the snake come out of the river, for in his eyes his sister's lover was a snake. He watched him eating and drinking, but when he began to make love to his sister, he was so angry that he took his dao and killed him. When he did this the girl turned into a bird. That bird's name is Taki-Rigo and to this very day whenever it cries 'Taki-Rigo', snakes come out of the ground to watch her.

The brother went home and now there were only three sisters left. The next day he told the second sister to remain behind, while he and other two went to the field, and to bring the food for them when it was ready. After the others had gone the girl went to the forest to get wood and leaves. She took her dog with her, for this dog was very helpful—he picked leaves for her, gathered wood, and caught birds and rats. She was pleased with him and soon they were making love to one another. As a result the girl took the food to the field very late. When she arrived, her brother asked her what had happened. She said that she had picked leaves, gathered wood and caught birds and rats and this had made her late. When they came home and saw the birds and rats they were very pleased.

This went on for a long time until at last the brother got suspicious, wondering how his sister managed to catch so many birds and rats. So one day, instead of going to the field, he hid in the trees nearby and when his sister went out with the dog he followed them and presently saw them making love to one another. He was so angry that he killed his sister.

The next day he went with the youngest sister to the field and left the other sister to cook the food and bring it to them. This girl used to go every day to get wood and leaves, and one day as she was doing this she met a tiger. She was very frightened, but the tiger said to her, 'Don't be afraid. I have been waiting for you here for a long time.' The girl had long wanted a husband and when she found the tiger so friendly she made love to him. This went on for some time, and every day the tiger used to give her the flesh of deer or wild pig to take home.

When this had happened for some time, the brother got suspicious, wondering where all this meat was coming from. So one day instead of going to the field he hid near the house and followed his sister to the forest. When he saw her making love to the tiger he was so angry that he killed her.

Now there were only the brother and one sister left and they could not do all the work of their field by themselves. They grew poorer and poorer and used to wander through the forest digging up roots and picking leaves to eat. The girl was grown up and anxious to find a husband, but they could not get anyone for her. One day as she was going through the forest the memory of her three sisters came to her and she began to weep. Hearing the noise a bear came out of the undergrowth and asked her what was the matter. The girl told him all that had happened and said, 'Now-a-days we are always hungry and I spend my time looking for roots.' The bear dug up a great many roots and gave them to her, and the girl took them home. She used to do this every day and the bear helped her to get roots.

After some days the girl said to herself, 'This bear gives me such a lot of help that I must take some rice and beer for him.' Already she had begun to love the animal who was so kind and friendly. So the next day she made rice and beer and took it to him. He soon got drunk on the beer and made love to her. After that whenever the girl went to the forest she used to make love with the bear and the bear would give her roots to take home. Every day she used to put on good clothes, but in the evening when she came back the clothes would be torn and dirty.

When the brother saw this he wondered where all the roots were coming from and why his sister's clothes were always getting torn. So one day, instead of going to work, he hid near the house and followed his sister into the forest. When he saw the drunken bear making love to his sister and tearing her clothes with his feet he was very angry, and when the girl started home with her load of roots he caught hold of her and killed her.

After that the brother lived alone.

2

MINYONG

Pangin, Siang F.D.

A man lived in the forest with his three sisters.[7] One of the sisters lived at home ; the other two used to go with their brother to work in their clearings. One day the brother noticed that the eldest sister had prepared mithun-flesh, rice and beer and was taking it to the forest. 'Where can she be going?' he wondered and he left his work and followed her secretly. She went down to the bank of the Siang River and stamped on the ground. A great snake came from the water and coiled himself round her. When the act of love was over, the girl fed the snake and they sat together for a time and then parted. The boy, full of anger, returned home. But he said nothing to the others, and the following day went by

[7] This story combines in an interesting way a number of motifs that appear in other tales.

himself to the river and stamped on the ground. When the snake appeared, he cut him to pieces with his dao.

The next day, the girl again prepared mithun-flesh and rice and beer and took it to the river. She stamped on the ground but no snake appeared. She searched everywhere and soon found signs that her lover was dead. Full of sorrow she hanged herself from a tree. When the brother saw her hanging there, he was angry and cut her belly open with his dao. A great number of little snakes poured from her and the boy ran away in fright. The snakes followed him. When he stood still and looked back, they ran away, but when he went on they followed him. Since then there has been enmity between men and snakes.

Such was one sister. The second sister used to make very good leg-bands and one day she sat for a long while making them. Her brother asked her, 'Why are you making so many?' 'It is my pleasure,' she replied. The next day he peeped through the wall and saw the girl tying the cords round and round the legs of a dog. He went in and said, 'Why are you doing such a strange thing?' 'Because this dog is my husband.' The brother was so angry that he went away to another place. But the girl went with her dog-husband to the forest and built a good house. The couple cleared a field and made their living there. In due time three puppies were born.

Meanwhile the brother returned home and began to search for his sister. At last he found her house, but when he arrived both the girl and her husband were working in the field and only the puppies were at home. When they saw their uncle they were very happy and barked loudly, crying, 'Our uncle has come to see us.' Presently the girl and the dog came home and were glad to see their visitor, the girl because he was her brother, the dog because he was his brother-in-law. They gave him rice and beer, and the dog jumped into the loft and threw down mithun-flesh. The boy ate the rice but quietly threw away the flesh, for he would not eat the gift of the dog.

The following day the girl and the dog bade farewell to the boy and went to work in the field. The boy prepared to return home, but the puppies barked loudly crying, 'Our uncle is going away.' This annoyed the boy and he cut off the head of one of the puppies with his dao. As he did so there came a voice from inside the hearth saying, 'When my parents-in-law return, I shall tell them what you have done.' Astonished, the boy lifted the first stone of the hearth, but there was no one there.

The puppies continued barking and the boy cut off the head of another of them. As he did so there came a voice from inside the hearth saying, 'When my parents-in-law return, I shall tell them what you have done.' Astonished, the boy lifted the second stone of the hearth, but there was no one there. Then he cut off the head of the third puppy. As he did so the voice came yet again from inside the hearth saying, 'When my parents-in-law return, I shall tell them what you have done.' Astonished, the boy lifted the third stone, and found a fat grub beneath it. He picked him up and took him home.

After a few days the boy went hunting. He found the bark of a certain tree and threw it on the ground for the grub who began to eat it with great enjoyment. He said, 'Take me to the forest and put me on this tree and I will do well.' The next day, therefore, the boy took the grub to the forest and left him on the tree. The grub stayed there for a long time eating the leaves and bark of the tree, but in the end he went away. Presently the youth went to find him, but there was no trace of him anywhere. He asked the birds where he was, but they could not tell him. He asked the animals where he was, but they could not tell him. At last Siggo-Pareng the water-bird said, 'I know where he is, but you cannot go there alone. Prepare rice-flour for me and I will lead you to the place.' The boy prepared rice-flour and when the bird had eaten it, his droppings turned white and the boy was able to follow him through the woods. The bird led him to a great rock, and there beneath it was the grub. He was busy making metal bowls (*dankis*),[8] for he had become Ninur-Botte Wiyu.

Ninur-Botte said, 'I cannot come with you, but you may have these bowls, for I have been making them for you. Carry them away one by one, but as you pass the monkeys' village, see that you make no sound or they will come out and kill you.' The youth accordingly took several of the bowls back to his house, but one

[8] These *dankis* are said to be imported from Tibet. I saw a fine specimen at Riu, decorated with a number of symbols such as the Wheel of Life, the Lotus, the Conch. The *dankis* are rarely used for cooking, being regarded as a form of currency. A rich man has bamboo symbols of the *dankis* in his possession hung before his tomb.

evening as he passed the monkeys' village, he accidentally knocked one of the bowls against a tree and it made a ringing sound. The monkeys were offering sacrifice in their *dere* (dormitory) at the time and when they heard the sound they rushed out. The boy dropped the bowls and ran for his life. The monkeys took their bows and arrows and searched for him everywhere ; they did not find him but they did find Ninur-Botte, and they shot him to death with their arrows.

When he heard this, the boy was very angry, and decided to revenge himself on the monkeys. When he reached their village he found that they had gone to the Siang River to fish. He followed them and found that they had left their bows and arrows in a great pile on the bank, and were playing about in the water. 'Now is my opportunity,' he said to himself, and he hurriedly tied up the strings of all the bows so that they could not be used. Then he threw a great stone, plop, into the river. The monkeys, realizing that an enemy had come, rushed to shore and scrambled for their bows. Each thought he had his neighbour's bow when he found his was useless and they were soon quarrelling among themselves. As they were shouting at each other, a bird cried from the sky. The monkeys were frightened and ran to the boy and stood before him. 'What was that noise?' they asked. 'It was a dreadful thing,' he said, 'a most evil thing and it will devour you all.' 'What shall we do?' 'Come with me and I will hide you.'

The boy took the monkeys, who were now shivering with fear, through the forest until he found a great hollow tree. 'Go in there,' he said, 'and you will be safe. I will build a door of wood and leaves and no one will know where you are.' 'That is very good of you,' said the monkeys.

But directly the door was made, the boy lit a fire with his flint and burnt them all to death. But one girl monkey, a very little one, escaped. As she ran away she rubbed her blackened hands on her face and ever since the monkey's face has been black. When she had grown up a little, she lay down one day on her back with her legs and arms outstretched. 'Let something fall on me,' she cried to Doini-Pollo. At that a tiny bamboo leaf fell from the sky ; it entered into her and she conceived. A monkey son was born and when he grew up he married his mother, for there was no one else to marry, and the monkey-tribe began again.

When the monkeys had increased in number they asked their grandmother if they might make bows and arrows as of old. But she said to them, 'Beware of men. They are stronger and wiser than we are. It was the madness of fighting them that led to our destruction. Now live peacefully in the forest and forget your bows and arrows.' So ever since the monkeys have lived among the trees and have eaten fruit.

So of the three sisters, one had married a snake and died ; the other had married a dog and gone away. Only the youngest sister was left. But one day the brother saw this girl also prepare mithun-flesh and rice and beer and take it to the forest. As before he followed her secretly, and what did he see? He saw his sister meet a tiger and, when the act of love was done, she fed him with rice and flesh and gave him beer to drink. When she came home, the boy asked her in sorrow and anger if she was going the way of her sisters. 'I am going to marry my tiger,' she declared. And the very next day she made a great feast and married the tiger and went to live with him in the forest. There they built a splendid house and every day the tiger went hunting and brought home lots of meat.

After a time, the brother felt sorry and went to see his sister and make friends. The girl was at home when he arrived, but the tiger was out hunting. Although the girl was happy to see her brother, she was frightened that if the tiger came home he would eat him. The brother said, 'Somehow or other you must save me.' So the girl fed him and then hid him up in the rafters and covered him with a basket.

When the tiger came home, he asked for a basket, and the girl put one before him. 'No, I want the one up there,' he said. 'That one is dirty,' said the girl and found another. The tiger was sick into the basket, and his vomit was bits of meat. For this was how he brought the meat home. The girl picked the bits of meat out of the vomit and spread them on the drying-rack above the hearth. The tiger sat down and spread his legs before the fire. He took some rice-beer and when he was warm and at ease, he said, 'Let us have a *ponung*.'[1] 'And where,' asked the wife, 'are the girls for a *ponung*? We can never have a dance, for you must always eat up all the dancers.' 'Anyway,' said the tiger, 'there is

[1] The characteristic Adi dance.

a most peculiar smell in the house today. It smells to me like a man.' 'Don't be stupid,' said the girl. 'How could a man be here?' 'It's not only a man,' said the tiger. 'It's the smell of a brother-in-law.' 'What a creature you are,' exclaimed the girl. 'Always smelling something! Have some more beer and go to sleep.' The tiger considered his wife's advice and found it good. He had another gourdful of beer and went to sleep. The brother lay up in the rafters all night, but in the morning, when the tiger went out to hunt again, he came down and said, 'Well, I have had enough. I must be on my way home.' His sister fed him with rice and beer, but he refused the meat which his brother-in-law had vomited, and took his dao and prepared to go away. The girl warned him to be careful, and gave him a red skirt and a dog. 'Let the dog go ahead. If he comes running back, you will know that my lord is on the way. Then cut a plantain, tie the dog to it and wrap the skirt round him at the bottom. And you yourself hide somewhere.'

The youth left the house and began to make his way home. He climbed hill after hill, crossed torrent after torrent ; the rocks thundered past him as he went. Then suddenly the dog came running back towards him. What did he do? He cut a plantain, tied the dog to it and put the red skirt below. Now it looked like a Gallong girl on her way to Pasighat. The boy hid behind a tree, and the tiger appeared. As he sprang with a great roar upon the dog, the boy came out from his hiding-place and killed him with his dao.

When the tiger did not return home that night his wife wept and in the morning, anxious and afraid, went out to find him. She saw his body on the ground and her own red skirt in the bushes near by. At this she felt very sad, and, although it was her own fault, furious with her brother.

Some time afterwards, the youth decided to bring his sister home to live with him. 'She is all I have left,' he thought, 'and at least she makes good beer.' So he went to bring her home. But she was full of anger against him for killing her husband. She showed him nothing but friendliness, however, and made him sit down and gave him food. As he was eating, she took an egg and a knife and slipped away behind the house. Her brother saw this and said to himself, 'What is she up to now?' He got up and quietly went to see what she was doing. He saw her break the egg and smear the yoke over her head and body. She put the knife into her mouth, and as she did so she turned into a great tigress. But he was ready for her and killed her with his dao before she could do him harm.

3

PANGGI

Geku, Siang F.D.

Peddong-Dorum had a tree called Ramjo: it was like a son to him. There was a man called Kare-Botte and he cut the tree, not from below, but from above, so that only the branches suffered. Some twigs fell down through the earth to Polo-Irgong-Lilong, underground-home of the Wiyus, where they turned into pigs. A big branch of the tree fell on the hills and became a deer ; another branch became a mithun, another a porcupine, a fourth a squirrel. In this way animals came to the world.

4

SHERDUKPEN

Shergaon, Kameng F.D.

Long ago, a woman was born on a high mountain of bare rock. There were no trees or streams ; she grew very thirsty, and went to find water. Presently she came to a great lake in the middle of which was a small forest-covered island. There was a Lama on this island, and when the woman arrived, he was bathing and washing his loin-cloth. The dirty water flowed across the lake and the woman drank it and went away.

After a few months her belly began to swell. She said to herself, 'What has happened? I have eaten nothing, so how is my belly full?' Presently, she laid five eggs and, astonished, broke them open to see what they were. From the first, there came a human child, a girl ; from the second came a monkey, from the third a tigress, from the fourth a cow and from the fifth a bitch. They gathered round her clamouring for food. The woman was frightened and ran down to the lake, thinking that what had happened must be due to the water she had drunk.

She saw the Lama sitting on his island and told him what had happened. 'These are your children,' she said. 'You must give them food.' The Lama told her to look on the little girl as her daughter and keep the cow and bitch in her house. But he sent the monkey and the tigress to live in the forest.

5

SINGPHO

Dumba, Tirap F.D.

There was a rich man called Chaumau. One day a Lama came to his house and he prepared a seat for him, anxious to honour so holy a man. But the Lama refused to sit down saying, 'I will take my seat only if you promise to do whatever I bid you.' Chaumau said, 'I will certainly do whatever you tell me.' The Lama then sat on the seat and Chaumau said, 'You may always live in my house.' The Lama was pleased at this and made his home there.

In due time a male child was born to Chaumau's wife and the father went to tell the Lama about it. The Lama said, 'Take this child and bury him in the ground.' Chaumau, mindful of his promise, took the child and buried him.

After a year a second child was born to Chaumau's wife and the father went to tell the Lama about it. The Lama said, 'Take this child and bury him in the ground.' Chaumau, mindful of his promise, took the child and buried him.

After a year a third male child was born to Chaumau's wife and the father went to tell the Lama about it. The Lama said, 'Take this child and bury him in the ground.' Chaumau, mindful of his promise, took the child and buried him.

When Chaumau saw that his three children were dead, he said to himself, 'Why have I allowed this Lama to live in my house, and why I have promised to do whatever he tells me?'

And now for the fourth time Chaumau's wife gave birth, this time to a baby-girl, and the Lama said, 'Take this baby and put her on the path where the elephants go to and fro.' Chaumau again did what he was told. A thousand elephants passed by but not one of them hurt the child, and when the Lama heard about it he told Chaumau to bring the baby home.

The Lama then said to Chaumau, 'Go to the place where you buried your three children and lie down on the ground pretending to be asleep, and listen to any voice you may hear.'

Chaumau went to the place where he had buried his three children and lay down on the ground pretending to be asleep. Presently the three ghosts began to talk to each other and the first child said, 'How unhappy I am that the Lama made my father bury me here! If he had not, I would have drunk the blood of my parents. But now I shall become a leech and at least drink their blood that way.'

The second child spoke from the grave and said, 'Had the Lama not ordered me to be buried, I would have devoured my parents, but I shall become a tiger and eat their flesh anyway.'

The third child spoke from the grave and said, 'Had the Lama not ordered me to be buried, I would have cast my parents into a deep sleep and would have used up all their wealth. But now I shall become a snake and bite them and all men.'

Hearing this Chaumau went to the Lama and said, 'You did well in making me bury the three children, for had I not done so they would have destroyed us.'

In due time the first child turned into a leech, the second into a tiger and the third into a snake.

THE BEAR

6

BUGUN (KHOWA)

Senchong, Kameng F.D.

Long ago there was a Dhammai who lived at home with his sister. They had no one to help them, and since the man himself spent the whole day drinking and smoking, the girl had to do all the work of the house and fields.

One day the man said to his sister, 'Go to the forest and get me some really sweet fruit.' When the girl reached the forest she found that all the best fruit was high in the trees and though she tried to climb up she could not reach it. She was very upset by this, for she thought that if she came back without anything, her brother would beat her. She continued searching frantically until at last she came to a tree where a bear had climbed high in the branches and was enjoying the fruit. When she saw him she thought that if she could only make friends with him he would get some fruit for her. So she stood beneath the tree and sang him a little song:

'My elder brother has sent me to fetch fruit,
But I cannot climb the trees to get it,
If you would bring some down for me, how
happy I would be!'

But the bear replied, 'This fruit is mine and I need it for myself; how then can I give it to your brother?' The girl said, 'I saw you some time ago and liked you so much that I have come to see you again.' The bear said, 'All right, I'll give you some fruit, but what will you give me in return? If you marry me I'll give you as much fruit as you want every day of your life.'

When the girl heard this proposal she burst out laughing and said, 'Of course, I'll be only too glad to marry you.' So the bear threw some fruit down to her from the top of the tree and she picked it up and took it home for her brother.

Now this fruit was so delicious that the brother said, 'You must go every day to the forest and get me some.'

After that the girl went daily to the forest and there she met the bear and every evening she came home with a load of fruit.

But the bear was a clumsy lover and when he took the girl in his arms he tore her clothes with his claws. When the girl returned home with her clothes torn her brother used to ask what had happened and she would reply, 'The difficulty is that the trees which have this particular kind of fruit are covered with sharp thorns and when I climb them they tear my clothes!' The brother gave her new clothes the first day and the second day and in fact every day he had to give her new clothes, and as they were very expensive he decided at last to follow her to the forest and see if what she said was really true.

This time, when the girl reached the tree, the bear had arrived before her and was already up the tree collecting the fruit. The girl called to him but he took no notice and did not reply. But in the end, after she had called to him several times, the bear sang to her saying:

'Is the fruit sweet or am I sweet?'

The girl sang in return:

'The fruit is not sweet, for it is for my brother,
But you are very sweet, because you are for me.'

When the bear heard this he came straight down from the tree and made love to the girl. Then he climbed up the tree again and threw down the fruit. The girl picked it up and started to return home.

The brother had heard the songs and watched everything that happened. So he quickly went home and arrived before the girl returned. This time when he saw her clothes torn and dishevelled he said angrily, 'How did you tear your clothes?' And the girl, alarmed by his tone, replied, 'If this bothers you so much, I won't go to get fruit for you again.' 'No, no, that doesn't matter at all. All I want you to do is to bring me this lovely fruit.'

The next day when the girl went to the place the bear was not at the tree, but she called loudly to him and he came. The bear said, 'I don't know what is the matter with me today, but I feel sick and giddy as if I were going to die.'

Now this time the brother had followed with his bow and arrows and when he saw the bear he took careful aim and shot him dead. When the bear fell down, the girl looked round in fright and saw her brother. She rushed at him screaming and crying, 'That was my husband. Why have you killed him?' He replied, 'You are a human being and you ought to marry a human being. How can you marry an animal like a bear?' He caught hold of her and dragged her home.

It is because this happened long ago that Dhammai women never touch bear's flesh.

7

TARAON (DIGARU) MISHMI

Machima, Lohit F.D.

There was a Chin girl who lost both her parents when she was very small. She and her brother were very fond of each other: They went about everywhere together, ate together, played together and slept together. At last when they grew up, they lived as man and wife and in time the girl became pregnant.

They were very ashamed of this and thought that everybody

would laugh and look down on them, so they decided to go and live in the forest. One day they were thirsty and could not find water anywhere. But there was a great rock from which there came a little brackish water that tasted salty. They drank it and turned into bears.

8

TARAON (DIGARU) MISHMI

Tushe, Lohit F.D.

Long ago, there were two brothers. The elder wanted to have a house to himself and tried to turn his younger brother out and send him to live in the forest, but he refused to go.

One day, when the elder brother went to work on the hillside, he saw a large honey-comb. The next day the younger brother saw the same comb and climbed up and took it down. When the elder brother saw what had happened, he was very angry but could not do anything about it, for the younger boy was the stronger of the two.

But the elder brother did not forget and one day he went to the hornet and said, 'When my brother next climbs a tree, sting him so that he will fall down and die.' The hornet waited till the younger brother climbed up a tree and then stung him on his bottom. The boy clasped his bottom with his hands to protect it and fell to the ground. As a result of this his back became crooked and he could not walk properly. He sent for a Goak-Drong (a great medicine-man) called Kronye to offer sacrifice for him, but though this went on for eight years, he hardly got any better and at the end of the eighth year, he decided that the expense was more than he could manage and turned himself into a bear.

As a bear he attacked every man he saw. So his elder brother made a cage and shut him up in it. But he cut through the wood with his teeth and escaped, and the bars of the cage turned into the thorny bombax tree.

When the elder brother saw the bear escaping, he ran after him and caught him by the tail, but the bear dragged him along the ground until the tail came off. This is why the bear has such a short tail.

9

WANCHO

Jaboka, Tirap F.D.

Once upon a time a crow, a bear, a monkey and a man went to work together in their clearing on the hillside. They laboured till noon and when the work was done they sat down to eat their food. The man had brought a basket of cooked rice with him, but when he went down to a little stream to wash, his friends stole it and ate it all.

When the man returned and found there was nothing left for him to eat, he was very angry and hit the bear on his neck. Since then the bear has had a white mark there. The crow was so frightened that he flew away from the hills and went to live in the plains. The monkey climbed up a tree and has lived there ever since.

Since then all the animals have been afraid of man. The bear has brains but cannot use them. Man too has brains but he can use them and this is the advantage he has over the animals.

The Buffalo

10

HRUSSO (AKA)

Hussigaon, Kameng F.D.

A tiger was hunting in the forest. As he went along he met a wild pig and said, 'O pig, I'm very hungry and I'm going to eat you.' 'The matter of eating me,' said the pig, 'can be taken up later, but first of all we must fight. If I am defeated then you can certainly eat me, but not otherwise.'

The tiger said, 'But when we fight, who will be the judge?' The pig said, 'You can run very quickly. Go and find a judge and come back with him for our fight.' Hearing this, the tiger went to find a judge.

There was a man called Rariu-Jija who was hunting in the same forest, and the tiger approached him, but he was so frightened that he began to run away. But the tiger called to him and said, 'Don't be frightened.' Rariu-Jija said, 'But haven't you come to eat me?' The tiger swore an oath saying, 'I haven't the least intention of eating you. All I want is that you should act as judge in a fight between the wild pig and myself.' So then Rariu-Jija agreed to go with the tiger.

In the meantime the pig had covered himself with wet and slippery mud. When the tiger reached the place with Rariu-Jija, he said, 'Now you must decide who is the winner.' The pig and the tiger began to fight, but the pig shook himself and the mud flew into the tiger's eyes and he was so frightened that he turned round to run away. When he saw this, Rariu-Jija declared that the pig was the winner and even the tiger agreed.

So the pig escaped, but the tiger was still hungry and said to Rariu-Jija, 'I'm very hungry and I'm going to eat you after all.' Rariu-Jija protested saying, 'But you took an oath that you would not eat me. You really can't change your mind now.' But the tiger replied, 'If you had declared me the winner I would have eaten the pig and would have had no need to eat you, but since you have declared the pig the winner and allowed him to run away I have got nothing else to eat but you.' When he heard this, Rariu-Jija ran for his life until he was so tired that he could run no more and took refuge in a tree. This tree was very tall with great branches. The tiger could not climb up, so he sat down at the foot of the tree, planning to eat Rariu-Jija when he came down.

Now this tree was a favourite resting-place of a herd of wild buffaloes and every evening they used to gather there for the night. When they came that evening as usual, they drove the tiger away.

In the morning the buffaloes went to their grazing-grounds and when they had gone Rariu-Jija came down from the tree and cleaned the place and then climbed up again. He did this for many days. When the buffaloes saw that every evening their resting-place was clean, they began to wonder what was going on and said to one another, 'How can we catch whoever is responsible for cleaning the place?' An old she-buffalo said, 'I am too old to go the grazing-grounds, so I will hide here tomorrow and catch him.' The other buffaloes approved of this suggestion and promised that each of them would bring her a little food when they returned in the evening.

So next morning all the others went away, leaving the old she-buffalo behind, and she lay down on the ground as if she were dead. Rariu-Jija descended from the tree as usual and cleaned the place, but when he saw the she-buffalo lying there, he mourned for her and began to wash her body. As he was doing so, the she-buffalo tried to catch him between her legs. He was so startled by this that he jumped away just in time and hastily went back to his place in the tree. In the evening the other buffaloes returned and when they heard what had happened, they wer angry and refused to give the old she-buffalo her food.

The next morning, however, the old she-buffalo said, 'This time I won't fail. I will certainly catch him today.' Rariu-Jija came down again and after the usual cleaning, thinking that now the she-buffalo was really dead, washed her body carefully. But while he was doing it she caught him and he could not get away. In the evening the other buffaloes returned and when they saw the man held firmly by the legs of the she-buffalo they were very pleased. They said to him, 'Don't be afraid. You have done us a great service and we will help you in every way we can. From today you will be able to drink our milk.' So saying they gave the old she-buffalo the food hat they had brought for her.

Henceforward Rariu-Jija lived happily with the buffaloes. He used to clean their resting-place every day and whenever any buffalo was sick or too weak to go to the grazing-grounds he would fetch food for him from the forest. In return he was allowed to drink as much milk as he wanted.

One day the buffaloes said to Rariu-Jija, 'Sometimes we go on journeys and when we do, how shall we know whether all is well with you or not? Make two flutes, one with a single pipe and another with two pipes. When we hear you playing on the single pipe, we will know all is well and will continue on our way, but when you play on the two pipes we will return at once.'

One day Rariu-Jija went down to a stream to bathe and some of his hair fell out. He thought that this hair was so precious that it should not be thrown away, so he made a wooden box for it. He threw the box into the water and it floated down stream.

Far below, the daughter of the Raja of Assam was bathing. She saw the box floating down and brought it to the bank and when she opened it and saw the beautiful hair, she said to herself, 'This is so fine that I must marry the man it belongs to.' She went home and refused to eat or even to speak to anybody. Her parents asked her anxiously what was the matter and said, 'What do you want? Tell us, we'll give you anything so long as you don't go on sulking.'

The girl showed them the box and the hair inside it and said, 'I want to marry the man whose hair this is.'

The Raja and Rani called men, animals and birds and asked them whose hair it was, but nobody knew anything about it. At last the crow said, 'I will go and find him.' He flew all over the place and at last came to the tree where Rariu-Jija was living. He was wandering about with a flute in each hand. The crow flew down and pecked him on the head. Rariu-Jija beat at the crow with his hands to drive him away and in doing so dropped both his flutes. The crow picked them up and carried them to the girl. 'Now certainly,' he said, 'this man will come to you.'

The girl began to play on the single flute and the buffaloes continued on their journey but after a little while she wondered what the double flute would sound like and began to play it, whereupon the buffaloes came running to her. Rariu-Jija saw them passing and supposed that they must be going to whoever had got his flutes. So he followed them until he came to the girl's palace. He went to her and asked her to give the flutes back, but she replied, 'I will only give them back if you will marry me.'

Rariu-Jija was entirely agreeable to this, and the two were married at once. When the Raja heard that his son-in-law had so many buffaloes and possessed a pair of flutes that could control them at will, he decided that he ought to have them. So he secretly stole the flutes and drove his daughter and her husband out of the house.

Rariu-Jija said to his wife, 'Don't let us stay here ; we will go to the tree where I lived for so long.' They went there and had many daughters. But none of them would eat any meat, for their mother was a Raja's daughter. This is why our woman do not eat the meat of pigs, mithun, goats, or fowls, but only fish and a certain kind of deer. This is also why there are many buffaloes in Assam today.[10]

[10] This story contains three motifs that are well known in other parts of village India. The hero who goes to serve a herd of buffaloes and wins their affection and support is paralleled in, for example, a Lohar story from the Raipur District of Madhya Pradesh, where a Raja's son, lost in the forest, serves cows beneath a mango tree. A Muria story describes how a boy hides in the branches of a great banyan tree, beneath which a herd

11

BUGUN (KHOWA)

Senchong, Kameng F.D.

Once upon a time there was a woman in Assam called Mujmi She conceived but died before the child was born and her body was taken out into the jungle and buried there. Five days after her death the people of her village, according to custom, went for a hunt and Mujmi's husband went with them. In the course of the hunt they came to the burial place and the husband tripped over the mound of his wife's grave and broke it open. From the grave there came out a cow and her calf ; these were the woman herself and the child that was in her womb.

When Mujmi's husband saw them he said to himself, 'I must not kill these creature, since they came out of my wife's grave, but I must look after them very carefully.' So he made a fence round the place to protect them from thieves and wild animals. The cow and the calf stayed on in the place and when the calf grew up he went to his mother and from her many calves were born. But they could not escape from the enclosure in which they had been kept.

After a time some Buguns came down to Assam to trade and they passed by the enclosure where the cows were living. They broke the fence and stole some of them and took them back to their country and the other tribes of this region purchased them.

of wild buffaloes have their resting-place. He makes friends with them and looks after their calves and in return they feed him with their milk.

There are many stories of the two magic flutes which can send a message over great distances. In the Lohar, as in the Hrusso, tale, these flutes are given to the hero by the leader of the cows and, when the boy gets into trouble, he plays the Flute of Sorrow and the cows run to help him. He loses the flutes but marries a Raja's daughter in the end. In Kuruk and Muria stories from Bastar, a Raja gives his young wife a Flute of Joy and a Flute of Sorrow. In a Dhoba story from Mandla, the hero marries a monkey: Bhagavan gives him two flutes—when he plays one, she remains a monkey, but when he plays the other she turns into a beautiful girl.

The idea of a message being carrled by a stream to someone bathing lower down is equally common. Often it is the beautiful hair of the hero or heroine ; in a Dhammai story recorded in Chapter III, a girl spits in the water and her future lover sees it.

For references, see my *Folk-Tales of Mahakoshal* (Bombay, 1944). pp. 138, 173, 202, 427, 386.

12

HILL MIRI

Chemir, Subansiri F.D.

There were two brothers living and working together. One was clever, but the other was very clumsy. When he went to the clearing, he could not work with his hands ; all he could do was to scrape the ground with his feet. His brother said, 'Why don't you work properly?' He said, 'I have no mind to this sort of thing. I want to travel.' His brother said, 'Very well, let us see how far you can go.' And at that the deer leapt into the air and with great bounds ran into the forest.

13

SHERDUKPEN

Shergaon, Kameng F.D.

Long ago, when Apapek and his three sons were living together, the old man took his eldest and youngest sons to the forest to hunt. They saw a deer and their dog chased it round and round in a circle and Apapek shot it with a poisoned arrow. But the poison did not kill the deer ; it only made it drunk with a kind of madness. Apapek and his sons tried to catch it but it danced among them ; it did not run away or fall down and die, but simply went on dancing.

This went on for a long time until Chungba-Sangyat came to them and said, 'Don't kill this deer, but let it go.' Apapek said, 'But I have already shot it and there is poison in its body. How can we let it go?' Chungba-Sangyat said, 'Even so, let it go, for it would be a sin to eat its flesh.' The boys agreed but Apapek said, 'I don't know anything about sin. I am an old man now and am hungry for meat, so whether you like it or not, I am going to eat it.' But Chungba-Sangyat still refused to let him do this and since Apapek continued to demand the meat he removed the poison from the deer's body and it ran away.[11]

[11] This is the story behind the Sherdukpen Deer Dance, which is performed with great vigour by a man wearing a mask which represents a deer's head with spreading antlers.

14

SHERDUKPEN

Rupa, Kameng F.D.

There were two brothers ; the elder was a Lama and the younger made his living by hunting. When the hunter brought the meat home the Lama used to eat it, even though he was not supposed to. But one day he repented and said, 'Don't go hunting any longer, for it is a sin to take the life of others.' His brother said, 'But how can I give up my only means of livelihood?' They argued for a long time and finally the Lama said, 'I shall turn into a red deer. If you can kill me you will be a great hunter and without sin. But if you cannot kill me, great sin will rest upon your head.' The hunter agreed to this.

The Lama went to the forest and there turned into a deer. Soon afterwards the hunter came with his dog to find him. He sat down to rest and gave some food to the dog and as the dog ate it the belly of the deer was filled. When this happened the Lama in the shape of the deer said to himself, 'My belly is full, how will I be able to escape?' Then the hunter rubbed his bow-string with leaves and tightened it. As he did so, the Lama relieved himself. At this he was still more afraid and said, 'Now that my belly has been filled and I have relieved myself without any reason, my brother will certainly kill me.'

The hunter waited by a stream and sent his dog to chase the deer. After a time the deer came to the water and the hunter said, 'Brother, shall I shoot or not?' The Lama replied, 'Brother, you must not shoot. From today I will be a man no longer but will live in the forest as a deer.' It was from this Lama that the race of deer began.

THE DOG

15

BORI

Mega, Siang F.D.

At the beginning there were only Abo-Tani and Taru. There were no other people in the world. So they naturally wondered how they were to get wives. They travelled round and round the hills until they came back to the place where they had been born, and there they found two bitches cooking their food. The brothers watched them for some time and then said to one another, 'We've not been able to find wives anywhere. These two bitches seem hard-working and are obviously good cooks. So why shouldn't we marry them?' They sat down by the fire with them and asked where they came from and if they were already married. The bitches replied, 'We have no home, but live where we feel inclined. No, we are not married.'

Abo-Tani said, 'We two brothers are in search of wives and we have fortunately met you, so let us get married.' The bitches replied, 'How can we get married, for you are one thing and we are another?' Tani said, 'That doesn't matter. We will get married.' So in the end the brothers each married one of the bitches.

One day some time after they were married, Tani and Taru quarrelled and Taru with his wife went away towards Tibet. Tani, however, remained with his wife and lived very happily and lovingly with her. They used to go everyday to hunt and got plenty of food to eat. But one day Tani did not go hunting and they had nothing to eat. In fact, Tani got so weak and hungry that he could not even stand up. But his wife went about as usual and never complained that she was feeling hungry. Tani wondered how it was that she did not feel hungry and suspected that she must be getting some food secretly. So the next day he hid himself and watched and found that his wife was eating his excreta. He was very angry at this and turned her out of the house.

The bitch went away to the forest and met a deer. The two became friends and both enjoyed criticizing Tani, the deer because he had killed so many of his relations, the dog because he had turned her out of the house.

One day the deer said to the dog, 'Let us go to Mite-Mitang Wiyu.' So they went together to see him. The Wiyu was very pleased at meeting them and killed a pig for them as a present. He cut up the meat and wrapping the pieces in leaves, gave them to the deer and said, 'This is for both of you.' But he took the dog into his house and said, 'There are a few things that I would like you to take for Tani, but don't tell that other fellow.' So saying, and looking round to see they were not observed, he put every kind of seed in the dog's ear.

While this was going on, the deer put the meat into a pocket which he had in his rump and went away, thinking that it would be stupid to share such good meat with anyone else. The dog came out at that moment and, seeing the deer running away, ran after him. After a long chase she caught up with him and pulled the meat out of his pocket and with it some of the deer's own flesh. The dog then went back to Tani and without saying anything turned her head on one side and shook herself and the seeds dropped out of her ear onto the ground. She was about to go away but Tani stopped her saying, 'Don't go, for although you will not be my wife, we can live together as friends.' So the bitch stayed where she was and lived with Tani. Since that time dogs have always lived with men.

And the reason why the dog and the deer are now at loggerheads is that the deer long ago stole the dog's food. This too is why, when a dog attacks a deer, he always catches his backside.

16

HILL MIRI

Chemir, Subansiri F.D.

Abo-Teni had a son who was very fond of hunting. One day he went to the forest and killed a deer. He had no knife, so he tore it to pieces with his teeth and gorged himself on the flesh. He ate so much that he could hardly breathe.

He went home and tried to tell his father that he had killed a deer, but no one could understand him, for his belly was so full that he could only say *'Kok-Kok'*. Abo-Teni lost his temper and knocked him down. He crawled away on all fours crying *'Kaiyen'*. Abo-Teni said, 'From today you will be a dog, and eat your meat raw, and be without the power of speech.'

17

KAMAN MISHMI

Lohit Valley, Lohit F.D.

Once a man and his wife lived together but had no children. As the house seemed empty without them, the husband brought a dog whom they both came to love and care for like a son.

One day the man went on a long journey leaving his wife and the dog at home. Now in the neighbourhood there lived a handsome young man with whom the woman had long been in love. When her husband had gone she called her lover and they spent the time together. But the dog watched everything the woman did and when her husband returned told him all about it.

The husband rebuked his wife, but she denied everything and declared that the dog had made up the entire story out of jealousy. The husband was very angry with the dog and, believing that his wife had been true to him, he comforted her but caught the dog and cut his tongue into two pieces. Ever since the dog has been unable to speak.

But when the woman saw the dog miserable in the corner of her house, she felt sad because she had been cruel and said to him, 'Henceforth, you will live in our house like a king and won't have to do any work. All my life I will serve you by giving you a share of whatever food I cook.'

Since that day the dog has lived with human beings, enjoying an equal share of the meals prepared for the family and has not done any work about the house.[12]

18

MINYONG

Komsing, Siang F.D.

There was once a great tree. At that time, there were no human beings on earth, only this tree. The Wiyus said to one another, 'How can we kill the tree?' A Wiyu who had the form of a rat was living in his hole and when the others called him, he came out and made a ladder on which he climbed the tree, but it broke and he fell down backwards with his legs in the air. Ever since, the rat's legs have been crooked.

Doiying Botte Wiyu thought to himself, 'Why hasn't the rat killed the tree?' He himself cut it with his dao, but it did not fall. Now this tree stood on a hillside above a river. As the Wiyu cut it, some of the chips fell on the hill and turned into animals, some fell into the river and turned into fish.

[12] Recorded by T. K. Barua.

But one chip of the wood went down through the earth to Kine-Dene, who was living in the underground home of the Wiyus. There it turned into a dog. When Kine-Dene saw it, he was pleased and said, 'This is my dog.'

Kine-Dene had all the seed in the world. When men were born and began to clear the forest and cultivate, they went to him to ask for seed. He said, 'I cannot give you seed without asking Doiying-Botte. If he agrees, I will certainly give it to you.' He asked Doiying-Botte who replied, 'Very well, give it to them.'

It was Engo-Takar who had asked for seed. Kine-Dene put every kind of seed in the ear of the dog and sent it to him. In gratitude, Engo-Takar offered the Mopun sacrifice to Kine-Dene. Ever since we have given him fowls and pigs in exchange for the food he gave us. We also give bits of our food to the dog who brought us seed. This is why the dog now lives with men and not with Kine-Dene.

19

NOCTE

Laptang, Tirap F.D.

A certain man had a dog and a pig, who did nothing but eat; they were far too lazy to do any work. After a time their owner decided to make them do something for their living and told them to go and plough his fields.

The pig worked all day, scratching the soil with his jaws until the entire surface was broken up. But the dog lay down in the shade of a tree and slept.

In the evening the pig went home and, directly he was gone, the dog got up and went round the field, rubbing out the pig's footprints and leaving his own in their place. Then he too went home.

That evening the man asked the dog and the pig what they had done. The pig said, 'I ploughed the whole field, but this dog slept all day under a tree.'

The dog said, 'It was I who ploughed the field. It was the pig who slept all day under a tree.'

The man said, 'I don't believe either of you. Tomorrow I myself will go to see the field.'

Next day, when the man went to his field he saw the dog's footprints everywhere, but not a single print of the pig. He returned and abused the pig, saying, 'You didn't do any work at all.'

Ever since, the pig has had to live below the house, and when he is offered food he is called with the words *'Mo-mo'*. This means 'No, no, you did no work.'

But the dog is allowed to live inside the house, and is called with the words *'Ko-ko'*, which mean 'Yes, yes, you did your work.'

20

NOCTE

Laptang, Tirap F.D.

In the old days dogs had horns and fought other animals with them, but did not bite as they do now. They could take their horns off and put them aside when they wanted to rest.

A dog and a goat lived together in someone's house, but the goat had no horns and was rather afraid of the dog.

One day the dog saw some husked rice in the mortar, and since no one was about, he removed his horns and ate it. As he was doing so, the goat came up secretly, picked up the horns and fixed them on his own head.

When the dog had finished eating the rice he looked round for his horns but saw that someone had stolen them. When he saw them on the goat's head he rushed at him, but the goat butted him and drove him away.

21

WANCHO

Jaboka, Tirap F.D.

The dog and the pig used to live with men. One day a man asked them to go and work in his clearing. The pig worked hard all day, but the dog lay down and slept under a bush. In the evening he came home first and told the man that he had worked all day but that the pig had done nothing but sleep. The man was angry with the pig and turned him out of his house and told him to live on excreta. But he allowed the dog to live with him as his own brother.

22

WANCHO

Longkhao, Tirap F.D.

Formerly the goat and the dog were friends. They used to husk grain in the same mortar. The dog had very beautiful ornaments in his ears and in order to husk the grain more easily he used to take them out and put them on the ground. One day, while the dog was busy husking, the goat stole the ornaments and ran away. He put them on his head and they turned into horns. This is why the goat has horns and the dog is still his enemy.

THE ELEPHANT

23

DHAMMAI (MIJI)

Sachung, Kameng F.D.

Long ago there was a god called Luchonmu-Bui who lived with his wife Jusung-Nui-Muhu among the mountains. One day she gave birth to an elephant, the first in the world. The mother fed him at her breast but could not give him enough milk. Then she gave him a little food but could not satisfy him and he was always crying for more. He grew very big, but was so weak and thin that he could not do any work, he could not even walk.

One day the two great gods of the forest, Lujuphu and Jasuju, invited all the animals, birds and fish to a feast. But the elephant was so weak that he could only crawl slowly along and when he reached the place all the food was finished. When the others saw the poor thin creature crawling along on the ground and realized that there was no food for him, they felt sorry and each of the animals, birds and fish took a little food from his belly and gave it to him. In the end the elephant had so much that he grew fat and strong.

This is why he is so strong today and why in his body there are various kinds of flesh.

24

IDU MISHMI

Taraon, Lohit F.D.

Inni-Abromai was the first person ever to build a granary. When he had done this he made himself a fine house, but after a few years it fell down and turned into a great animal, as long as a Mishmi house. The pillars on which the house stood turned into his legs ; the roof projecting at one end became the head ; and the ladder leading to the door turned into the trunk. This was the first elephant.

25

KHAMPTI

Lalang, Tirap F.D.

Long ago there was a man and his wife who had no children. They grew old and said to one another, 'We are growing old and we have no child'. They went therefore to a holy tree and offered it sacrifice. Every day they used to pour water on the tree and salute it. After they had done this for many days, a spirit came out of the tree and asked the old man and his wife, 'Why have you been making these offerings to me for so long?' They replied, 'We are now old, yet we have never had a child and we have been offering you water so that we may have one.'

The god replied, 'Good. You will have a child and you need not make offerings to me any longer.' When the old people heard what the spirit of the tree said, they returned home.

On that very day the old woman conceived and when ten months were complete she gave birth to a tortoise. The parents complained to one another, 'After the immense trouble we took to please the spirit of the tree all he has given us is a tortoise.' But afterwards they thought, 'At least we have some kind of child, even if he is only a tortoise.'

The old woman tried to feed the tortoise at her breast, but he refused to take it and asked for rice instead. They thought that the baby would only eat very little, but he demanded two large leaf-bundles of it. This was on the second day and on the third day he ate three bundles. On the fourth day he ate four bundles and thereafter every day he ate one extra bundle, until when he was twenty days' old he ate twenty bundles of rice in a single day.

The old parents, seeing that their entire store of rice was being exhausted, were alarmed and sighed for the day when they had no family. 'This child is not even a human being and because of him we are likely to be entirely ruined. If he eats as much as this when he is only twenty days old, what he will do when he is grown up?'

So they went to the tree and said to the spirit who lived there, 'We don't want this child, please take him back.' But the spirit took no notice of them.

Now his parents had called this tortoise Ailung, and since the spirit of the tree did not take him away, his mother said to him, 'You are eating up all our food and yet you do no work.' Ailung replied, 'Mother, ask my father to make me a really good dao.' His mother said, 'But Ailung, what will you do with a dao?' The tortoise replied, 'I'll go to the forest and make a field there.' Although the mother wondered how the child could use a dao since he had no hands, she said to her husband, 'Ailung wants a dao,' and he made his son not one but two.

Ailung took the daos to the forest. When he arrived there, he turned into an elephant, using the two daos as tusks. In a single day he cut the trees of three hillsides, but there was a very tall rubber tree standing between the hills and he left it standing, for he thought, 'This is a beautiful tree and we can rest in its shade.'

In the evening Ailung removed his tusks and turned them into daos and became a tortoise again. When he returned home his father asked him how much forest he had cleared. Ailung said, 'Don't ask me now, but when I have completed the work and the harvest is ready for reaping I will show you.'

Now in the rubber tree which Ailung had left standing there lived a great spirit who had many children. When he saw that all his forest was cut, he was afraid that his own tree would also be destroyed and he would have nowhere to live, so he sent his children into the clearings. He played his flute and as he did so, the children raised up all the trees and made them as they were before. When the forest had been restored the children returned to the rubber tree and stayed with their father.

Next day when Ailung returned to the place and saw what had happened, he was very angry. He turned himself into an elephant and in a towering rage again destroyed the forest. This time he decided that he would not spare a single tree, but when he came to the rubber tree the spirit and his children came out, and fought against him. It was not much use, for Ailung was very strong and soon had them at his mercy. But the tree-spirit said, 'We will do anything you want us to do, but don't kill us.' Ailung said, 'Set fire to whatever I have cut and make the clearings properly and then sow seed in the ashes.' So the spirit and his children prepared the clearings and sowed the paddy-seed that Ailung gave them. When the harvest was ready Ailung saw it and was very pleased with the spirit and his children. He said to them, 'Do one more thing. Reap the harvest and winnow out the grain and bring it to my house.'

Ailung then took his tortoise form and went home and said to his parents, 'The harvest is ready and the porters will soon be bringing the rice to the house.' They did not believe that their son had actually made any field, but presently the spirit and his children appeared carrying great loads of rice, so much that there was nowhere in the house to store it. Ailung said to his parents, 'Give all these labourers a good meal. Henceforward I will not live with you any longer, but will go to dwell in the forest.'

In their presence Ailung changed into an elephant and put his daos as tusks and then went away into the forest. He was the first of all the elephants. Since the parents treated the spirit and his children so generously the gods have ever since lived happily on earth with men. But if men do not treat them properly and feed them well, they give them all kinds of diseases.

26

MINYONG

Kebang, Siang F.D.

The elephant was a stupid and clumsy child and so his mother got angry with him and hit him on the face with an axe. She tried to get it out, but it stuck and grew there and became his trunk. But he was still very stupid and did not even try to learn how to prepare his food, or winnow out the corn. So one day when they were winnowing together she picked up the big winnowing-fans, one in each hand and hit him over the head with them—hard. So hard that they too stuck there and became the great flapping ears he has to this day. But yet he remained very foolish and helpless and his mother threw the tongs at him one day when he was unusually provoking, and they became his tusks. And then the elephant went away into the forest: but as a punishment for his laziness and stupidity he wears rice-pounders on his feet and you can still see the marks of them, down in the country where the elephant lives.

27

MINYONG

Pangin, Siang F.D.

There was a woman who left her village, but she could not do without her home, and took it with her, but as she went along, it turned into an elephant. She was naturally annoyed at this and struck the great animal in the face with a dao. The dao stuck in the bone and became a long nose hanging to the ground. When the woman reached the place where she wished to live, she borrowed rice-grain from the neighbours and began to clean it in a basket. She told the elephant to help her, but he refused. She struck him on the side of the head with the basket and it stuck there as an ear. Every day she used to abuse the elephant for his laziness, and once she poked his face with two bits of firewood and they turned into tusks. Finally she fixed the largest and heaviest pestles she could find to his legs and drove him into the forest. Since then the elephant has had legs like rice-huskers.

28

MOKLUM

Longke, Tirap F.D.

Rang originally made the elephant with wings so that he could fly about in the sky. But whenever the great creature flew down, he broke the trees and crushed the crops growing in the fields and even destroyed houses and granaries. When Rang saw this, he took the wings away from him and fixed plantain trunks to his body for legs and gave him a pestle as a trunk.

29

MOKLUM

Khimiyang, Tirap F.D.

There was an idle and disobedient girl. One day her father beat her so hard that she ran away from home. But when evening came and there was no supper the father repented, for he realized that without his daughter he would have no one to cook for him. He followed her and begged her to come back, but she said, 'I'll never come home again.' He went on imploring her to come but she still refused. In the end he put some rice on a leaf under a tree saying, 'Whenever you feel hungry, you will find some rice for you here.'

Next morning when he went to put more rice under the tree he found a great animal instead of his daughter. He was going to run away when the elephant said, 'Don't be afraid, my father, I am your own daughter. During the night I ate the rice you gave me and immediately changed my shape.' The man examined what was left of the rice and found it sour but tasty. The girl assured him that she had taken nothing but the rice. This was how people learnt to make rice-beer. It is said that a woman should not take too much of this or she will become as fat as an elephant.

30

NOCTE

Laptang, Tirap F.D.

One day, long ago, an elephant came flying down from the sky. He was very strong, but did not know how to use his strength. Men were weak, but had the knowledge to use what strength they had. So they tamed the elephant and put him to work for them.

There was a tiger in the sky. He saw what men were doing to the elephant and thought that he might do the same to men. He flew down to earth and found a little boy playing with part of a snake-gourd. He asked what it was and the boy replied, 'My mother made it to tame the tiger.' The tiger was afraid and flew back to the sky.

31

SHERDUKPEN

Shergaon, Kameng F.D.

Once there was a great hunter who lived all alone in the forest, for his parents were dead and he had no wife. He built himself a good house and used to go out every day to hunt. In this way he collected a great deal of meat, of which naturally he could only eat a little. The rest he dried in the sun and stored in an enormous basket in the loft of his house. Gradually the basket became full of dried meat.

One day, when the hunter came home from the forest, he found his food ready cooked. He was a little surprised but he knew that anything could happen in this world and sat down and ate his supper thankfully. This happened day after day for a whole year. And then he thought it would be interesting to see who was cooking for him, so the next morning, instead of going to hunt as usual, he hid behind his house. Presently a beautiful girl appeared ; she swept the place, fetched water, cooked the food and went away. The hunter returned home and ate his supper. The next day, however, he hid just behind the door and when the girl came out, caught her in his arms. But she said, 'Let me go. If you want me, you must wait a week. I cannot come to live with you now.' But the hunter, who was overjoyed at finding a wife, refused to let her go. The girl said, 'The trouble is that if you forget your love and quarrel with me, I will disappear at once. So you had better let me go.' But he still refused saying, 'How could I quarrel with anyone so beautiful as you?' Then he asked her, 'Where have you come from and who are your parents?' 'I am born,' she said, 'from the dried meat stored in your house. If you don't believe me, go and see if there is any meat left.' He went to look and there was no meat. But even then he would not let the girl go. So she said, 'Very well, but you must never taunt me by saying that I have no parents and was born from dried meat.' After this they began to live together very happily.

A year went by and then one day they quarrelled, and the hunter exclaimed, 'Why have I married a girl who has no parents and was born from dried meat?' As he said this the girl ran out of the house. Her husband followed her until they came to a great river in flood. She crossed the water without difficulty, but he remained on the bank on the near side. She threw her cloth over her head so that it hung down before her like a trunk and called to him, saying, 'Now I'll always be like this and you will never be able to live with me again.' So saying, she turned into an elephant.

This is why the elephant obeys man, for she used to be his wife and has breasts and organs like a woman.

And since the elephant was originally born of a mixture of all kinds of meat, so when the Hrussos eat elephant's flesh they feel as if they were enjoying at once beef, pork and venison.

32

TAGIN

Serra, Subansiri F.D.

There was a wild boar who had four children. They were very small. This boar loved wild roots so much that she used to neglect her litter and go rooting in the forest. In the evening she would bring back some roots to feed the children.

One day she said to herself, 'Every day I go to the forest, and my children remain behind crying with hunger. If I spend three whole days on it and gather a big pile of roots, then I needn't go out for a long time and can stay at home with the children.'

So thinking the boar said to her babies, 'I won't be coming back for three days. But don't be afraid: I'll send your food with someone or other.' She went away and at the end of three days had a big pile of roots. She tried to get porters to carry them home, but no one would help her. At last Tapeng the bat flew down and the sow said, 'Look at all these roots. Take them to my house, give some to the children and store the rest for me. You shall have your share.' Tapeng promised to do this, but instead of taking the roots to the boar's house, he took them far away to his own hut on a high mountain.

The boar went home and as she neared her house there was a great noise of the children crying, for they were ready to die of hunger. She hurried in, and there were no roots, no Tapeng, and the children starving. 'We have never even heard of this Tapeng,' said the children.

The boar fed her children as well as she could and then in a great temper went off to look for Tapeng. But she could not find him, for he was up on his mountain.

One day a porcupine went to Tapeng's hut and stole some of the roots. As he was bringing them down, the boar met him and recognized her roots. 'Where did you get those?' she asked. The porcupine said, 'O these are Tapeng's: he's got a grand store of them up on the hill.' The boar told the porcupine what had happened and asked him to catch Tapeng for her. 'Certainly,' said the porcupine.

The porcupine caught Tapeng and brought him to the boar. 'I thought it best to store the roots in my house,' said Tapeng. 'I was intending to send them to you directly I could get porters.' 'Is this really true?' 'I swear it on the Sun and Moon.' So the boar let him go.

Tapeng went home and continued to eat the roots, but not a single one did he send to the boar.

Then the wild boar said to herself, 'The only thing to do now is to report the matter to the elephant.' She went to the elephant and laid her case before him. 'I myself will catch the fellow,' said the elephant. 'I will punish him and make him return your roots.'

The elephant set out and, after a long day's search, managed to find Tapeng. 'Why do you tell so many lies?' he said. 'Because I have got something,' said Tapeng. 'That's why I have to tell lies.' 'What thing is this?' 'O just a thing.' 'Then show it to me.' 'But it's not here, it's in my house. Why not come and see it?' For he knew the elephant could never climb the hill to his house.

The elephant said, 'I can't possibly go as far as that. Go and fetch it.' Tapeng put a pole in front of the elephant and said, 'When this pole breaks of its own accord, I will return.' He went away, leaving the elephant standing in front of the pole and watching it with both his eyes.

Tapeng returned home and continued to stuff himself on the roots. The boar went to dig for more and her babies cried with hunger. But the elephant stood before the pole waiting for it to break. He just stood there: he did not lie down or sit down. And ever since the elephant has slept standing up.

33

TARAON (DIGARU) MISHMI

Machima, Lohit F.D.

Jebmallu worked so hard in his fields and got such a fine crop that he had to build two granaries to store it. He built them high on four pillars so that the rats would not be able to get in. He filled each granary with his grain and hung the baskets and winnowing-fans, in which he had carried it, beside the door.

Next day he found the granaries had disappeared. They had turned into elephants and gone away into the forest. The four pillars had become legs ; the ladders up to the door had turned into trunks. The large baskets were heads and the winnowing-fans had become ears.

34

WANCHO

Longkhao, Tirap F.D.

The elephant got his body from both gods and animals. He has a great belly, for Rang filled it with leaves. The snake gave him a trunk. Rang put two winnowing-fans for ears and spears for tusks. He added a rat's tail. He made the feet from the flesh of animals and men, the eyes with two stones.

35

WANCHO

Senua, Tirap F.D.

In the old days the elephant was very proud. As he had such a fine and splendid body. Rang asked him to go and live with him in the sky. But the elephant thought he was so big that no one would be able to injure him and that he would be quite safe on earth. So he refused to go and this annoyed Rang who said, 'One day you will be sorry.'

Years later men learnt how to catch elephants and make them work, carrying their loads and moving their timber. Today whenever the elephant has to pull a big log of wood, he weeps and raises his trunk to the sky saying to Rang, 'You were right. I would have reigned in heaven as a king if I had come when you called me, but instead I now have to serve as a slave on earth.'

The Horse

36

BUGUN (KHOWA)

Senchong, Kameng F.D.

In Suttum-Kabo, which lies beyond Lhasa, there was a great lake in which a mighty serpent used to live. From this snake the first horse was born beneath the water. A man called Chong-Phu-Norbu-Jangpu saw it and thought to himself, 'There is some sort of animal below the water. It would be a good thing if I could catch it and make it work for me.' So he made a long rope and caught him. But when the horse came out of the water he wanted to eat the man, who managed, however, to escape by climbing a tree. He kept hold of the rope and tied it to one of the branches and then stayed up in the tree for several days, not daring to come down for fear of the horse.

Presently the horse got so weak for hunger that he lay down to sleep as if he were dead. The man then came down from the tree and tied his four legs together and began to give him a little food.

Then he called his friends and they slung the horse on a pole and carried him home.

This is how the tribes of this region came to keep horses.

THE MITHUN

37

BUGUN (KHOWA)

Senchong, Kameng F.D.

Hanai the Sun is the wife of Habia the Moon. They have a son called Jomi and a daughter called Lomi. One day when the two children were about sixteen years old their parents went away somewhere and brother and sister lay together. As a result, Lomi became pregnant. Brother and sister were terrified of what their parents would do, and the girl hid among the clouds until she gave birth to her child. This child was not a human being but a mithun and they threw him down to earth, so that their parents would not know anything about it. The mithun fell in a place where there was a great rock surrounded with water. He climbed on to the rock but was afraid to go anywhere across the water.

One day a party of Hrussos came hunting and they saw the mithun. He was very hungry and they made a great pile of grass on the bank of the lake in order to tempt him across but he would not come. Then they made a pile of soft green leaves and when he saw it he came over. The Hrussos caught him and kept him in their house.

38

DAFLA

Solo (Palin Valley), Subansiri F.D.

The two Wiyus, Gyomane and Himane, were husband and wife. One day Himane gave birth to a baby girl and they called her Garmane. Her father made baskets and a stick for her but she did not know how to use them. One day he got annoyed at this and said, 'Become a mithun, become a mithun,' and as he spoke the girl changed into a mithun. Jingma's son was Teni and he was the first to see the girl after her change. This is why all the descendants of Teni keep mithuns.[13]

[13] Recorded by B. K. Shukla.

39

DHAMMAI (MIJI)

Nakhu, Kameng F.D.

Long ago three brothers lived in Jangdaphang-Nadmu. The eldest went towards Lhasa, the youngest to Assam and the middle brother, Sajo-Lang, went to Chang-Darrou among the mountains.

When they had left Jangdaphang-Nadmu, the god Kan-Nui-Nuchu appeared. He looked on every side but could see no other living being and said to himself, 'I am all alone. I have no one.'

Kan-Nui-Nuchu cut some wood and made a great creature with four legs and two horns, plastered it with mud and covered it with plantain leaves. It was strong and beautiful but there was no life in it. The god was pleased but he felt very tired after his work and lay down to sleep. While he slept the creature became alive as a mithun and ate Kan-Nui-Nuchu's clothes and drank his rice-beer. This was all right but she realized that the god would be angry when he woke up and ran away in fear. Presently she saw the footprints of a man and followed them until she came to Chang-Darrou. There Sajo-Lang, the second of the three brothers, saw her and thought to himself, 'What a fine animal this is! The meat will be delicious.' He ran for his bow and arrows but before he could shoot, the mithun said, 'Don't kill me. I have come to live with you and will help you and your children'. So Sajo-Lang tied her up with a piece of rope and took her to his house, and from her many other mithuns were born.

Some time after the mithun had run away, the god Kan-Nui-Nuchu awoke and found his cloth and beer had disappeared. Since he supposed that there was no other living being in the world he wondered how this could have happened. Then he looked for the creature he had made and this too had disappeared. Full of anger he followed the mithun's footprints until he came to Sajo-Lang's house and saw her tied up outside. He was very annoyed at this and made Sajo-Lang's children ill.

Sajo-Lang called for a priest who fell into trance and told the story of all that had happened. He declared that in return for the mithun they must give cloth and beer in sacrifice to Kan-Nui-Nuchu. Ever since this day the Dhammais have offered cloth and beer inside their houses to Kan-Nui-Nuchu and in return he protects them and their cattle.

40

HILL MIRI

Chemir, Subansiri F.D.

From Sippu and his wife Riggu were born two brothers, Nikkum and Sukkum. Nikkum was born in the morning, Sukkum in the evening. So Nikkum was the elder and more important of the two. When they grew up, they lived together in the same house, and made their clearings in the forest.

Nikkum cut a clearing in one day, but Sukkum cut three clearings. Nikkum often had to go to drink water, but Sukkum only drank once a day. Nikkum used to sleep as all men do, but Sukkum never slept: he ate and worked night and day. This worried Nikkum, for he knew he could never work like this, and he decided to send his brother away. He also objected to Sukkum's habit of relieving himself anywhere and everywhere, in the house while he was eating, when he was talking to you, at any time.

Nikkum said, 'Don't do this: it makes a horrid mess.' Sukkum took no notice, and Nikkum lost his temper and said, 'You make beer and I'll make beer. Whoever makes it ready and drinks it first will be the victor.' They agreed on this and both went to make the beer. Nikkum's was ready first and he got drunk.

There was no iron in those days, so Nikkum made a wooden dao and went to beat Sukkum with it. 'Is your beer ready?' he asked. 'No.' 'Then I shall kill you,' said Nikkum. Sukkum said, 'Consider, we are brothers. Don't kill me. I will have children and they will serve you. Tie me up with a rope and tether me outside your house. I and my wife will both serve you.'

But Nikkum took no notice of this, and raised his dao to strike his brother. At that moment, Si-Duinye came to the house, and begged Nikkum not to strike. 'But what can he do to serve me?' said Nikkum. 'When you are ill,' said Si-Duinye, 'you can sacrifice his children: when you want wives, you can buy them with his children.' So Nikkum made a rope and tethered his brother outside the house, and he was the first mithun.

And now when a mithun is sacrificed, the Nibo-priest tells this story to him and says, 'Do not be sorry for your death. This is the old agreement. The gods will eat half your flesh, and half will be for men.' Sometimes, when he hears this, tears fall from a mithun's eyes.

41

HRUSSO (AKA)

Buragaon, Kameng F.D.

Buslu-Ao had three sons and three daughters. The boys' names were Sijji-Jao, Machlo-Jao and Chalo-Jijao and the girls' names were Phibi-Chisi, Machlo-Chisi and Chalo-Michisi.

When they grew up the boys could not find wives and the girls could not find husbands and their father decided that his sons and daughters would have to marry each other. So Sijji-Jao married Phibi-Chisi, Machlo-Jao married Machlo-Chisi and the four of them lived happily together and worked hard in their houses and their fields. But Chalo-Michisi was not happy with Chalo-Jijao, for she said, 'How can I sleep with my own brother?' And she refused to go to her husband or work for him. In this way a whole year went by in constant quarrelling until they all said to the boy, 'Your wife is useless. She doesn't love you and she won't work.' Chalo-Jijao put up with it for a long time, but one day he beat his wife and she went and lay down in a corner of the house in a fit of sulks.

But when the others went to the fields, she got up, took bamboo vessels in her basket and a gourd to fill them and went down to the river for water. When she reached the river, she put the basket on her head and placed the gourds as horns on either side ; she put the strainer used for rice-beer as a tail and tied the bamboo tubes to her arms and legs. Then she ate her own clothes and this made both her sides swell. In this way she turned into a mithun and wandered away into the jungle and stayed there.

In the evening when the others returned from the fields and did not find her in the house they supposed she was hiding somewhere and was still cross after the quarrel, so none of them went to look for her.

Two days passed without any news of the girl and then Chalo-Jijao got into a state and went to find her ; he had hardly started when the bumble-bee told him that she had turned into a mithun and was in the jungle, a little distance from the water-point. Chalo-Jijao hurried to the place and there sure enough was Chalo-Michisi in the form of a mithun. Bursting into tears, he caught her and led her back to the house. He called the whole family and showed them what had happened. They were all astonished, and Buslu-Ao said, 'We cannot allow my daughter to wander about in the jungle. We must make proper arrangements for her. I suggest we tie her up near the house.' He made a strong rope of cane and tied her to a pillar. They offered her food and water, but she refused to eat or drink ; she just stood there weeping.

Then Buslu-Ao, seeing the tears rolling down the mithun-face, said, 'You are my daughter—in fact you are both daughter and daughter-in-law, but the great Mathi-dao has turned you into a mithun. What can we do? Don't take on so ; you should eat just as we eat.' The mithun replied, 'It is true that Mathi-dao has turned me into a mithun and I am quite happy about it, but at the same time I am a woman and I cannot possibly live without a husband. Let me go and I will find a mate.' When her father heard this, he released her and she wandered away in search of a husband, but it was not so easy to find one.

First of all she met a dog and thought to herself, 'If I can marry him, that will be very good.' But when she approached him, she saw that he was too small and decided that he wouldn't do.

So she left the dog and went wandering along until she met a pig. At first she thought it to be very good to marry the pig, but when she came a little nearer, she thought, 'The colour of this pig is the same as my own, but he too is far too small.'

Then in the distance she saw a horse and was very happy, for she thought that here at last was a suitable mate. When she came a little nearer, however, she saw that he had a different kind of legs, a different tail, a different face and decided that he wouldn't do either.

So the mithun left the horse and went wandering along until she met a great deer. At first she thought that he would do, but when she came a little nearer she saw that he was altogether different ; for one thing the horns were too big. In this way she met a bear, a tiger, a monkey and all the animals of the forest in turn, but not one of them was sufficiently like her to be her husband.

At last she came to the place of the rising of the sun. She crossed the river of cold waters and the river of hot waters, and there at last she found, standing in the sandy bed of the stream, a male mithun. When she saw him far off she was thrilled and called to him and the male mithun answered her. She went nearer and saw that he had the same colour, the same kind of face, the same kind of legs and the same kind of tail and knew that at last she had found her mate. They came together at once and had two calves.

In the meantime the mithun's human husband Chalo-Jijao fell ill and the family called the priest to see what was the matter. He declared that the boy would only be cured if they sacrificed a mithun. 'But where shall we find a mithun?' they asked. The priest replied, 'There are mithuns, but far away, beyond the cold river and the hot river.' So the two elder brothers, Sijji-Jao and Machlo-Jao, went to find them. They came to the place of the rising of the sun and crossed the cold river, but they could not cross the hot river. So they stood where they were on the bank with leaves and salt in their hands and called to the mithuns on the far side, and when they saw the salt they began to cross the river. But the heat was too great for them, and only the mithun who had been Chalo-Michisi and her two calves survived. The brothers brought them home and tied them up in front of the house.

Then Buslu-Ao's wife came out to look at them and realizing that this was her own daughter said, 'We can't possibly sacrifice her.' But Buslu-Ao said, 'It is true that she was once our daughter, and the gods desire to have her. We just have to sacrifice her.'

That was that, and they tied her up and tried to kill her, but could not even break the skin with their axes. Then Buslu-Ao's wife said, 'I told you so. She is our daughter and it's not possible for us to kill her, unless perhaps you tell her that it is her duty to die.

Buslu-Ao's wife went to her mithun-daughter and whispered in her ear, 'You were once a human being and it would not have been possible to sacrifice you, but now you are a mithun and it is your time to die.' Then the old lady moved aside and the others struck the poor creature with their daos and killed her. But as she was dying she said, 'I am dying and my blood will fall in your eyes and injure them.' And the blood did, in fact, spurt out of the mithun's body into the eyes of Buslu-Ao's wife. It was after this that diseases of the eyes came to the world.

42

MINYONG

Pangin, Siang F.D.

Sedi-Botte and his wife Melo-Nane were old when two sons were born to them. Yet a third child was in the mother's belly. He grew and was big, but she could not deliver it ; it was worse than having twins. Sedi-Botte called a Miri and told him of his wife's trouble. The Miri felt the belly: he examined chicken's livers and pig's livers ; he looked at rice ; but he could not say what the matter was. Then Sedi-Botte himself declared: 'The trouble is that Limir-Sabbo is in her.' As he said this, his wife was delivered of a mithun.

Limir-Sabbo grew quickly: he had great horns: in fact he was so dangerous to men that his brothers decided to kill him. When they had done so, they planted his organ in their clearing. After five days Sedi-Botte went to look and there was a tree growing from the organ. He called the Miri to say what it was, but he did not know. Then Sedi-Botte himself declared: 'It is a pumpkin.' The creeper grew and grew and great pumpkins presently hung from it. Sedi-Botte and his sons put their ears to one of them and heard a noise *bulung-bulung*. They asked the Miri what it was, but he did not know. Then Sedi-Botte himself declared: 'This is none other than Tapung-Taiyo.' He cut the pumpkin and out came a silkworm. They asked the Miri what it was, but he did not know. Then Sedi-Botte himself said, 'Take this worm to Doini-Pollo.'

When they took the worm to Doini-Pollo, he fixed the head, horns and legs of the dead mithun to it and made a new mithun, smaller and tame to man. There was a quarrel as to whose he was, but in the end the Kebang decided that he was the son of Doini-Pollo.

THE MONKEY.

43

DHAMMAI (MIJI)

Nakhu, Kameng F.D.

Long ago a Raja called Bunui had a frog and a monkey as his servants, for in those days these animals could talk like human beings. Now the monkey was deceitful and ambitious and plotted to kill the Raja and reign in his place. He was very conceited and when the Raja gave him work to do, he never did it properly.

One day the Raja sent the frog to get him fish and the monkey to bring him sweet fruits from the forest. The monkey went to the forest, but he ate every fruit he picked and when his belly was full he lay down and slept. In the evening he woke up and was rather frightened, for he thought that the Raja would beat him for not bringing him any fruit. So he covered himself with mud and hurried home. On the way he met the frog who was carrying a heavy load of fish.

When the monkey saw that the frog was bringing home so much and he himself had nothing, he was still more disturbed, for he thought that the Raja might promote the frog above him. So he threw the frog with his fish into a stream. When the frog came out he said to him, 'You had better tell the Raja that you couldn't catch any fish and that is why you have come home without anything. After all why do you bother about this fellow? One day I am going to kill him and when I myself am Raja, I will give you a good job with very little work to do.'

The monkey and the frog went to the Raja and told him that they had not been able to get him anything, either fruit or fish. The monkey said, 'I personally searched everywhere and climbed a hundred trees until I fell down, as you can see from my whole body being covered with mud and dust. What could I do? There was nothing to get. But look at this frog. All day long he has been bathing in the stream and hasn't even tried to catch any fish. Had he really tried he wouldn't be as clean as he is now.'

The Raja saw the monkey dirty and dishevelled and the frog clean and shining. This made him very angry and he beat the frog on the head crying, 'Did you go to fish or to bathe?' This is why even now the top of the frog's head is flat.

The frog was very angry and told the Raja all that the monkey had said. Then he went in a huff out of the house to the river and has lived there ever since.

At that time the monkey had no tail. One day he went to the forest and collected all his relatives. He armed them with bows and arrows and made arrangements to attack the palace and kill the Raja. But when the Raja heard what they were planning, he quickly made a black paste and coloured his face with it and then sat quietly waiting for his enemies to come.

At first the monkey came by himself, leaving his army hiding in the trees outside. When he saw the decorations on the Raja's face he was very pleased and said, 'Where did you get that paste? I would like to have some for myself.' The Raja said, 'I went to a hollow tree and got my servants to put me inside. They collected a lot of wood and set fire to it and the smoke made my face black. If you would like to look as nice as I do, then collect plenty of wood and take it to the hollow tree.'

The monkey went out and called his relatives and they collected a lot of wood and piled it round the hollow tree. Then the Raja tied each monkey to his fellow with a rope round the waist and sent them into the hollow of the tree. When they were all inside, he set fire to the wood. Very soon the monkeys began to scream, 'Let us out, let us out. We are quite black enough.' But the Raja piled up more and more wood until they were burnt to death.

But high up in the tree a pregnant she-monkey managed to escape, for the rope that held her was burnt by the fire, leaving a piece hanging down behind. This monkey gave birth to a son and when he grew up she married him and they had many children. But they were so ashamed that they lived ever afterwards in the forest. This is why the monkey has a tail and his face is black and it is in memory of this that even now the Dhammais make black marks on their faces.

44

HILL MIRI

Meli, Subansiri F.D.

At first monkeys were like men and lived with men. But when they went together to work in their clearings, the monkeys only played about and did none of the real work. And when houses had to be built, the men had to do everything: the monkeys spent the time climbing trees and pulling one another's tails. At last the men said to the monkeys, 'Brothers, you are no use to us ; we can't keep you here.' And they drove them away into the forest.

There were also bears living with men at that time. But the bears were very quarrelsome ; there was not a moment's peace in a village in those days. So after a time, the men said, 'Brothers, you are too quarrelsome, go and live in the forest.'

Even now, when a number of bears are together, they cannot keep from quarrelling, and this is why they live solitary.

45

IDU MISHMI

Koronu, Lohit F.D.

Essoe was the mother of all the monkeys and Amme was her eldest son. In her day men and monkeys lived together, worked together and went out hunting together. The arrows used by the monkeys were made of bamboo, but those used by men were tipped with iron.

One day they had a competition when both men and monkeys shot their arrows at a tree, but the monkeys shot much better and the men mostly missed.

Then one day the men and monkeys went together to shoot fish at a place where two streams joined. They closed one stream so that all the water flowed in a single channel and they all put their bows and arrows together in the stream they had closed. While they were having some food one of the monkeys opened the dam and the water carried off the bows and arrows. The bamboo ones floated but the iron ones sank and the men were able to recover them.

Then the men said to the monkeys, 'Your bows and arrows have been carried down the stream, go and find them.' The monkeys plunged into the water and went downstream, but could not find their bows and arrows and came back shivering.

In the meantime, the men had heated some large stones and they said to the monkeys, 'Sit down and make yourselves warm.' But when the monkeys sat on the hot stones, their bottoms were burnt and they jumped in fright into the trees and have lived there ever since.

46

MINYONG

Siang Frontier Division

(From G. D. S. Dunbar, *Abors and Galongs*, p. 46)

Long ago men and monkeys were almost alike, neither wore clothes and both had bows and arrows. At first they lived peaceably together, but afterwards they fought. One day, when the monkeys were catching fish by throwing stones and chestnuts at them from the branches above a pool, the men came up unnoticed. First they took the monkeys' bows and knotted and tied the strings, so that they were useless ; then they took the fish the monkeys had already caught and put them in their satchels. After that, they rushed at the monkeys with their daos. The startled monkeys ran to their weapons but found that they were useless, for the strings were too short for the bows. Many of them were killed and the rest fled away. But the men followed them, and called out after them saying that they wanted to make peace. And at last the monkeys were reassured and came back again. The terms of peace were that the monkeys should no longer live in houses, as they had before, but in trees ; and the men burnt all their houses. After this they all gathered together for a feast, the men and the monkeys that had not been killed. The feast was held in the trunk of a huge decayed hollow tree, for the entrance of which the men had made a big door of leaves and branches. First of all they started singing, and while this was going on the men excused themselves for a little, while they went off to get their food. But when all the men were outside they shut the door and set fire to the tree. And the monkeys, unable to get out, were burnt to death—all except one, that escaped half burnt, with its face all black and charred. That is why monkeys nowadays have no weapons, nor any house, and why their faces are black.

47

MINYONG

Komkar, Siang F.D.

At first men and monkeys lived together as friends ; there were no distinctions between them. But gradually quarrels arose and at the Kebangs the monkeys were often clearer in speech than the men, and the men decided to be rid of them. So one day when the monkeys had gone to catch fish in the Siang River, the men followed them. They found their bows and arrows and quietly tied the strings of the bows so that they could not be used. Then they attacked the monkeys with their daos. The monkeys ran for their bows and arrows, but found them useless. 'This is not mine,' cried one ; 'it is useless ; it must be your's.' 'No, this is your's,' cried another, 'Mine was in good order when we went to the river.' As they were quarrelling between themselves, the men killed them.

But a few escaped into the forest. So the men sent a messenger to them and offered to make peace on condition that from that day the monkeys should live in trees, and should no longer use bows and daos. The monkeys agreed and the men burnt the monkey village. They arranged a great feast to show that peace had been made. There was a hollow tree, and the men made a door of leaves and branches for it. They asked the monkeys to dance a *ponung* inside: 'it is very cold outside,' they said. The monkeys began to dance, and then one of the men struck a flint, and as the sparks flew the monkeys cried, *'Goning-ening goning-ening.'* Gradually the men slipped out of the tree, then banged the door and shut up the monkeys inside. The man with the flint made fire and burnt the monkeys to death. Only one escaped, and she ran to the forest rubbing her burnt hands over her face. Ever since monkeys have lived in trees in the forest and their faces and hands have been black.

48

MINYONG

Pangin, Siang F.D.

Long ago two brothers lived together. The younger had many children, so many that the elder wearied of providing for them and planned to kill them. One day, therefore, he said to them, 'Let's go to the forest and collect plantain leaves, and I'll thatch a fine house for you.' They started out and on the way their uncle found a hollow tree. He said, 'Here is the very thing. It will make a splendid house, warm, and free of wind.' The children went into the hollow tree and their uncle at once shut them in with the dry plantain leaves they had gathered and set fire to them. All were killed except one girl who escaped and ran away to another village. Somehow there was a child in her belly. When it was born, she took her son to live in the forest. Many days passed and the child was a man. The mother said, 'Let us marry each other.' Her son said, 'You are my mother: how can we marry?' But the mother insisted and they came together. But they were so ashamed that they never again went into any village and lived as monkeys in the forest.

49

NOCTE

Kothung, Tirap F.D.

There was a man with two wives who were always quarrelling. The elder wife had a boy-child whom she loved very much. But presently she died and her son fell into the hands of the younger wife. This woman abused the boy and beat him until in despair he ran away to the forest. There was no fire there to cook with, so the boy lived on raw fruit and leaves. He had no clothes and to keep warm he grew hair all over his body. He never returned to the village and his children were the first monkeys.

50

TARAON (DIGARU) MISHMI

Tetuliang, Lohit F.D.

A woman lived in Ring-Lembum, the country of the Sun. She was pregnant for eight years and then gave birth to a shell. She filled a basket with grass and put the shell in it just as if it was an egg. She kept the shell there for eight years and then eight baby-boys were hatched from it. The first was a Chin, the next an Idu, the third a Khampti, the fourth a Singpho, then a Taraon, an Assamese, a Naga and a Lama. When they grew up, each went to live in his own country.

The Taraon boy went wandering over the mountains in search of a wife. After a long time, he found a rat and married her, and the human being and the rat lived together. When a child was born it looked exactly like a rat. The Taraon man said, 'You have not given me a good child. You don't work or cook properly. I won't keep you as my wife any longer.' So the rat was ashamed and went away and dug a hole in the ground. This is why rats live in holes.

Then the Taraon boy went again over the mountains in search of a wife. After some time, he found the black and white bird called Ta, who lives on the banks of rivers, and he married her. The bird was soon pregnant and, when the time for delivery came, flew to a mountain. There she gave birth to some kind of child, but no one knows what it was. She flew back and the Taraon boy asked, 'Where is my child?' The bird said nothing. Her husband said, 'You must have eaten your own child. You do no work and don't cook properly. I won't keep you any longer.' The bird was ashamed and flew away to the riverside. This is why the Ta bird always lives on the banks of rivers.

Once again the Taraon boy wandered over the mountains in search of a wife and this time he found a she-monkey. She soon became pregnant and in due time bore a child called Taruinya. He flew up into the air making a loud noise like an aeroplane and disappeared. He became a very evil spirit who makes men quarrel and fight each other. He is always watching us, ready to make things go wrong.

Then the monkey gave birth to a human boy and a girl and after them to a tiger. Directly the tiger was born, he ran away to the forest but he got no food there and when he was very hungry, he said to himself, 'I'll go and eat my mother.'

The tiger came to the house and caught hold of his mother, the monkey. When he saw it, the human son abused the tiger and said, 'How can you eat her who bore you?' The tiger said, 'I would not ordinarily, but I am very hungry.' 'But you can't possibly do it,' said the boy. Then the tiger lost his temper and said, 'When I finish eating my mother, I'll take you by the scruff of the neck and eat you as well.' The boy shouted back, 'You just try and I'll kill you with my arrow.' The tiger said, 'I don't care what you do. I am going to eat this monkey, whether she is my mother or not. I dare you to try to stop me.'

But the boy shot at the tiger and killed him and threw the body into the river. The tiger floated down and at last drifted to the bank, where he sank in the mud. A tiger cub was born from every hair of his body and this is why there are tigers all over the world.

The two human children of the monkey married when they grew up and from them came the Mishmis.

51

TARAON (DIGARU) MISHMI

Machima, Lohit F.D.

Men and monkeys were born of the same mother and at first looked like each other. For a long time they lived happily together, but one day there was a great quarrel and both men and monkeys went out into the jungle to make bows and arrows to protect themselves. The monkeys made better bows which could shoot much farther than those made by the men, and when the men saw it, they said to one another, 'We can't defeat our younger brothers in war ; we must subdue them by trickery.'

So they went down to the river and made traps to catch fish. The monkeys followed them ready for a fight. The men said, 'You have come to fight while we are peacefully making traps. We have dropped our weapons into the water, so what can we fight you with? Go into the water and find our bows and arrows and then we can fight you.' The younger brothers went far down the stream, but could not find the missing weapons.

While they were away, the men quickly built a great fire, heated a large stone and put it on one side. When the monkeys returned trembling with cold, the men said, 'Sit on the stone and warm yourselves before the fire.' The monkeys did so but the stone was so hot that it burnt the skin off their bottoms and they jumped up into a tree.

Ever since these monkeys have lived in trees and their bottoms have been red and without skin.

52

WANCHO

Banfera, Tirap F.D.

At first, monkeys were men. The big monkey was the big brother, the little monkey was the little brother. They were the sons of a very old man and woman. The parents did all the work in the clearings and the brothers never went to help them, but preferred to work in the house. The younger brother did the cooking and the big brother husked the grain. But they did nothing else. Since they sat in the house, they used to eat up everything and there was nothing left for the old people, who got very angry with them and told them to go away. One day the father beat them so hard that they ran into the jungle. The younger brother had a wooden spoon in his hand and took it with him. He said, 'I am not going to do any work, whatever the old man says. I cannot be bothered to build a house or work in the clearings ; I shall live on fruit in the jungle.' As he went, he tied the spoon to his back as if it was a dao. It turned into a tail and he became a monkey.

As for the big brother, he went to husk grain and his hands got black with the chaff and dirt. He rubbed his face and it turned black. When his father beat him he ran away, tying the pestle to his back. This became a long tail and he too turned into a monkey.

53

WANCHO

Nisa, Tirap F.D.

Formerly men and monkeys were brothers. In a certain house there was a family in which a man was the elder brother and there were three younger brothers who were monkeys. The man used to do all the work and the monkeys sat about chattering and drinking rice-beer. The elder brother was always abusing them and trying to make them work. Sometimes he refused to give them food because they were so idle. In the end, the monkeys went off to the forest saying, 'We would rather live on fruit and leaves among the trees than live with you and have to work.'

54

WANCHO

Nisa, Tirap F.D.

In the old days monkeys used to live with men, looked like them and shared the life of their homes. One day a monkey was husking rice with a pestle. Suddenly for some reason or other, he quarrelled with the man in whose house he was living and the man seized the pestle to beat him. The monkey snatched it back, tucked it between his legs and ran away with it. As he ran he became a real monkey and the pestle turned into his tail.

THE PIG

55

HILL MIRI

Meli, Subansiri F.D.

Abo-Teni and his wife Chittu-Teni went to Si-Duinye the Sun and said, 'We want something special.' 'What is that?' asked Si-Duinye. 'It must be something which will first be very fat; second, useful for marriage and sacrifice: third, able to clean the mess made by us and our children.' Si-Duinye said, 'I know of nothing that has all those qualities.'

So Abo-Teni himself made an image of a pig and said, 'It should be something like this.' Si-Duinye said, 'I cannot give it to you, but Nikkum, Eji and Po-um should be able to.' So Abo-Teni and his wife went to Wiyu-land to see them. When Nikkum heard what they wanted, he caught hold of Eji and cut off his buttocks and made them into a pig. He cut out his ribs and made them into a goat. He cut out his eyes and made them into a fowl. When these things were ready, he gave them to Po-um and Po-um gave them to Abo-Teni.

Because the pig was made of a pair of buttocks, he is full of fat and eats excrement. Because the fowl was made from an eye, the Nibos can use her to divine with: they can see the truth by looking at her eggs and liver.

56

MINYONG

Riga, Siang F.D.

Sedi-Libom was neither rock nor soil, neither animal nor human being. He looked like a rock, but he was not one, for he could go about. Sedi-Karki-Milli Wiyo saw him and, wondering what he was, struck at him with his dao, and cut him in half. Out of his broken body came a large grub. Sedi-Karki-Milli picked it up and found it alive. 'If I kill it,' he said to himself, 'Doini-Pollo will see me, so I will let it be.' In the end he took the grub to Doini-Pollo, who was pleased with it and gave it a head and tail and four legs. Its snout was very soft, but Doini-Pollo put a bit of iron there so that it could dig for roots with it. He gave it a bitter fruit to eat and sent it away.

The pig wandered away to the field of Engo-Takar, who had planted it with many roots. The pig ate them all, and Engo-Takar came running to curse him, but he denied that he was the thief. 'Then,' said Engo-Takar, 'vomit up whatever is in your belly.' The pig brought up all he had, but the roots had disappeared: there were only the seeds of the bitter fruit given by Doini-Pollo. When Engo-Takar saw that, he let the pig go.

For this reason, one should never put rice-beer near a place where a pig has vomited, even if this has happened underneath the house. For a pig's vomit is bitter and spoils the beer.

57

MOKLUM

Longke, Tirap F.D.

Sengwa and Phengwa gave food to everyone and taught men how to cook. But there were so many demanding food that they forgot to give anything to the pigs. This is why the pig has to eat excreta. But men who are sometimes kinder than the gods give him rice to eat as well.

THE RAT

58

SHERDUKPEN

Shergaon, Kameng F.D.

There was a Sirinpu called Dut-Gepu-Langdir who was a great enemy of the Lamas and whenever they planted flowering shrubs for sacrifice, he cut them down as soon as they grew up. What could they do? They decided that the only thing would be to kill him, and they fought against him but he was too strong for them. Then they called the villagers to help, and they did the Ajilama dance hoping that the Sirinpu would come to watch it and that they then could kill him with their arrows. When the dance began, a great crowd assembled but he did not come.

Now Dut-Gepu-Langdir had three daughters. They saw the dance and ran home to call their father saying, 'There's a great dance ; you come and see it.' The Sirinpu hurried to the place, but when he arrived the people shot him. Many arrows stuck in his body and he fell groaning to the ground, but he did not die.

His eldest daughter cried to him, 'Father, die: how can you bear this pain? I will pick all the flowers of the Lamas and put them on your tomb.' But the Sirinpu could not die.

Then the second daughter cried to him, 'Father, die: how can you bear this pain? I will prepare poison and kill the Lamas with it.' But still the Sirinpu could not die.

Then the youngest daughter cried to him, 'Father, die: how can you bear this pain? From me a rat will be born and it will destroy the Lamas' books and the cloth and grain of ordinary men.' When the Sirinpu heard this, he died.

After the Sirinpu's death the villagers tried to cremate his body, but it would not burn. It was only when they cut it into little pieces that it caught fire. Even then they said to one another, 'Possibly from the ashes something evil may be born.' So they collected the ashes and threw them into the river. But among them they found one small bit of bone unconsumed, and for fear that some evil might be born from it they ground it up and threw it into the wind.

From the dust of this bone were born the first mosquitoes and dim-dam flies.

From the youngest daughter the first rat was born and ever since rats have eaten the books of the Lamas and have destroyed the cloth and grain of ordinary men.

The Tiger

59

BORI

Payum, Siang F.D.

There were four brothers: Tani, Taro, Taiyo and Taki. Their father, Turi, had a dao and when he died Tani got it and valued it so greatly that he kept it always with him ; not for a moment did he lay it down.

One day Taiyo quarrelled with Tani saying, 'Whatever land our father left—you should give me my share.' Tani replied, 'We are four brothers and whoever has most children will get most land. But since none of us have any children at present, there is no point in talking about dividing the land to-day.'

One day Tani and Taiyo went hunting and killed a deer. Tani said to Taiyo, 'Go and get fire and we will cook the meat and eat it.' Taiyo went to find fire but did not go very far and after a time he came back and said falsely that he had searched everywhere and could not find it. So Tani said, 'Then I will go and find the fire: you stay and watch the deer.' When Tani came back he found Taiyo eating the raw flesh and said, 'Why are you doing this?' Taiyo said, 'Because I like it.' Tani was very angry with Taiyo and in his rage dug up the ground with his feet and dropped his dao. Taiyo snatched it up and put it in his mouth. Immediately it turned into great teeth and his body was transformed into a tiger.

Tani said, 'You are an animal and not a human being and therefore your share of our property will be the forest.'

60

BUGUN (KHOWA)

Senchong, Kameng F.D.

Zongma, the greatest of all, had a son called Phumphulu. When the boy grew up he left his home and went to find a wife. He travelled towards the east where there was living a daughter of the Sun whose name was Muinini. Phumphulu loved her and they lived together as man and wife. In due time Muinini gave birth first to a tiger-cub, then to a human boy, then to a dog, then to every kind of grain, then to wild roots and at last to a human daughter. They all lived together and at first were very happy.

But when the tiger grew up, his teeth became long and sharp and he went to his mother and said, 'I am hungry ; give me some meat to eat.' His mother said, 'There is no meat here ; what can I give you?' The tiger said, 'If you don't give me some meat to eat, I will eat my brother and sister and the dog.' Muinini was frying maize at the time and in her anger she beat the tiger with the hot spoon.

The tiger ran weeping to his father who was stringing his bow before going out to hunt. The tiger told him how hungry he was and said, 'I shall eat my mother.' His father got very angry at this and beat him with his bow, telling him to get out of the house at once.

Ever since, the tiger has lived in the forest and has carried on his body the marks of his beating with the bow and the spoon.

61

BUGUN (KHOWA)

Kapsi, Kameng F.D.

Long ago there was an old man called Phumphulu who had a wife called Muinini. Phumphulu was too weak and frail to do any work and his wife did everything, cultivating in the forest and fetching wood and roots to eat.

Although they were old, one day Muinini found herself pregnant. When her time came, she gave birth to a child which was not human, but crawled on four legs. When Phumphulu saw it, he said to his wife, 'We are old and our child is some sort of animal. Had it been a real human child we could have fed him on what we eat ourselves, but how can we feed this creature?' The child heard what his parents said and although he was only a baby he spoke to them. 'Mother and father,' he said, 'don't worry. I will go every day to the forest and bring you back sufficient meat so that you'll have more food and not less than you had before.' Hearing this, the parents were very pleased.

The child grew up quickly and was soon going to the forest to hunt. Sometimes he would kill a pig, eat half of it himself and bring half for his parents ; another day he would kill a deer, eat half of it himself and bring the other half for his parents. In this way he killed many kinds of animal and always brought half of the meat for Phumphulu and Muinini.

After some time Muinini conceived again and this time gave birth to a dog. The parents were very worried at having yet another animal in the family and wondered what they were to do for him. But the puppy said, 'Mother and father, don't worry. I will be the guardian of your house and I will always show you what path to take. Wherever you go, I will go too and look after you.' When they heard this the parents were consoled.

One day the tiger-child said to his parents, 'I am going on a long journey to hunt ; you both follow me as far as Lora-Phong and I will meet you there with plenty of meat.' Having said this the tiger-child went away.

Phumphulu and Muinini prepared food and rice-beer for their son and started off for Lora-Phong and the puppy followed them. When they reached the place they found a great rock, beneath which they made their camp. They made a fire and began to cook some rice, anxiously watching the path for the moment when their tiger-son would bring them the meat. Two days passed but the tiger did not come. The puppy said to the old couple, 'My elder brother hasn't come, so I'll go and look for him.' He went a very long way and presently found his brother lying asleep by the path. He woke him up and said, 'What are you doing? We were all expecting to see you at least two days ago and our parents are very hungry and yet here you are lying asleep by the side of the path.'

'Ever since I left the house,' said the tiger, 'I've not been able to catch a single animal. Nor have I had a bite to eat, and that has made me weak which is why I've been sleeping here.' As he looked at his younger brother the tiger felt even more hungry and he said, 'Why did you wake me up? I am going to eat you.' At that the puppy ran away all the way back to his parents at Lora-Phong. But he did not tell them what had happened and when they asked him about the tiger, he said that he was on his way.

A few days later the tiger-child reached Lora-Phong, and his parents did not welcome him but abused him saying, 'You were going to bring us plenty of food ; where is it?' The tiger replied, 'Ever since I left home I have had nothing to eat and now I'm so hungry that I'm going to eat you all. First of all I'll eat you, mother.' He tried to kill his mother but she hit him with a bamboo spoon. So he turned away from his mother and attacked his father, but he hit him with a bamboo arrow. The tiger backed away growling and his parents said to him, 'We are your father and mother and yet you want to eat us. After this you will always live in the forest. If now you go down to the plains of Assam, the people there will certainly catch you in their nets and kill you. If you go to the country of the Monpas, they will kill you with their cross-bows. If you go to the country of the Hrussos, they will kill you with their poisoned arrows. If you go to the country of the Buguns, they will kill you with their traps.'

When he heard this the tiger was frightened and ran away into the forest and has lived there ever since.

Phumphulu and Muinini went home and their dog followed them. This is why the dog always looks after people's houses and when they miss their way on their journeys he leads them back to the right path.

The marks on the tiger's body are those made by Muinini when she beat him with the bamboo spoon.

62

DHAMMAI (MIJI)

Nakhu, Kameng F.D.

Many years ago two brothers, Nummo and Nuhung lived with their parents in Chang-Darrou. Every day the two boys used to go out hunting and set traps for birds. But it was Nummo who did all the work: Nuchung only watched. One evening Nummo set his traps and next morning he said to his brother, 'Go and see what has been caught.' Nuhung went and found some birds and rats. He ate half of each bird and rat uncooked as it was and put the rest in his basket. When he came home Nummo asked him why there were only bits and scraps of meat. Nuhung said, 'I do not know. I've just brought what I found.' After this he used to do the same thing every day and grew fat and strong.

One day Nummo set a trap for a wild pig and next morning said to his brother, 'There is sure to be a pig in the trap. Go and fetch it.' But when Nuhung went to the place he followed him secretly and saw him take the pig from the trap and tear it to pieces with his teeth. The pig screamed in pain and Nummo hurried to the place and said, 'Why are you eating the meat raw?' Nuhung was ashamed and jumped up saying, 'Don't tell anybody.' Nummo said, 'So this is why you only bring half of every animal caught in our traps. Are you an animal or human being?' Nuhung replied, 'I am a man but I am also partly an animal.'

Nuhung had a small knife in his hand and he put it in his mouth where it turned into a set of great teeth. 'From today,' he cried, 'I am a tiger. Whatever I stole from you I will return, but on no account tell anyone that your younger brother is a tiger living in the forest. If you so much as whisper the story to our parents I will devour you.'

Nummo took home what was left of the pig and his parents were pleased, but they asked, 'Where is Nuhung?' Nummo said, 'He has gone to get wood from the forest.' Many days went by and, when the boy still did not return, the old people got very anxious but Nummo kept them quiet by saying, 'He has gone to some other village in search of a wife.'

At last when they had given up all hope of their youngest son, his parents wept saying, 'You have killed your brother and that is why you won't say where he is.' Nummo replied, 'I can't tell you what happened now, but I will tell you after two days.' He spent these two days building a strong fence round his house thinking, 'How can he come and kill me when I am protected by this fence?' But every evening the tiger-brother used to sleep beneath the house, for he was anxious to know whether Nummo had revealed his secret or not.[14]

At last Nummo told the whole story to his parents and the tiger heard him. Next time Nummo went outside his fence, the tiger was waiting for him, crouched ready for the spring. But his parents ran forward and stood before him and said, 'Nuhung, you have become a tiger, so live out in the forest. Nummo, you are a man, you must live at home. But since you are brothers, you must never quarrel or hurt one another.'

And indeed for many years the Dhammais and the tigers lived at peace with one another, but presently the tigers began to kill the Dhammais' mithuns and horses, and since then there has been war between them.

63

GALLONG

Sokki, Subansiri F.D.

The two brothers Niso and Niyu used to go hunting in the thick forest on the banks of the Sipi River. They set traps for squirrels and birds and returned home at sunset. But Niso, who was the elder of the two, used to get up very early in the morning and eat half of whatever was in the traps ; there was no way of cooking it, he ate the meat raw. Then he would come home before Niyu was awake.

When they went out later, they would find the traps robbed and Niyu used to wonder what sort of man it could be who ate so much raw meat.

This went on for many days. Then one evening, Niyu pretended to be very tired and went to rest early. But as soon as Niso was asleep, he got up quietly and went to hide behind a tree near the place where the traps were set. In the early morning, he saw his brother come and remove a squirrel from the trap, tear it in half and begin to eat it.

Niyu came from his hiding-place and cried, 'Brother, why do

[14] It is interesting to find the same motif in a Gallong story from a remote and isolated village in the Sipi Valley of north-east Subansiri. The main difference is that the Dhammai tale has a happy ending. The motif also occurs in a Dhanwar story from central India. See my *Folk-Tales of Mahakoshal*, p. 462.

you do this? These things belong to both of us ; take them and cook and eat them properly.' But Niso said, 'I can only get strength from raw meat. If you don't like what I have done, I am sorry. From today I shall live in the forest and eat all my food raw. I have been robbing you for a long time, but now I shall repay my debt and give you all the help I can.'

As he spoke, his body changed its form and he became a tiger. He said, 'Whenever you go hunting I will help you, but on one condition, that you tell no one that your elder brother, in order to eat raw meat, has turned into a tiger of the jungle. If you tell anyone, I shall hear of it, and I shall take the form of a black dog and pursue you. There will be war between us. If you can kill me, well ; but otherwise I shall kill you.' Niyu said that there was no need of this gloomy talk, for he would certainly tell nobody. The tiger, pleased, went away into the jungle.

After this Niyu used to go often to hunt and every time his tiger-brother caught a deer or wild boar for him. So Niyu lived well and grew rich and fat. But in time he grew old and one day, as he sat by the hearth, his children and grandchildren asked him about Niso. 'We once had an uncle: where has he gone?' Niyu said not a word for fear of the black dog.

Then Niyu grew so old that he had no strength, not even to go out of the house. His children went on pestering him for news of their uncle. Niyu said to himself, 'I am old now ; my hunting days are over. Even if the black dog does come, what can it do to me?' So Niyu told his children and grandchildren what had happened.

But Niso was listening and heard all that passed. He turned into a black dog and sat below the house. Niyu was there by the hearth, tugging at his hair with his comb. But somehow he dropped the comb and it fell through the floor to the ground below. Niyu said to one of his sons, 'My comb has fallen down ; go and get it for me.' When the boy went down, he could not find the comb, for the black dog was sitting on it. He climbed up into the house again and told his father.

Then the black dog moved a little and allowed part of the comb to show. Niyu looked down through the floor and saw the comb and the black dog sitting on it. He took his bow and arrows and climbed down from the house. Then Niso became a tiger again and sprang at his brother. At the same moment Niyu fired his arrow. The arrow pierced the tiger and killed it, but in its spring it hurled Niyu to the ground: he was old and he too died.

So now, if anyone sees a tiger in a dream he must sacrifice eggs and a fowl saying, 'You are my brother: do not trouble me.' If he does this, the tiger will protect his mithuns and other animals and does not injure them.

And if anyone kills his brother, by accident or in a quarrel, he is taboo: he must go to live like a tiger, by himself in the forest, for a time.

64

IDU MISHMI

Koronu, Lohit F.D.

A woman became pregnant. In due time she gave birth to a daughter and after a few days the god Konpa flew down in the form of a bird and perched outside the house crying *'Anchi Anchi.'* When the mother heard this, she gave her daughter the name of Anchi.

When the girl grew up she married and her husband came to take her to his house. But as they were going along through the forest, Konpa met them and caught Anchi by the hand saying, 'What are you doing with this girl? She is my wife, not your's.' The husband said, 'No, she is mine,' and took her by the other hand. Each pulled the girl in a different direction, but in the end Konpa carried her off to his house on the top of a hill.

There the god gave Anchi every kind of pretty cloth and she spread it out in the sun and far away the people living below in the valleys saw it.

As she went on living with the god, Anchi's appearance gradually changed and white and black marks appeared on her body. Soon after the birth of her first child, she said to herself, 'I've not seen my mother for many days. There's a cock of mine there which I left behind. I'll go and see her and fetch my cock at the same time.'

When she reached her home, her mother and her younger brother were in the house, but they didn't recognize her and were rather frightened. But Anchi explained how it was that she was now looking different and her mother took her into the house and fed her well and gave her the cock.

Anchi took the cock home to her husband and when she reached the house, he crowed. This cock used to be heard on earth until the Great Earthquake but no one has heard him since. This is why a certain hill-village is called Anchi-Elomi.

The following year Anchi went again to see her mother and brother, for at the time of her wedding she had not given them a feast. On the way she caught a tiger and took him with her as a present for her mother, but when the old lady saw him, she screamed with fright. Anchi said, 'What you are afraid of? It is only a sort of goat.' 'Are you mad?' cried the mother. 'It is a tiger and will kill us all. But if you yourself will kill him, then we will eat him.'

There was no dao or knife in the house but only the wooden sword used in the loom. Anchi picked it up and killed the tiger and they all feasted on the meat.

Anchi's younger brother was very small, too small to do much work in the fields. Anchi said to him, 'Prepare some rice and beer and take it to the field, divide it into five parts and put it in five different places and I'll send my own child to work for you.' So saying, she went away.

The next day Anchi's old mother and brother took the rice and beer to the field and put it in five places in five different bamboos. Then they went down to the lower slope of the hill and began to clear the forest. But higher up Anchi's little son came and made a great clearing. He ate the rice and drank the beer and went away, but the mother and son could not see him.

Then Anchi went to her mother and asked if the clearing was ready. 'Yes,' said the mother, 'but we never saw your son. We only knew that he had been there because the rice and the beer was finished.' Anchi said, 'Yes, it was my son but his father is a god and you will never see him.'

Since that day the Taraons have eaten the flesh of tigers.

65

IDU MISHMI

Dibang Valley, Lohit F.D.

After the great flood which destroyed all living creatures in the world the god Ekamo desired to fill it again with men and animals.

He sought everywhere for a wife who would give him children to people the world, but the only other woman was his own daughter Erraye, beautiful and charming. Because she was so beautiful and also because there was no one else, Ekamo told her that she would have to marry him. But she declared that she would rather die, and ran from the house and climbed up a nearby tree for safety. But Ekamo sent a rat to cut the tree down and after some days it fell crashing on the house.

There were many cocks and hens there and when the tree fell, they cried, 'What is the matter? What has happened?' Since that day whenever a cock hears any sound in the night, it cries out, 'What is the matter?'

Now Erraye could not escape from her father and they lived together as husband and wife. After some time, the girl gave birth to a small creature with black stripes on his body. She was frightened of him and asked her husband to leave him in the forest. Gradually the creature grew into a splendid animal.

Erraye now became the mother of another child who proved to be a strong and handsome boy. He grew up and one day while he was wandering in the forest, he suddenly met a great striped creature crouched before a deer. The tiger recognized his brother and they became friends. The younger boy asked the tiger how he had killed the deer and the tiger replied, 'My teeth are the weapons with which I kill and in my stomach is the fire with which I cook.' The boy then asked for some meat for his parents but the tiger replied angrily, 'My parents deserted me in the forest when I was young and unable to look after myself. I will not give them anything ; all I want is to eat both of them.'

The boy went home quickly to warn his parents about the tiger, and Ekamo told him to kill him in any way he could.

Again after some days, as the boy was going through the forest, he met the tiger and challenged him to fight. He knew that he would certainly be defeated in a real duel, so he suggested that whoever could cross a certain stream and first reach the other bank would be victorious over the other. The tiger immediately jumped into the water, but the boy remained on the bank and when the tiger was in the middle of the stream, he shot a poisoned arrow at him and pierced his back.

The tiger died and was carried down the stream. The god Gallan saw this and was sad. He sent two water-gods, Sillin Dingino and Eton Dingino, to sit on the bones of the dead animal. After a time many tigers came from the bones and Gallan sent some of them to the plains and kept some of them with him in the hills.[15]

66

IDU MISHMI

Ichuli, Lohit F.D.

Long long ago a boy was born with all his teeth, and a great shock of white hair ; he began to talk at once. But in spite of this he was as tiny as an ordinary baby.

At his birth fire began to burn within the earth and this frightened the rat out of his hole. Then the water covered the earth and fish swam into the houses and filled the baskets where the hens were roosting. The women were pleased at getting so many fish.

The god Silli Anjome was born as a man to send the water away but he was so tall that he could not stoop down to dig the channels which would carry off the water, and he went away to China. The Illu (Brahmaputra) River became so full of water that it rose up to the Lama Mountains.

Then the girl Anjome Milli was born. She too was very tall and the wind came from her ; it blew so strongly that the water and even the trees and grass were dried up. The wind picked up small boys and girls and carried them away, no one knew where. There was a pregnant woman whom the wind blew to the top of a tree—she fell from it and died.

Then the god Mimmu-Me was born and created fire. With this fire he burnt the trees which had been withered by the wind.

Then the god Anju-Aru was born. He went like a bird to the place where the fire was raging and then flew here and there about the world to see what was happening. He saw that the water was again flowing and bringing down human bones. The bones caught in the branches and stumps of trees and when Anju-Aru saw them he thought, 'These are men's bones: where have they come from? They are very fine bones.' He fell in love with the bones and danced and sang before them. From his dance the goddess

[15] Recorded by T. K. Barua.

Aru-Mai-Milli was born and Anju-Aru married her, and in due time she gave birth to a boy Eri and a girl Ekko-Mu.

When his children grew up, Anju-Aru thought to himself, 'There is no boy for the girl and there is no girl for the boy. They must marry each other and then, gradually, from them all human beings will be born.' So he said to Ekko-Mu, 'You must marry your brother.' The girl was very shocked at this and exclaimed, 'How can I marry my brother? I will die if I do,' and she ran out of the house and climbed up a tree. Anju-Aru called for a swarm of rats and they burrowed under the tree and brought it down. Ekko-Mu said, 'It is no use trying to escape. Where can I go?' So she married her brother. Before long she conceived, and on the left side her belly went *put-put-put,* but on the right side it was quiet. She wondered what could be making this strange noise inside her and asked her husband whether the thing would kill her or save her.

After some time a tiny little creature was born from her left side. He was covered with black stripes and had four legs and a tail. Ekko-Mu called her husband and they decided that if they let him grow up he might destroy them. So Erai took him to the forest and left him there.

Then from the girl's right side there was born the god Kera in human form. This boy was strong and beautiful and, when he grew up, his father made him a bow and arrow.

One day Kera went out hunting and met a tiger. He did not realize that this was his brother born from the same womb but the tiger knew at once and said, 'You are my younger brother ; why have you come here?' The boy said, 'I have come to hunt.' The tiger said, 'Come then, let us go hunting.' They hunted all day and Kera got nothing. But the tiger caught a deer and Kera said, 'Brother, give me a little of the meat to take home.' The tiger was annoyed and said, 'Eat as much of it as you can.' The boy said, 'How can I cut it and how can I cook it?' To this the tiger made no reply. Then Kera said, 'How do you cut up your meat and cook it?' The tiger showed his teeth and said, 'This is my dao and my stomach is my kitchen.' Kera said, 'My teeth are not strong enough and my stomach is not big enough. So let me take the meat home.' The tiger said, 'I'll not let you take anything home, for our parents threw me away in the jungle. I am not going to give anything to such wicked people and if I can catch them, I'll kill and eat them.'

Kera went home and told his parents what had happened. His father was angry and said, 'If ever you meet my son the tiger again kill him.' He prepared a poisoned arrow and gave it to the boy. So next day Kera went out hunting again and met the tiger and said, 'Brother, my father has told me to kill you, so I am going to shoot you.' The tiger said, 'You cannot kill me like that. We have got to have a fight first.' When Kera saw the great teeth of his brother, he was frightened and thought he could never win in a straight fight. So he said, 'Here is a river. Whoever crosses it first will be the winner.' The tiger agreed. The boy said, 'You go first.' And the tiger went into the water and, as he was struggling across, Kera shot him dead.

The tiger's body was swept downstream to a place called Dingubiyudu and was caught in the reeds by the banks. The god Dingu-Aneni saw the bones and said to himself, 'These are not ordinary tiger's bones. They were born from a human womb. I wonder how they have come here.' So he collected them in a pile and sat on them for ten years and at the end of that time all kinds of cats, tigers, leopards, wild cats were born and began to run about.

This is how the race of tigers first came to the world.

67

MINYONG

Pangin, Siang F.D.

Peddo-Doban-Banji-Botte and Peddo-Doban-Banmang-Nane were husband and wife. In due time the woman conceived. She used to go daily to work in the fields, but her husband stayed at home dancing and drinking beer. When her time came, the woman had no one with her ; there was no fire, no food, no water. In such a state, she was delivered of twins. She was very hungry. She said to the elder child, 'Son, go to the forest and get me meat' and he went out to hunt. She said to the younger, 'Son, go and get fire.'

The younger son went to Nimkir-Nomnan's house. This man had killed a lot of rats and had made a great pile of them in a corner of his house. He was sitting by the fire roasting them when the boy came in and he threw one of them to him to eat. When the boy saw the pile of rats he was so pleased that he forgot all about his mother and stayed by the warmth of the fire, eating rats. In this way he turned into a cat.

The elder brother went far into the forest. There he killed a barking-deer. When he tasted the blood he found it so sweet that he forgot all about his mother and stayed where he was. In this way he turned into a tiger.

68

MINYONG

Komkar, Siang F.D.

Peddong-Nane was the wife of Kadung-Botte. Though Wiyus, they were human in form, but their son was an animal. When they saw him, they were sad and sent him to live in the forest.

The child wandered through the forest until he came to the place where Banji-Botte had killed Polung-Sabbo. There he found Banji. The child kicked a pot and knocked it over: he was so hungry that he licked up the spilt blood. He could not eat, for he had no teeth. Banji-Botte asked him, 'Why have you no teeth?' He put Polung-Sabbo's teeth into the child's mouth. The child said, 'What shall I do with these?' 'You may eat flesh and drink blood.' This is how the child became a tiger.

69

MOKLUM

Magantang, Tirap F.D.

Originally the tiger had a long beard. One day a man saw it and thought it looked very nice. He asked the tiger for it and the tiger gave it to him. But the woman wasn't there and that is why women don't have beards.

Rang had three dogs whom he sent to earth. The biggest of them he painted with black stripes and told to live in the forest and eat the larger animals. He sent the second also to the forest and told him to eat the small animals. He told the third dog to live with men. This is how the tiger, the wild dog, and the ordinary dog came into being.

70

NOCTE

Tut, Tirap F.D.

Formerly, men and tigers were brothers and they used to live together and go to work in their clearings together. One day they saw a deer and both wanted to have it, for both were equally hungry. This led to a quarrel, and, since they could not agree, they became enemies, and the tiger declared that he would no longer live with men and ran away to the forest.

But the tiger had no fire in the forest and felt very cold, so he sent a cat to steal it from his former friend's house. But when the cat got to the house, she was so comfortable and warm that she stayed there. The tiger was very angry at this and declared that he would eat the cat whenever he could catch her. This is why the cat is so frightened of a tiger and hides her droppings with earth for fear that he may discover where she lives.

71

WANCHO

Banfera, Tirap F.D.

In the old days it was tigers who had guns ; men only had sticks. The tigers used to hunt men and shoot and eat them, so men grew very timid. But there was one clever man who made friends with a tiger and won his trust. One day this man said to the tiger, 'Let's go hunting.' The man had a stick, the tiger took his gun. They saw a deer and the tiger said, 'You kill it.' The man said, 'No, you kill it.' The tiger fired his gun and the deer fell. The tiger said, 'Let's eat it,' but the man said, 'Not without cooking it ; it tastes much better when cooked.' 'But there are no vessels here,' said the tiger. 'Then we will carry it home and cook it there,' said the man. He cut a branch from a bombax tree and removed the thorns from one end. He tied the deer to it and placed the thorny end on the tiger's shoulder. The tiger cried, 'I can't carry this, for the thorns hurt me.' The man said, 'They don't hurt me.' 'You men are very strong,' said the tiger. The man said, 'I will get some men to carry it home.' At that the tiger went away. The man dragged the deer into the forest, put it in a hole in the ground and covered it with earth.

But the tiger thought things over, and presently went to the man and said, 'If you call other men to help us carry the deer, we will have to give them a share of it. Let's cut up the flesh and take it home bit by bit.' But when they went to the place, there was no deer to be seen. The man said, 'You didn't shoot it properly, it has got up and run away. Now let's see which is best, my stick or your gun. You shoot and I will beat the ground.' The tiger fired his gun but nothing happened. The man went to the place where he had hidden the deer and beat the ground with his stick, the earth fell away and there was the deer. The tiger was very pleased and said, 'Your stick is better than my gun,' and he gave his gun to the man and took the stick. Ever since then men have had guns and tigers have been afraid of them.

72

WANCHO

Khanu, Tirap F.D.

The Wangham (Chief) and the tiger at first were real brothers. In those days men had long pointed teeth and tigers had little teeth. The Wangham used to call the tiger friend and the tiger used to call the Wangham friend. But the Wangham was more astute than the tiger.

One day he went to the forest and killed a deer. He told the tiger that as it was evening they had better carry the carcass home. As they were doing so the tiger got tired and told his friend that he could not carry it any longer. So the Wangham suggested that they should cut it up and carry it home that way. When they had done this, the Wangham asked the tiger to fetch some water. Directly he had gone, the Wangham hid the meat. The tiger returned and asked what had happened to it. The Wangham said, 'It is somewhere or other and whoever can find it can have it all. But the one who can't find it will have to give his teeth to whoever does find it.' In the dark the tiger could not find the meat but the Wangham could, for he knew where it was. So the tiger gave his teeth to man and man gave his great pointed teeth to the tiger.

73

SHERDUKPEN

Rupa, Kameng F.D.

In Tibet lived an old man Apapek and his wife Janmu. They had three sons—Gappasambru, Tepagalu and Dagyesambru. The two old people, who were very rich, divided their property between Gappasambru and Dagyesambru but they gave nothing to Tepagalu. He went to them and asked for his share, but they refused to give him anything.

As a result of this Tepagalu was very sad and said to himself, 'I have no share of the property and I have nothing to eat ; what is the use of living here? I will go anywhere I can get food.' He left his home and went to Chungba-Sangyat and told him his story. 'Tell me,' he said, 'if I will ever get a share of my parents' wealth.' Chungba-Sangyat said, 'You will never get it.' He went to the spirits and said, 'Tell me if I will ever get a share of my parents' wealth.' And the spirits too said, 'You will never get it.' Then he went to the Wind and said, 'Tell me if I will ever get a share of my parents' wealth.' And the Wind too said, 'You will never get it.'

So at last in despair Tepagalu went to the forest. As he pushed his way through the trees, he came to a great cave in the side of a hill. There were streams of water flowing down both sides of the cave leaving a dry path in the middle. The boy went into the cave and, though it was very dark, made his way deep into the ground. After he had gone a long way, he found an enormous bird call Jatung-Tung-Karmu sitting on three great eggs. He greeted the bird and said, 'Whatever do you eat in a place like this?' 'I eat rice,' said the bird. 'I have been hungry for many days,' said the boy, 'and I am weak through fasting. Could you give me a little rice?' The bird replied, 'I have no rice myself, for I usually go out and find it. But I can get some for you. The difficulty is that I am sitting on these three eggs and if I leave them they will get cold and be spoilt.' The boy said, 'Go and get the rice: I'll keep your eggs warm.' The bird agreed to this but said, 'Whatever you do, don't turn these eggs upside down.' The boy promised that he would not touch the eggs at all but would simply hold his hands above them to keep them warm. So the bird went away and the boy warmed the eggs with his hands.

But presently he got curious and picked up the eggs to examine them and put them back upside down.

After some time the bird returned with the rice and gave it to Tepagalu, but when she saw that her eggs were upside down she was very angry and went away.

When the bird had gone, the boy wept for loneliness and wondered what he should do. But presently he remembered that God was merciful and that he might allow something to come out of the three eggs. He took one of the eggs in his hand and called on Chungba-Sangyat saying, 'Have pity on my despair ; allow something to come from this egg to help me.' He broke the egg with his stick, and a white yak came out of it and went flying through the air to Chungba-Sangyat. The boy broke the second egg and a red yak came out of it and went flying to the spirits of the forest. The boy cried, 'There is but one egg left ; allow this at least to be of use to me.'

He broke the egg open and a black yak came out of it and went down into the water. The boy then came out of the cave and, taking a rope in his hand, sat outside by the stream for a whole year. All this time the black yak remained in the water, but at the end of the year she raised her head above the surface and Tepagalu caught her with his rope. He took her home and kept her with him. After a time she bore a calf and the boy got milk and ghee. In three years the yak had three calves.

When Apapek heard of this, he came with his two other sons and they all lived together and danced in honour of the animal that gave them their food.

Fabulous Monsters

74

APA TANI

Reru, Subansiri F.D.

When the Apa Tanis first came to their country, they found it all mud and water and surrounded by forest. We cut the forest and guided the water into channels and drained the swamp, so that we were able to make our fields there. When we were doing this three *burus* came out of the swamp. They were like enormous pigs and their bodies were covered with white stripes. We killed them and buried them. They were not animals but Wiyus.[16]

[16] For a full account of the traditions regarding this legendary creature, see R. Izzard, *The Hunt for the Buru* (London, 1951).

GLOSSARY OF TRIBES

ADI—A word now used instead of the rather derogatory 'Abor', which means 'unruly' or 'independent', formerly given by the people of the plains to the tribesmen of Siang and the Padams of Lohit.

APA TANI—The Apa Tanis are unique among the people of NEFA in living in a single homogeneous area of only twenty square miles, which accommodates their seven villages and nine thousand inhabitants, as a result of a meticulous division of land and a system of irrigated fields which does not allow even the slightest waste. The villages are administered by councils of elders and are divided into three groups, each of which constitues a ritual unit, and Apa Tani society consists of an upper and a lower classes, which do not intermarry. The Apa Tanis are often tall and good-looking ; they dress very like the Daflas but can be distinguished by a tattoo mark over the chin and by the famous cane 'tail'. The women coil their hair on the top of the head, wear nose-plugs and are heavily tattooed. They are excellent weavers and in the past supplied the Daflas and Hill Miris with their cloth. They bury their dead. Lively and detailed descriptions of them, as they were ten years ago, will be found in Mrs Bower's *The Hidden Land* and C. von Furer-Haimendorf's *Himalayan Barbary*.

BORI—A small group of Adis, closely allied in appearance, dress and custom to the Bokars, Ramos and other northern tribes, who live in the Syom and Sike Valleys—an isolated and little known area lying between Mechuka to the west and Karko to the east. They are good weavers in wool and cotton, keen hunters and fishermen, and maintain communal dormitories for boys and girls. To some extent they act as middlemen in trade between the Minyongs and Gallongs and the wilder tribes of the west.

BUGUN—The Buguns, who are popularly known as Khowas, occupy seven villages in the neighbourhood of the Sherdukpens and Hrussos. There are only some 1,500 of them and ever since their migration from the north to their present habitat, they have had a dependent status ; they have had to work for the Hrussos whom they regard as their overlords and they early got heavily into debt to the Sherdukpens, who acted as merchants to supply them with goods from the plains. They have no weaving and few arts and have always been poor. In dress and appearance they are like the Hrussos and Dhammais. They bury their dead and their religion is of the general tribal type, but slightly influenced by the prevailing Buddhism of the area in which they live. The Administration has now done much to lift the burden of servitude which previously lay heavily upon them.

DAFLA—The name 'Dafla' has been given by the people of the plains to a large tribe calling itself Bangni (a word which simply means 'man') which is distributed over a great tract of wild and difficult country in the east of Kameng and west of Subansiri. The Daflas have been known as independent and turbulent since the days of Aurangzeb, and although the majority of them have settled down to a life of peace under an ordered administration, their appearance, with the hair tied in a knot above the forehead, remains proud and dignified. In the past they kept many slaves who were generally prisoners of war, and in Subansiri they used to raid the Apa Tani villages. Today, however, they live in close economic symbiosis with the Apa Tanis, whom they supply with cotton and other goods in exchange for cloth and rice. Although the Daflas live in villages, the real social unit is the house which is often very large and accommodates an entire joint family. The Daflas have few dances and, apart from a little weaving and excellent cane-work, are not proficient in the arts. They bury the dead near their houses. Detailed descriptions will be found in the books by Mrs Bower and Dr C. von Furer-Haimendorf mentioned above.

DHAMMAI—The people known as Miji to the outside world call themselves Dhammai. There are about 5,000 of them inhabiting 25 villages in the Kameng Frontier Division. To the north and west of them are the Monpas, to the south the Hrussos, to the east the Bangnis. There is a tradition that long ago they lived in the plains and later migrated to the mountains, but there is little sign of this in their culture. In appearance and way of life there is little to distinguish them from the Hrussos, with whom they sometimes intermarry. Both men and women let their hair grow long and they have adopted certain elements of Monpa dress, the women being very fond of silver ornaments. They have little weaving and purchase most of their cloth from their neighbours or from the plains. They are divided into two classes, the Nyubbu and the Nyullu, who do not intermarry. Their religion is of the tribal type but, like the Hrussos, they have come under a certain amount of Buddhist influence.

DOBANG—A name given by the plains-people in Dunbar's day to the Adis of Basar and Daring. It is no longer current and was never used by the Adis themselves.

GALLONG—The word Gallong covers a number of small groups in

Siang and northern Subansiri, among whom are the Paktus, Riba-Basars, Tai-padis, Nali-bags, Tatar-tanis, while the Ramos, Bokars and Tagins are closely related to them. Gallong village and political organization is built up on the clan system, each village consisting of a single clan. Houses are generally substantial and in contrast to the neighbouring Minyong houses, are square rather than rectangular. They do not have communal dormitories. The marriage arrangements of the Gallongs are unusual: male children are betrothed before birth ; a man may marry his mother-in-law and there is a slight but definite strain of polyandry. The art of weaving had largely died out among them, but some of their beautiful traditional patterns are now being revived. The Gallongs differ from the Minyongs and Padams in keeping their hair long, and are an attractive-looking people of fine physique. See G. D. S. Dunbar, 'Abors and Galongs', *Memoirs of A. S. B.*, Vol. V (1913-17).

HILL MIRI—The group of clans, which for want of a better name, is commonly known as the Hill Miri, lives in scattered villages throughout northern Subansiri. There is actually no generic name for these people, who call themselves after their village, which in turn depends on the clan ; there has been some attempt to classify them as Saraks, Tarbotias, Panibotias and so on, or to call them Nisu—but this is a classification not accepted by themselves. They are broadly similar in appearance, culture and language to the Daflas and Apa Tanis. See E. T. Dalton's *Descriptive Ethnology of Bengal* for an interesting early account.

HRUSSO—The Hrussos are commonly called Aka which means 'painted'—for they have a custom of painting their faces with black marks. Though they are a very small tribe of only about one thousand individuals, they figure frequently in the historical records. They have a tradition that they migrated from the east and had relations with the Ahom kings. In the early years a Hrusso Chief, Tagi Raja, gave a great deal of trouble to the Government of the day, and Hrusso raids on the plains continued almost to the end of the last century. Today, however, the Hrussos are peaceful progressive people who have come under a certain amount of Hindu and Buddhist influence. They build very long and substantial houses and are keen traders, acting as middlemen for the Dhammais and other neighbouring tribes. They purchase cloth, blankets and swords from Bhutan and other articles from the Assam plains, and are themselves well dressed and prosperous in appearance. See C. H. Hesselmeyer's article, 'The Hill Tribes of the Northern Frontier of Assam', in the *Journal of the Asiatic Society of Bengal*,

XXXVII (1868) and some notes by R. S. Kennedy in his *Ethnological Report on the Akas, Khoas and Mijis and the Monbas of Tawang*.

IDU MISHMI—The Idu Mishmis, popularly known as Chulikattas or 'crop-haired' from their custom of cutting the hair round the head in Padam-Minyong fashion, live mainly in the Dibang Valley of north-western Lohit. It has been suggested that they are the earliest of the Mishmi migrants from Burma, from whom the Taraons split away to enter the Lohit Valley some five hundred years ago. Their legends associate them with the Padams, whom they resemble in general appearance and in the style of their textiles, but from whom they differ in having no communal dormitory and little dancing. The Idu, like all Mishmi, houses are long and narrow, occupied by a large number of persons, and villages often consist of not more than two to six buildings. The Idus kept slaves and were formerly notorious for their violent and suspicious treatment of strangers but, with the opening up of their country, they have proved friendly and amenable. There is a convenient summary of the early literature on the Mishmis in J. P. Mills' article 'The Mishmis of the Lohit Valley, Assam' in the *Journal of the Royal Anthropological Institute*, Vol. LXXXII.

KAMAN MISHMI—The Kaman or Miju Mishmis live in the upper reaches of the Lohit River, in valleys leading down to it and in the Khamlang Valley. There is a tradition that they migrated to their present home from the Kachin Hills of Burma. They are similar in appearance to the Taraons, wearing their hair long and weaving textiles of the same designs and colour. Like all Mishmis, they are keen traders and some of them come down regularly to the plains for cane-cutting at which they are expert. They are fond of opium and tobacco, but are indifferent cultivators.

KHAMPTI—The Khamptis are allied to the Shans and seem to have migrated from Bor-Khampti near the source of the Irrawady to the south of Lohit and Tirap about two hundred years ago. There are about 5,000 of them in India. They speak an Indo-Chinese language of the Tai group and are the only people in NEFA with a script of their own. They are Hinayana Buddhists by religion and maintain a number of shrines and temples. They are keen traders and expert craftsmen ; today many of them are literate, and one of them has been Member of Parliament for NEFA in two successive legislatures.

MINYONG—The Minyongs, who are closely allied to the Padams, are a strong and influential Adi tribe who live in about 70 villages on both banks of the Siang river, and in scattered settlements to the west of the Siang, and across to the Siyom river. There are some 17,000 of them and they live in large villages which may have as many as 400 houses ; these are grouped according to clans in separate divisions. Like the other Adi groups, they have dormitories for boys and young men and in some cases dormitories for unmarried girls. They are enthusiastic dancers and good weavers. Like the Padams and Idus, both men and women cut their hair short. The Minyongs are strongly democratic, being governed by a Kebang or Council of elders, and women hold a high position in their society ; there are female shamans who have considerable influence. Formerly a warlike and aggressive people, with many slaves, they have been unusually successful in adapting themselves to the pacific conditions of ordered administration.

MOKLUM—One of the sub-groups of the tribe which is now called Tangsa. The Tangsas live along the Burmese border in the Tirap Division and have many domestic and economic ties with Burma.

MONPA—An important tribe, some 20,000 strong, living in the north-west of the Kameng Frontier Division. They are Buddhist by religion with Tibetan affinities, their religious allegiance centering round the great monastery at Tawang. Another important Monpa centre is Dirang Dzong and there is some difference in dialect between the Tawang and the Dirang Dzong Monpas. These people dress mainly in Tibetan fashion, build substantial houses of stones and wooden planks and, in addition to jhum cultivation, are expert in growing rice on irrigated terraces which they manure both with cowdung and oak-leaves. Some of them, however, are mainly graziers and they are all enthusiastic breeders of horses, yaks and other livestock. They are exceptional among the NEFA tribes in drinking milk (which is taboo to most of the others) and in making ghee. They trade widely both in Tibet and Bhutan, and with the neighbouring tribal people in Kameng. They are good wood-carvers, weavers, carpet-makers, and also make paper from local materials. Their dance-pantomimes are of great variety and involve the creation of splendid masks and elaborate dresses.

NOCTE—The Noctes live in the neighbourhood of the administrative headquarters at Khonsa, between the Wanchos and Tangsas, in the Tirap Frontier Division. They have had contacts with the plains for many years and, though formerly headhunters, have now lost much of their traditional culture. They are the only people in NEFA who claim to be Hindus, for they follow a modified Vaishnavism, which has not, however, influenced their habits of food and drink.

PADAM—The Padams, one of the Adi groups living in the Pasighat area and in western Lohit, number some 9,500 persons and are very similar in appearance, dress and custom to the Minyongs.

PANGGI—A small group of not more than 3,500 individuals, living on the left bank of the Siang River. In dress, hair-style and custom there is little to distinguish them from the Minyongs and Padams.

PHOM—The Phoms are a small tribe living between the Changs and Konyaks in the Tuensang area. Hutton considers them closely allied to the Changs, but there is some evidence to associate them with the Konyaks.

SHERDUKPEN—The Sherdukpens are a small tribe of only about 1,500 persons, living mainly in the two villages of Rupa and Shergaon in the south of the Kameng Frontier Division. They have traditions of migration with Tibet from which their present social organization is believed to be derived. They are divided into two classes, the Thongs who are descended from the third son of the king of Lhasa, and the Chaos who are the descendents of his porters and servants. These, in turn, are divided into sub-groups, who still must work for their Thong overlords. There is no intermarriage between the two groups. The Sherdukpens do not build special dormitories for unmarried boys and girls, but organize them according to their group divisions. The Sherdukpens plough the level fields in their beautiful valleys and also practise jhum cultivation. But their main interest is in trade, for which every year they migrate to the low country. In many ways they resemble the Monpas and perform the same kind of pantomimes, obtaining their masks from Dirang Dzong or Tawang. Their dress, however, is slightly different and they affect a pleasant black cap of yak's hair decorated with a white cockade. Their religion is an interesting blend of Buddhist and tribal ideas.

SHIMONG—The Adis of Shimong and allied villages along the left bank of the Upper Siang River, between Karko and Tuting are commonly known as Shimongs. There is, however, little to distinguish them from the Minyongs.

SINGPHO—The Singphos are allied to the Kr-Khyan people of Burma, and were once a powerful and warlike tribe who spread across the border into the Assam Valley. The date of their migration is given approximately as the end of the eighteenth century, when they came from the neighbourhood of the Irrawady river through Tenga Pani, east of Sadiya to their present home in Tirap and Lohit. The men tie their hair in a knot on the crown and the women generally put on turbans. Many of them are addicted to opium. They are Buddhist, but have adopted many elements of the tribal religion of their neighbours. Their previous mortuary custom, which is reflected in one of the stories given in this book, was to defer a burial until all the relations of the deceased could pay respect to the corpse. There is an early account of them in Dalton's *Descriptive Ethnology of Bengal.*

TAGINS—The Tagins are to be found in the west of the Siang and north-east of the Subansiri Frontier Divisions. They live in small villages, scattered in lonely and desolate valleys, and the conditions of their life are perhaps harder than any in NEFA. In the past they carried on an extensive trade in slaves and until recently were hostile to visitors. Many of them went about naked, though they all had cloth for use on occasions, much of it being an attractive and durable woollen import from Tibet.

TARAON MISHMIS—The Taraons, often called Digarus, live to the west of the lower reaches of the Lohit Valley and in appearance and culture are closely allied to the Kamans, though their language is said to be nearer to the Idu. The Taraons have legends of migration from Burma and seem to have split off from the Idus some hundreds of years ago. They are addicted to opium and like other Mishmis make the house rather than the village the unit of their society. They have always been traders, bartering their products both with the Tibetans and the Assamese ; important local products are musk, the *coptis teeta* (at one time greatly in demand as a febrifuge), aconite, bees-wax, ginger, ivory and rubber. They are excellent weavers.

WANCHO—The Wanchos live in southern Tirap. Their society is divided into strictly defined classes, of which the Wangpan or serf-class is the lowest. The houses of the Wanghams are enormous and these Chiefs are still of great influence. In the old days many Wanchos went naked. They still, like the Konyaks, dispose of the dead by exposure. They were formerly ardent head-hunters, though the custom has now disappeared. Their wood-carving is strong and vital and their weaving, though not extensively practised, is interesting.

BIBLIOGRAPHY

BERESFORD, G. W.—*Notes on the North-Eastern Frontier of Assam* (Shillong, 1881 ; reprinted, 1906).

BOR, E.—*Adventures of a Botanist's Wife* (London, 1955).

BOR, N. L.—'The Daflas and their Oaths', *J. R. A. S. B.*, Vol. II (N.S., 1936), pp. 27-39.

BOWER, U. G.—*The Hidden Land* (London, 1953). About the Subansiri area.

BUTLER, J.—*A Sketch of Assam, with Some Account of the Hill Tribes* (London, 1847). Early descriptions of Abors, Akas, Daflas, Khamptis, Mishmis and Singphos.

COOPER, T. T—*New Routes for Commerce ; the Mishmee Hills : An Account of a Journey made in an Attempt to Penetrate Thibet from Assam to Open New Routes for Commerce* (London, 1873).

DALTON, E. T.—*Descriptive Ethnology of Bengal* (Calcutta 1872). Gives accounts of the Khamptis, pp. 1-9 ; Singphos, pp. 9-13 ; Mishmis, pp. 13-21 ; Abors, pp. 21-35 ; Daflas, pp. 35-37 ; Akas, pp. 37-38 ; Nagas, pp. 38-44.

DUN, G. W.—*Preliminary Notes on Daphlas* (Simla, 1896).

DUNBAR, G. D. S.—*Other Men's Lives. A Study of Primitive Peoples* (London, 1938). Includes a popular account of Daflas and Abors at pp. 230-345.

DUNBAR, G. D. S.—'Abors and Galongs', *Memoirs of A. S. B.*, Vol. V (1913-17). A full and valuable account.

ELWIN, VERRIER—*Folk-Tales of Mahakoshal* (Bombay, 1944).

ELWIN, VERRIER—*Myths of Middle India* (Bombay, 1949).

ELWIN, VERRIER—*Tribal Myths of Orissa* (Bombay, 1954).

FURER-HAIMENDORF, C. von—*Ethnographic Notes on the Tribes of the Subansiri Region* (Shillong, 1947).

FURER-HAIMENDORF, C. von—'The After-Life in Indian Belief', *J. R. A. I.*, Vol. LXXIII (1953).

FURER-HAIMENDORF, C. von—'Religious Beliefs and Ritual Practices of the Minyong Abors', *Anthropos*, Vol. XLIX (1954).

FURER-HAIMENDORF, C. von—*Himalayan Barbary* (London, 1955). On the author's travels in the Subansiri F.D.

GAIT, E.—*A History of Assam* (Calcutta and Simla, 1926). Brief accounts of the relations of Government with the NEFA tribes.

GILLE, A.—'An Account of an Expedition among the Abors in 1853', *J. R. A. S. B.*, Vol. IX (N. S., 1913) pp. 107-122. Describes Father Krick's visit to Membu.

GOSWAMI, P.—*Folk-Literature of Assam* (Gauhati, 1954).

GRAY, J. Errol.—*Diary of a Journey to the Bor Khampti Country and Sources of the Irrawady made by Mr J. Errol Gray, Season 1892-93, from Assam* (Simla, 1893).

GRIERSON, G. A.—*Linguistic Survey of India*, Vol. III, Tibeto-Burman Family, Part I (Calcutta, 1909). Accounts of the Aka, Abor, Miri, Dafla and Mishmi languages.

HESSELMEYER, C. H.,—'The Hill Tribes of the Northern Frontier of Assam', *J. A. S. B.*, Vol. XXXVII (1868), pp. 192-208. On the Akas.

IZZARD, R.—*The Hunt for the Buru* (London, 1951).

KENNEDY, R. S.—*Ethnological Report on the Akas, Khoas and Mijis and the Monbas of Tawang* (Shillong, 1914).

KINGDON-WARD, F.—*A Plant Hunter in Tibet* (London, 1934). There are two chapters about the Mishmis.

KINGDON-WARD, F.—*Assam Adventure* (London, 1941). References to Monpas.

KINGDON-WARD, J.—*My Hill So Strong* (London, 1952). Contains a vivid account of the 1950 Earthquake as it affected the Lohit F.D.

MACGREGOR, C. R.—'Notes on Akas and Akaland', *Procs. A. S. B.* (1894), pp. 198-212.

MACGREGOR, C. R.—*Military Report on the Kampti-Singpho Countries* (Calcutta, 1887).

MACKENZIE, A.—*History of the relations of the Government with the Hills Tribes of the North-East Frontier of Bengal* (Calcutta, 1884). Contains in Part I a historical account of the dealings of Government with the Akas (pp. 21-26), the Daflas (pp. 27-32), the Abors and Miris (pp. 33-46), the Mishmis (pp. 47-54), the Khamptis (pp. 57-60) and the Singphos (pp. 61-72). Appendix C (pp. 399-404) contains a note by P. T. Carnegy, dated 1873, on the 'Seebsaugor Nagas in 1873', and Appendix J (pp. 537-550) consists of extracts from the Assam Census Report of 1881: this gives some brief notes on the Hill Miris, Abors and Daflas.

MILLS, J. P.—'A Brief Note on Agriculture in the Dirang Dzong Area', *Man in India*, Vol. XXVI (1946), pp. 8-11.

MILLS, J. P.—'Tours in the Balipara Frontier Tract, Assam', *Man in India*, Vol. XXVII (1947), pp. 9-35.

MILLS, J. P.—'A Preliminary Note on the Senjithongji of the Balipara Frontier Tract, Assam', *J. Ind, Anthr. Inst.*, Vol II (1948), pp. 1-8.

MILLS, J. P.—'The Mishmis of the Lohit Valley, Assam', *J. R. A. I.*, Vol. LXXXII.

NEEDHAM, J. F.—*Outline Grammar of the Khamti Language* (Rangoon, 1894).

NEUFVILLE, J. B.—'On the Geography and Population of Assam, 1823', *Asiatic Researches*, Vol.XVI (1828).

SHAKESPEAR, L. W.—*History of Upper Assam, Upper Burmah and North-Eastern Frontier* (London, 1914).

SHAKESPEAR, L. W.—*History of the Assam Rifles* (London, 1929).

STITH THOMPSON—*The Folktale* (New York, 1946).

STONOR, C. R.—'The Feasts of Merit among the Northern Sangtam Tribe of Assam', *Anthropos*, Vol. XLV (1950).

WORD-LIST

ABHANG—The traditional epics of the Adi tribes.
APONG—The Adi word for rice-beer.

CHUNGA—A piece of bamboo used for carrying water or as a drinking vessel.

DAO—An implement, universal throughout NEFA, used as a weapon and for cutting wood or bamboo.

GAM—A village Chief or headman.

JHUM—Axe-cultivation, in the course of which the forest is felled and fired, the seed being sown in the ashes.

MITHUN—The *bos frontalis,* a species of Indian bison.
MORUNG—Men's house, in which all the unmarried youths sleep.
MOSHUP—The men's dormitory or club among the Padams ; by the Minyongs it is called *dere* and by the Boris and other northern groups *bango*.

PONUNG—The characteristic Adi dance.

WIYU—A god, demon, or spirit. The word is often pronounced 'Ui' and is used throughout the Siang and Subansiri Frontier Divisions.

INDEX